REMEMBERING THE SECOND WORLD WAR

Remembering the Second World War brings together an international and interdisciplinary cast of leading scholars to explore the remembrance of this conflict on a global scale. Conceptually, it is premised on the need to challenge nation-centric approaches in memory studies, drawing strength from recent transcultural, affective and multidirectional turns.

Divided into four thematic parts, this book largely focuses on the post-Cold War period, which has seen a notable upsurge in commemorative activity relating to the Second World War and significant qualitative changes in its character. The first part explores the enduring utility and the limitations of the national frame in France, Germany and China. The second explores transnational transactions in remembrance, looking at memories of the British Empire at war, contested memories in East-Central Europe and the transnational campaign on behalf of Japan's former 'comfort women'. A third section considers local and sectional memories of the war and the fourth analyses innovative practices of memory, including re-enactment, video gaming and Holocaust tourism.

Offering insightful contributions on intriguing topics and illuminating the current state of the art in this growing field, this book will be essential reading for all students and scholars of the history and memory of the Second World War.

Patrick Finney teaches in the Department of International Politics at Aberystwyth University. He has published widely on collective memory, especially in relation to the Second World War, and on the international history of the twentieth century, especially in relation to the inter-war period. He is currently writing a book entitled *How the Second World War Still Shapes Our Lives*.

REMEMBERING THE MODERN WORLD

Series Editors: David Lowe and Tony Joel

The *Remembering the Modern World* series throws new light on the major themes in the field of history and memory in a global context. The series investigates relationships between state-centred practices and other forms of collective and individual memory; looks at the phenomenon of anniversaries and national days in the context of global and national identities; shows how some cities and sites play active roles in generating acts of remembrance; and asks why some phenomena and events are remembered more widely and easily than others.

Titles in the series:

Remembering the Cold War
David Lowe and Tony Joel

Remembering Genocide
Nigel Eltringham and Pam Maclean

Remembering the First World War
Bart Ziino

Remembering the Second World War
Patrick Finney

Forthcoming titles in the series:

Remembering Women's Activism
Sharon Crozier-de Rosa and Vera Mackie

Remembering Independence
David Lowe, Carola Lentz and Jonathan Ritchie

REMEMBERING THE SECOND WORLD WAR

Edited by Patrick Finney

LONDON AND NEW YORK

First published 2018
by Routledge
2 Park Square, Milton Park, Abingdon, Oxon OX14 4RN

and by Routledge
711 Third Avenue, New York, NY 10017

Routledge is an imprint of the Taylor & Francis Group, an informa business

British Library Cataloguing in Publication Data
A catalogue record for this book is available from the British Library

Library of Congress Cataloguing in Publication Data
Names: Finney, Patrick, 1968– editor.
Title: Remembering the Second World War / edited by Patrick Finney.
Description: Abingdon, Oxon ; New York, NY : Routledge, 2017. |
Series: Remembering the modern world | Includes bibliographical references and index.
Identifiers: LCCN 2017004186 (hardback : alk. paper) |
(pbk. : alk. paper) | (ebook)
Subjects: LCSH: World War, 1939–1945–Influence. |
World War, 1939–1945–Social aspects. | Collective memory.
Classification: LCC D744 .R43 2017 | DDC 940.54/6–dc23
LC record available at https://lccn.loc.gov/2017004186

ISBN: 978-1-138-80813-3 (hbk)
ISBN: 978-1-138-80814-0 (pbk)
ISBN: 978-1-315-17890-5 (ebk)

Typeset in Bembo
by Out of House Publishing

To Elsa, Arthur and Harriet

CONTENTS

FIGURES

CONTRIBUTORS

Margaret Atack is Professor of French at the University of Leeds. She has published widely and extensively on French literature, thought and culture in the twentieth century. She is currently writing a book with Christopher Lloyd, entitled *Narratives of the Second World War in France: Remapping the Landscape.*

Joan Beaumont is a Professor in the Strategic and Defence Studies Centre at the Australian National University. She has published widely on Australia in the two world wars, Australian defence and foreign policy, the history of prisoners of war and the memory and heritage of war. Her current research projects include *Serving our Country: A History of Australian Aboriginal and Torres Strait Islander People in the Defence of Australia* and *Second Shock: Australia's Great Depression and the Legacy of World War I.*

Joyce van de Bildt is a PhD candidate in History at Tel Aviv University writing her dissertation about the contested memory of the 1952 revolution in Egypt during the periods of rule of Anwar al-Sadat and Hosni Mubarak. Her research interests include contemporary Egyptian history, collective memory, commemorations and identity politics.

Tim Cole is Professor of Social History at the University of Bristol. He has wide-ranging interests in social and environmental histories, historical geographies and digital humanities and also works within the creative economy. He has published extensively on the Holocaust and its commemoration and his most recent monograph is *Holocaust Landscapes* (London: Bloomsbury, 2016).

Gerald Figal is a Professor of History and of Asian Studies at Vanderbilt University. He has extensive interests in modern Japanese cultural and intellectual history, war memorialisation and cultural studies. He is currently working on a book project entitled *The Medium is the Monster: Supernatural Circuits and Consumer Fantasies in Contemporary Japan*, which concerns the intersection of media, consumerism and the monstrous in contemporary Japan.

Patrick Finney teaches in the Department of International Politics at Aberystwyth University. He has published widely on collective memory, especially in relation to the Second World War, and on the international history of the twentieth century, especially in relation to the inter-war period. He is currently writing a book entitled *How the Second World War Still Shapes Our Lives*.

Jeremy Hicks is Reader in Russian Culture and Film at Queen Mary University of London. He has research interests in Soviet film, the Holocaust and the Second World War and in Soviet literature from the 1920s to the 1940s. His most recent monograph is *First Films of the Holocaust: Soviet Cinema and the Genocide of the Jews, 1938–46* (Pittsburgh: University of Pittsburgh Press, 2012).

Eva Kingsepp teaches in the Department of Geography, Media and Communication at Karlstad University. She completed a PhD dissertation at Stockholm University in 2008 on *Nazi Germany in Popular Culture: Memory, Myth, Media* and carried out postdoctoral work on the popular history and cultural memory of the Second World War in North Africa and the Middle East.

Jie-Hyun Lim is Professor of Transnational History and Director of the Critical Global Studies Institute at Sogang University. He has extensive interests in global history, historical theory and historiography and the history of mass dictatorship. Recent publications include *The Palgrave Handbook of Mass Dictatorship* (New York: Palgrave, 2016), co-edited with Paul Corner.

Bill Niven is Professor of Contemporary German History at Nottingham Trent University. He has published widely on the history and memory of Nazi Germany, the history of East Germany and German film, theatre and literature. He has recently completed a monograph on Hitler and film.

Caroline Norma is a Lecturer in the School of Global, Urban and Social Studies at the Royal Melbourne Institute of Technology University. She lectures in translation and interpreting and has research interests in prostitution, pornography and trafficking in Australia, Japan and South Korea. Her most recent monograph is *The Japanese Comfort Women and Sexual Slavery during the China and Pacific Wars* (London: Bloomsbury, 2016).

Edward Vickers is Professor of Comparative Education at Kyushu University. He has extensive research interests in the contemporary history of education in Chinese societies, with a particular focus on the role of schools and other public institutions in political socialisation and their relationship to nationalism and the politics of identity. His next book is *Education and Society in Post-Mao China* (London: Routledge, 2017), co-authored with Zeng Xiaodong.

Tatiana Zhurzhenko is Director of Research for the Russia in Global Dialogue and Ukraine in European Dialogue programmes at the Institute for Human Sciences (IWM), Vienna. Her research focuses on post-Soviet borders and borderland identities, on memory politics in Eastern Europe and on gender politics and feminism in Ukraine.

ACKNOWLEDGEMENTS

This book has had a long and somewhat troubled gestation, but I am delighted to acknowledge the assistance of all those who have facilitated its completion. I am grateful to the editors of the *Remembering the Modern World* series, David Lowe and Tony Joel, for commissioning the volume and for their guidance and encouragement. At Routledge, I must primarily thank Eve Setch for overseeing the commissioning of the work and Amy Welmers, who guided the manuscript to completion with extraordinary patience and understanding. I am grateful to Maria Whelan for meticulous copy-editing and to Eleri Pipien and all her colleagues at Out of House Publishing for their production work. The volume was originally conceived in collaboration with Stephan Petzold of the University of Leeds who had a significant input into determining its structure and the topics of some of the contributions. I am grateful to the contributors for producing such thoughtful and exciting work, and for their positive and cooperative responses to my suggestions and requests for revisions during the editorial process. The proposal was reviewed for Routledge by four anonymous referees who provided insightful comments at a formative stage; I am very grateful to them and to those numerous colleagues who peer reviewed the contributions for me. The Department of International Politics at Aberystwyth provided as congenial an atmosphere in which to work as one could hope for in the neo-liberal University and I am grateful for the research leave and teaching relief which helped me to complete the project. As ever, my most important debt is to my wife, Laura, who makes everything worthwhile with her love, understanding, humour and insight.

INTRODUCTION

Patrick Finney

The cycle of seventieth anniversary commemorations of the Second World War concluded over the summer of 2015, terminating with a lavish parade in Beijing on 3 September in which the People's Republic of China marked the victory over Japan by showcasing its contemporary military might.[1] This grandiose ending was in keeping with the scale and extent of commemorative activity across the globe over the previous few years which had rendered the war insistently visible. The ubiquity of remembrance was not always welcomed. Great Britain, for example, was saturated with commemorative events from 2009; the summer of 2010 was particularly frenzied as the successive anniversaries of the landmarks of the 'finest hour' of 1940 – from Dunkirk, through the Battle of Britain and to the onset of the Blitz – were marked with public ceremonies, museum exhibitions and an avalanche of media coverage, but the cycle continued as the calendar moved round. In May 2013 an editorial in *The Guardian* lamented:

> This week, it was the Dambusters – their wartime air raids against German dams commemorated once again, 70 years on. Last week, it was the Arctic convoys – their survivors gathering in the Highlands, again 70 years on from their wartime exploits. Only a few days before that, it had been the turn of the Bevin Boys – commemorated in a new memorial to their war years in the coalmines. What will it be next? … Do we need any more memorials, plaques and statues? Can we not decide, maturely and respectfully, that enough is enough? Can we at last move on?[2]

This sentiment about commemorative excess is often voiced but appears to be entirely in vain. However disabling or solipsistic this nostalgic obsession with the war might be, the juggernaut of British remembering nonetheless rolls on. Moreover, the phenomenon is by no means limited to Great Britain (whatever the specificities of its peculiar relationship to the wartime past): the Second World War remains extremely salient in contemporary societies, far and wide across the globe, as the current unfolding of a seventy-fifth anniversary commemorative cycle testifies.

The conflict is evoked and invoked ubiquitously in myriad political and cultural discourses, and is an object of serious contestation: far from being empty signifiers, representations of the war play crucial roles as vehicles for the negotiation of collective identities and meditation upon political action. The period since the end of the Cold War, moreover, has seen a dramatic upsurge in contemporary remembering of the earlier conflict (Stone 2014). Diverse factors including geopolitical change, globalisation, the development of digital and networked technologies, the rise of new norms of apology and human rights and the imminent passing of the wartime generation have produced a dramatic quantitative increase in memory and important qualitative shifts in its character. For close on three decades, we have been living through a time of intense dynamism in global Second World War remembrance. Amidst a blizzard of claims and counter-claims, older myths have been demolished and new ones have emerged, venerable taboos have been breached and fresh ones have been erected and national memory cultures have acquired new nuances, just as they have been undermined and cross-cut by new transnational forces and processes. New practices of remembrance have emerged to complicate and thicken our relationship to the wartime past, and to raise new ethical questions about relativisation and normalisation (Rosenfeld 2015). It is therefore little wonder that the cultural historian Dan Stone has been moved to observe: 'remarkably, the further we get from the Second World War, the more fierce the battle over its meaning grows' (Stone 2010: 467).

This real world activity is matched by a profusion of scholarly studies of collective remembrance of the same conflict. The explosive proliferation of work on collective remembering across the humanities and social sciences is one of the most remarkable scholarly phenomena of the last three decades. The interdisciplinary field of memory studies is now firmly established as a dynamic and fertile area of inquiry, with its own apparatus of dedicated journals, degree courses, book series, conferences and collaborative research projects. The remembrance of the traumas of the Second World War lies at the heart of this endeavour. Exploration of the impact and legacy of the Holocaust was initially crucial to the emergence of the study of memory as a legitimate, even urgent, scholarly project. Analysis of how the heritage of the war shaped reconstruction, the renegotiation of national identities and the fabric of political, social and cultural life across the post-war decades has supplied much of its subsequent energy. Moreover, although we are now more than seven decades from the outbreak of the war, scholars continue to explore how the conflict remains visible and contested across the globe, with little indication that their enthusiasm will soon be exhausted (although cf. Rosenfeld 2009).

This volume brings together an international cast of leading scholars, both distinguished, established names and emerging, early career talents, drawn from a wide range of disciplines, to map the state of the art in the field and to chart new ways forward. In terms of conceptual underpinning, it is premised on four recent and ongoing developments within memory studies at large and the field of global Second World War memory in particular. The first of these is the wide-ranging questioning of nation-centric approaches. Much early work in this field focused squarely on processes of remembrance within national borders. This made sense, given the public prominence and cultural authority of official remembering and the important relationship between it, processes of post-war reconstruction and the renegotiation of national identity. Yet scholars have increasingly begun to investigate the operation of memory at other levels, including the sub-national – the local and sectional – and the transnational or transcultural. As one important recent collection on transnational memory puts it:

> Globalized communication and time-space compression, post-coloniality, transnational capitalism, large-scale migration, and regional integration: all of these mean that national frames are no longer the self-evident ones they used to be in daily life and identity formation. As a result, the national has also ceased to be the inevitable or preeminent scale for the study of collective remembrance.
>
> *(De Chesari and Rigney 2014: 2)*

The pieces in this collection respond to this provocation, yet also elucidate the enduring pertinence and utility – albeit in an expanded field – of the national frame.

The second development is a shift of emphasis from static approaches to remembrance – often involving formal analysis of specific texts, monuments or sites – towards ones that prioritise fluidity and mobility. Against a previous tendency to conceive of mnemonic objects or acts as possessing particular stable characteristics and residing within bounded containers – whether it be a nation or a culture – this approach would instead emphasise the transcultural travels of memory: 'memories do not hold still – on the contrary they seem to be constituted first of all through movement' (Erll 2011: 11). To an extent, this is simply to build on the myriad scholarly contributions that have long stressed the processual character of memory, but recent formulations extend the implications of this considerably. As Astrid Erll puts it:

> The term 'travelling memory' is a metaphorical shorthand, an abbreviation for the fact that in the production of cultural memory, people, media, mnemonic forms, contents, and practices are in constant, unceasing motion. … I claim that *all* cultural memory *must* 'travel', be kept in motion, in order to 'stay alive', to have an impact both on individual minds and social formations. Such travel consists only partly in movement across and beyond territorial and social boundaries. On a more fundamental level, it is the ongoing exchange of information between individuals and the motion between minds and media which first of all generate what [Maurice] Halbwachs termed collective memory.
>
> *(Erll 2011: 12)*

These ideas have fuelled particularly productive work on transcultural memory (Bond and Rapson 2014).

The third development is an affective turn in memory studies, as elsewhere across the humanities and social sciences. In part this involves an empirical shift as scholars have begun to look for evidence of mnemonic activity beyond familiar source materials – such as novels, films and political speeches – and to explore instead practices of remembrance – such as dark tourism, re-enactment and videogaming – in which emotive and somatic responses are more in play. Yet this move is also clearly connected to conceptual developments such as the articulation of the notion of 'prosthetic memory' to capture the ways in which new technologies and experiential forms allow an individual to 'take on a more personal, deeply felt memory of a past event through which he or she did not live' (Landsberg 2004: 2). The question of the transmission of memory across generations is a closely related concern. The term 'postmemory' has been coined to connote how the descendants of trauma survivors gain vicarious experience of events they '"remember" only by means of the stories, images, and behaviors among which they grew up'; such experiences, it is argued, can be transmitted 'so deeply and affectively as to *seem* to constitute memories in their own right'. Whilst originally intended to refer to intra-familial relations, many scholars have pondered whether and how such processes might 'extend to more distant, adoptive witnesses or affiliative contemporaries' (Hirsch 2012: 5–6). This quest has assumed added urgency in relation to the Second World War given the imminent passing of the participant generation; this has created wide-ranging cultural anxieties about authenticity and how memories might best be preserved for the future (Finney 2017).

The fourth development concerns the way in which memories of different pasts, and different traumas, inter-relate. Simple observation tells us that memories of multiple pasts are often in play simultaneously: just recently, after all, the closing stages of the Second World War seventieth anniversary cycle overlapped and intersected with the beginning of the First World War centenary commemorations. Too often, perhaps, the pragmatic necessity to delimit subjects in manageable ways for analysis has led us to obscure or under-estimate the way in which remembrance of one trauma is informed by remembrance of another. Conceptually, another problem arises from the common tendency to conceive of memories of different pasts as necessarily antagonistic and as competing for occupancy of a finite quantity of space in the public realm, as if the consequence of choosing to remember one conflict must be mnemonic oblivion for all others. Michael Rothberg has famously proposed a counter-model:

> Against the framework that understands collective memory as *competitive* memory – as a zero-sum struggle over scarce resources – I suggest that we consider memory as *multidirectional*: as subject to ongoing negotiation, cross-referencing, and borrowing; as productive and not privative.
>
> *(Rothberg 2009: 3)*

Rothberg's particular concern was the fruitful interaction between memories of the Holocaust and memories of decolonisation. The former has become especially important in this context given the emergence in the post-Cold War period of a cosmopolitan Holocaust memory, through which the Holocaust has become sacralised as the defining atrocity of modernity, serving as 'a moral touchstone in an age of uncertainty and the absence of ideological master narratives' (Levy and Sznaider 2006: 18). The emergence of new norms of apology, restitution and regret and human rights – with which Holocaust memory is intimately, indeed, constitutively connected – has also established a framework which promotes productive, if not always harmonious, conversations between memories of different traumatic pasts. It also makes it less problematic to frame a study of Second World War remembrance in global terms – while the signifier yokes together numerous conflicts in many different theatres, this new normative fabric endows the mnemonic field with coherence, just as there are clearly common factors at work precipitating and fuelling the upsurge in Second World War-focused commemorative activity over recent decades in Europe, the Americas and Asia (on global memory, see Assmann and Conrad 2010).

The essays comprising this volume are arranged into four thematic sections, the structuring logic of which speaks to the four-fold conceptualisation above though without precisely replicating it. The contributors were not instructed to adopt any particular theoretical or conceptual position but their contributions nonetheless cohere around this set of inter-related concerns. While they constitute significant original treatments of their specific subjects, and can be read for profit in themselves by those interested in those empirical topics, they also collectively illuminate the conceptual terrain and the current state of the field and are suggestive of its likely future direction.

The first section of the book probes the continued validity and potential of nation-centric approaches to Second World War remembrance. Although the scholarly tide has turned somewhat against the national, this does not mean that this perspective has been entirely abandoned (Bragança and Tame 2016). The nation remains an important realm of mnemonic production and consumption, even if it needs now to be understood as always existing in relation to other levels and scales – the local, the transnational and the global (De Cesari and Rigney 2014). Margaret Atack offers an overview of the long run of Second World War memory in France since 1945, making a powerful argument that the specificities of the French case mean that the national remains a necessary organising principle. She also provides a compelling reading of how several 'myths of silence' have operated there which demonstrates that our capacity to generate new interpretations of developments within the national frame is by no means exhausted. Bill Niven analyses recent developments in the memory of the Nazi past in Germany, another country where – because of the burden of guilt – a strong *prima facie* case might be made for national specificity. Whilst adopting a nation-centric approach, Niven is alive to the influence of transnational forces and the role of internal contestation – specifically, in this instance, inter-generational conflict. Finally, Edward Vickers considers recent memory politics in the People's Republic of China, yet another good test case for nation-centric approaches given how fervently the Beijing regime has sought to manage and instrumentalise memory of the war since the 1980s. By exploring how this project is received in parts of China with different historical experiences and contemporary priorities, Vickers underlines the importance of not discounting the nation-state as a mnemonic actor and yet demonstrates the fissures, fractures and tensions in 'Chinese' memory.

The second section shifts the focus more squarely onto transnational forces and processes. My own essay on the memory of the British Second World War considers what can be gained empirically and conceptually by adopting the lens of empire to explore remembrance in the European former colonial powers. Thinking about how the Empire has been largely excluded from British war memory helps us to understand how that memory has in fact been shaped by the transnational forces and processes of decolonisation. Moreover, thinking about the competing national war memories produced across the former imperial space, in conversation with those of Britain, brings into focus another dimension of transnational co-production. Tatiana Zhurzhenko's essay on the Soviet war memorial in Vienna, and associated memory discourses, casts light on several transnational processes. On the one hand, she explores how Austrian war remembrance has shifted in recent decades to move into closer alignment with a pan-European memory paradigm focused on Holocaust recognition. On the other hand, she explores how post-Soviet Russia has made use of war memorials across the continent to assert its geopolitical influence, and how members of the Russian diaspora – and specific embodied performances of remembrance – have been enfolded into that process. Finally, Caroline Norma explores the transnational campaign to secure justice for former 'comfort women' in East Asia. She traces how the campaign emerged in the 1990s and how a transnational network of feminist activists – centred on a Korean-Japanese nexus – came together to pressurise the Japanese government to offer recognition and restitution. She also explores how it is fruitful to locate this campaign in relation to the transnational movement to abolish prostitution, illustrating the fundamental interconnection of war memory with larger political, ethical and normative concerns.

The third section addresses local and sectional memories, though here too the transnational is in fact also prominent. Gerald Figal explores local war memories on the island of Okinawa, and how and why war commemoration there has grown up in tension with that on mainland Japan. He identifies and anatomises a local tradition of 'activated war memory' in which war remembrance is intimately entwined with contemporary peace education and political struggles against Japanese (and American) militarism. Joan Beaumont both explores a locale – the Yokohama cemetery for Allied servicemen in Japan – and analyses a sectional memory – that of the relatives and ex-comrades of the fallen interred there, who have enjoyed a somewhat uneasy relationship with currents of national and official memory in Australia. Intriguingly, she also discusses how it is that the Yokohama cemetery has failed to become a more significant site of memory. Finally, Joyce van de Bildt tells the story of the commemorative work of those associated with the Joop Westerweel resistance movement in the Netherlands. Owing to certain unique characteristics, this community developed a distinctive sectional memory that was in tension with dominant memories of resistance in the Netherlands; it also possessed palpable transnational dimensions, since much of the memory work occurred in Israel, and embodied some distinctive commemorative practices, such as the planting of a forest.

The final section deals with practices of remembrance, opening up more directly consideration of authenticity, affect and embodiment. Jeremy Hicks analyses the life and times of the Soviet Victory Banner, the flag flown over the Reichstag after its capture by the Red Army in 1945. He traces the use made of the flag in museum displays and through deployment at Victory Day parades, and demonstrates the auratic power it possessed as a tangible and authentic physical object; this power was such, indeed, that it also seems to have invested the facsimile copies that have been authorised for use in parades and re-enactments in Vladimir Putin's Russia. (This illustrates, incidentally, that these innovative and embodied forms of memory certainly can be harnessed to nation-building and other political projects.) Eva Kingsepp considers videogaming as a way of performing and experiencing memory. She surveys the various types of Second World War games, analysing them as texts – how they represent the war and the narrative progression built into them – and concluding that they generally contain significant sanitising omissions, seldom, for example, broaching the Holocaust. She also considers how they are consumed – the ludic experience which gamers enjoy – and the potential for them to trigger serious critical reflection on the past outside game time. Finally, Tim Cole explores embodied experiences of Holocaust tourism, considering artistic endeavours to walk the landscapes of the Holocaust, educational programmes in which visiting Holocaust sites plays a central part and the return journeys of Holocaust survivors to the places where they were incarcerated and persecuted. These experiences are fraught with ambiguities and tensions and Cole concludes with a warning that for most of us the act of entering Holocaust landscapes in the hope of achieving authentic connection or identification will produce profoundly disappointing results, for all its seductive promise.

In a brief afterword Jie-Hyun Lim draws back our focus in order to consider how Second World War and Holocaust remembrance is entangled with memories of other traumatic experiences, especially those of Stalinism and decolonisation. He also elucidates how the contemporary terrain of memory is characterised by conflicting forces of reterritorialisation and deterritorialisation with national memory cultures both resurgent and in flight. His thoughts resonate with others throughout the contributions and point to the irony that, in a sense, the contemporary state of the field renders the title and framing of this collection – as dealing with the remembrance solely of the Second World War – somewhat obsolete. Future scholars in the field will need to acknowledge the tensions this creates and seek to work them productively and creatively.

Notes

1 'China Military Parade Commemorates WW2 Victory over Japan', *BBC News*, 3 September 2015, www.bbc.co.uk/news/world-asia-china-34125418.
2 'Unthinkable? Putting the Second World War to Rest', *The Guardian*, 17 May 2013, www.theguardian.com/commentisfree/2013/may/17/unthinkable-second-world-war-editorial.

References

Assmann, Aleida and Conrad, Sebastian. eds. 2010. *Memory in a Global Age: Discourses, Practices and Trajectories*. London: Palgrave Macmillan.

Bond, Lucy and Rapson, Jessica. eds. 2014. *The Transcultural Turn: Interrogating Memory Between and Beyond Borders*. Berlin: De Gruyter.

Bragança, Manuel and Tame, Peter. eds. 2016. *The Long Aftermath: Cultural Legacies of Europe at War, 1936–2016*. Oxford: Berghahn.

De Cesari, Chiara and Rigney, Ann. 2014. 'Introduction'. In *Transnational Memory: Circulation, Articulation, Scales*, edited by Chiara De Cesari and Ann Rigney. Berlin: De Gruyter. 1–25.

Erll, Astrid. 2011. 'Travelling Memory'. *Parallax*, 17, 4: 4–18.

Finney, Patrick. 2017. 'Politics and Technologies of Authenticity: The Second World War at the Close of Living Memory'. *Rethinking History*, 21, 2: 154–70.

Hirsch, Marianne. 2012. *The Generation of Postmemory: Writing and Visual Culture after the Holocaust*. New York, NY: Columbia University Press.

Landsberg, Alison. 2004. *Prosthetic Memory: The Transformation of American Remembrance in the Age of Mass Culture*. New York, NY: Columbia University Press.

Levy, Daniel and Sznaider, Natan. 2006. *The Holocaust and Memory in the Global Age*. Philadelphia, PA: Temple University Press.

Rosenfeld, Gavriel D. 2009. 'A Looming Crash or a Soft Landing? Forecasting the Future of the Memory "Industry"'. *Journal of Modern History*, 81, 1: 122–58.

Rosenfeld, Gavriel D. 2015. *Hi Hitler! How the Nazi Past is Being Normalized in Contemporary Culture*. Cambridge: Cambridge University Press.

Rothberg, Michael. 2009. *Multidirectional Memory: Remembering the Holocaust in the Age of Decolonization*. Stanford, CA: Stanford University Press.

Stone, Dan. 2010. 'Beyond the "Auschwitz Syndrome": Holocaust Historiography after the Cold War'. *Patterns of Prejudice*, 44, 5: 454–68.

Stone, Dan. 2014. *Goodbye to All That? The Story of Europe since 1945*. Oxford: Oxford University Press.

PART I

National memory cultures?

1

A NATION UNITED? THE IMPOSSIBLE MEMORY OF WAR AND OCCUPATION IN FRANCE

Margaret Atack

Is France more obsessed with its wartime past than other nations? Many commentators and historians seem to think so. True or not, it would certainly be hard to overstate the importance of the memory of the Second World War in France over the seven decades which followed. It has been argued over from many different standpoints; it has been a vector for different currents in other conflicts; it became, towards the end of the twentieth century, a cultural phenomenon in its own right. Dominated from the 1970s on by the trope of 'breaking the silence' and the interminable repetition of 'revelations' of material that was often already in the public domain, the rhetoric of outrage, of taboos and myths to be swept aside, was underpinned by a most misleading impression of the immediate post-war decades. Conan and Rousso's important 1994 study *An Ever-Present Past* – whose original French title, *Un passé qui ne passe pas* (Conan and Rousso 1994), punningly combined a food metaphor of indigestibility with the notion of the interminable resistance in the present to letting the past be past – itself became a vector of the memory industry, perpetuating the extraordinary phenomenon that it had sought to analyse and explain. But through all the outpouring of material and the at times bitter controversies, a more complete picture has now certainly been established in public awareness, one that, in its acknowledgement of the key role of the Franco–French wars within the Franco–German war, points to the enduring relevance of the Franco–French framework in the historian's methodological armoury. That is not to say that external factors have had no influence: colonial wars, the Cold War and globalisation have all played a part; yet the overriding conclusion must be that the national framework is vital to any understanding of the way memories of the Second World War have developed and evolved in France.

By virtue of the diversity of experience of the French and the divisions within the nation during the war years, these memories were diverse and divided. France was one of the combatant nations until its defeat in June 1940, and again after the

Liberation of Paris and much else of its territory in August 1944; as a defeated, occupied country between those dates it was in a singular position which, while not unprecedented – after all, the north of France had been occupied for four years during the First World War – was markedly different from those of its allies. The commemoration and memory of France at war and of the Occupation constitute interlocking, overlapping, yet at times very distinct thematic topics in France's invocation of its past.

France was a splintered and divided country during the Occupation, with seven different zones, each with different lived experiences and different histories. Resistance, Vichy, collaboration: these are umbrella terms for complex and plural phenomena that also evolved and changed over the four years of Occupation; the extreme polarisation of the months of fighting at the Liberation is often back-projected over the whole period, effacing many of the complexities governing choices, activities and trajectories in the preceding years. Individual, collective, official and public memories of the war-time years are multiple, fragmented, and of course conflicting, as the divisions of these years undercut the possibility of uncomplicated national commemoration. By the 1990s, the expression 'war of memories' had become commonplace and chronology, important for understanding the Occupation itself, is equally important here: if the past haunts the present, the present also haunts the past, and the memory of the war years has its own history.

La mémoire courte

'*Français, vous avez vraiment la mémoire courte*' ('My fellow countrymen, you really have a short memory') is the phrase famously pronounced by Philippe Pétain on 17 June 1941, exactly a year after his first broadcast announcing the defeat. He was berating the French for having forgotten what a dreadful state they had been in at that time and how much had been achieved since (Pétain 1941: 122). It is a phrase that echoes down the post-war years, emblematic of the arguments over memory and the trope of forgetfulness that is so often at the heart of its rhetoric. Jean Cassou, a Resister and a poet who famously memorised poems during a spell in prison in 1943, appropriated the phrase for *La Mémoire courte*, a polemical essay angrily attacking the French for their complicity with German behaviour during the Occupation, and deploring the post-war failure to live up to the Resistance ideals (Cassou 1953). His is one of many voices lamenting the perceived failure of the *épuration* as well as the fact that the heritage of the Resistance is wilting under sustained attack.

Although the notion that from 1944 onwards the celebration of the Resistance and a nation united silenced all other views has obtained wide credence, the reality could not have been more different. Certainly, the period following the liberation of Paris saw many national commemorations of victory and the Resistance, both formal and informal. De Gaulle's walk down the Champs Elysées on 26 August 1944, flanked by leaders of the French armed forces and leaders of the internal Resistance forces, cheered by over a million lining the route and followed by a *Te Deum* in Notre Dame, was unforgettable for those who witnessed it, as was the experience of Liberation. Years later, the historian Stanley Hoffmann, who spent the war as a child in hiding in the south of France, expressed well the sense of joy:

> Who did not live, in a French town or village, the weeks just before and after the Liberation, does not know the bliss of being alive at the end of an unspeakable ordeal, or the bliss of being happy with and proud of those amidst whom one had come through.
>
> *(Hoffmann 1975: xxv)*

The insurrection and his acclamation by the people of Paris, metonymically standing for France, were for de Gaulle the key legitimation of France as a combatant nation. His famous speech at the Hotel de Ville was not primarily about memory but focused on persuading the French that they now had a '*devoir de guerre*', a moral duty to pick up arms again and defeat Germany. In his view, Paris in August 1944 proved that only a handful of wretched traitors had accepted German sovereignty over France; Pétain and the Vichy government had misled many French people of good faith, but Paris showed the French were massively committed to France and her freedom and independence, and would take up arms again in order to enter Germany as conquerors. His framing of the war and the Resistance never varied: the Resistance had been the beacon of hope lighting the way forward. This vision of the Resistance as the spearhead of the nation at war during the dark years informed the Armistice Day commemoration of 11 November 1945, when the coffins of twelve Resisters, men and women, were brought to the Arc de Triomphe and laid around the tomb of the Unknown Soldier, before being carried for burial at Mont Valérien, where so many executions by firing squad had taken place during the Occupation. De Gaulle's vision of the Resistance as his special group of companions carrying the nation forward was reiterated in all his speeches of his wilderness years, from his resignation in 1946 to his return to power in 1958, and this structure was repeated in his vision for his political movement, leading the fight for the salvation and restoration of France's greatness.

For the French Communist Party too, invocation of the Resistance and its own leadership was situated within a political discourse of contemporary war. The Communist Party emerged with great legitimacy from its Resistance activities and electoral success, and joined the government until May 1947. But a combination of factors – exclusion from the government having refused to support a vote of confidence, the Cold War and their unconditional support for Stalin and the political interests of the Soviet Union – subsequently placed them firmly in an oppositional role. Resistance heroism was celebrated, but always with a purpose, as with their continuing lionisation of the Groupe Manouchian, the mainly foreign and Jewish communist resisters arrested, tried and shot in 1944 (Association des anciens FFI-FTPF 1951). The Communist memory was focused on a narrative of popular resistance, militancy and insurrection in a national fight against Nazism led by the Party and seamlessly integrated into its political discourse to bolster its own ideological imperatives.

Nonetheless, alongside these political discourses celebrating a nation united in pursuit of victory, the aftermath of the Occupation was a socially and politically turbulent time. Henry Rousso chronicles the political, ideological and juridical conflicts that dominated the early years of the ill-loved regime of the Fourth Republic (Rousso 1990). The trials of the *épuration*, both of prominent collaborators and, across the country, of thousands of otherwise obscure people, articulated a strong demand for justice against Vichy and its leaders, and against writers, journalists and entertainers; the extreme polarisation of the months of often brutal fighting in 1944 had coloured attitudes to the whole Occupation. Together with the trials and petitions for grace in certain cases, such as that of the journalist and writer Robert Brasillach, an ideological war of words in books and articles was also raging. While much of the right was discredited by association with collaboration, and the Communist Party came out of the first post-war elections as the largest party, angry denunciations of the Communist Resistance became commonplace in many right-wing books and pamphlets, together with virulent attacks on de Gaulle and defences of Vichy, particularly of Pétain as the protector of national interests against the Germans. The political use of Resistance for personal advantage and the shallow or non-existent moral credentials of the *maquis* whose actions and atrocities, it was argued, were only too similar to German crimes, were pejoratively dubbed '*résistantialisme*' (Desgranges 1948). Defence of Pétain was central to Louis Girard's polemical works, one of which bequeathed the important phrase 'the Franco-French War' to the memory debates of later decades (Girard 1950).

Documenting the anti-Semitism of Vichy and the horrors of the deportation of 70,000 Jews from France has, since the 1980s, been an important strand in the reversal of a heroic myth of French national Resistance. Yet it is worth noting that the Centre de Documentation Juive Contemporaine published a range of titles from 1945 to comprehensively present the crimes against the Jews in Hitler's Europe, and in France in particular; some of these, such as the authoritative study by Joseph Billig on the Commissariat aux questions juives (Billig 1955–1960) and Léon Poliakov's famous *Bréviaire de la haine: le IIIe Reich et les Juifs* (Poliakov 1951), had a strong impact. Commemoration and constitution of an archive were inseparable in this work. The anti-Semitic legislation of the 'pseudo-government of France at Vichy' (Lubetzki 1945: 5) that sought to define and isolate France's Jews, the internment camps set up across France (Weill 1946), the pillage of Jewish belongings (Cassou 1947), Jewish resistance movements and other organisations (Knout 1947; CDJC 1947), all received detailed attention. Georges Wellers, who would again be prominent in the fight against anti-Semitic revisionism in the 1980s, wrote an important study of the internment camp at Drancy to the north of Paris which would become a focal point of arguments about French complicity and occultation in later decades (Wellers 1946). None of these books side-stepped the role of the French people who contributed – as legislators and as police – to the marginalisation and persecution of Jews.

While the Cold War was an important factor in the extreme polarisation of debates around Communism and the French Communist Party's defiant invocation of its Resistance past, the Algerian War of Independence of 1954–62, which might also be seen as a pressure emanating from outside France, posed acute questions about French national identity. For both left and right, the Algerian war meant that the ideological battles of 1940–44 continued to be fought as the vocabulary of Resistance and collaboration was mobilised across the political spectrum. Use of torture by the French military was widely equated by the left to the actions of the Gestapo, with the colonial occupation likened to the German Occupation. France was now in the position of the hated occupier, as Sartre underlined in his play *Les Séquestrés d'Altona*, where the German soldier and torturer of Russian partisans during the Second World War is called by the near homonym Frantz, and where the *magnétophone* he uses to record his views for the judges of the future recalled clearly for contemporary audiences the '*magnéto*', the apparatus of torture administering electric shocks (Sartre 1959). 'If one day there is another Nuremberg tribunal we will all be found guilty; we are making new Oradours every day', reported a French soldier (Comité résistance spirituelle 1957: 55).

The Resistance was an integral part of the political orchestration of historical spectacle to support de Gaulle's return to power, though he can hardly have enjoyed parallels drawn in the press between himself and Pétain.[1] In September 1958, on the anniversary of the declaration of the Third Republic in 1870, de Gaulle unveiled the new constitution for a Fifth Republic on the Place de la République. He was introduced by André Malraux, who had fought in the Resistance under the alias 'Colonel Berger':

> No-one can remake France without the French, and the Republic is repeating to them what the muffled voice of the Republic in exile used to say: I want to become France once more. Many of you here will have heard, night after night: 'This is London. The French are speaking to the French. *Honneur et patrie*. You are about to hear the Général de Gaulle.' [...] This is Paris! *Honneur et patrie!* Once again, French men and women keeping the rendezvous with the Republic and with history, you are going to hear the Général de Gaulle.[2]

By 1961 the terrorist anti-independence Organisation Armée Secrète (OAS) had been formed; many of its leaders had been active in the Resistance and saw themselves as continuing the same patriotic fight for France. An OAS document of 20 October 1961 is notable for its use of '*la Résistance*' to describe their own movement,[3] while questions asked in Parliament about the killings of Algerians in Paris on 17 October 1961 explicitly recalled the German Occupation (Beauvoir 1963: 435–7). In other words, in the political turbulence throughout the Fourth Republic and beyond, reference to the Occupation was part of the living fabric of that turbulence, rather than merely a self-conscious memorialisation (though the latter was also visible in some official national and local commemorations).

La Mémoire Courte, a documentary film made in 1962 by Henri Torrent and his wife Francine Premysler, encapsulates the approach to the Second World War and the Occupation in this period before the extraordinary shift in perspective of the post-'68 years. The film takes a global view, with military and domestic footage from France, Germany, Japan, Italy, the Soviet Union, Great Britain and the United States, as well as from Spain. The sections on the Occupation of France cover many aspects: high life in Paris, at fashion shoots and the races, women dyeing their legs and painting the seam on the back to simulate real stockings, speeches of collaborators like Alphonse de Chateaubriant, Jacques Doriot or Philippe Henriot haranguing huge crowds, crowds cheering Pétain, the queues for food, Vichy's youth cult and the *chantiers de jeunesse*, the *maquis*, and the huge *rafle* (round-up) of 16–17 July 1942, known as the '*rafle du vél d'hiv*' after the velodrome where many thousands of Jews were detained before transit to the camp at Drancy. Apart from one acerbic comment within the film, relating to the capacity of Germans to erase instantly from their memory all knowledge of who might be responsible for the concentration and extermination camps when angrily challenged by the liberating armies, the term '*la mémoire courte*' is here future-oriented. The film ends with footage of Germany under the rubble, images of the misery and suffering of war that the audience is exhorted to remember; it must avoid '*la mémoire courte*' and not let this happen again. As if to prove its point, *Hitler connais pas* was the provocative title of Bertrand Blier's compelling 1963 film about young people who, in a series of interviews, talk of their own past and present circumstances, their difficulties and aspirations. The war is passing into history, and the war is not their concern.

By the end of the Algerian war, then, and in the years following, the Gaullist narrative of world war and sacrifice was framing the memory of the Occupation, with de Gaulle himself combining military and Resistance in his person. The Resistance centred on de Gaulle was exploited to heal division and forge memorable images of a nation united, as in the famous 1964 ceremony at the Panthéon to receive the ashes of Jean Moulin, the envoy sent by de Gaulle to unify the Resistance movements in France in 1943 and a figure plucked from some obscurity at the time for the occasion (Piketty 2000). Two years later, the appearance of Gérard Oury's *La Grande Vadrouille*, a comedy of individual and fairly anarchic Resistance to the Germans involving famous comic actors and extremely well worked German and English caricatures that held the record for the most successful French film for over four decades, suggested a relaxation of tension over the traumatic defeat of 1940; it was followed by many other highly popular film comedies. And throughout the years of the Fourth and early Fifth Republics, hundreds of novels and large numbers of films about the war and Occupation appeared. It has been noted that most of the Goncourt prizes were awarded to novels presenting far from heroic sides of the Occupation, in which they were quite typical of large numbers of others (Jacquet 2000). The Goncourt rewarded André Schwartz-Bart's *Le Dernier des justes* (Schwartz-Bart 1959), that included reference to Drancy and deportation, and Anna Langfus' *Les Bagages de sable* (Langfus 1962), recreating the intensely painful world of a Holocaust survivor in post-war France; Simone de Beauvoir's novel of the crushingly soulless values of consumer society, *Les Belles Images*, draws on the atrocities of the deportations of Jews and the Algerian war as part of its political critique (Beauvoir 1966).

Far from silencing them, the major narrative of France at war accommodated a multiplicity of other stories about the Occupation within the edifying portrait of a nation having overcome its defeat and integrated the internal Resistance forces into the French army, marching once more, and this time to victory.

La mode rétro

The end of the 1960s saw very significant changes in France. The massive political and social upheaval of May '68, exploding out of rigid hierarchical social and cultural structures and mores, was primarily intending to change the future, and to reimagine political, cultural and professional relationships. Yet the students and workers on the streets invoked the past in support of the values of insurrection, revolution and the resistance to oppression: 'CRS-SS', equating the French riot police with the Nazis, was a common slogan. De Gaulle had been in power for ten years and was now a figure of established authority rather than one representing any kind of rebellion: so the protestors reconfigured the Resistance in the image of Third World movements of national liberation (Atack 1999: 114–15). Made in 1969 for television, *Le Chagrin et la pitié* (*The Sorrow and the Pity*) was the emblematic film of its times, and its impact can hardly be overestimated. In spite of its topic and because of its topic, this four-hour long documentary on life in Clermont-Ferrand during the Occupation was not broadcast by the state-owned French television. Instead, in 1971 it was shown in a Paris cinema, provoking massive press coverage and generating long queues.

Framed as subversive by its 'banning', with its intensely melancholic title and the sense of an ambitious, totalising and comprehensive document on the Occupation conveyed from the outset by its very length, *The Sorrow* effected a massive paradigm shift, ushering the Occupation into the public arena anew as an object of public and private memory. The Occupation had previously been a battleground for its protagonists and had provided a set of living references, yoked to new political discourses; now it was at centre stage within a problematic of multiple memories that fractured the homogeneity of what the film actually created, *a contrario*, as the authorised version of the Occupation. Its 'banning' meant that an authorised, official, necessarily Gaullist version of the Occupation, which had official, Gaullist, national Resistance at its core, was *de facto* under attack. The reception of this indubitably pro-Resistance film focused almost entirely upon what it had to say about collaboration and division; the notions of myth and counter-myth were extensively discussed, with the film being charged by some with replacing a Resistance myth with a myth of collaboration.

In over thirty interviews, interspersed with contemporary newsreels, a wide range of people recall their memories of the time: resisters, collaborators, officials and politicians such as Pierre Mendès-France, Anthony Eden and Georges Bidault.

(The latter had been chosen by de Gaulle to replace Jean Moulin after his arrest, had walked down the Champs-Elysées with de Gaulle on 26 August, and, as one of the leaders of the OAS convicted in the courts in his absence, had only just returned to France from exile.) *The Sorrow* gives us a people-focused, bottom-up Resistance; de Gaulle was conspicuous by his absence. Those who come out worst are those who are unthinkingly complicit with Nazi or Vichy oppression: the German former officer, the lycée teachers who watched their students being arrested and still did nothing or Marius Klein, the shopkeeper who is cruelly mocked for putting up a notice explaining to his customers that he was not Jewish. (The film could, however, be criticised for failing to explain the complexity of Vichy's anti-Semitic laws that created a climate of confusion and paranoia, or how the scale of denunciations had placed individuals in the situation of having to prove to the authorities that they were not Jewish, a situation that would later be explored in Joseph Losey's kafkaesque film *M. Klein* (1976).) A royalist upper-class Resister comes across as ridiculous, whereas Christian de la Mazière – who actually fought for Germany in a German uniform, as a member of the Division Charlemagne, and who explains his choices with articulate fluency in terms of family and class rebellion – does not. The picture is one of complexity.

To the authenticity of the individual voice of lived experience is added a powerful use of popular music, with Maurice Chevalier's familiar songs deployed in a defamiliarising context, accentuating the immediacy of affect that the film creates with its compelling interviews and supporting footage. Similar techniques had been used in *La Mémoire courte*, but that film had not inserted itself into public memory in the way the Moulin ceremony or the Gaullist-focused historical narrative presented in school books had done (Citron 2008: 103–5). The different framing devices in each of the two films, from global warfare to multiple French experiences and memories of behaviour, lent the documentary footage in each a very different character.

After the controversy surrounding *The Sorrow and the Pity*, the floodgates in film and fiction seemed to open through the 1970s: the psychological flaws and political compromises of a nation were insistently depicted in an explicit or implicit rejection of the heroic grandeur and martyrdom that had characterised the reception of Jean Moulin into the Panthéon. Other individual voices were also making themselves heard, including those of the next generation coming to grips with marginalised memories of collaboration. Patrick Modiano and Marie Chaix both wrote novels about the Occupation that placed collaboration and anti-Semitism at their centre (Modiano 1968; Chaix 1974). Representations of fascism, decadence and sexuality, in the wake of Visconti's *The Damned* and Cavani's *The Night Porter* – the story of a sadomasochistic relationship between a former inmate and former guard of a concentration camp – was an integral part of what was now being called '*la mode rétro*', the fashion for the look, feel and deviant behaviour of the Occupation years. Louis Malle's 1974 *Lacombe Lucien*, one of several films of these years about the Occupation but the most important and lasting filmic expression of '*la mode rétro*', conveys two messages of ambiguity: the ambiguity of power, sexuality and violence centred around fascism, and the ambiguity of commitment – it suggests that choices between engagement in the Resistance and in collaboration were more often the product of chance than ideological fervour. The decadence of the collaborationist milieu with its nightclubs, rich food and drink was one of the established tropes of discourses on the Occupation: the soundtrack of Django Reinhardt and the Quintette du Hot Club de France places the whole film, while set in the rural south, under the sign of Paris by night.

De Gaulle had left office in 1969 and died in 1970. Michel Foucault famously argued, in a discussion of '*la mode rétro*', that these years signalled the break with a dominant pro-Resistance narrative and the emergence of a counter-memory of the Occupation years, pointing to Giscard d'Estaing, president from 1974, as the first without a Resistance past (Foucault 1974). In fact Georges Pompidou, who succeeded de Gaulle in 1969, would have been an equally pertinent example: his pardon for the former Vichy paramilitary Paul Touvier in 1971 became a national scandal. Reintroducing the Occupation with the claim that it was a poorly understood and mythologised period of French history, *The Sorrow* and '*la mode rétro*' set the frame for the maelstrom of public debates in the 1980s that would deepen and broaden this approach. But this was also taking place within a wider context, where a generic interest in the past was at the same time becoming all-consuming; this is perhaps the single most important instance of outside factors shaping the national agenda.

1980 was decreed '*l'année du patrimoine*' or 'heritage year'. This move did not command universal political approval but public enthusiasm was widespread and genuine, and it was a huge success, particularly at the local level (Nora 1996). Already in the 1970s, *Le Cheval d'orgueil*, a story of rural Brittany, had been a runaway bestseller (Hélias 1975), and there had been a surge of popularity for programmes featuring rural France on television (Bosséno 1976). The rural location of *Lacombe Lucien*, feeding off this burgeoning passion for heritage, surely contributed to its success. This turn towards an 'authentic' lived experience of regional heritage has been widely interpreted as a response to the anonymising processes of globalisation and consumerism, with the individual and collective recall of a lived past being a privileged vector of French specificity (Kuisel 1993; Nora 1996). Pierre Nora's multi-volume *Lieux de mémoire* offered a sophisticated theorisation of these processes, his argument being that in a world of accelerating and continual change, France's connections to its memories had been broken (Nora 1984–92). 'We speak so much of memory', Nora wrote, 'because there is so little of it left.' The groups and collectivities that sustained memory as an organic living thing had gone and the French were condemned to forgetfulness and to constructing mere representations of memory. The sites of memory are not what is being remembered but are rather laboratories where tradition is being produced (Nora 1989: 7). The French are no longer within memory but detached from it, with the result that its contours have become visible and can be studied.

Coincidentally no doubt, in 1980 the important Comité d'histoire de la deuxième guerre mondiale (Committee of the History of the Second World War) was to re-establish itself as the Institut d'histoire du temps present (Institute for the Study of the Present Time); its first major project was to research the troubled and troubling relations the French had with the memory of the Second World War (Damoi and Rioux 1986). This brought together a large number of studies of commemoration from different parts of France, showing the extent to which they varied and the ways in which local details created specific tensions and solutions. The importance of the commemoration of 11 November meant it retained its place in the calendar, establishing a continuity between the two world wars; but other resonant dates, such as 18 June (the anniversary of de Gaulle's 1940 radio address from London), would be marked or not according to the configuration of local politics. Commemoration of the anniversary of the end of the war in Europe on 8 May 1945 was often subdued or subsumed into other local festivities on proximate dates; this was not entirely because on the same day French police had massacred hundreds of Algerians in Sétif, though great play was subsequently made of this coincidence in anti-colonial discourse. In 1954 the anniversary was palpably overshadowed by the defeat of the French expeditionary force at Dien Bien Phu the previous day. So while it is impossible to get to grips with local and regional memories without understanding the relationship of the protagonists to the national picture, it is also true that the complexities of the national landscape are refracted and reconfigured at the local and regional levels in multiple different ways, according to the political complexion of the local authorities and the specific experiences and historical dynamics of each area.

The enthusiasm for heritage, intersecting with the 'memory as revelation' dynamic of '*la mode rétro*', helped sustain the Occupation as a central mnemonic narrative, and this was also fuelled by the controversies associated with a series of public trials and by scandals over historical revisionism and contemporary anti-Semitism. Klaus Barbie, the head of the local Gestapo in Lyon – known as the 'butcher of Lyon' for his personal torturing of Resistance members – was brought to France from Bolivia to stand trial. His defence was led by Jacques Vergès who challenged the right of the French state, in his view guilty of war crimes in the Algerian war, to try him; he also mobilised the now dominant scepticism about the legitimacy of the Resistance, particularly attacking the reputation of Jean Moulin who had died during his transfer to Germany after being tortured in Lyon at Barbie's hands. At the same time, Holocaust revisionism became a national scandal. Robert Faurisson, a professor of literature and active Holocaust denier, published a series of inflammatory high-profile statements denying the existence of homicidal gas chambers; as anti-Semitic violence returned to the streets of Paris with bombs in the rue Copernic in 1980 and the rue des Roziers in 1982, this was as much a matter of present politics as of memory. Jean-Marie Le Pen, head of the extreme-right National Front party, commented in 1987 that the gas chambers were just a historical footnote or minor point of detail. Pierre Vidal-Naquet, whose parents had been deported to Auschwitz to their deaths, was an important figure in the refutation of revisionism (Vidal-Naquet 1987, 1995); he was also one of a group of significant intellectuals who had survived the war as children in hiding and who had started in the 1960s to re-examine their personal heritage (Suleiman 2015).

It was not, however, possible to cast these views as simply those of an extremist fringe beyond the mainstream of French society. The audience of millions who watched *The Sorrow* when it was finally shown on television in 1981 heard Pierre Mendès-France, one of those at the centre of President François Mitterrand's investiture a few months earlier, describe in a forty-minute interview being put on trial by Vichy with the former prime minister Léon Blum. Bernard-Henri Lévy's *Idéologie française* argued powerfully that racism was inherent in Republican ideology and that Frenchness therefore relied on exclusion (Lévy 1981). His historical analysis to support this was more than shaky, but more serious works exploring French fascism began to appear in numbers too. The historical journal *Vingtième siècle* reprised Girard's title of 1950 for a special issue on 'Les guerres franco-françaises' in 1985 (Azéma, Rioux and Rousso 1985). Historiography had already contributed to the framing of memorialisation, as when Robert Paxton's study of Vichy France complemented the lessons of *The Sorrow* (Paxton 1973).

This happened to an even greater extent in 1987 when the first edition of Henry Rousso's *Le Syndrome de Vichy* appeared, a study devoted to the memory of Vichy (Rousso 1990). This work above all others has established itself as a primary reference point, in popular and scholarly work alike, with its identification of a Resistance myth that Rousso dubbed '*résistancialisme*', namely the mythic instrumentalisation of Resistance to signify the whole of France. Although Rousso was too sophisticated to say this, his work was used to support the argument that the only public discourse about French behaviour during the Occupation ever since 1944 had been one of national heroic Resistance, until the silence about collaboration, complicity and anti-Semitism was finally broken by *The Sorrow*. Rousso presented the post-war controversies and invocations of Vichy as a 'syndrome', a continual return to and pathological working through of the unfinished business of mourning, culminating in the '*résistancialiste*' myth of the 1960s, which mobilised Gaullist pronouncements of 1944 in foundational support. The trope of the return of previously repressed and occulted memories and of the breaking of taboos has remained central to much subsequent public discourse on the war, even where this has often involved the re-presentation of material that can clearly be shown to have been already in the public domain; the repeated efforts of historians to break this particular dynamic have been resisted, and Rousso's work thus – and ironically – created a new syndrome beyond the one he sought to subject to analysis.

If '*la mode rétro*' had focused initially on the issue of collaboration, the end of the 1980s was dominated by Jewish memory: by the Holocaust and the active French involvement in the deportation from France of 70,000 Jews, ranging from the very elderly to small babies. Claude Lanzmann's nine-hour 1985 epic *Shoah* reconstructed the scale and cruelty of the Final Solution and Louis Malle's highly successful 1987 *Au revoir les enfants* told the story of Jewish children hidden in Izieu and deported to Auschwitz after a raid by Barbie's men. Crime fiction, which had had a new lease of life as a highly politicised genre in the 1970s, became in the hands of Didier Daeninckx and others the perfect vehicle for the exploration of state crimes and their cover-up. The continuity of state criminality from Vichy to the Algerian war and beyond appeared to be encapsulated in the person of Maurice Papon, a government minister in the late 1970s whose role in the deportation of Jews as a Vichy official and in the deaths of Algerians in Paris on 17 October 1961 as chief of police was being repeatedly discussed in the early 1980s in the left-wing press. As crimes of the past contaminated the present, *Meurtres pour mémoire* (*Murders in Memoriam*) (Daeninckx 1983), presenting Papon's story in fictionalised guise, became an iconic text for unravelling the complexities of the layering of memories of the Algerian war and the Occupation. National amnesia seemed to some to have become a defining French characteristic (Nicolaïdis 1994).

'*La mode rétro*' established the modalities by which understanding of key elements of the war years would be revised: with the shock of revelation, the uncovering of hidden crimes and the ending of years of official silence. It brought the Occupation into the public arena as the focus of a maelstrom of competing positions. In the following decades memories of the Occupation would enter into the heart of the state, its laws and its institutions.

Le devoir de mémoire

The 1990s saw a veritable explosion of historical works, novels, films, testimonies and autobiographies examining all aspects of the culture, politics and practices of Vichy France, including the camps and deportations and other painful memories such as the shaving of women's heads at the liberation, now seen as a sexual crime. The Gayssot law criminalising the denial of the Holocaust was passed in 1990 (Bienenstock 2014). The expression '*lieux de mémoire*' entered the dictionary, underlining the pervasive new importance of commemoration. This was further reinforced by the commemorative cycle marking the fiftieth anniversary of key events in the war through the first half of the decade, and by the establishment of many new museums and memorials dedicated to the Resistance or to wartime atrocities (such as that at Oradour-sur-Glane). The television channel France 2 devoted a whole evening to the fiftieth anniversary of the '*rafle du vél d'hiv*' on 16 July 1992: a screening of Michel Mitrani's 1974 film *Les Guichets du Louvre*, an adaptation of Roger Boussinot's 1960 novel (Boussinot 1960), was followed by a round table discussion with schoolchildren.

These years were intense in their recall of the Occupation. The sense that the pressing issue of the moment was the integration of the Holocaust – and most particularly the complicity of Vichy in the deportations – into French memories was reinforced by the shocking desecration of a Jewish cemetery in Carpentras in 1990. The phrase '*devoir de mémoire*', commonly if rather awkwardly translated as 'duty to memory', became central to the memorialisation of the war. After being used in a ceremony at the deportation memorial in the Ile de la Cité in 1992 and placed in the headline of *Le Monde*'s subsequent report (Ledoux 2011: 23–4), it became omnipresent from 1995 (Ledoux 2011 : 31–40), and dominated public and pedagogic memory of the war (Coquio 2015: 133–57). A question was devoted to it on the philosophy paper of the *baccalauréat* in 1992 (Lalieu 2001) and, indeed, it provoked important work from philosophers reflecting on the relationships between individual and collective memory and the renewed role of the witness within this framework of memory as imperative (Ricœur 2000).

The ever-complex relations between historians and the surviving actors of the war years (Rousso 2012: 11–12) came to a head when veteran Resistance heroes Raymond and Lucie Aubrac were interviewed – many would say interrogated – by historians about their dealings with the Nazis. Klaus Barbie had raised suspicions at his trial about possible Resistance complicity in the arrest of Jean Moulin at Caluire and questions had also been asked about the circumstances in which Raymond Aubrac had escaped from a Gestapo prison. Lucie Aubrac had written her memoir of the Resistance (Aubrac 1984) to counter Barbie's slurs but the affair nonetheless developed into a major 'political-media' scandal (Veillon and Alary 2000: 184). This latest controversy only seemed to confirm that '*la mode rétro*' and its aftermath had robbed the Resistance of its pristine reputation and of much of its voice in the national arena.

In 1995 France's new president Jacques Chirac, who would be dubbed the '*président du devoir de mémoire*' when he stepped down in 2007 (Ledoux 2011: 31), pronounced the first official acknowledgement and apology for French culpability in the deportations of Jews. This was in marked contrast to his predecessor Mitterrand who had followed de Gaulle's line that the Republic was not responsible for the illegitimate Vichy regime's actions, a distinction that by this time had become untenable. Mitterrand was a thoroughly controversial figure by the end of his presidency in 1995, for his role in Vichy prior to his joining the Resistance had become public knowledge, as had, no doubt more damagingly, his friendship with former Vichyiste René Bousquet (Péan 1994). He unveiled a memorial to the deported children of Izieu but also sent flowers every year to Pétain's grave. The sense that those at the heart of the French state had consistently covered up French crimes became overwhelming. Bousquet, who had been the senior police officer organising the '*rafle du vél d'hiv*' with the Germans, was finally charged in 1993, though he was murdered at home before he could be brought to trial. Papon's trial for crimes against humanity relating to his role in deportations finally took place in 1998. Paul Touvier, who had been protected by the Catholic Church, was finally convicted for his role in the Vichy paramilitary *milice* in 1994.

In 1997 Patrick Modiano published *Dora Bruder* (Modiano 1997). Modiano had long been dissecting the more troubling aspects of the Occupation in his elusive, fragmented, fiction, exploring how the trope of memory as revelation itself actually generated anxieties about forgetfulness. This latest novel was a masterly exploration of loss: the loss of Dora Bruder and her family, deported from Paris to Auschwitz, and the loss of any secure material presence of the past. As the narrator walks the streets of Paris, he remembers his father whose path may or may not have crossed with that of Dora, his own adolescence during the Algerian war, and Dora's past as he conjectures it to have been. As fictionalised as it is documented, the novel celebrates the power of the imagination even as it records its limitations. Dora is realised, becomes real, in the narrative that cannot recapture her; she is both recovered and lost in the same gesture. In its will to resist the anonymising force of history, its focus on the unique value and tragic fate of this, and by implication every, victim of deportation from France, Modiano's text represents the best aspects of the often controversial and indeed sometimes tyrannical injunction of '*le devoir de mémoire*'.

The focus upon the crimes of the deportations and French complicity in the Holocaust brought the French nation-state and its institutions back into focus. There was undoubtedly a drive to give palpable, permanent, public form to memory, whether in the apparatus of the law, the setting up of national and local memorial institutions, or the commemoration of the victims. So the Mémorial de la Shoah in Paris, opened in 2005, contains a poignant Wall of Names listing every single person deported to the death camps because they were Jewish.

The twenty-first century

The new century seemed set to continue the ways of the old. Jonathan Littell's 700-page novel *Les Bienveillantes* (*The Kindly Ones*) (Littell 2006) flew off the shelves as it harnessed once more the trope of the shock of revelation and confirmed the effectiveness of scandal as a strategy to dominate the public arena. This is the story of Maximilien Aue, an officer of the SS who witnesses and describes in detail the massacres at Babi Yar, the siege of Stalingrad and the operation of the death camps. Its provocative opening sentence – 'Human brothers, let me tell you how it happened' – with its Baudelairean overtones placed this story of a perpetrator of extreme violence, massacres and individual murders firmly within, and claiming kinship to, French culture. This is further thematised in Aue's stays in occupied Paris, moving in collaborationist circles, and in the echoes of Sartre's *Les Mouches*. Redefining the relationship between history and fiction, and demonstrating the porous nature of historiography, public memory and media, it was closely followed by other hybrid novels with a central European theme including Laurent Binet's *HHhH*, on the assassination of Heydrich (Binet 2010), and Yannick Haenel's *Jan Karski*, on the heroic Polish resister who reported to the Allies on the appalling situation of the Jews in Poland (Haenel 2009).

The Resistance also found a voice: Stéphane Hessel's pamphlet *Indignez-vous* (*Time for Outrage!*) (Hessel 2010) sold nearly a million copies in ten months. In 2004 many major Resisters and deportees including Hessel had signed an appeal to commemorate the sixtieth anniversary of the programme of the Conseil national de la Résistance of 15 March 1944. In common with other former Resistance fighters, Hessel subsequently grew steadily more angry at the efforts of President Nicolas Sarkozy to appropriate the memory of the movement for conservative patriotic ends after his election in 2007. They organised an annual commemoration at the site of a major massacre of Resistance figures where Sarkozy had previously given a key campaign speech, to keep what they saw as the true radical values of the Resistance alive. Hessel's 2009 speech at this event would end up being printed as *Indignez-vous*, an appeal to the spirit of Resistance that was turned to the present and the future, not the past. He urged the young to mobilise Resistance values to fight for human rights and against the depredations of neo-liberal capitalism, with a neat and pointed call for a '*devoir d'indignation*'. As president, Sarkozy controversially ordered the last letter of Guy Môquet, shot as a Resister at the age of seventeen, to be read in every school and proposed that every 10-year-old primary school child should adopt the memory of a deported Jewish child in order to transmit the memory across generations; Simone Veil, a former minister and a deportee herself, described this suggestion as 'unbearable', a mnemonic intervention likely only to traumatise the young.[4]

Alongside these major controversies in the public arena and the institutions of the state, individual voices and new studies continue to extend and deepen the densely complex fabric of multiple war memories. New topics with obvious contemporary piquancy include the role of North Africans in the Resistance. Ivan Jablonka's award-winning memoir of his grandparents – political activists, illegal immigrants to France and then deportees to Auschwitz – joins the growing transnational literature in which the third generation grapples with the damaging legacy of the war (Jablonka 2012). Hélène Berr's diary detailing the daily life of a Jew in Paris until her deportation (Berr 2007), and the television drama series *Un Village français*, demonstrate in different ways how public appetite for the war years remains remarkably strong.[5]

The decades of controversy and revelation have made a difference: the most painful realities of life under Vichy and foreign occupation are integrated into public awareness of the period at all levels, including the school curriculum, and not at the expense of the Resistance. To an extent, there is much greater comfort with complexity: the combination of allegiance first to Vichy and then to the Resistance that was so shocking in Mitterrand's journey when it was first revealed is now accepted as having been commonplace (Vergez-Chaignon 2008: 747). Awareness that war and occupation involved a complex patchwork of multiple experiences is embodied in *La Vie des Drancéens 1939–1945* (*Life of the Inhabitants of Drancy*) (Moreau 2004), produced in the commune of Drancy, site of the detention camp for deportations to the east. With a simple chronological organisation, local history and war memories converge in a compilation of the experiences of the inhabitants and the events in the neighbourhood from mobilisation to liberation. Scrapbook, testimony, commemoration, archive, it is a collective record of hundreds of individual lives and events with resonance beyond the locality (for example, every departure for Auschwitz is recorded), interspersed with comments from protagonists who are still living in the area.

Conclusion

While things have shifted as the years of competing memory wars and shocking revelations have given way to an acknowledgement of diverse, conflicting and painful realities, what has remained absolutely tenacious is the 'myth of the myth': the myth that a silence fell on all this from de Gaulle's words at the Hotel de Ville in August 1944 until *The Sorrow and the Pity* in 1971. Witness, for example, Jacques Mandelbaum welcoming the re-release of *La Grande Vadrouille* in July 2016:

> Twenty years after the end of the second world war, you can see here the last lights of the Gaullist myth gleaming, of a France united against the oppressor, freed from oppression with honour and dignity regained. [...] The beliefs carried by *La Grande Vadrouille* are soon going to shatter (recognition of collaboration, revolt of May 1968) but the myth will continue to lull the collective consciousness.[6]

In 2013, Laurent Douzou reviewed two 'iconoclastic' books (Douzou 2013) which he suggested should have had a greater impact: Pierre Laborie's *Le Chagrin et le venin* (*The Sorrow and the Poison*) and François Azouvi's more recent *Le Mythe du grand silence* (*The Myth of the Great Silence*) (Laborie 2011; Azouvi 2012). Both challenge the notion that there was silence in France about crimes and collaboration after the war, yet this remains a commanding discourse. Why, the French might well ask, have we forgotten that we had not forgotten?

Part of the answer may lie in the force of the nation as a singular subject of the history and the memory of the war. For de Gaulle '*la France*' was the central protagonist; the only reason for the military and political struggles of the war and the Fourth Republic was to restore France to her glory and greatness. '*La France blessée*' was his recurrent image of the years of the Occupation. Henry Rousso's later historiographical model of the post-war years as years of unfinished mourning and repression maintained the nation as a psychological subject. There is an undeniably powerful naturalising effect in the model of the nation as a consciousness with repressed memories, where unity can only operate as a false memory, especially in a country with a central allegiance to the 'Republic one and indivisible' being coterminous with France itself.

Historiographical analysis of the ways France has remembered the Second World War needs to recognise the limitations of any national model for understanding a particular locality and also the interaction of national and international factors at various points; but the strength of the national as an organising principle is the overwhelming factor in France's fractured and fracturing memorialisation of the war.

Notes

Unless otherwise indicated, all translations are my own.

1 See the material collected under anonymous editorship in *L'OAS parle*, published in Paris by Julliard in 1964; here at 24.
2 Transcripts of Malraux's speech and that of de Gaulle which followed it can be found at http://fresques.ina.fr/de-gaulle/fiche-media/Gaulle00020/discours-place-de-la-republique.html.
3 *L'OAS parle*, 102.

4 'Mémoire de la Shoah: Simone Veil juge « insoutenable » la proposition de Nicolas Sarkozy', *Le Monde*, 2 February 2008, www.lemonde.fr/politique/article/2008/02/15/shoah-simone-veil-juge-insoutenable-la-proposition-de-nicolas-sarkozy_1012067_823448.html.
5 Manu Bragança, '« Un Village français »: les clefs d'un succès', *The Conversation*, 20 September 2015, http://theconversation.com/un-village-francais-les-clefs-dun-succes-46367.
6 Jacques Mandelbaum, 'Reprise: « La Grande Vadrouille », duo de pieds nickelés dans une France occupée', *Le Monde*, 13 July 2016, www.lemonde.fr/cinema/article/2016/07/12/reprise-la-grande-vadrouille-duo-de-pieds-nickeles-dans-une-france-occupee_4968084_3476.html.

References

Association des anciens FFI-FTPF. 1951. *Pages de gloire des vingt-trois*. Paris: Immigration (CFDI).

Atack, Margaret. 1999. *May 68 in French Fiction and Film: Rethinking Society, Rethinking Representation*. Oxford: Oxford University Press.

Aubrac, Lucie. 1984. *Ils partiront dans l'ivresse*. Paris: Seuil.

Azéma, Jean-Pierre, Rioux, Jean-Pierre and Rousso, Henry. eds. 1985. 'Les guerres franco-françaises'. *Vingtième siècle*, 5: 3–154.

Azouvi, François. 2012. *Le Mythe du grand silence: Auschwitz, les Français, la mémoire*. Paris: Gallimard.

Beauvoir, Simone de. 1963. *La Force des Choses*. Paris: Gallimard.

Beauvoir, Simone de. 1966. *Les Belles Images*. Paris: Gallimard.

Berr, Hélène. 2007. *Journal 1942–1944*. Paris: Tallandier.

Bienenstock, Miriam. ed. 2014. *Devoir de mémoire?: les lois mémorielles et l'histoire*. Paris: Editions de l'Eclat.

Billig, Joseph. 1955–1960. *Le Commissariat général aux questions juives (1941–1944)*. 3 vols. Paris: Editions du Centre.

Binet, Laurent. 2010. *HHhH*. Paris: Grasset.

Bosséno, Christian. 1976. 'Télévision et monde rural'. *La Revue du cinéma: image et son*, 311: 44–59.

Boussinot, Roger. 1960. *Les Guichets du Louvre*. Paris: Denoël.

CDJC. 1947. *Activité des organisations juives en France sous l'occupation*. Paris: Editions du Centre.

Cassou, Jean. 1947. *Le Pillage des œuvres d'art et des bibliothèques appartenant à des Juifs en France*. Paris: Editions du Centre.

Cassou, Jean. 1953. *La Mémoire courte*. Paris: Editions de minuit.

Chaix, Marie. 1974. *Les Lauriers du lac de Constanze: chronique d'une collaboration*. Paris: Seuil.

Citron, Suzanne. 2008. *Le Mythe national: l'histoire de France revisitée*. Paris: Editions de l'Atelier.

Comité résistance spirituelle. ed. 1957. *Des Rappelés témoignent*. Paris: Clichy.

Conan, Eric and Rousso, Henry. 1994. *Vichy: un passé qui ne passe pas*. Paris: Fayard.

Coquio, Catherine. 2015. *Le Mal de vérité ou l'utopie de la mémoire*. Paris: Armand Colin.

Daeninckx, Didier. 1983. *Meurtres pour mémoire*. Paris: Gallimard.

Damoi, Evelyne and Rioux, Jean-Pierre. eds. 1986. *La mémoire des Français: quarante ans de commémorations de la seconde guerre mondiale*. Paris: Editions du CNRS.

Desgranges, Abbé. 1948. *Les Crimes masqués du 'résistantialisme'*. Paris: Editions de l'Elan.

Douzou, Laurent. 2013. 'Deux relectures iconoclastes: de la mémoire de l'occupation'. *Critique*, 798: 889–905.

Foucault, Michel. 1974. 'Anti-rétro'. *Cahiers du cinéma*, 251–2: 5–17.

Girard, Louis. 1950. *La Guerre franco-française*. Paris: Editions André Bonne.
Haenel,Yannick. 2009. *Jan Karski*. Paris: Gallimard.
Hélias, Pierre-Jakez. 1975. *Le Cheval d'orgueil*. Paris: Plon.
Hessel, Stéphane. 2010. *Indignez-vous*. Paris: Indigène Editions.
Hoffmann, Stanley. 1975. 'Introduction'. In *The Sorrow and the Pity: Chronicle of a French City Under the German Occupation: A Film by Marcel Ophuls*.Translated by Mireille Johnston. St Albans: Paladin. vii-xxvi.
Jablonka, Ivan. 2012. *Histoire des grand-parents que je n'ai pas eus*. Paris: Seuil.
Jacquet, Michel. 2000. *Une occupation très romanesque*. Paris: Editions La Bruyère.
Knout, David. 1947. *Contribution à l'histoire de la résistance juive en France 1940–1944*. Paris: Editions du Centre.
Kuisel, Richard F. 1993. *Seducing the French: The Dilemma of Americanization*. Berkeley, CA: University of California Press.
Laborie, Pierre. 2011. *Le Chagrin et le venin: la France sous l'occupation, mémoire et idées reçues*. Paris: Bayard.
Lalieu, Olivier. 2001. 'L'invention du devoir de mémoire'. *Vingtième siècle*, 69: 83–94.
Langfus, Anna. 1962. *Les Bagages de sable*. Paris: Gallimard.
Ledoux, Sébastien. 2011. *Le 'devoir de mémoire' à l'école: essai d'écriture d'un nouveau roman national*. Sarrebruck: Editions Universitaires Européennes.
Lévy, Bernard-Henry. 1981. *L'Idéologie française*. Paris: Grasset.
Littell, Jonathan. 2006. *Les Bienveillantes*. Paris: Gallimard.
Lubetzki, J. 1945. *La Conditions des Juifs en France sous l'occupation allemande 1941–1944: la législation raciale*. Paris: Centre de Documentation Juive Contemporaine.
Modiano, Patrick. 1968. *La Place de l'étoile*. Paris: Gallimard.
Modiano, Patrick. 1997. *Dora Bruder*. Paris: Gallimard.
Moreau, Daniel. ed. 2004. *La vie des Drancéens 1939–1945*. Paris: Ed Papyrus drancéen, section Diméné.
Nicolaïdis, Dimitri. 1994. *Oublier nos crimes: l'amnésie nationale, une spécificité française?*. Paris: Autrement.
Nora, Pierre. 1984–92. *Les Lieux de mémoire*. 3 vols. Paris: Gallimard.
Nora, Pierre. 1989. 'Between Memory and History: *Les Lieux de Mémoire*'. Translated by Marc Roudebush. *Representations*, 26: 7–24.
Nora, Pierre. 1996. '1980 l'année du patrimoine: la ruée vers le passé'. *Le Magazine littéraire: La Passion des idées, 1966–1996*. (hors série). 68–70.
Paxton, Robert. 1973. *La France de Vichy*. Translated by Claude Bertrand. Paris: Seuil.
Péan, Pierre. 1994. *Une jeunesse française: François Mitterrand 1934–1947*. Paris: Fayard.
Pétain, Le Maréchal. 1941. *Paroles aux Français: Messages et écrits, 1934–1941*. Lyon: Lardanchet.
Piketty, Guillaume. 2000. 'De l'oubli relatif à la commémoration nationale'. In *Jean Moulin face à l'histoire*, edited by Jean-Pierre Azéma. Paris: Flammarion. 325–33.
Poliakov, Léon. 1951. *Bréviaire de la haine: le IIIe Reich et les Juifs*. Paris: Calmann-Lévy.
Ricœur, Paul. 2000. *La Mémoire, l'histoire, l'oubli*. Paris: Seuil.
Rousso, Henry. 1990. *Le Syndrome de Vichy de 1944 à nos jours*. 2nd edn. Paris: Seuil.
Rousso, Henry. 2012. *La dernière catastrophe: l'histoire, le présent, le contemporain*. Paris: Gallimard.:
Sartre, Jean-Paul. 1959. *Les Séquestrés d'Altona*. Paris: Gallimard.
Schwartz-Bart, André. 1959. *Le Dernier des justes*. Paris: Seuil.
Suleiman, Susan Rubin. 2015. 'Orphans of the Shoah and Jewish Identity in Post-Holocaust France'. In *Post-Holocaust France and the Jews 1945–1955*, edited by Sean Hand and Steven T. Katz. New York: New York University Press. 118–38.

Veillon, Dominique and Alary, Eric. 2000. 'Caluire: un objet entre mythe et polémique'. In *Jean Moulin face à l'histoire*, edited by Jean-Pierre Azéma. Paris: Flammarion. 184–94.

Vergez-Chaignon, Bénédicte. 2008. *Les Vichysto-résistants de 1940 à nos jours*. Paris: Perrin.

Vidal-Naquet, Pierre. 1987. *Les Assassins de la mémoire: 'Un Eichmann de papier' et autres essais sur le révisionnisme*. Paris: La Découverte.

Vidal-Naquet, Pierre. 1995. *Les Juifs, la mémoire et le présent*. Paris: Seuil.

Weill, Joseph. 1946. *Contribution à l'histoire des camps d'internement dans l'anti-France*. Paris: Editions du Centre.

Wellers, Georges. 1946. *De Drancy à Auschwitz*. Paris: Editions du Centre.

2

GENERATION WAR AND POST-DIDACTIC MEMORY

The Nazi past in contemporary Germany

Bill Niven

Germany is entering a period of what I call post-didactic memory in respect of the Nazi past and the Holocaust. This term should not be misunderstood. The implication is not that Germany will soon no longer believe in teaching the Holocaust, nor should it be inferred that Germans no longer believe it necessary to convey to younger generations the importance of learning lessons from the past. The term 'didactic', however, rarely means simply 'designed to teach'. The online Merriam-Webster dictionary, for instance, points out that the adjective 'didactic' can be used to 'describe someone or something that tries to teach something (such as proper or moral behavior) in a way that is annoying or unwanted'.[1] Another online dictionary suggests, as a meaning, 'inclined to teach or lecture others too much', or 'teaching or intending to teach a moral lesson'.[2] The term 'post-didactic' engages critically with the negative connotations of didacticism by suggesting a new form of approach to Nazism which is free of moralisation. The expression 'post-didactic' refers to a change of cultural mentality.

In Germany, writing and speaking about German war crimes was for a long time bound up with a kind of moral mission. Underlying many cultural or political pronouncements on the topic was the assumption that the Germans, marked by the stigma of Nazi atrocities, were in need of special guidance or ethical reorientation. If there had been a special path to Nazism, then it would need – so the implication – a special path to steer the Germans away from it. In East Germany that special path was antifascism, which was predicated on the belief that an elite group of resistance heroes should provide moral education to the masses which had followed fascism. In the Federal Republic, Western liberal democratic values were offered in a process of 're-education'. Didactic memory operates on the basis that there are teachers who are gifted with moral and corrective insight, and the recipients of teaching who are prone to be susceptible and unstable. Didactic memory informed the essays and speeches of Günter Grass, the novels of Christa Wolf, the films of Fassbinder, the posturing of the 1968 generation and the speeches of German politicians of both Social Democratic and Christian Democratic stripe. It has also informed the veritable explosion of memorials in Germany since reunification.

The placing of these visible markers pointing to Nazi crimes reached a high point with the inauguration of the Holocaust Memorial, constructed in the very heart of Berlin, in 2005. Germany's commitment to the construction of such markers is a commendable indication of its will to acknowledge national wrongdoing; in this respect, other nations would be well advised to take a leaf out of Germany's memorial book. Yet the proliferation of memorials in Germany also bespeaks a certain distrust of the populace: the Germans need to be reminded, runs the implicit message, because they cannot be relied upon to remember without such prompts. Nor is it purely by chance that Germany has become the land of memory, memory theory and memory philosophers; one only needs to think of the seminal work on communicative and cultural memory by Jan and Aleida Assmann (Assmann 1992, 1999). In a country where forgetting the Holocaust would constitute what Ralph Giordano famously called 'the second guilt' (Giordano 1990), reflecting on memory's inner workings, its social, political and cultural character has become something of a compulsion, with reflection and moralising never far apart.

In recent years, doubts have begun to surface about this overly didactic approach to memory. This chapter explores the causes of these doubts, doubts that, seen cumulatively, are both symptomatic of and responsible for a gradual shift towards a post-didactic memory. I use this term to designate a memory culture in which the core assumption of didactic memory – namely that the lessons of Nazism must be imparted to Germans in a manner which presupposes their need for ethical instruction – no longer obtains. Post-didactic memory is based on trust, didactic memory on distrust. The former operates on the basis that the lessons of Nazism, by and large, have been learned. It accepts that Germans must be given more freedom to determine their own ways of thinking and feeling about Nazism. This acceptance is based on the belief that most Germans, schooled in democracy since 1945, are not likely to fall prey to fascist sympathies. They are not ethically fallible. Nazism does not need to be taught in a top-down, condescending, moralising way.

The difference between didactic and post-didactic memory can be illustrated by the discussion surrounding how best to react to the end of the ban on the republication of Hitler's autobiography *Mein Kampf* (*My Struggle*), a prohibition which has been in place since 1945, but which lapsed in 2015 when copyright expired.[3] The Bavarian government which had imposed the original ban reacted to the lapsing of copyright by authorising the Centre for Contemporary History in Munich to produce a critically annotated edition (Hartmann *et al.* 2016). Others have pointed out that such annotated editions already exist (Zentner 1991) and that it is, anyway, not necessary to embed *My Struggle* in a forest of footnotes because today's Germans, should they want to read it (which is unlikely), do not need a critical edition to be able to comprehend and feel disgusted by its racist and bellicose message. The German-Turkish comedian Serdar Somuncu has become famous in Germany for taking *My Struggle* 'on tour', reading excerpts to school and adult audiences (Somuncu 2015). In one performance he makes the point that, while it would of course not be appropriate to laugh at *My Struggle*, the audience might still feel their diaphragms contract with laughter.[4] Didactic memory would preach that there should be no laughter; post-didactic memory recognises it will happen anyway because to the modern German Hitler's sentences and sentiments are simply absurd. Somuncu, in a talk show in 2012, stated that in his experience German schoolchildren (aged fourteen upwards) had a great desire to get to grips with German history, but wanted to do so 'without restrictive prescriptions', whether this be from politicians, teachers or anyone else. In other words, they need and can be trusted to find their own way.[5] His readings are an invitation to them to do exactly that.

Germany finds itself at a 'memory watershed'. The causes and symptoms I explore below fall into several categories, but all are interlinked. The first, and most obvious, has to do with a generational shift. Young Germans today grew up in united Germany, a country which has faced the Nazi past in a more comprehensive and much less blinkered way than was possible in East or even West Germany. At the same time as this young generation was and is growing up, the older generations responsible for transmitting the moral lessons to be learnt from Nazism have fallen into discredit. This affects both the 1968 generation – i.e. the student generation of the late 1960s – and the intellectuals of the so-called '*Flakhelfer*' ('flak helper') generation born in the mid-1920s, so called because this generation helped to man the anti-aircraft batteries at the end of the Second World War. Whereas the 1968 generation rebelled against their parents, the recent rebellion against the 1968 generation has to a significant degree come from former 68ers themselves, while the intellectuals of the 'flak helper' generation have been brought into disrepute by the discovery of their involvement in Nazism.

These national generational developments have been complemented as elements in the emergence of post-didactic memory by important transnational factors. In 2014, 100 years after the outbreak of the First World War, high-ranking European politicians acting and speaking on the international commemorative stage seemed in broad agreement that no one country was specifically to blame for that war (although the blame game did remain a popular pastime in some states). In 2015, seventy years after the liberation of Auschwitz, speechmakers at former camps lamented the passing of the survivor generation and stressed the greater responsibility for remembering that now falls to contemporary generations. The calls for vigilance in the face of tyranny and discrimination, however, really seemed to be directed – albeit implicitly – against Vladimir Putin's Russia. No-one seriously believes Germany is likely to launch a new and destructive imperialism. These recent commemorative developments, as well as the intensifying global transformation of the Holocaust into a universal symbol of evil, and the spate of publications on the collaboration of non-Germans in the Holocaust or on the predations of Stalinism (e.g. Gross 2003; Snyder 2010), have taken some historical-moral pressure off Germany. How Germany responds to this external easing of stigmatisation, though, remains a national, internal matter.

A good place to begin discussion of the issues at the heart of this chapter is probably the 2012 publication *Das Menschenmögliche: Zur Renovierung der deutschen Erinnerungskultur* (*What is Humanly Possible: On the Renovation of German Memory Culture*), by the sociologists Harald Welzer and Dana Giesecke. The generations visiting memorial sites today, the authors write in their introduction, are the fourth and fifth post-Holocaust generations: 'it would be to do them an injustice to go on deploying that historical-moral pathos which, while justified in the struggle for memory, has become stale and musty' (Giesecke and Welzer 2012: 30).[6] In his contribution to the book, Welzer takes issue not with the importance of Holocaust memory, but with the superfluous insistence on the need to remember. He argues that schoolchildren largely acknowledge and accept this need. The goal of education, then, would seem to have been achieved. Yet according to statistics, Welzer tells us, 40 per cent of young people today believe they have to behave in a 'politically correct way' in respect of the Nazi period, while 43 per cent feel obliged to show '*Betroffenheit*' – a difficult German word to translate, conveying as it does a deep sense of moral shock, dismay and, in the context of German responsibility for the Holocaust, shame (Giesecke and Welzer 2012: 179). Welzer expresses concern that, if young people feel limited in their freedom by the way the Holocaust is being taught to them, then this is the exact opposite of what they are supposed to be learning in an education system for which the ability to think democratically and civil courage are central goals (Giesecke and Welzer 2012: 184). That teaching the Holocaust may on occasion take on a quite totalitarian cast is demonstrated by Welzer through an anecdote. When two schoolchildren refuse to take part in a trip to Auschwitz, the teacher responds by declaring: 'either we all go, or no-one does' (Giesecke and Welzer 2012: 193). Welzer paints a picture of a Holocaust education that is autocratic, moralising, prescriptive and ultimately counterproductive because it is not conducted in a democratic spirit. While it may have made sense to assume that many Germans were reluctant to face up to the Holocaust in earlier post-war decades, it makes little sense now. With the widespread acceptance of the need to remember, assuming the resistance of audiences to the ethical lessons of the Holocaust is not only anachronistic, but disrespectful to those audiences.

Welzer and Giesecke do not blame any particular older generation for the overbearing approach to Holocaust education and commemoration which they criticise. The social and cultural historian Ulrike Jureit, however, certainly does. For Jureit, the representatives of the 1968 student generation – once rebels, now established members of the social, political and cultural hierarchy – have imposed their model of remembering the Holocaust on Germany; a specifically generational memory, then, has been institutionalised and quite literally set in stone in the form of Berlin's massive Holocaust Memorial, dedicated in 2005. This generational memory is characterised by an empathic identification with the Jewish victims. Rather than see themselves as in any way connected to their parental generation, a generation mired in the crimes of Nazism, the 68ers lined up alongside the Holocaust victims, an association made all the easier by their belief that they, like the Jews under Hitler, were living under fascist conditions in West Germany.

According to Jureit, this empathic model of remembering obviates the need to deal with the legacies of perpetration. For this reason, empathic memory might seem an attractive memory model for subsequent generations, too, but Jureit is sceptical. She points out that when the German parliament decided on the construction of the Berlin Holocaust Memorial in 1999, it did so because, according to the minutes of the session, it wanted to keep the memory of an 'unimaginable event' in German history alive and warn 'all future generations, never to violate human rights again'. If we follow Jureit, this appeal to later generations presupposes two things: firstly, that the parliamentarians were speaking as a collective representing the morally enlightened second post-war generation and, secondly, that they regarded the generations following them as less ethically stable because they do not possess the same empathic identification. The Holocaust Memorial, with its emotive evocation of the plight of the Jews, was supposed to address this perceived deficit. Its function was thus fundamentally didactic. While Jureit accepts that younger generations may indeed lack the same empathic identification with Jewish victims, she does not see this difference to the aforegoing 68ers as a failing: 'it is typical of a generation which still feels itself to be morally invulnerable to perceive this difference as a fault and a deficiency' (Jureit 2005: 265).[7]

Neither Welzer nor Jureit reflect, in the cited publications, on their own generational positions (Welzer was born in 1958, Jureit in 1964). Nor does Jureit address the fact that Lea Rosh, without whose commitment the Holocaust Memorial in Berlin would never have materialised, was too old to be reckoned among the 68ers (she was born in 1936). Eberhard Jäckel, another key initiator of the project, was also too old (he was born in 1929). Whether German parliamentarians who in reality belong to a range of generations see themselves as the collective voice of the 'second generation' is also open to debate. What is certainly true is that Jureit's critique of the assumed moral superiority of the 1968 student generation is symptomatic of a contemporary trend so widespread in Germany that it threatens – or promises – to oust the positive image this generation generally enjoyed. This trend stems in part from an increasing irritation in Germany at the prohibitive and judgemental rules imposed on acting, thinking and speaking by Germany's powerful memory culture, rules castigated by Martin Walser in his provocative 1998 speech in receipt of the Peace Prize of the German Book Trade (Walser 1999). Condemnation of the 1968 generation emerged from the desire to find someone to blame.

It would be hard to pin a date on the beginnings of this critique, but 1998 would be a possible candidate. The thirtieth anniversary of the 1968 student revolts saw a number of critical assessments appear in national newspapers. When the Red–Green government came to power in the same year, it was inevitable that some former 68ers like Joschka Fischer would find themselves subjected to less than charitable assessments of their development from rioters against the state to its foremost representatives. The critique of Fischer, of course, reached its highpoint in 2013, when he stood accused of having assaulted a policeman in May 1976. A few years earlier, in 2008, the feature film *Der Baader-Meinhof Komplex* (*The Baader-Meinhof Complex*) reached German cinemas; it was produced by Bernd Eichinger, earlier the producer of *Der Untergang* (*Downfall*), the acclaimed but controversial 2004 account of Hitler's last days. While opinions on the film were divided, the objections raised in the left-wing media that it reduced the history of the Rote Armee Fraktion (Red Army Faction or RAF) to one of mindless violence – violence, in other words, that appeared to have no roots in the social, political and economic atmosphere of the time – were not without justification. What became clear from Uli Edel's film, too, was that the 1968 generation was being judged *pars pro toto* by the behaviour of that part of it which went on to commit such violence. This conflation of 1968 with the RAF has now become the norm in Germany. One only needs to think of the exhibition *RAF – Terroristische Gewalt* (*RAF – Terrorist Violence*) shown in 2015 in Berlin's German Historical Museum and originally conceived by the House of History in Baden-Württemberg.[8] For all its impressive displays of artefacts and original film clips, the exhibition is an exercise in historical decontextualisation. Violence seems to grow *sui generis* out of the 1968 revolt, rather than having wider roots, and no attempt is made to ask why some 68ers went on to commit violence while the vast majority did not. The failure to acknowledge the variety of paths that led out from 1968 encourages the impression that the rebellion's real significance was as a prelude to savagery.

The conventional view that 1968 represented a positive turning-point in the history of West Germany has, then, been turned on its head. Indeed, alarming continuities are construed between 1968 and Nazism. If 2008 was indeed a kind of decisive moment for what can only be called 1968 revisionism, then a central role was played by Götz Aly's controversial book *Unser Kampf 1968: Ein Irritierter Blick zurück* (*Our Struggle 1968: An Irritated Look Back*). Aly's construction of a 1933 generation which he understood structurally and psychologically as the forebear of the 1968 generation provocatively reversed the standard chronological pattern of thinking: instead of the 68ers progressively preparing the way for later generations, in Aly's model they appear as a reactionary force extending the authoritarian and intolerant thinking and conduct characteristic of a generation which supported Nazism.

Particularly striking was Aly's rather glib dismissal of the standard view that the 1968 student generation had made a significant contribution to '*Vergangenheitsbewältigung*' ('coming to terms with the past'). Aly argues that 1968 represented in many ways the high point of the judicial process of confronting Nazism that had begun in West Germany in the late 1950s. Yet the 68ers, according to Aly, were not interested in any of this: 'in their specific turning away from reality', Aly writes, 'the severe social turbulences of 1968 must be interpreted rather as a flight from the German crimes, which at that time were being addressed more and more and were becoming ever more visible' (Aly 2008: 150). If the students in the late 1960s addressed the issue of Nazism, Aly suggests, then they did so only to attack the supposed fascism of the Americans – an attitude encapsulated in the slogan 'USA-SA-SS' – or of the Israelis. Aly contends that the 1968 generation's construction of Israel as a nation of perpetrators effectively blocked any acknowledgement of or empathy with Jews as victims of Nazism. If Jewish victimhood was evoked, then this was done only to enable the 1968 generation through questionable comparisons to stylise themselves as the new victims. Aly's views were not without their critics, and 2008 also saw the publication of quite a few books which took a more benign view of 1968 and upheld the position that the revolt had provided positive impulses for West German society; an example is Ingrid Gilcher-Holtey's study (Gilcher-Holtey 2008). But Aly's polemic captured an increasingly hostile mood towards 1968, encapsulating a trend towards interpreting the revolt as an expression of German totalitarianism and the RAF as its logical and organic extension.

About the same time as the 1968 generation were being discredited, another was coming in for criticism: the so-called 'flak helper' generation. While this expression *usually* refers to those born between 1926 and 1928, in recent public debates in Germany it has acquired an elasticity, being used as a label for Germans born anywhere between 1922 and 1930. The same elasticity applies in the case of the rather loose use of the term '68er' to include Germans born from the mid-1930s through into the early 1940s. It often suits critics of either of these generational cohorts to expand their temporal boundaries so that as many of those who are to be criticised as possible are brought within their range. The criticism of the very broadly defined 'flak helper' generation began in earnest in 2003, following the publication of an international lexicon of Germanists (König 2003). Encyclopedic in scope, the three-volume set was able to benefit from research conducted at Berlin's Federal Archives, which since 1994 have been in possession of the Berlin Document Centre files which the American occupying forces had rescued from destruction in 1945. Those files, among other things, contain lists of Nazi Party memberships – including those, so König's editorial team established, of authors Walter Höllerer, Peter Wapnewski and Walter Jens, each of them significant figures, to put it mildly, in post-war West German literary life.

The flak was now directed, so to speak, at the 'flak helpers' (Herwig 2013). How could it be that the paragons of democratic literary rebirth after 1945 had formerly been Nazi Party members? In 2007, it became public knowledge that writers Martin Walser, Siegfried Lenz and the cabaret show veteran Dieter Hildebrandt had also been members of the Nazi Party. A year before this, in 2006, the shocked world had woken up one morning to the news that Nobel Prize laureate Günter Grass had been a member of the Waffen SS. Up to this point – and again in 2007 – the suddenly embarrassed public intellectuals had argued that they had had no idea they were Party members. Could it not have been that their names had simply been added along with those of many others by subaltern Nazi officials keen to do their bit for bolstering recruitment? While some historians accepted this argument, others pointed out that the membership papers had been signed, and that no-one was drafted into the Party without his or her knowledge. In the case of Günter Grass, there could be no such excuses. He had known he was a member of the Waffen SS, and had not admitted it subsequently (Kölbel 2007).

If the image of the 1968 generation had been subjected to a kind of iconoclasm, then the image of the 'flak helper' generation went up in flames almost by itself.

The literary intellectuals who had dispensed the lessons of Auschwitz to the nation, long accorded an almost priest-like status on the basis of an apparently unimpeachable moral probity and intellectual integrity, now appeared as hypocritical and insincere. Their pronouncements on the ethical health of the nation, long seen as wisdom issuing from above, were exposed as cheap psychological tactics: by arrogating to themselves the right to speak about the past and act as judges of the degree to which it had or had not been overcome, they sought to conceal their own past complicity or compensate for their own bad conscience. The word '*Moralisierung*' ('moralisation') has a Janus face: it can imply the injection of morality into a system of action and thinking where that injection is desirable, and it can imply the undesirable overloading of a system of action and thinking with moral judgements. It is this latter meaning that increasingly captures the sentiments of the critics of Germany's memory of the Holocaust, and its semantic equivalent is stigmatisation: young people, who bear no responsibility for the Holocaust, are made to feel that they do.

The critique of moralisation as a pathological generational project of guilt evasion and transference is bound up with an insistence on the need to overcome taboos. The topic of German wartime suffering, through the bombing war, or through flight and expulsion, has recently found expression in blockbuster television films such as *Dresden* (2006) and *Die Flucht* (*March of Millions*) (2007). These films were accompanied by claims that their topics had long been taboo, that the Germans had not been allowed to mourn their own pain and loss, and that the 1968 generation was to blame for imposing this prohibition. To counter such claims, evidence was provided of a long-standing cultural preoccupation with precisely these supposedly taboo themes (in, for instance, film and literature; e.g. Hage 2003). Yet such counterevidence cannot undermine the argument that there was a reluctance to address them within the family. Also, and this is more important in the current context, the numerous protests at ostensible 'prohibitions' by the 68ers may stem only in part from a genuine belief that taboos need to be overcome. The by now almost ritualised claims that the Germans have not been allowed to remember their own wartime suffering are designed to create a climate of indignation which makes it easier to delegitimise the right of the 68ers to occupy the moral high ground. If the educators of 1968 have been denying the right to remember, then they have been violating the principles of democracy they supposedly wish to foster. If, by giving open and emotional expression to the memory of German suffering at the hands of the Allies during the Second World War, Germans are exercising a fundamental right to freedom of memory, then nothing, not even Auschwitz, can legitimately be mobilised against it. We are witnessing the acting out of a moral drama, set in motion by the sense that the 68ers can only be beaten using their own weapons.

One would be mistaken in thinking the protagonists in this drama are only members of competing generations, here the younger, there the older. In fact, some of the most vehement critics of the perceived moral duplicity of the 68ers are members of the 1968 generation itself, such as Götz Aly. Another member of the 1968 generation who has taken a generally critical line on its supposed achievements is the author Bernhard Schlink, several of whose works – from the world-famous 1995 novel *Der Vorleser* (*The Reader*) through to his most recent *Das Wochenende* (*The Weekend*) (2008) – question the 68ers' contribution to overcoming legacies of Nazism (see also Schlink 2003). Relevant here, too, are the writings of Thilo Sarrazin, born one year after Schlink in 1945. While Sarrazin directs his ire towards a political establishment not prepared to face the failure of Germany's multi-ethnic society, his sweeping criticism of supposed forms of political correctness towards Muslims living in Germany is linked to a rejection of the legacies of 1968 (Sarrazin 2010). Aly's anger at his own generation is part of a process of self-reckoning (and thus a more extreme form of the self-reckoning typical of other 1968 intellectuals such as Peter Schneider; see Schneider 2008). By contrast, Schlink's and Sarrazin's seems to spring from a different source. Their views represent, perhaps, those sections of the 1968 generation whose more detached stance towards the student movement has long gone unnoticed. Neither Schlink nor Sarrazin was particularly rebellious in their youth. Nor, for that matter, were most West German students. Through Schlink and Sarrazin, the long-silent majority have found their voice. Critical reactions to the legacies of 1968 are therefore intragenerational as well as intergenerational.

They are also not restricted to ethnic Germans. In 2014, the Turkish-German writer Akif Pirinçci raced to the top of the bestseller charts with his rant *Deutschland von Sinnen: Der Irre Kult um Frauen, Homosexuelle und Zuwanderer* (*Germany is off its Head: The Crazy Cult of Women, Homosexuals and Immigrants*). He launches tirade after tirade against the German '*Gutmensch*', a difficult term to translate: perhaps 'do-gooder' comes closest. In Pirinçci's eyes, the '*Gutmensch*' is also the product of the 1960s and 1970s, whose alternative values have now become social and political gospel in an act of mainstreaming which has marginalised traditional values such as heterosexuality and the family. Like Sarrazin, Pirinçci lambasts the left-liberal establishment and the media for their role in keeping watch over supposed deviations from left-liberal norms, norms Pirinçci regards as abnormal, even perverse. Coming to terms has gone too far, is the message: warning against the effects of anti-homosexuality, effects made clear under Nazism, is one thing; promoting homosexuality at the expense of heterosexuality is another (Pirinçci 2014). There is here, then, the suggestion that the legacy of 1968 is righteous over-vigilance, a political correctness sustained at the expense of majority German interests.[9]

Before moving on to consider what a culture of post-didactic memory might look like, it is important to stress another important factor in the critical momentum which is giving rise to its emergence: a noticeably strident reassessment of the actual extent and relative severity of Germany's historical guilt. This reassessment has been in progress for a while, and of course is intimately bound up with the question of how the German past should be taught: for if Germany's guilt, in some key respects at least, is not quite so clear, or so unique, then a top-down moralising style of education is also inappropriate for this reason. The reassessment has not been an all-German affair, far from it. Certainly, one of the causes of it was the 'Germans as victims' discourse which seemed to take a grip of the German public realm in the first decade of the new millennium (Niven 2006). But German publications such as Jörg Friedrich's *Der Brand* (*The Fire*) (Friedrich 2002), which does not pull its punches in its critique of the Allied bombing war, were complemented by English-language books on the Allied air raids which were also not without critical force, particularly Dagmar Barnouw's *The War in the Empty Air* (Barnouw 2005; see also Grayling 2006). The German decision to create a Centre against Expulsions in Berlin will seem only too justified to any reader of R. M. Douglas' ironically titled *Orderly and Humane* (Douglas 2013), a searing portrait of the suffering of Germans expelled from Eastern Europe at the end of the Second World War; the book was quickly translated into German, to wide critical acclaim. As one commentator has recently argued, to a degree a 'new World War II revisionism' is making itself felt in international war historiography (Rosenfeld 2015). One aspect of this revisionism is the gradual acceptance outside of Germany that the Allies also committed war crimes between 1939 and 1945, not just the Germans. Another is the increasing awareness that the Holocaust, while a primarily German venture, was implemented with varying degrees of collaboration on the part of other nations and nationals. Timothy Snyder's recent two books (Snyder 2010, 2015) make clear connections and interdependencies between the Nazi and Soviet systems, with the most recent showing how the legacies of Stalinism in the lands subsequently occupied by the Nazis created a fertile ground for anti-Semitic atrocity. Roger Moorhouse's book on the Hitler–Stalin Pact similarly makes clear how much the Second World War's beginnings are rooted in a joint responsibility (Moorhouse 2014).

This reassessment is not a redistribution. Germany's guilt for the Second World War and the Holocaust does not diminish as a result of the collaboration or crimes of others. It is more a question of extending the scope of moral criticism. But this very act of extension does release Germany to a significant degree from the burden of being some kind of exception. The shame that many Germans feel in respect of Nazism relates not just to the severity of Nazi crimes, but also to the stigma that comes with the view that these crimes cannot stand comparison with others or that they were 'uniquely German'. This view is now being undermined. Also challenging the culture of shame on which didactic memory is built is the realisation that, of all countries in the world, Germany is the one that has made the most serious attempt to come to terms with its past. The 2015 commemoration of the seventieth anniversary of the liberation of Auschwitz and other Nazi camps was overshadowed not by neo-Nazism in Germany – although this certainly exists – but by Putin's seizure of Crimea and his sabre-rattling towards Ukraine. Commemorative events in honour of the dead at Auschwitz were perturbed not by any concerns over Germany, but by tensions between Poland and Russia.[10] Russia appears not to have learnt from the moral catastrophe of Stalinist imperialism; indeed, for Putin, one might argue, the Second World War is not really over. No-one could accuse Germany of venturing down Hitler's path again.[11]

In another and wider sense, recent historical revisionism has involved a redistribution of guilt, because the centenary commemorations of the outbreak of the

First World War across Europe were accompanied by a conciliatory recognition that no one nation was to blame. This verdict, to be sure, was not unanimous, not least in Britain, but the very fact that the question of German guilt for triggering the Great War was hotly debated in the British media and among politicians was a sign that it was no longer a given.[12] Moreover, not all those who still believed in seeking to assign blame targeted Germany. Shortly before the centenary commemorations, Serbia made much of a 1913 letter which supposedly exculpated Serbia of historical guilt for the war while incriminating the Austro-Hungarian Empire.[13] The diffusion of blame that characterised many publications and commemorative pronouncements around Europe in 2014 did not go unnoticed in Germany. Christopher Clark's book *The Sleepwalkers* (Clark 2012, 2013), which appeared to 'eschew the blame game', as one reviewer put it, proved a great hit when published in German translation.[14] German historian Heinrich August Winkler wrote that if Clark were right that the First World War had resulted from a common European political culture, then this would let Germany 'off the hook'.[15] While Winkler appeared concerned by this, the four intellectuals who put their names to a manifesto entitled 'Why not only Germany is to blame' in the German daily *Die Welt* welcomed, in reference to Clark's book, what they saw as a 'paradigm shift'. For Sönke Neitzel, Thomas Weber, Dominik Geppert (all historians) and Cora Stephan (a publicist), this shift meant that Germans could finally take leave of the sentiments of guilt which had crippled thinking and feeling. They pleaded for more patriotism, even nationalism.[16] Post-didactic memory, then, a memory released from moral censure, could pave the way to more national pride.

This chapter concludes by examining one or two examples of what form a post-didactic memory might take. In 1992 James Young introduced the term 'countermonuments' to designate a trend towards self-critical memory in Germany unmatched in any other country. Memorials, after all, are usually designed to celebrate; 'Where', Young pointedly asked, 'are the national monuments to the genocide of the American Indians, to the millions of Africans enslaved and murdered, to the kulaks and peasants starved to death by the millions?' (Young 1992: 270). I argued recently that German countermonuments to a degree overlapped with and were being replaced by what I termed 'combimemorials': a combination of memorial with archive and exhibition (Niven 2013). There are many aspects to the motivation for this combination, but I want to highlight one here: the wish to overcome the traditional division between memorial and public. Most countermemorials, in fact, still uphold the basic separation of the two: the memorial remains sacrosanct, the observer in a relation to it of ethical inferiority. Combimemorials, by contrast, are the result of a collaboration between public and artist that presupposes their equal position and equal right to codetermine the location and content, if not always the form, of memorials. Thus Günter Demnig's '*stolpersteine*' ('stumbling stones'), brass plaques set into the pavements outside the former homes and workplaces of deported Jews, the first laid in 1995, can only be installed in a particular street if a group of local residents sponsor them and do the necessary research. Once laid, the stones act as memorials, and as archival evidence of Jewish presence (the names of the former residents are engraved upon them). A comparable project, '*Denksteine*' ('think stones') by Horst Hoheisel (who died in 2011), involved the participation of schoolchildren who were invited to do research into the fate of local Jews and to commit what they discovered, and any associated thoughts, to paper. In Kassel, these texts were wrapped around stones and the stones, deposited in archive boxes, put on display at Kassel station. Hoheisel's installation exhibits an archive of the present as well as of the past. It integrates Germany's youngest generations, as equals, in the production of a memorial enterprise. Rather than receiving knowledge – the basic principle behind didactic memory – schoolchildren are trusted to create it. Memory is not imposed, by *fiat*, but emerges from their own engagement with history.

Post-didactic memory principles are also at work on German screens, never more so than in the two blockbuster TV series produced by the team of Nico Hofmann (producer), Stefan Kolditz (scriptwriter) and Philipp Kadelbach (director): the 2013 production *Unsere Mütter, Unsere Väter* (*Generation War*), about a group of young Germans and a German Jew hurled into the turmoil of the Second World War; and the 2015 *Nackt unter Wölfen* (*Naked among Wolves*), a remake of a 1963 East German feature film about communist resistance at Buchenwald concentration camp.

There is a scene in *Generation War* which shows a German Jew, Viktor, and a fellow prisoner, a Pole, jumping from a train probably bound for Auschwitz. While they escape the Nazi hell, they end up in the clutches of anti-Semitic Polish Home Army partisans. In that moment where they allow the prisoners to jump from the train, the filmmakers made a decision to show a different but parallel history to that of Auschwitz. Indeed beginning the film as they do with the evocation of a harmonious image of Jewish-German friendship in 1941 was already such a decision. Poland objected with outrage to this portrayal of Polish anti-Semitism, particularly in a German film; the Polish ambassador to Berlin wrote letters of protest. Adam Krzeminski, a famous Polish journalist and expert on Germany, declared that the film constituted an attempt to make Poland share 'guilt for the gas chambers'.[17] German historians pointed to the absurdity of suggesting that the norm in 1941 was German-Jewish solidarity or that there would have been young Germans as yet untouched by Nazism.[18] These are important criticisms. But they can themselves be challenged: a number of (non-German) historians, for instance, have pointed to anti-Semitism as a feature of the Home Army (Marrus 1989: 27). *Generation War* partakes of recent international trends in reminding its viewers that anti-Semitism was not merely a German phenomenon during the war.[19] It does so in an almost programmatically post-didactic way, pulling viewers' attention away from the train headed for Auschwitz and making them concentrate on events in a Polish forest. *Generation War* points to different trajectories. In showing the diametrically opposed development of two brothers in war, a development that is surprising in the light of their respective characters and inclinations, it questions traditional biographical, sociological and ideological framings of Nazi criminality. This is, certainly, a kind of revisionism, but it does not go hand-in-hand with any wish to play down German guilt, which is a constant theme through the TV film. Rather, it trusts its German audiences to be mature enough to handle historical complexities without drawing the wrong conclusions.

Naked among Wolves is a very different kind of TV film, but it shares some of the operational principles of *Generation War*. Systematically – and, one would have to say, over-zealously – Kadelbach and Kolditz deconstruct what they see as the anti-fascist didacticism of the original 1963 East German cinema film of Bruno Apitz's 1958 novel *Naked among Wolves*. That novel and film showed the communist prisoners as heroes who offered resistance to the SS and saved the life of a young child. Kadelbach and Kolditz remove all suggestions of heroism with a surgeon's precision and they also remove all teleology. There is no point to the suffering we see and it is shown to extreme. What is left is a set of morally compromised characters, as well as images that shock, horrify and move, but do not seem to add up to any coherent narrative. This is the TV film's weakness *as a film*: it lacks drama and direction. But the intention was to create a film which showed reality, in contrast to the version of Buchenwald which had been served up to East German audiences to persuade them of the moral superiority of communism. Here again, the filmmakers trusted their audiences to be able to face the horrors of concentration camp history without emerging from this confrontation equipped with some kind of simultaneously uplifting and humbling moral message about how to become a better person, and who to look up to. This is post-didactic memory pure.

'These shameful deeds: Your guilt!' ran the title of a famous poster which, showing piles of corpses at liberated Dachau, was displayed in public places in the American zone after the end of the war. It encapsulated the basic principles of didactic memory: an assumption of general German responsibility for Nazi crime, the assertion of a moral divide between those administering criticism and those receiving it and the wish to engender a sense of moral failure and debt. What the Allies began, and what was continued in politically inflected or otherwise tendentious forms of pedagogy in East and West Germany is, as the Germans might say, an '*Auslaufmodell*': an obsolete, or at least obsolescent model. In its place are coming, will come, forms of engaging with the National Socialist past that are multi-perspectival, more open to popular participation and negotiation and more broadly historicising. This development is unthinkable without, and is an expression of the emergence of, new generations utterly free of any moral taint from Nazism and even of the psychological fallout of its post-war legacies. It has also been accelerated by the fact that we live in a post-totalitarian era in which comparisons of Stalinism with Nazism are commonplace (if still contested), and in which, with the rise and rise of comparative genocide studies, it is less and less the norm to regard the Holocaust purely in terms of its own history. Germany can be trusted to embrace these complexities without losing sight of responsibility for memory of the Holocaust (although the globalisation of Holocaust memory inevitably also disperses this responsibility over many countries). And it can be trusted to build Freedom and Unity memorials (planned for Leipzig and Berlin) in celebration of 1989–90 without losing sight of the darker past of the Holocaust. Trust is the motor of post-didactic memory.

Notes

Unless otherwise indicated, translations from German are my own.

1 See www.merriam-webster.com/dictionary/didactic.
2 See http://dictionary.reference.com/browse/didactic.
3 For a good account of the history of *My Struggle*, see Kellerhoff 2015.
4 See Serdar Somuncu, 'Aus dem Tagebuch eines Massenmörders Teil 1', www.youtube.com/watch?v=qfsmOxkf9AA.
5 See Anne Will, 'Hitlers Mein Kampf im Klassenzimmer: Man wird doch wohl noch lesen dürfen', *ARD*, 2 May 2012, www.youtube.com/watch?v=dMXvZn1TNIs.
6 All page numbers to this text refer to the Kindle edition.
7 See also Jureit and Schneider 2010. In this later book Jureit further develops her concern about German over-identification with Jewish victims, coining the phrase '*gefühlte Opfer*', roughly translatable as 'felt victims', to designate this condition.
8 For an English summary, see the German Historical Museum website, *RAF: Terrorist Violence*, www.dhm.de/en/ausstellungen/archive/2014/raf.html.
9 Pirinçci himself came to feel the effects of the vigilance he lambasts. Following a controversial speech he gave at a 2015 demonstration staged by PEGIDA – a populist right-wing organisation opposing the 'Islamicisation of the West' – the German book trade effectively boycotted the sale of his works. His speech was widely misinterpreted as suggesting that a good solution to the refugee crisis would have been concentration camps – had they still existed. In fact, he implied that, if the camps still existed, then that's where Germany's politicians would have liked to put anyone who did not share their views (e.g. on the refugee question). The German media, perhaps deliberately, falsely contextualised his reference to concentration camps to make it seem worse than it was.
10 Adam Easton, 'Poland-Russia Row Sours Auschwitz Commemoration', *BBC News*, 26 January 2015, www.bbc.co.uk/news/blogs-eu-30957027.
11 Except the Greeks, perhaps, who blamed the 'Nazi Germans' for an EU austerity package imposed on them. But such comparisons are the result of wounded anger; they bear little resemblance to reality. See Dan Bloom, 'Angry Greeks Compare Germans to Nazis', *Mirror*, 13 July 2015, www.mirror.co.uk/news/uk-news/angry-greeks-compare-germans-nazis-6059006.
12 Thus the BBC provided on its website 'Ten Interpretations of Who Started WW1', *BBC News*, 12 February 2014, www.bbc.co.uk/news/magazine-26048324. Conservative politician Boris Johnson, then mayor of London, and the Labour Party education spokesman Tristram Hunt clashed spectacularly and with great media to-do over the question of German guilt for the Great War: Boris Johnson, 'Germany Started the Great War, but the Left can't Bear to Say so', *Daily Telegraph*, 6 January 2014, www.telegraph.co.uk/news/politics/10552336/Germany-started-the-Great-War-but-the-Left-cant-bear-to-say-so.html.
13 Nemanja Cabric, 'Serbia Says Letter Absolves it of WW1 Guilt', *Balkan Insight*, 10 January 2014, www.balkaninsight.com/en/article/serbia-washes-away-wwi-guilt.
14 A.W. Purdue, 'Book Review: *The Sleepwalkers: How Europe went to War in 1914*', *Times Higher Education*, 27 September 2012, www.timeshighereducation.com/books/the-sleepwalkers-how-europe-went-to-war-in-1914-by-christopher-clark/421230.article.
15 Heinrich August Winkler, 'Und erlöse uns von der Kriegsschuld', *Die Zeit*, 18 August 2014 www.zeit.de/2014/32/erster-weltkrieg-christopher-clark.
16 Dominik Geppert, Sönke Neitzel, Cora Stephan and Thomas Weber, 'Warum Deutschland nicht allein schuld ist', *Die Welt*, 4 January 2014, www.welt.de/debatte/kommentare/article123516387/Warum-Deutschland-nicht-allein-schuld-ist.html.
17 Konrad Schuller, 'Über Widerstand und Antisemitismus', *Frankfurter Allgemeine Zeitung*, 9 April 2013, www.faz.net/aktuell/feuilleton/medien/unsere-muetter-unsere-vaeter/diskussion-in-polen-ueber-widerstand-und-antisemitismus-12138685.html.

18 Ulrich Herbert, 'So wären die Deutschen gern gewesen', *taz*, 22 March 2013, http://herbert.geschichte.uni-freiburg.de/herbert/beitraege/2013/So%20waeren%20die%20Deutschen%20gern%20gewesen.pdf.

19 See, for instance, the Polish film *Pokłosie* (*Aftermath*) (2012), as well as Jan T. Gross' book about the Polish involvement in the massacre of Jews in Jedwabne in July 1941 (Gross 2003).

References

Aly, Götz. 2008. *Unser Kampf 1968: Ein irritierter Blick zurück*. Frankfurt am Main: Samuel Fischer.

Assmann, Aleida. 1999. *Erinnerungsräume: Formen und Wandlungen des kulturellen Gedächtnisses*. Munich: Beck.

Assmann, Jan. 1992. *Das kulturelle Gedächtnis. Schrift, Erinnerung und politische Identität in frühen Hochkulturen*. Munich: Beck.

Barnouw, Dagmar. 2005. *The War in the Empty Air: Victims, Perpetrators and Postwar Germans*. Bloomington, IN: Indiana University Press.

Clark, Christopher. 2012. *The Sleepwalkers: How Europe Went to War in 1914*. London: Allen Lane.

Clark, Christopher. 2013. *Die Schlafwandler: Wie Europa in den Ersten Weltkrieg zog*. Munich: DVA.

Douglas, R. M. 2013. *Orderly and Humane: The Expulsion of the Germans after the Second World War*. New Haven, CY: Yale University Press.

Friedrich, Jörg. 2002. *Der Brand: Deutschland im Bombenkrieg, 1940–1945*. Munich: Propyläen.

Giesecke, Dana and Welzer, Harald. 2012. *Das Menschenmögliche: Zur Renovierung der deutschen Erinnerungskultur*. Hamburg: Edition Körber-Stiftung. [Kindle edition].

Gilcher-Holtey, Ingrid. 2008. *1968: Eine Zeitreise*. Frankfurt am Main: Suhrkamp.

Giordano, Ralph. 1990. *Die zweite Schuld oder Von der Last Deutscher zu sein*. Hamburg: Rasch und Röhring.

Grayling, A. C. 2006. *Among the Dead Cities: Was the Allied Bombing of Civilians in WWII a Necessity or a Crime?* London: Bloomsbury.

Gross, Jan T. 2003. *Neighbours: The Destruction of the Jewish Community in Jedwabne, Poland*. London: Arrow.

Hage, Volker. ed. 2003. *Hamburg 1943: Literarische Zeugnisse zum Feuersturm*. Frankfurt am Main: Fischer.

Hartmann, Christian, Vordermayer, Thomas, Plöckinger, Othmar and Töppel, Roman. eds. 2016. *Hitler, Mein Kampf: Eine kritische Edition*. Munich: Institut für Zeitgeschichte.

Herwig, Malte. 2013. *Die Flakhelfer: Eine gebrochene Generation*. Munich: Deutscher Verlags-Anstalt.

Jureit, Ulrike. 2005. 'Generationen als Erinnerungsgemeinschaften: Das Denkmal für die ermordeten Juden Europas als Generationsobjekt'. In *Generationen: Zur Relevanz eines wissenschaftlichen Grundbegriffs*, edited by Ulrike Jureit and Michael Wildt. Hamburg: Hamburger Edition. 244–65.

Jureit, Ulrike and Schneider, Christian. 2010. *Gefühlte Opfer: Illusionen der Vergangenheitsbewältigung*. Stuttgart: Klett-Cotta.

Kellerhoff, Sven Felix. 2015. *'Mein Kampf': Die Karriere eines deutschen Buches*. Stuttgart: Klett-Cotta.

Kölbel, Martin. ed. 2007. *Ein Buch, ein Bekenntnis: Die Debatte um Günter Grass, Beim Häuten der Zwiebel*. Göttingen: Steidl.

König, Christoph. ed. 2003. *Internationales Germanistenlexikon 1800–1950*. 3 vols. Berlin: De Gruyter.

Marrus, Michael. 1989. *The 'Final Solution' Outside Germany: Volume 1*. Westport, CT: Meckler.

Moorhouse, Roger. 2014. *The Devil's Alliance: Hitler's Pact with Stalin*. London: Bodley Head.

Niven, Bill. ed. 2006. *Germans as Victims*. London: Palgrave Macmillan.

Niven, Bill. 2013. 'From Countermonument to Combimemorial: Developments in German Memorialization'. *Journal of War and Culture Studies*, 6, 1: 75–91.

Pirinçci, Akif. 2014. *Deutschland von Sinnen: Der Irre Kult um Frauen, Homosexuelle und Zuwanderer*. Waltrop: Manuscriptum Verlagsbuchhandlung.

Rosenfeld, Gavriel D. 2015. *Hi Hitler! How the Nazi Past is being Normalized in Contemporary Culture*. Cambridge: Cambridge University Press.

Sarrazin, Thilo. 2010. *Deutschland schafft sich ab: Wie wir unser Land aufs Spiel setzen*. Munich: Deutsche Verlags-Anstalt.

Schlink, Bernhard. 1995. *Der Vorleser*. Zurich: Diogenes.

Schlink, Bernhard. 2003. 'Die Erschöpfte Generation'. *Der Spiegel*, 1: 134–5.

Schlink, Bernhard. 2008. *Das Wochenende*. Zurich: Diogenes.

Schneider, Peter. 2008. *Rebellion und Wahn: Mein '68*. Cologne: Kiepenheuer and Witsch.

Snyder, Timothy D. 2010. *Bloodlands: Europe between Hitler and Stalin*. New York, NY: Basic Books.

Snyder, Timothy D. 2015. *Black Earth: The Holocaust as History and Warning*. London: Bodley Head.

Somuncu, Serdar. 2015. *Der Adolf in mir: Die Karriere einer verbotenen Idee*. Cologne: Wortartisten.

Walser, Martin. 1999. 'Erfahrungen beim Verfassen einer Sonntagsrede'. In *Die Walser-Bubis-Debatte: Eine Dokumentation*, edited by Frank Schirrmacher. Frankfurt am Main: Suhrkamp. 7–17.

Young, James E. 1992. 'The Counter-Monument: Memory against Itself in German Today'. *Critical Inquiry*, 18, 2: 267–96.

Zentner, Christian. 1991. *Adolf Hitlers Mein Kampf: Eine kommentierte Auswahl*. Berlin: List.

3

REMEMBERING AND FORGETTING WAR AND OCCUPATION IN THE PEOPLE'S REPUBLIC OF CHINA, HONG KONG AND TAIWAN

Edward Vickers

> In ['the World Anti-Fascist War'], the Chinese People's War of Resistance against Japanese Aggression started the earliest and lasted the longest. ... The unyielding Chinese people fought gallantly and finally won total victory, ... thus preserving China's 5,000-year-old civilisation and upholding the cause of peace of mankind. ... This great triumph crushed the plot of the Japanese militarists to colonise and enslave China and put an end to China's national humiliation.[1]

Thus declared President Xi Jinping of the People's Republic of China (PRC), in his 2015 speech commemorating the seventieth anniversary of victory over Japan. Just two months earlier, the president of the Republic of China (ROC), Ma Ying-jeou, in his own commemorative speech, emphasised the wartime role of the Kuomintang (KMT) regime: 'The victory of the war of resistance was the result of our entire citizenry's heroic struggle led by Generalissimo Chiang Kai-shek. No one should tamper with or distort [this truth]'.[2] But in fact both presidents spoke in very similar terms, hailing the role of the united 'Chinese people' or 'citizenry'; Xi hardly mentioned the Communist Party in his 3 September oration. Meanwhile, in Hong Kong, the Special Administrative Region (SAR) government organised a slew of events celebrating China's glorious triumph. The chief executive, C. Y. Leung, having attended the September commemorative parade in Beijing, later presided over a local event, hailing the contribution to victory of Hongkongers along with 'other Chinese people'.[3] In publicly marking the war's seventieth anniversary, then, the leaders of these three Chinese polities were singing from essentially the same hymn-sheet.

However, this official harmony belied a profound fragmentation of popular memories of the war and interpretations of its political significance. Though by no means confined to Taiwan and Hong Kong, this fragmentation is most apparent there, correlating closely with divisions vis-à-vis relations with China itself. On the mainland, the narrative of united and steadfast national resistance during the so-called 'Anti-Japan War of Resistance' (hereafter AJW) has formed a central theme of 'patriotic education' since the 1990s. Hong Kong and Taiwan also experienced Japanese occupation, while the ROC defines itself as the rump of the very state that defeated Japan in 1945. Uplifting stories of the AJW thus seem ideally suited to fostering a shared consciousness of Chineseness. The problem for the PRC authorities, however, is that the very harnessing of AJW memories to the Communist Party's legitimating narrative fuels cynicism amongst those notional 'compatriots' for whom Beijing, not Japan, seems the real threat today.

In recent years, a number of scholars have analysed Chinese memories of the AJW with a particular focus on implications for relations with the West (e.g. Wang 2012; Gries 2004) or with Japan (e.g. Rose 1998; Reilly 2012; He 2013). Most such studies effectively equate 'China' with the PRC. Here, I focus instead on the memory divides within and especially between the mainland PRC, Hong Kong and Taiwan. I argue that the centrality of memory of 'national humiliation' in general, and the AJW in particular, to notions of patriotic identity on the mainland exacerbates the mutual alienation between Chinese 'patriots' and Hongkongese and Taiwanese for whom other memories and identities have come to assume more immediate significance.

In writing about a concept as slippery as 'memory' it is necessary to be clear exactly what one means by the term. Rather than attempting the daunting task of probing individual or collective consciousness, I primarily examine the ways in which various media have been used to shape, manipulate or reflect popular understandings of the AJW. I draw to some extent on previous analyses of school curricula and textbooks by myself and others; for an educationalist, unlike an international relations specialist, the insight that 'to understand a country,... one must read its textbooks' (Wang 2012: 7) comes as no startling revelation. But while school texts remain influential, their significance has arguably waned with the spread of new media and the rapid growth of heritage-related tourism. Popular media, especially on the mainland, may serve as alternative vehicles for official narratives, but also operate in a marketised environment in which the need to appeal to viewers or visitors cannot be ignored. I therefore make some reference to the portrayal of the AJW in film and on television. Finally, in assessing the political significance of war memory in Hong Kong and Taiwan, I discuss briefly how patterns of popular political activism reflect evolving understandings of history and identity, especially among the young. Throughout, the analysis is concerned as much with what is forgotten or omitted from official narratives as with what is remembered and actively commemorated.

Tropes of war memory discourse

Before discussing in turn the mainland PRC, Taiwan and Hong Kong, however, it is useful first to identify several tropes important to the framing of war memory.

These include victimhood, trauma and humiliation, and the relationship between assertions of unique Chinese suffering and claims to national moral superiority. In discussing what he characterises as China's 'Chosenness-Myths-Trauma' complex (Wang 2012), Wang argues that a group starting out with a particularly exalted conception of its relative status is likely to experience especially profound shock when this is overturned: the further they fall, the harder they land. This was the predicament of Chinese elites following the Opium War, which initiated the destruction of their self-conceit as Heaven-ordained masters of a civilisational universe. By the end of the century, nationalists had begun to redefine China as just one nation amongst many. The AJW is remembered as the brutal culmination both of a 'Century of Humiliation' and of a half-century of concerted Japanese aggression. Rendering the consequent subjugation all the more galling was Japan's traditional status on the periphery of China's civilisational sphere; in the familial metaphor beloved of Confucian-heritage societies, the younger brother was rebelling against the elder, transgressing a fundamental law of human relations.

This enduring sense of China's rightful place in the East Asian international order lends special force to a second set of tropes, concerning the steadfast resistance of the Chinese people and eventual victory over their usurping neighbours. As Mao famously declared at the foundation of the PRC, and as every Chinese schoolchild knows, following victory over both the Japanese and the supposedly imperialist-backed KMT, in 1949 the Chinese people 'stood up'. The PRC's more recent emergence as an economic superpower and key geopolitical force has reinforced the sense that China's proper place in the global order is at last being recovered. This perhaps lends extra significance to a teleological narrative of heroic resistance to foreign oppression ('this is what they fought for!'), enhancing retrospective indignation at the temerity of Japan's earlier subversion of Heaven-sanctioned hierarchy.[4]

Themes of both victimhood and resistance permeated President Xi's 3 September 2015 speech, but mainland coverage of the war's seventieth anniversary featured little discussion of the experience of occupation or of the related issue of collaboration. There is nothing extraordinary in this, of course – for societies subjected to invasion and occupation, dealing with the legacy of collaboration presents formidable challenges (see Margaret Atack's chapter on France earlier in this volume). However, the day-to-day struggle to secure the necessities of life and the awkward compromises this may entail constitute, for most, a more salient aspect of wartime reality than resistance heroics. As Diana Lary has recently emphasised, for up to eight years (or longer in the North-East), life went on under Japanese occupation – in relative comfort for some – but memories of occupation remain largely unrecorded.[5] In Hong Kong and Taiwan, however, this history has in recent years received an increasingly public, albeit selective, airing. In those societies, collaboration with the Japanese occupiers is nowadays represented not simply as vile treachery, but sometimes as responsible pragmatism, or even as one strand in the tapestry of a proudly flaunted 'multicultural' identity.

Finally, when considering the selection and packaging of war memory for public consumption, we need to bear in mind that 'the public' in such cases increasingly extends beyond national borders. A China with an enhanced sense of its global status demands foreign, especially Western, validation of its war record, and the moral and political status that this confers or reaffirms. This is one instance of a broader internationalisation of the politics of heritage across East Asia, manifested in the increasing politicisation of the UNESCO World Heritage process (Meskell 2013). Meanwhile, the penetration of popular culture by Western influences to some extent determines what aspects of the wartime past are deemed significant or worth remembering. As we shall see, this can produce some incongruous results.

The mainland PRC – victimhood, resistance and the 'end of humiliation'

The authorities in both Beijing and Taipei have at times evinced considerable ambivalence over the commemoration of the AJW. In the first decade after the 1972 restoration of Sino–Japanese ties, when the PRC was desperate for Japanese investment and know-how, official rhetoric was generally oriented more towards the future than the troubled past. And in the post-Tiananmen years, when China was temporarily ostracised by most Western states, the PRC authorities were at pains to accommodate Japanese sensibilities – in 1991 even cancelling their own commemoration of the Nanjing Massacre for fear of offending the visiting Japanese premier (Chang 2001: 136). But 1991 also witnessed the initiation of a 'patriotic education campaign', intended to shore up support for the regime in the aftermath of the 1989 student movement. A central theme of this was the history of China's 'century of humiliation', in particular the heroic struggle against brutal Japanese aggression. The significance of 'patriotic' themes to the legitimation of Communist rule was further enhanced when, from 1992, the relaunch and intensification of market-oriented reforms signalled the effective abandonment of socialism.

Contrary to a widespread perception in Japan itself, war-related anti-Japanese sentiment was not conjured out of nothing by Party apparatchiks. As China opened up, media liberalisation brought greater awareness of foreign affairs, including controversies within Japan over school history texts. Although discussion of suffering endured during Mao's mass campaigns was no longer entirely taboo – as witnessed by the 1980s 'scar literature' – debate over its causes remained so. By contrast, blame for the earlier sufferings inflicted by 'Japanese militarists' could be directed safely outwards, minimising the divisive political side-effects that delving into Maoist atrocities might involve. The public airing of memories of the Japanese invasion was thus licensed and occasionally encouraged by the regime, as an adjunct to Beijing–Tokyo diplomacy or a buttress for domestic legitimacy. And while it might seem paradoxical that memories of Japanese atrocities should be publicly rehearsed less by the actual victims than by their children or grandchildren, Denton, citing

Ian Buruma, suggests that this is because 'those who suffer real historical trauma tend to want to forget; it is the next generation … that does the remembering and develops … "a pseudoreligion of victimhood"' (Denton 2014: 134). In any event, it was the evident popular appeal of public commemorations of the AJW that led Party leaders during the 1990s to make the history of that war a key focus of the 'patriotic education campaign'.

The fiftieth anniversary of the war's end, in the summer of 1995, was the focus for an orchestrated propaganda campaign. Indignation at continuing Japanese 'distortion' of history was whipped up by President Jiang Zemin, even though the early 1990s had witnessed moves by Japan's government towards greater openness over and contrition for the wartime past (Chang 2001: 137–9).[6] The construction of monuments or memorials to the Japanese invasion, which had begun during the early- to mid-1980s (witness the memorials to Unit 731 in Manchuria and to the Nanjing Massacre), continued apace (Denton 2014). For example, the Memorial Hall of the Chinese People's War of Resistance against Japan at Lugouqiao, south of Beijing, was first opened in 1987, extended in 1997, and further extended and renovated in 2005 and 2015, for the sixtieth and seventieth anniversaries of the war. In such museums, as elsewhere, by the mid-1990s alongside the 'victor narrative' that had dominated in public commemoration of the war during the 1980s, a narrative of 'victimhood', emphasising Japanese brutality and Chinese suffering, was increasingly to the fore (Gries 2004).

The 1995 commemorations also stressed the Communist Party's role as the 'mainstay' of the anti-Japanese forces, but increasingly, as the 1990s gave way to the early 2000s, this message was displaced by an emphasis on the 'united' character of Chinese resistance – encompassing both KMT and CCP forces (Mitter 2000). Acknowledgement of KMT 'patriotism' in the face of Japanese aggression reflected the shift towards nationalism and away from socialism as the regime's core legitimating ideology, but was also related to concerns over growing support for independence on KMT-ruled Taiwan (Coble 2007). By 2004, visitors to Nanjing could inspect the renovated Presidential Residence and have their pictures taken in Chiang Kai-shek's restored state rooms, posing in front of a portrait of the Generalissimo himself – a spectacle unthinkable even ten years earlier. In the face of burgeoning Taiwanese nativism and opposition to 'reunification', the CCP and KMT found themselves once again on the same side of history – for the first time since the anti-Japanese struggle of 1937–45.

However, celebration of KMT–CCP camaraderie, alongside insistence on the supreme significance of the struggle with Japan, involved not just 'new rememberings' (Coble 2007), but also new – and old – forms of forgetfulness. The KMT–CCP Civil War, until the 1980s central to the foundation myth of 'New China', experienced a historiographical demotion. That conflict, officially commemorated as a glorious revolutionary triumph, was if anything even more brutal and destructive than the preceding Sino–Japanese War (Dikötter 2013). Novelist Liu Zhenyun, describing his reasons for writing the novella *Remembering 1942* about the famine of that year in his native Henan (a consequence of the Japanese invasion), professed 'perplexity' at the fact that this catastrophe had apparently been 'forgotten'. He recalled a conversation with his grandmother:

> When I ask her about 1942 she responds: '1942? What about it?' I tell her it was the year many people died of starvation. 'People died of starvation all the time', she replies. 'What's so special about that year?'[7]

Official historiography has drawn a veil over the nature and extent of suffering inflicted *by* Chinese *on* Chinese during other twentieth-century struggles, from the Civil War to Mao's disastrous mass campaigns – the Great Leap Forward (1958–62) and the Cultural Revolution (1966–76). Also systematically excluded from the public record are accounts of Chinese aggression against other nations or peoples. The mantra that 'China has never invaded another country' enjoys widespread popular credence. The long history of China's territorial expansion is explained by reference to an osmosis theory of assimilation, whereby neighbouring peoples are irresistibly attracted to 'advanced' Han Chinese civilisation (Vickers 2015). Conviction of the essentially peaceable nature of 'Chineseness' lends a sometimes hysterical intensity to popular outrage at foreign 'bullying', past or present.

Also largely forgotten, as already noted, is the experience of Japanese occupation. In the North-East, Beijing, Shanghai, Guangzhou and points in between, while numerous museums and memorials now commemorate key battles or atrocities, the realities of life under Japanese rule are mostly occluded from the public record. Shanghai – the economic hub of occupied China from 1937 to 1945 – has its monument to the 1937 Battle of Songhu, renovated and substantially expanded for the seventieth anniversary in 2015. Here, the permanent exhibition, entitled 'Blood Drowned Songhu', recounts the heroic if doomed defence of the city by KMT-led troops, placing it within the broader context of China's united and victorious resistance to Japanese aggression. But the narrative jumps from the conclusion of the 1937 battle to the post-1945 reckoning with Japanese 'war criminals', without relating what happened in the intervening eight years. The same gap is evident in the Shanghai Municipal History Museum (Jiang and Vickers 2015), as well as in textbook accounts of the war (Vickers and Yang 2013).

One of the most notable depictions of occupied Shanghai, and one that engages with the vexed issue of collaboration, is Taiwanese director Ang Lee's 2007 film, *Lust/Caution*. Adapted from a short story by the famous Shanghainese author Eileen Chang, this depicted a torrid affair between a senior official in the collaborationist municipal government and a female student assigned by the resistance to entrap him. But when the film was released in mainland China, censors decreed cuts to the graphic sex scenes and to footage showing the female protagonist walking past refugees lying dead on the city streets. Also removed were key lines of dialogue in the film's climactic scene, when the student warns her lover of the plot to kill him; the idea that love might trump patriotism was beyond the pale.[8]

Sex, in the form of rape and enslavement, was very much part of the experience of war and occupation for tens of thousands of Chinese forcibly conscripted as 'comfort women' by the Japanese army (Qiu, Su and Chen 2014). However, this is an issue the Chinese authorities have long been reluctant to publicise – partly (in the early 'Reform' period) for fear of offending Japanese investors and stoking domestic opposition to rapprochement with Japan, but perhaps also because it casts the Chinese government and people in a less-than-heroic light. Within a society where female chastity has traditionally been a totem of familial and communal honour, 'comfort women' symbolised collective shame and national weakness. For decades after the war, those victims who survived, dishonoured and destitute, were widely ostracised and persecuted. Nor has the Chinese state or the Communist Party ever offered them special assistance, insisting that responsibility lies solely with the Japanese Government. This remains so even today, when the PRC authorities – less in thrall to overseas investors, conscious of China's new-found status and keen to be seen to be standing strong against Japan's resurgent nationalists – are sponsoring efforts to have 'comfort women'-related documents officially entered on the UNESCO 'Memory of the World' register. In Nanjing, the Massacre Memorial now features an exhibition on 'comfort women', and in 2015 a former 'comfort station' there was opened as a museum. In Shanghai, a new 'comfort women' exhibition also opened in 2015, but within the campus of Shanghai Normal University, off-limits to the general public. In the city that was at the centre both of the network of wartime 'comfort stations', and of the pre-war (and present-day) sex trade, these aspects of the municipal past remain acutely sensitive (Jiang and Vickers 2015).

By contrast, an aspect of the occupation experience that has recently received rather lavish publicity relates to Shanghai's role as a haven for refugees. However, the refugees singled out for special commemoration are not the vast numbers of Chinese who streamed into the foreign settlements in 1937, depiction of whose neglected corpses was excised from *Lust, Caution* by mainland censors; nor the millions who later fled conflict or consequent famine – notably the Henan Famine of 1942 – some of whom headed for Japanese-occupied regions. They are the roughly 30,000 Jewish refugees from Europe who succeeded in reaching Shanghai in the late 1930s. This is a story that can be told in a manner that buttresses Chinese *amour propre* partly through appealing to Western sensibilities. The Shanghai Jewish Refugees Museum, established in 2007 but treated to a major makeover in 2015, depicts the Jews as sheltering under the protective wing of their Chinese elder brothers or sisters (see Figure 3.1). Displays at the museum – photographs of visiting foreign dignitaries, flags showing the nationalities of overseas visitors, and an entire room featuring an exhibition entitled 'Shanghai Jewish Refugees Museum Going Global' – again and again drive home the message that this episode in Shanghai's past enables the city and the 'Chinese people' to stand tall in the eyes of the world.

While it here provides the occasion for celebrating Chinese humanity in the face of European barbarism, the Nazi Holocaust simultaneously frames memories of China's own wartime victimhood. Chinese-American Iris Chang's 1997 best-seller *The Rape of Nanking* was subtitled – with an American readership in mind – 'The Forgotten Holocaust of World War II' (Chang 1997). By that point, millions of Chinese had already seen *Schindler's List* (Wald 2004: 10); millions more

FIGURE 3.1 The protective Chinese elder sister: a new statue at Shanghai's Jewish Refugees Museum, 2015. Photograph © Edward Vickers.

would subsequently view other Shoah-related films, such as Roman Polanski's *The Pianist* (2002), starring Adrian Brody. When *Remembering 1942* was transferred to the screen in 2012, with Brody again cast in a starring role (as *Time* correspondent Theodore H. Wright), author Liu Zhenyun described how his 'frame of reference' for the 1942 Henan Famine ('over 3 million deaths') had been the

FIGURE 3.2 Victimhood and righteous anger at the Nanjing Massacre Memorial. Photograph © Edward Vickers.

number killed at Auschwitz ('around 1 million').[9] Meanwhile, when the Nanjing Massacre Memorial was completely rebuilt in 2007, the new structure bore an uncanny resemblance to Israel's Yad Vashem memorial. In December 2014 the date of the massacre itself became a Chinese national holiday, marked by a solemn speech from the President and the ceremonial release of a flock of doves to signify 'peace'; China's 'forgotten Holocaust' was acquiring the ritual trappings of its Western counterpart. Evidence released by *Wikileaks* has shown the keenness of the Memorial's management to forge ties with memorials to the victims of Nazism, such as the Washington Holocaust Museum.[10] Nor are the Chinese alone in this: at one point in 2015, it looked as if China and Japan would simultaneously submit bids for UNESCO recognition for their wartime efforts to save Jews, each featuring a heroic 'Schindler' figure. Asian elites eager for international recognition have apparently concluded that nothing confers greater kudos in Western (especially American) eyes than saving Jews.[11]

The story of the Jewish refugees in Shanghai serves to reinforce an image of China as much more than a passive victim of war; here the magnanimous humanity of Chinese people is on display, burnishing Shanghai's reputation as a tolerant, cosmopolitan modern metropolis. (In the Jewish Refugees Museum, the rapid departure of most Jews after late 1945 is depicted as natural and inevitable; no reference is made to the rapid onset of the cataclysmic KMT–CCP Civil War.) Here the

Chinese emerge as paragons of moral strength and champions of justice – tropes also visible, in a somewhat different guise, in public accounts of the post-war treatment of the defeated Japanese. The relative clemency with which captured Japanese were treated by the victorious Chinese has long been a theme of Party propaganda – one which, Lary suggests, has some basis in historical fact.[12] But in recent war-related exhibitions, depictions of Japanese militarists submitting to the stern, orderly justice of the victorious Chinese have been accorded heightened prominence – even if in less official contexts the ministrations of justice are tinged with vengeful satisfaction. Nor is this simply a bilateral affair; today, school texts, museums and the media are at pains to remind PRC citizens that their nation was a key partner in the *global* alliance against 'fascism' (Vickers 2013). In Xi Jinping's China, then, the public commemoration of the Second World War mirrors a vision of today's PRC as a confident, powerful and morally irreproachable global actor.

Taiwan – learning to love China's enemy

The image of restored strength and national pride so important to the Communist Party's domestic legitimacy is threatened, however, by its continuing failure to resolve what it has long depicted as a key legacy of the 'century of humiliation': Taiwan's separation from the mainland. Under the presidency of Ma Ying-jeou from 2008 to 2016, China's Communists intensified a rapprochement with the KMT that had begun with a 2005 mainland visit by former KMT presidential candidate, Lien Chen. Alongside deals on cross-Straits trade and transport links, the two parties have highlighted wartime legacies to underline the shared heritage that unites Taiwanese with their mainland 'compatriots'. In February 2014, the first official KMT–CCP meeting in almost seventy years took place in China's pre-1949 capital, Nanjing, and in 2015 the KMT Vice-Chairman marked the seventieth anniversary of the AJW (and tenth anniversary of Lien's mainland tour) with a visit to the Nanjing Massacre Memorial.[13] As we have seen, Ma Ying-jeou himself, in his July 2015 speech, also sought to emphasise the continuing relevance of the war to the collective memory and identity of today's ROC 'citizenry'.

But on Taiwan today, this symbolism barely resonates beyond an elderly and diminishing constituency of core KMT loyalists, as witnessed by the steady decline in the proportion of Taiwanese self-identifying as primarily 'Chinese' (to less than 5 per cent by 2013).[14] The election of January 2016, a crushing defeat for the KMT, was dominated by livelihood issues but, as always in Taiwan, these were inextricably intertwined with identity-related concerns. Having promised significant economic rewards from improved ties with the mainland, at minimal cost to Taiwan's autonomy, the KMT was perceived by many to have failed to deliver. Worse, it was seen as having conceded significant commercial influence to China, in a context of rising inequality and economic stagnation at home. But, more fundamentally, resentment of Chinese influence or mainlander interlopers reflects the fact that most Taiwanese today do not see themselves as sharing in an all-encompassing Chinese citizenship, instead seeing PRC 'compatriots' very much as 'other'.

This weakness of shared identity is in part rooted in very different memories of or attitudes towards the legacy of Japanese occupation. While consciousness of past victimisation by and victory over Japan has become central to the PRC's national narrative, on Taiwan mainstream discourse has followed a diametrically opposite path. If the Nanjing Massacre and its associated Memorial have become the archetypal symbols of national victimhood for mainland Chinese, for many Taiwanese, memorials to the February 1947 '228 Incident' and subsequent 'White Terror' serve a very similar function. But the latter abuses were committed not by foreign imperialists, but by the KMT's mainlander troops and police as they sought to impose control over the newly 'liberated' Japanese colony.

For many on Taiwan, KMT oppression during the pre-1987 Martial Law period is nowadays seen as the freshest layer in the palimpsest of victimhood that is their island story (Vickers 2007). Supporters of Taiwanese independence typically tell this as a tale of repeated incursions by outside powers, including the Dutch, Spanish, Qing/Manchu and, finally, the KMT. Moreover, of all these the Japanese are depicted as by no means the worst. During its spell in power between 2000 and 2008, the pro-independence Democratic Progressive Party (DPP) enshrined this view in school textbook accounts, using equivalent terms to describe the 'rule' of these various outside invaders. But shortly before the February 2014 KMT–CCP summit in Nanjing, Ma Ying-jeou's government announced a rectification of textbook terminology, with the Dutch 'occupation' or Japan's 'colonial rule' to be clearly distinguished from the legitimate governance of the Qing Dynasty or the post-1945 ROC. References to 'China' would also need to be replaced with the more politically correct 'mainland China', to avoid any implication that 'Taiwan' was a separate entity.[15] This was the cue for street protests against government 'brainwashing', seen as part and parcel of the KMT's broader capitulation to Beijing. These demonstrations then fed into the 'Sunflower Movement' later that spring, which was fuelled by discontent at the government's trade deals with the mainland.

Testament to Taiwan's entrenched political pluralism, however, is the fact that even while the administration in Taipei was seeking to shore up the crumbling constitutional façade of 'One China', ROC state institutions elsewhere remained complicit in undermining it. In the southern pro-independence stronghold of Tainan, a state-funded National Museum of Taiwan History (NMTH), opened in 2011, presents a vision of the island's past profoundly at odds with the KMT's preferred narrative (Vickers 2013) At the NMTH, Taiwanese society and culture are depicted as the product of a diverse heritage consisting of indigenous (Polynesian), European, Chinese and Japanese elements. This emphasis on diversity, diluting the significance of the island's Chinese heritage, has been typical of 'nativist' discourse since the 1990s, informing numerous other cultural projects (Vickers 2009a). Taiwan, the message goes, is an *Asian* melting pot, rather than a purely Chinese artefact.

Nonetheless, key tropes of nationalist Chinese historiography find ironic echoes in the tendency of nativist narratives to depict Taiwan's people as harmonious multiculturalists victimised by a succession of external forces (Vickers 2009b).

Firstly, the image of Taiwanese as perennial victims obscures the extent to which the ethnically Han population's settler ancestors, who arrived on the island from the seventeenth century onwards, found themselves pitched into conflict with the indigenous inhabitants whose land they were colonising. Moreover, the contemporary fashion for claiming the indigenous tribes as 'proof' of Taiwan's primordial separateness from China both ignores the prior rejection and suppression of their heritage and betrays a fundamentally biological conception of nationhood characteristic of Chinese nationalism – thus mimicking the latter even while rejecting it. And when it comes to the history of the Pacific War, a narrative focused overwhelmingly on the victimhood of 'native' Taiwanese obscures the wartime suffering experienced by mainlanders who fled to the island after 1945, and the extent of Taiwanese complicity in its key cause: Japan's imperial project.

At the NMTH, the section on the Japanese colonial period, entitled 'The Great Transformation and the New Order', occupies the central space in the permanent exhibition. This depicts the Japanese as benevolent harbingers of modernity, bringing order, science and development to local society (Vickers 2013). Moreover, in depicting Taiwan's experience of the war the exhibition's resolute focus on Taiwanese victimhood and apparent disinterest in events beyond home shores is reminiscent of the stance of Japan's conservative establishment on that country's wartime past. In his discussion of the 1995 commemoration of the war's fiftieth anniversary, Chang noted how a 'pro-commemoration' group, strong within the ruling KMT, sought to emphasise the united resistance of all Chinese in the struggle with Japan – an approach that, as we have seen, has since become mainstream on the mainland.[16] By contrast, 'anti-commemoration' groups associated with the 'nativist', pro-independence movement, sought to emphasise *local* suffering – in particular of male military conscripts and female sex slaves (Chang 2001); in 2015, the latter were finally memorialised in Taiwan's first Comfort Women Memorial Hall, established by a local NGO, the Taiwan Women's Assistance Foundation. In the NMTH, meanwhile, a large diorama depicts a Taiwanese family bidding farewell to their conscripted son. But the exhibition is silent on the question of what Taiwanese conscripts got up to overseas, and has nothing to say about the wartime experience of those who came to Taiwan from the Chinese mainland after 1945. For that side of the story, one must look elsewhere.[17]

The seventieth anniversary year of 2015 witnessed various efforts by the KMT authorities to use the wartime past to shift the terms of debate over cross-Straits relations and to buttress their own legitimacy. These included academic conferences, exhibitions, parades, schools-based activities, television documentaries and films, and the issuing of commemorative publications, stamps and coins. The purpose, besides reminding all citizens of 'the glorious history of the gruelling struggle by all military and people during the War of Resistance', was to 'bring young people to recognise the true facts of the War of Resistance against Japan and its contribution to world peace'.[18] KMT leaders were at pains to stress that, in highlighting the history of the war and the contribution to victory of the KMT-led ROC, they were neither pursuing a retrospective rivalry with the Communists nor seeking to aggravate Japan. However, they were attacked by the opposition DPP for setting aside almost 100 million NT dollars (US$ 3 million) for commemorative activities – money which, it was pointed out, could have been spent on boosting military defences against the PRC.[19]

The KMT's vulnerability to such criticism was enhanced by the fact that many Taiwanese have become, if anything, more disposed to identify with Japan than with mainland China. Popular nostalgia for the Japanese colonial period has been on the rise at least since the 1990s, when democratisation and media liberalisation unleashed a veritable craze for all things Japanese. The nostalgic tone was epitomised in the opening scenes of Hou Hsiao-hsien's acclaimed 1990 film, *City of Sadness*, which depicts genteel Japanese families preparing to leave the island in 1945; their departure is followed by mounting discontent and disorder leading up to the '228 Incident'. In a less serious vein, Wei Te-sheng's 2008 romantic comedy *Cape No. 7* interweaves a contemporary romance between the Taiwanese male and Japanese female leads with a tale of star-crossed 1940s lovers (told in flashback): a Japanese teacher and a local Taiwanese girl. This remains (as of 2016) Taiwan's highest grossing domestically produced film ever. And in the anniversary year of 2015, *Wan Sheng Hui Jia* (Chen 2015), a book recounting the difficult post-war experiences of 'Taiwan-born Japanese' and the offspring of mixed marriages during the colonial era, rapidly became a bestseller, and the basis for a popular documentary film.

While the official commemorative rhetoric on Taiwan in 2015 may seem remarkably similar to that of 1995, in the intervening twenty years public consciousness, especially among the young, has shifted ever further away from identification with China's wartime travails. Meanwhile, for those seeking, as Alisa Jones puts it, to 'triangulate' their way to a distinctive Taiwanese identity, cultivating nostalgia for Japan's local legacies – developmental, cultural or genealogical – has come to seem an attractive strategy for balancing the claims of their Chinese heritage. Such nostalgia has been an important influence on coverage of the Japanese period in both museums and school textbooks from the 1990s onwards (Jones 2013). But there is much more to this than what the mainland media has often derided as cynical 'cultural separatism' (Vickers 2009b). Sepia-tinted romanticising of the colonial past can involve as much selective forgetfulness as Communist or KMT tales of indomitable Chinese heroism. However, in contrast to the transplanted narrative of China's war, colonial nostalgia has real roots in the local past, invoking memories of an external 'other' who, when all was said and done, left the island peacefully and threatens no forcible return.

Hong Kong

In contrast to Taiwan but like much of the Chinese mainland, Hong Kong experienced all the horrors of Japanese invasion and occupation from 1942–45 without any of the benefits of developmentalist colonial governance. According to Carroll, 'in three and a half years, at least ten thousand … civilians were executed, while many others were tortured, raped or mutilated' (Carroll 2007: 123). Moreover, refugees arriving in Hong Kong after 1945, during the KMT–CCP Civil War and subsequently, generally possessed memories of the Sino–Japanese conflict indistinguishable from those of their mainlander relatives. Differences with the mainland in terms of the representation of the Sino–Japanese conflict, or its local resonance, therefore cannot be traced to fundamentally different experiences of the war itself – as is partly the case for Taiwan. They must be explained primarily in terms of how subsequent experiences, and the local socio-political context, have refracted these earlier memories.

Most of Hong Kong's current population is descended from the hundreds of thousands who fled to the colony after 1945 to escape conflict, famine, persecution or poverty in the Communist-dominated mainland. While Beijing-affiliated groups enjoyed a substantial following during the postwar decades amongst sections of the local working class and New Territories villagers, most locals were thus viscerally anti-Communist. But they were also strongly conscious of their Chinese identity, a consciousness that was enhanced by the experience of living under British colonial rule. When, in the 1970s, younger Hongkongers (mostly locally raised, if not locally born) began to agitate for reforms to some of the more discriminatory colonial ordinances, they did so under the banner of 'Chineseness' – demanding, for example, that Chinese be made a second official language. During the mid-1970s, an attempt by the authorities to reform the teaching of Chinese history was scuppered by the forceful opposition of local teachers and students who suspected a 'colonial' plot to subvert their Chinese identity (Morris, McClelland and Wong 1997).

But during the 1970s – indeed, until the 1990s – the history of China's war with Japan, or of the other conflicts of the recent past, was barely taught in local schools; the syllabus for Chinese history effectively stopped in 1911, partly due to a British desire to make schooling as 'depoliticised' as possible. Neither did Hong Kong's own history feature in the curriculum until after 1997 (Vickers 2005). Therefore memories of the war were derived almost exclusively from popular discourse – family stories, the local press and other media – and, for most, were thus related to a sense of Chineseness rather than of local belonging.

The exception was the official commemoration of the war dead on Remembrance Day (11 November). This was a quintessentially British ceremony, presided over by the governor and senior military commanders, and taking as its centrepiece a replica of the Whitehall Cenotaph. In the latter years of British rule, this became the focal point for an ultimately successful campaign to secure British citizenship for surviving Chinese veterans of the Hong Kong Regiment and their widows (Schumacher 2014). But for most local residents, the story of the battle for Hong Kong against the Japanese, the wartime internment of captured Commonwealth soldiers and officials, their liberation in 1945 and the restoration of British rule doubtless seemed less personally relevant than China's War of Resistance.

Chinese patriotism, anti-Communism and resentment of Japan found common expression in the local movement to 'Protect the Diaoyu Islands'. Although, since 2012, the uninhabited Diaoyu/Senkaku Islands (north of Taiwan, southwest of Okinawa) have witnessed direct confrontation between Beijing and Tokyo, each side competing to assert its sovereign claims, previously the respective governments sought to contain or defuse tensions over this issue. It was groups of nationalist activists on both sides who made the running – based, in the Chinese case, not on the mainland, but in Taiwan and Hong Kong. These activists, many linked to pro-democracy groupings, were not seeking to bolster Beijing vis-à-vis Tokyo, but to embarrass the Communist (and KMT) authorities by highlighting their pusillanimity (Reilly 2012: 88–91). It was for this reason that grassroots activism over the Diaoyu can be traced back to two events in 1972: Japan's resumption of sovereignty over Okinawa (including the Diaoyu/Senkaku islands), and the formalisation of diplomatic relations between Japan and the PRC. Renewed tension over the issue in 1996, involving the accidental drowning of a Hongkongese activist, led to displays of anti-Japan outrage that caused some to observe that Hongkongers were finally embracing China's five-star flag (Matthews 2001).

By the 1990s, the Sino–Japanese War was receiving fuller treatment in school texts for Chinese history, with coverage of the national struggle against Japan converging with that in textbooks across the border. Since 1997, this convergence has continued, with locally published materials featuring greater emphasis on atrocities such as the Nanjing Massacre, and on the collective efforts of 'the Chinese people' as the key cause of ultimate victory. The influence of mainland trends is also evident in an increased stress on China's contribution to the global anti-fascist struggle, and a corresponding reduction in acknowledgement of the Allies' role in Japan's defeat (Morris and Vickers 2013). Textbook treatment of the war as a totemic symbol of Chinese national unity has reflected the broader post-1997 effort to permeate both the school curriculum and various extra-curricula activities with 'national education' (Vickers 2011; Morris and Vickers 2015).

But when it comes to officially sanctioned accounts of the war's impact on Hong Kong itself, significant divergences from the standard mainland narrative emerge. The nature of these differs depending on where one looks. In the Hong Kong Museum of History, and the Museum of Coastal Defence (the latter originally planned as a regimental museum for the Royal Hong Kong Volunteers), considerable attention is devoted to the experience of the British or Commonwealth soldiers involved in the battle for Hong Kong, and to the internment of captured soldiers, officials and their families for the duration of the war.[20] These museums, whose collections and historical narratives are still to some extent shaped by their pre-1997 origins, cater in part to foreign tourists, presumably including descendants of those who fought for Hong Kong during the war.

In school textbooks, however, the battle of Hong Kong and the experience of POWs receive very little attention.[21] Instead, the narrative focuses on the history of 'local Chinese society' under Japanese occupation. Popular textbooks for history (a separate subject from Chinese history) tend to assert that local Chinese leaders had little choice but to work with the Japanese, and that they thereby pragmatically secured concessions over food supplies and sanitation which alleviated the hardship of some Hong Kong citizens. Reviewing the sycophantic biography of a prominent local worthy, Shouson Chow (Zheng and Chow 2006), one author, noting that 'the Pacific War years are largely glossed over', commented:

> Few prominent local individuals covered themselves with glory in that difficult time, and Chow was no exception. Only one local member of either the Legislative or Executive Councils did not work with the Japanese in any way during their occupation of Hong Kong. … All the other members of the pre-war local elite – all of them – participated to some degree in the Japanese administration of Hong Kong.[22]

In discussing the war on the Chinese mainland, local texts roundly condemn elite collaboration with the Japanese, but when it comes to Hong Kong, the collaborators are depicted as loyal servants of the community, striving to maintain stability and a semblance of normality through difficult times. In this respect, there is little difference between textbooks and museums – all are virtually silent on the issue of collaboration, and devote little attention to the nature or extent of atrocities committed locally by Japanese troops.

Perhaps the most significant reason for this is the fact that those local Chinese leaders who worked with the Japanese throughout the war years resumed their collaboration with the British once the Japanese had departed. Moreover, their descendants remain prominent to this day amongst Hong Kong's elites, having transferred their allegiance to Beijing as the 1997 retrocession approached (Ching 1999; Studwell 2008). To the extent that their collaboration with the Japanese must be acknowledged, therefore, it suits both today's local establishment and the Beijing regime to allow a positive gloss to be given to accounts of the conduct of 'local Chinese leaders' during the occupation period.

More broadly, directing Hongkongers' attention towards the national rather than local theatre of the Sino–Japanese conflict is deemed more congruent with the regime's nation-building purposes. Or, at least, local elites appear to believe that they can thus better, and more safely, impress Beijing with their patriotic dedication. The commemorative activities organised by the Hong Kong authorities in 2015 consistently highlighted the pan-Chinese dimension of the struggle with Japan. They ranged from film shows, lectures, exhibitions and guided tours to the establishment of a dedicated commemorative website by the Home Affairs Bureau.[23] As on Taiwan and the Chinese mainland, commemorative stamps and coins were also issued. The Legislative Council, dominated by pro-Beijing elements, voted to make 3 September (the date of the Japanese surrender) a one-off public holiday in Hong Kong as on the mainland – a decision condemned by pan-democrat legislators for 'undermining local autonomy'.[24] And on 6 October, Hong Kong hosted a classic 'United Front' display of pan-Chinese unity, as representatives of the mainland authorities joined representatives from Hong Kong, Macau and 'China's Taiwan' to celebrate victory 'in the Chinese people's War of Resistance against Japanese Aggression and the recovery of sovereignty over Taiwan'.[25]

In Hong Kong as in Taiwan, however, the popular appeal of such messages, especially amongst local youth, is highly doubtful. The Hong Kong Film Academy did not divulge the size or age-profile of audiences for the September 2015 screenings of its newly acquired classic, *The 19th Route Army's Glorious Battle against the Japanese Enemy*, but they are unlikely to have included young veterans of the 2014 'Umbrella Movement'.[26] Local society remains deeply polarised between those identifying primarily or solely as Hongkongers, and others who prioritise their Chinese identity – partly because, to a far greater extent than in Taiwan, in Hong Kong the latter group is continually replenished by new arrivals from the mainland. However, even before the mass demonstrations of 2014, polling conducted by the Baptist University's Hong Kong Transition Project found that over 80 per cent of 18–40 year olds, and over 70 per cent of university graduates, would 'protect and promote' a sense of 'Hong Kong's identity as plural and international', rather than either a cultural or political sense of 'Chineseness'.[27] And this group includes those subjected, since the 1990s, to the various manifestations of the post-handover government's 'national education' campaign.

For many parents of the latter, who came to adulthood under British rule, the flaunting of anti-Japan patriotism – for example over the Diaoyu issue – was one way of asserting Chinese dignity while disavowing loyalty to the Communists. But with Britain now replaced by Beijing, ruling through the very same elites who dominated under the previous dispensation, that tactic has lost its appeal. If the 1989 Tiananmen Incident administered a profound shock to local patriots, the Beijing authorities' subsequent moves to seek new legitimacy by adopting the mantle of anti-Japan nationalism have profoundly altered the local resonance of patriotic messages. Where once declarations of fiery resentment against Japan were an expression of youthful rebelliousness, now they smack of fellow-travelling. And for many young Hongkongers faced with rampant inequality, outcompeted for jobs by mainlander graduates, priced out of the local housing market, and denied any say in shaping the system that allows this, hostility to Beijing and its local proxies increasingly eclipses any other sentiment. Japan is no longer the enemy.

Conclusion

Among the many ironies of contemporary mainland–Hong Kong–Taiwan relations is the fact that key elements of the PRC ideology that arouse cynicism in Taiwanese and Hongkongese youth today were mainstream in their own societies forty years ago. Many in Hong Kong and Taiwan took pride in the fact that they were preserving the traditions and culture of the ancient and hallowed Chinese civilisation, just as these were being obliterated on the Maoist mainland. Even amongst some Taiwanese otherwise dismissive of KMT propaganda, there was a widespread sense that they stood for a real and enduring 'Chineseness' threatened by Communist barbarism. For those who had fled from the mainland, the Communists were just the latest harbingers of China's unfolding apocalypse. Before them had come the

Japanese, from victory over whom the treacherous Reds had managed to manufacture a fresh national disaster. True Chinese patriotism for many in post-war Taiwan and Hong Kong combined anti-Communism and anti-imperialism, the most heinous exponents of the latter being Japan's military machine.

Today, while schoolchildren continue to study Chinese history and literature, the political significance of this cultural heritage for young Taiwanese and Hongkongers has been transformed. In a world where the Communist Party has nailed its colours to the mast of 'tradition', and seeks to extend its soft power through a global network of Confucius Institutes, solicitude for China's civilisational inheritance no longer distinguishes the PRC from non-Communist 'Greater China'. Meanwhile, the KMT and CCP can now agree in attributing victory in the AJW to the united efforts of 'the Chinese people', freely acknowledging each other's 'patriotism' and forgetting or suppressing old accusations of treachery. Seen from Beijing, the ideological basis for pan-Chinese rapprochement would thus appear strong.

However, it is precisely the link with Beijing's aspirations for political control that neuters the political significance of 'national' war memory for many in Hong Kong and Taiwan. By seeking to sanctify its new, ostensibly inclusive, narrative of the AJW, making it a litmus test for true Chinese patriotism, the Communist Party guarantees that its opponents will fail this test. For while the details of the official narrative may have changed, the fundamental premises underlying it have not. These include a singular, undifferentiated vision of 'the Chinese people' that denies the diversity of actual wartime experiences, let alone the legitimacy of discussing or commemorating this diversity. The same premises also preclude acknowledgement of how other experiences that have shaped Hong Kong and Taiwan, before and since the AJW, have influenced how many there interpret the significance of that conflict. The official story of the AJW is one of undifferentiated Chinese victimhood, universal commitment to the anti-Japan struggle and rejoicing at its teleological resolution in the monolithic unity of the PRC. True Chinese must take this whole package, or leave it.

As we have seen, however, victimhood was far from undifferentiated, resistance far from universal and the AJW by no means the only catastrophe to have seared itself into the folk memory of Chinese communities during the past century. The coyness of museums and officially approved textbooks in acknowledging the wartime compromises of Hong Kong's elites shows that, when it suits the interests of Beijing or its allies, the orthodox narrative of united patriotic resistance can be tweaked. But merely pointing out this inconsistency in the official narrative risks reinforcing or legitimising its founding premises. These include what Mitter terms the 'stark division between brave resistance and cowardly collaboration' that obscures 'the more complex realities facing many Chinese, such as the dilemma of whether to leave family, property and businesses' (Mitter 2013: 116). Nowhere, perhaps, is the complexity of those realities, and the memories through which they are refracted, greater than in Taiwan, which after half a century of Japanese colonial rule found itself on the other side of the AJW.

While the CCP may be extreme in its Leninist insistence on a singular historiographical orthodoxy, discomfort with acknowledging the complex consequences of invasion and occupation is, as already noted, far from unusual internationally. But in the Chinese case, Marxist-Leninist teleology is not the only ingredient in the mix; Social Darwinism and Confucianism are others. The moralising concerns of the latter infuse traditional Chinese historiography, encompassing high state politics, loyalty and disloyalty in the relationships that govern them, the commemoration of exemplary statesmen and themes of proper place, humiliation and revenge (Jones 2005). Like Leninists, Confucians have tended to see it as the role of the state, or the Party (which comes to the same thing), to hand down judgements of unimpeachable rectitude on historical fact. None of this encourages tolerance of nuance or diversity in historical interpretation, and goes some way towards explaining why, even in democratic Taiwan (long ruled by the Confucian Leninists of the KMT), the rival camps compete to construct separate monuments to their incompatible, but in some ways equally totalising, national narratives (Vickers 2009a). In their commemoration of war and occupation, the ways in which Chinese societies conduct their vehement arguments about the past reveal much about what still unites them, culturally if not politically.

Notes

Unless otherwise indicated, all translations are my own.

1 'Full Text of Chinese President's Speech at Commemoration of 70th Anniversary of War Victory', *Xinhua*, 3 September 2015, http://news.xinhuanet.com/english/2015-09/03/c_134583870.htm.
2 'Taiwan President Remembers Nationalist Victory in Sino–Japan War. July 4', *Reuters*, 4 July 2015, www.reuters.com/article/us-taiwan-military-idUSKCN0PE0HS20150704.
3 'HK marks 70th Anniversary of V-Day, Taiwan Recovery from Japanese Occupation', *Xinhua*, 5 October 2015. http://china.org.cn/china/2015-10/06/content_36748824.htm.
4 Here I crudely paraphrase themes discussed far more thoroughly and subtly by Wang 2012.
5 Diana Lary, 'After Victory: the Waves of Returning Exiles in China, 1945–1946-', WARMAP International Workshop, 7 January 2016, www.youtube.com/watch?v=C4ANFVntweg.
6 The apparent failure of such moves to mollify Chinese (or Korean) resentment contributed to a nationalist backlash in Japan that began around 1995, and has gathered pace, in fits and starts, ever since.
7 Liu Zhenyun, 'Memory, Loss', *The New York Times*, 30 November 2012, www.nytimes.com/2012/11/30/opinion/global/why-wont-the-chinese-acknowledge-the-1942-famine.html.
8 'Lee admits "political edit" of film', *Metro*, 8 December 2007, http://metro.co.uk/2007/12/08/lee-admits-political-edit-of-film-577763/.
9 'Memory, Loss'.
10 Mark Frost (lecturer in history at Essex University and Principal Investigator for WARMAP – the War Memoryscapes in Asia Partnership (www.warinasia.com/)), personal communication, 6 January 2016.
11 The Chinese and Japanese 'Schindlers' were, respectively, the diplomats Ho Fengshan (in Vienna) and Sugihara Chiune (in Vilnius).

12 Lary, 'After Victory'.
13 'KMT Vice-Chairman Hu to Attend Conference on Tenth Anniversary of Lien-Hu Meeting', *National Policy Foundation*, 22 April 2015, www.taiwannpfnews.org.tw/english/page.aspx?type=article&mnum=111&anum=16011.
14 According to surveys conducted by the Election Study Centre of National Chengchi University, Taipei.
15 'Ministry Approves New Brainwashing Curriculum', *Taipei Times*, 28 January 2014 www.taipeitimes.com/News/front/print/2014/01/28/2003582309.
16 The 1995 anniversary was the first to be commemorated with full pomp by the ROC Government on Taiwan, Cold War pressures and KMT links with Japanese right-wingers having previously discouraged the Party from indulging any lingering anti-Japan animus. The then ROC President Lee Teng-hui delivered a commemorative speech that strongly emphasised the theme of united anti-Japanese resistance under KMT leadership – a clear retort to official rhetoric on the Chinese mainland, which was then stressing the Communist Party's 'mainstay' role in the struggle.
17 For example to the National Military Museum in Taipei – an institution affiliated to the KMT.
18 '*Jinian kangzhan shengli ji Taiwan guangfu qishi zhounian: ningzhu quanmin aiguo xinnian*', *Xingzheng Yuan*, 14 September 2015, www.ey.gov.tw/News_Content2.aspx?n=F8BAEBE9491FC830&s=C252938FCA7F6DB5.
19 Zhou Siyu, '*Za yi yuan jinian kangzhan; guofang bu ai pi ben wei dao zhi*', *Ziyou Shibao*, 18 January 2015. http://news.ltn.com.tw/news/politics/paper/848399.
20 The Hong Kong Museum of History (HKMH) was closed in 1997 and reopened, on a new site, in 2001; the Museum of Coastal Defence opened in 2000. One significant change to the plan for the permanent exhibition of the HKMH, introduced following representations from the post-1997 Urban Council (a Beijing-appointed body), involved establishing a special section devoted to 'The role of Hong Kong in modern Chinese political history' – including its role in supporting the anti-Japanese war effort from 1937 to 1941.
21 It should be noted that, since the early 2000s, relatively few Hong Kong students actually study history or Chinese history – both subjects having become optional to make way for the teaching of Modern Standard Mandarin, ICT and other courses. So textbooks are indicative less of what all young people learn or know about the war than of what authors, publishers and educational officials deem it politically prudent to publish or teach.
22 Jason Wordie, 'Book Review: *Grand Old Man of Hong Kong: Sir Shouson Chow*', *The South China Morning Post*, 3 October 2010, www.scmp.com/article/726397/grand-old-man-hong-kong-sir-shouson-chow.
23 'HAB Launches Website to Commemorate 70th Anniversary of Victory of the Chinese People's War of Resistance against Japanese Aggression', *Hong Kong Government Press Releases*, 7 August 2015, www.info.gov.hk/gia/general/201508/07/P201508070786.htm.
24 'Hong Kong Lawmakers Vote for September 3 Holiday to Mark Anniversary of Japan's Surrender', *South China Morning Post*, 9 July 2015, www.scmp.com/news/hong-kong/politics/article/1835083/hong-kong-lawmakers-vote-september-3-holiday-mark.
25 'HK marks 70th Anniversary of V-Day'.
26 'Press Release: HKFA to Commemorate 70th Anniversary of Victory in Chinese People's War of Resistance against Japanese Aggression', *Hong Kong Leisure and Cultural Services Department*, 3 July 2015, www.lcsd.gov.hk/en/news/press_details.php?id=8455#.
27 Hong Kong Transition Project, *Constitutional Reform: Consultations and Confrontations*, Briefing Paper, Hong Kong Baptist University, January 2014, http://hktp.org/list/constitutional-reform-brief.pdf.

References

Carroll, John. 2007. *A Concise History of Hong Kong*. Lanham, MD: Rowman and Littlefield.

Chang, Iris. 1997. *The Rape of Nanking: The Forgotten Holocaust of World War II*. New York, NY: Basic Books.

Chang, Jui-te. 2001. 'The Politics of Commemoration: A Comparative Analysis of the Fiftieth Anniversary Commemoration in Mainland China and Taiwan of the Victory in the Anti-Japanese War'. In *Scars of War: The Impact of Warfare on Modern China*, edited by Diana Lary and Stephen MacKinnon. Vancouver: University of British Columbia Press. 136–61.

Chen, Xuan-ru. 2015. *Wan Sheng Hui Jia [The Taiwan-Born Return Home]*. Taipei: Yuan Liu.

Ching, Frank. 1999. *The Li Dynasty: Hong Kong Aristocrats*. Hong Kong: Oxford University Press.

Coble, Parks M. 2007. 'China's New Remembering of the Anti-Japanese War of Resistance, 1937–1945'. *The China Quarterly*, 190: 390–410.

Denton, Kirk. 2014. *Exhibiting the Past: Historical Memory and the Politics of Museums in Postsocialist China*. Honolulu, HI: University of Hawai'i Press.

Dikötter, Frank. 2013. *The Tragedy of Liberation: A History of the Chinese Revolution, 1945–1957*. London: Bloomsbury.

Gries, Peter Hays. 2004. *China's New Nationalism: Pride, Politics and Diplomacy*. Berkeley, CA: University of California Press.

He, Yinan. 2013. 'Forty Years in Paradox: Post-Normalisation Sino-Japanese Relations'. *China Perspectives*, 4: 7–16.

Jiang, Lei and Vickers, Edward. 2015. 'Constructing Civic Identity in Shanghai's Museums: Heritage, Ideology and Local Distinctiveness'. In *Constructing Modern Asian Citizenship*, edited by Edward Vickers and Krishna Kumar. London: Routledge. 217–39.

Jones, Alisa. 2005. 'Shared Legacies, Diverse Evolutions: History, Education and the State in East Asia'. In *History Education and National Identity in East Asia*, edited by Edward Vickers and Alisa Jones. London: Routledge. 31–64.

Jones, Alisa. 2013. 'Triangulating Identity: Japan's Place in Taiwan's Textbooks'. In *Imagining Japan in Post-War East Asia*, edited by Paul Morris, Naoko Shimazu and Edward Vickers. London: Routledge. 170–89.

Matthews, Gordon. 2001. 'A Collision of Discourses: Japanese and Hong Kong Chinese during the Diaoyu/Senkaku Islands Crisis'. In *Globalizing Japan: Ethnography of the Japanese Presence in Asia, Europe and America*, edited by Harumi Befu and Sylvie Guichard-Anguis. London: Routledge 153–75.

Meskell, Lynn. 2013. 'UNESCO's World Heritage Convention at 40: Challenging the Economic and Political Order of International Heritage Conservation'. *Current Anthropology*, 54, 4: 483–94.

Mitter, Rana. 2000. 'Behind the Scenes at the Museum: Nationalism, History and Memory in the Beijing War of Resistance Museum, 1987–1997'. *The China Quarterly*, 161: 279–93.

Mitter, Rana. 2013. *China's War with Japan, 1937–1945: The Struggle for Survival*. London: Allen Lane.

Morris, Paul, McClelland, Gerry and Wong, Ping Man. 1997. 'Explaining Curriculum Change: Social Studies in Hong Kong'. *Comparative Education Review*, 41, 1: 27–43.

Morris, Paul and Vickers, Edward. 2013. 'Unifying the Nation: The Changing Role of Sino-Japanese history in Hong Kong's History Textbooks'. In *Imagining Japan in Post-war East Asia*, edited by Paul Morris, Naoko Shimazu and Edward Vickers. London: Routledge.149–69.

Morris, Paul and Vickers, Edward. 2015. 'Schooling, Politics and the Construction of Identity in Hong Kong: the "Moral and National Education" Crisis in Historical Context'. *Comparative Education*, 51, 3: 305–26.

Qiu, Peipei, Su, Zhiliang and Chen, Lifei. 2014. *Chinese Comfort Women: Testimonies from Imperial Japan's Sex Slaves*. Oxford: Oxford University Press.

Reilly, James. 2012. *Strong Society, Smart State: The Rise of Public Opinion in China's Japan Policy*. New York, NY: Columbia University Press.

Rose, Caroline. 1998. *Interpreting History in Sino-Japanese Relations*. London: Routledge.

Schumacher, Daniel. 2014. '"Privates to the Fore": World War II Heritage Tourism in Hong Kong and Singapore". *World History Connected*, 11, 1. http://worldhistoryconnected.press.illinois.edu/11.1/schumacher.html.

Studwell, Joe. 2008. *Asian Godfathers: Money and Power in Hong Kong and Southeast Asia*. London: Profile Books.

Vickers, Edward. 2005. *In Search of an Identity: the Politics of History as a School Subject in Hong Kong, 1960s-2005*. 2nd edn. Hong Kong: Comparative Education Research Centre.

Vickers, Edward. 2007. 'Frontiers of Memory: Conflict, Imperialism and Official Histories in the Formation of Post-Cold War Taiwanese Identity'. In *Ruptured Histories: War, Memory and the Post-Cold War in Asia*, edited by Sheila Miyoshi Jager and Rana Mitter. Cambridge, MA: Harvard University Press. 209–32.

Vickers, Edward. 2009a. 'Rewriting Museums in Taiwan'. In *Rewriting Culture in Taiwan*, edited by Shih Fang-long, Paul-Francois Tremlett and Stuart Thompson. London: Routledge. 69–101.

Vickers, Edward. 2009b. 'Original Sin on the Island Paradise: Qing Taiwan's Colonial History in Comparative Perspective'. *Taiwan in Comparative Perspective*, 2: 65–86.

Vickers, Edward. 2011. 'Learning to Love the Motherland: "National Education" in Post-Retrocession Hong Kong', in *Designing History in East Asian Textbooks: Identity Politics and Transnational Aspirations*, edited by Gotelind Müller. London: Routledge. 85–116.

Vickers, Edward. 2013. 'Transcending Victimhood: Japan in the Public Historical Museums of Taiwan and the People's Republic of China'. *China Perspectives*, 4: 17–28.

Vickers, Edward and Yang, Biao. 2013. 'Shanghai's History Curriculum Reforms and Shifting Textbook Portrayals of Japan'. *China Perspectives*, 4: 29–37.

Vickers, Edward. 2015. 'A Civilising Mission with Chinese Characteristics? Education, Colonialism and Chinese State Formation in Comparative Perspective'. In *Constructing Modern Asian Citizenship*, edited by Edward Vickers and Krishna Kumar. London: Routledge. 50–79.

Wald, S. S. 2004. *China and the Jewish People: Old Civilisations in a New Era*. Jerusalem: The Jewish People Policy Planning Institute.

Zheng, Victor and Chow, Charles W. 2010. *Grand Old Man of Hong Kong: Sir Shouson Chow*. Hong Kong: Hong Kong University Press.

Wang, Zheng. 2012. *Never Forget National Humiliation: Historical Memory in Chinese Politics and Foreign Relations*. New York: Columbia University Press.

PART II

Transnational transactions

4

ISAAC FADOYEBO'S JOURNEY

Remembering the British Empire's Second World War

Patrick Finney

Isaac Fadoyebo left his home village in South-Western Nigeria early in 1942 after enlisting in the Royal West African Frontier Force, one of over 500,000 African soldiers to serve the British Empire in the Second World War. These men may well have expected to end up fighting the Germans: Roald Dahl recalled in his memoirs how, working for Shell in East Africa at the outbreak of the war, he explained it to his Tanganyikan servant as a struggle against 'Bwana Hitler who wishes to conquer the world' (Dahl 2008: 236). But 16-year-old Fadoyebo and 120,000 others instead made the long sea voyage to India and thence to Burma to fight the Japanese. In February 1944, while breakfasting on the banks of the Kaladan river, Fadoyebo's platoon was ambushed by the Japanese; his right femur was shattered by a bullet and, grievously wounded, he was left for dead. Local villagers – Muslim Rohingya – then saved his life. Emerging from the jungle, they brought food and water and bandaged his wounds; when Fadoyebo was well enough to be moved he was sheltered in the house of a local farmer, at considerable personal risk. Fadoyebo, together with another surviving soldier, was protected by the Rohingya for nine months until British Ghurkha forces finally recaptured the area in December 1944. Fadoyebo was hospitalised and then repatriated, going on to enjoy a successful post-war career as a civil servant. His remarkable story of survival was rediscovered in 1989 when the BBC Africa Service broadcast a series of programmes to commemorate the fiftieth anniversary of the outbreak of the war. Fadoyebo sent his manuscript memoir to the BBC, which led to its publication, and he was subsequently the subject of a documentary film. The film-maker delivered a letter of thanks from Fadoyebo to the family of the farmer who had sheltered him just before the Nigerian died in 2012.[1]

The mobilisation of African troops for Britain in the Second World War represented 'the largest single movement of African men overseas since the slave trade' (Killingray and Plaut 2010: 293). It was also part and parcel of an unprecedented transnational movement of peoples consequent upon the waging of a global war by European global empires. This process not only had a transformative impact on the lives of millions of individuals such as Fadobeyo, it also had consequences for the future of those empires. Although the relationship between the war and post-war decolonisation is complex, and the extent to which colonial veterans were radicalised by the war should not be exaggerated, some certainly did return home emboldened to play a part in nationalist politics (Killingray and Plaut 2010: 203–35). Thus another Nigerian veteran proudly recalled: 'Every soldier who went to India got new ideas and learnt new things. We came back with improved ideas about life. We, the ex-servicemen, gave this country the freedom it's enjoying today. We gave this freedom and handed it over to our country.'[2] The impact of the war also lingers on into the present. Many veterans received only meagre pensions and 'returned to a life of squalor and inadequate medical care', suffering increasing indignities as they have come towards the end of their lives.[3] Other groups entangled in this far-flung war of empires experienced abiding hardship. The Karen tribesmen who fought the Japanese alongside the British in Burma in the hope of securing their independence after the war never received any formal recognition or recompense. After the war they waged a secessionist insurgency that called forth brutal repression from successive post-war Burmese regimes and by 2010 many elderly veterans were reported to be surviving on scanty charitable donations, even as they still spoke of their former British commanders with 'stirring fondness'.[4]

The core myths which have dominated British remembrance of the Second World War have not allowed much space for experiences such as these; indeed, they might be said to have forcefully excluded them. The iconic events in British war remembrance – Dunkirk, the Battle of Britain, the Blitz, D-Day – are fundamentally focused on the mother country, or at best the European theatre of war; this has given rise to long-standing laments that other important events and theatres have been 'forgotten' (Connelly 2004: 248–66). The dramatic progressive narrative of the 'People's War', in which the nation united against fascism and for the construction of a new post-war settlement between citizens and state, is similarly focused on the metropole and generally gives little visibility to non-white actors. A parallel 'People's Empire' myth, emphasising partnership between the constituent parts of the Commonwealth, flourished in wartime propaganda but rapidly faded thereafter: 'once the war was over, the part played by Africans, Caribbeans, Indians, and Maori was generally forgotten' (Webster 2007: 88). Non-white servicemen from the Empire found tolerance transmuting into 'outright hostility' after the war; as large-scale Commonwealth in-migration began, they were 'rapidly re-configured as unwanted foreigners who ought to "go back home"' (Ugolini 2014: 104): The chief conservative counterpart to the 'People's War' myth was the Churchillian narrative that emphasised the glorious history and peculiar virtues of a proud British people accustomed to standing alone against aggression; it may have been frank about the fact that this was an imperial people, but the viewpoint of the 'island race' predominated here too.

This chapter explores what difference it makes to our thinking about British war remembrance – both empirically and conceptually – if we bring the imperial dimensions of the war and its aftermath more fully into the picture. On the one hand, it explores British war memory 'at home', and how it was that the imperial nature of the conflict was suppressed for so long, only recently to come into focus. This raises a series of questions about the relationship between war memory and processes of decolonisation, and especially how the former may have served to retard the British coming to terms with the loss of Empire; bound up with that is the role of the significant change to the composition of the remembering subject caused by immigration linked to decolonisation. The underpinning assumption here is that we neglect the role of transnational influences in the generation of national memories at our peril. On the other hand, the chapter explores British war memory 'abroad', and how it is fruitful to conceive of the former imperial space as a field in which multiple memories of the war are in play, and often in contestation, as a consequence of the unfolding of decolonisation. Locating British war memory in this larger transnational context again illustrates the need to supplement the national with consideration of the other layers and scales of memory with which it is entwined.

The 'rediscovery' of Empire

Bringing the problematic of empire into focus in relation to the memory of the Second World War makes obvious sense given the widespread debates about the nature and legacy of the British Empire which have raged in recent years. These are in part a product of large-scale political and cultural shifts. British involvement in new wars in Afghanistan and Iraq over the last fifteen years following '9/11' triggered fresh questions about the toxic legacy of colonialism there. Simultaneously, across the west, multiculturalism has come under strain in the face of rising inequality and neo-liberal globalisation, mass movements of refugees and migrants and Islamist political violence. More narrowly, scandals have erupted around specific episodes in Britain's colonial past; witness the high-profile legal case through which former Mau Mau fighters in Kenya won compensation payments in 2013 for abuses and torture inflicted by the British armed forces and colonial administration. (This case cast light not only on the violence of imperial rule but also on the careful efforts made to manage its memory, with the revelation that a huge collection of official papers, including a 'migrated' colonial archive relating to the abuses in Kenya, had been hoarded, in breach of the Public Records Act, at a British government facility at Hanslope Park (Cobain 2016).) The debate on empire has in part been conducted through high-profile historical works, ranging from nostalgic neo-conservative defences to fierce postcolonial denunciations (e.g. Ferguson 2003; Gott 2011; Kwarteng 2011; Mishra 2013). Politicians have also invoked the imperial past as a reference point – witness the Brexit referendum campaign – and activists have vigorously campaigned to rid Britain's universities of statues and other symbols honouring imperial 'heroes' such as Cecil Rhodes.[5] Further, the salience of empire in our contemporary consciousness has occasioned significant cultural interventions such as a major exhibition at Tate Britain in 2015 entitled 'Artist and Empire: Facing Britain's Imperial Past', which itself fuelled further impassioned debate.[6]

In this context, the historiography on the role of the Empire in Britain's Second World War has blossomed. Ashley Jackson's magisterial 2006 one-volume survey insisted that this conflict

> ought to be recognized as a global struggle, and particularly as an *imperial* [sic] one, in which apparently disparate British battles and strategic concerns formed part of one interconnected whole, and in which every campaign that the British fought was fought alongside imperial allies for imperial reasons.
>
> *(Jackson 2006: 1)*

Writing again a few years later, Jackson continued to bemoan the hegemony of Eurocentrism in 'the standard British war story' which obscured 'the reliance that Britain placed upon colonial resources in prosecuting the war, and the war's impact on colonized peoples' (Jackson 2015: 559). Yet important new contributions were appearing with increasing frequency. Some of them tackled broad themes and areas, such as Christopher Bayly and Tim Harper's twin volumes on the war and the end of empire in South-East Asia (Bayly and Harper 2004, 2007), or a landmark edited volume on *Africa and World War II* (Byfield, Brown, Parsons and Sikaingi 2015). Other contributions focused on specific countries, including, for example, a run of impressive monographs on India. Madhusree Mukerjee explored the inter-connections between the 1943 Bengal famine and British imperial strategy in an acerbic assault on *Churchill's Secret War* (Mukerjee 2010), while Yasmin Khan offered a social history of *The Raj at War* (Khan 2015) and Srinath Ragavan produced a comprehensive account of both India's contribution to the war and the latter's impact on India's politics, economy and society (Ragavan 2016). Yet other works explored the contribution of particular actors, such as Stephen Bourne's studies of the role of black Britons on the home front and of black servicemen and women from across the Empire (Bourne 2010, 2012). In addition to the contextual factors already adumbrated, this scholarship drew strength from the recent rejuvenation of imperial history and the related emergence of new forms of global and transnational history-writing.

Historical scholarship is itself a discourse of memory, of course, but the Empire was simultaneously becoming more visible in other commemorations of the war. (There is a parallel with the case of the First World War, where the imperial aspects of the conflict are receiving unprecedented attention during the rolling cycle of centenary events.[7]) In 2002, the Queen opened the Commonwealth Memorial Gates in Hyde Park to honour the contribution of servicemen and women from the Indian sub-continent, Africa and the Caribbean who served in the two world wars, with particular recognition for those seventy four who won George and Victoria crosses. When the Imperial War Museum North (IWMN) opened in

2002, one of its six thematic 'silos' was dedicated to 'Empire, Commonwealth and War', and this has been a recurring emphasis ever since: over the summer of 2016 the IWMN hosted a temporary exhibition entitled 'Mixing It: The Changing Faces of Wartime Britain', based on oral testimonies from service personnel and civilians who came to Britain during the war, which gives prominence to many from the Empire.[8] Andrea Levy's multiple prize-winning novel *Small Island* was also noteworthy in raising consciousness of the imperial aspects of the war, telling the story of the migration to Britain in the war and the later 1940s of a West Indian couple, Hortense and Gilbert, the latter having served in the Royal Air Force (RAF) in the war (Levy 2004); the book was subsequently adapted into a very popular BBC mini-series in 2009. Catching and shaping this mood, the Imperial War Museum (IWM) launched a comprehensive scoping study in 2012 entitled 'Whose Remembrance? Communities and the Experiences of the Peoples of Britain's Former Empire during the Two World Wars'; this set out to audit the visibility of imperial themes in historical scholarship, museum exhibitions and films, novels and the theatre.[9]

Postcolonial melancholia?

This 'rediscovery' of Empire ineluctably leads us to question why and how the imperial dimension of the British experience of the Second World War was previously occluded, and for so long. As previously discussed, a 'People's Empire' myth was assiduously cultivated in British wartime propaganda to assist with the mobilisation of imperial resources. Yet the flourishing of this narrative of partnership and common struggle co-existed with persistent racial tension and discrimination in the mother country and the colonies; moreover, it could not mask the contradictions inherent in an imperial power fighting an anti-fascist war for democracy and liberty while denying those self-same rights to its own colonial subjects (Rose 2003: 239–84). After the war, the myths that came to dominate British remembering left scant room for the Empire. The 'People's War' myth stood centre stage as Clement Attlee's Labour government enacted the collectivist settlement: its grand narrative of communal solidarity and 'popular democratic accomplishment' long served 'as the rhetorical binding of the postwar consensus' (Eley 2001: 821). In the 1950s, this myth itself had to make room for a resurgence of more conservative understandings in a Churchillian vein: British war films, for example, increasingly forsook themes of collectivist egalitarian endeavour in favour of martial masculinity and elite heroism (Ramsden 1998). The 'People's Empire' myth, in any event becoming 'increasingly fragile' following the outbreak of colonial wars in Cyprus, Kenya and Malaya, was therefore pushed aside (Webster 2007: 56). As decolonisation and the slide from great power status proceeded apace, victory in the Second World War began more and more to function as an integrative myth, a pre-eminent symbol of national grandeur offering reassurance and consolation to a country unnerved by post-war decline. Recalling the imperial character of the war could not but be inimical to the strategic purpose memory now served.

When the war was represented, empire was effaced in diverse ways. First, it was simply neglected or ignored. Winston Churchill's six volumes of war memoirs profoundly shaped British understandings of the war, yet their treatment of the Far East was scanty and misleading. While this was in good part a product of Churchill's eagerness to manage his own reputation by concealing his personal responsibility for crucial errors and misjudgements, it nonetheless fuelled a larger amnesiac discourse (Wilson 2014). Similarly, the Far East seldom featured in British war films, and when it did the focus was overwhelmingly on Western prisoners of war (Noakes and Pattinson 2014: 15). Second, careful handling of imperial themes and events could neutralise disruptive connections and resonances. The desert war in North Africa and the Middle East, for example, was a relatively popular topic in 1950s war films, yet it threatened to raise a series of uncomfortable questions about the history of Western colonial oppression and violence in the region. These were evaded by various means, including the deployment of the trope of the 'empty desert' which rendered local populations invisible and allowed this to be presented as 'essentially a European war, which, while it took place on the continent of Africa, involved fighting with European weapons against a European enemy' (Francis 2014: 111).[10]

Over subsequent decades, and in changing political circumstances, the core myths of the war waxed and waned. The 'People's War' narrative lost its ideological power as the collectivist settlement to which it was sutured broke down in the 1980s, even as much of the public retained a sentimental attachment to its symbolism; in tandem, the Churchillian nationalist and individualist narrative resurged, at least from the time of the Falklands War, and moralising rhetoric and appeasement analogies have been a staple in British foreign policy well into the present century (Finney 2010: 188–225). Above and beyond these vicissitudes, however, remembering the war as a moment of glorious triumph served a continuous purpose as a 'security blanket' for a nation perpetually disappointed by the present, which all too often involved the continued invisibility of the imperial dimension.[11]

It was only as circumstances shifted again and permitted the emergence of a new critical discourse on the imperial past in general that the relationship between the war and the Empire began to be more fully explored in history and memory. Some commentators assign particular significance here to the re-engineering of national identity effected by the New Labour governments from 1997, in which diversity and multiculturalism came to be celebrated as the positive essence of Britishness (Travers and Ward 2016: 85). Certainly, during the fortieth and fiftieth anniversary celebrations of the end of the war in 1985 and 1995, the contribution of non-white troops – especially in the Far East – remained largely invisible in the official ceremonies and the products of the memorabilia industry (Watson 2014). Yet just a few years later the Commonwealth Memorial Gates were dedicated. The staging of an exhibition at the IWM entitled 'From War to *Windrush*' in 2008 – to mark the sixtieth anniversary of the voyage of the *Empire Windrush* carrying West Indian immigrants to London – was symptomatic of this rethinking (and driven both by top-down official initiative and grassroots bottom-up pressure). Telling the stories of black men and women from the West Indies and Britain in the two world wars, it aimed to create 'a powerful iconography of Black belonging in the national narrative' whilst challenging the 'exclusionary vision of racial whiteness' that had too often characterised the 'dominant imagery of the Second World War'.[12]

The New Labour years certainly did not entail a rejection of the notion of the Second World War as a 'good war' and a signal achievement in modern British history, but this no longer seemed automatically to require the suppression of the imperial dimension which could instead be incorporated and valorised. Yet in the complex and multifaceted landscape of British war memory, progress towards more capacious or critical understandings is always at risk of reversal. So more recent nostalgic discourses of austerity chic – perhaps the most significant mode whereby the 1940s past is publicly engaged today – are largely evasive about the Empire, performing a 'whiting-out', both of the wartime past and of 'the syncretic cultures that developed here from the 1950s onwards' (Hatherley 2016: 200).

Scepticism about the capacity of British remembrance of the war to evolve to more fully acknowledge the imperial dimension is echoed in the work of Paul Gilroy. Writing in the immediate aftermath of the Iraq war, Gilroy was profoundly unpersuaded by the New Labour project, and the extent to which it had broken with older nationalist discourses of identity or enabled the nation to really begin to come to terms with the legacy of empire. For Gilroy, marginal changes in the content of commemoration of the Second World War were somewhat beside the point; what mattered was how talking about that war worked strategically to facilitate a larger silence about the Empire. Secular obsession with the Second World War was a symptom of 'postcolonial melancholia', whereby a neurotic fixation on 'that particular mythic moment of national becoming and community' functioned as a compensatory displacement, as a form of unresolved mourning for the lost Empire. A corollary of this strategic role for war memory was the perpetuation of racist and xenophobic attitudes, especially towards post-war Commonwealth immigrants. Nostalgic longing for the supposed last moment of 'homogeneity', 'before the country lost its moral and cultural bearings', coupled with a failure to confront or acknowledge 'the profound change in circumstances and moods that followed the end of Empire and consequent loss of imperial prestige', worked to delegitimise and denaturalise their presence: 'the incomers may be unwanted and feared precisely because they are the unwitting bearers of the imperial and colonial past' (Gilroy 2004: 95–132). Gilroy thus offers a more nuanced version of the general claim adumbrated above that the long-standing British preoccupation with victory in the war offered a means of clinging to national grandeur as it in fact ebbed away. Moreover, he helps us to understand the apparent paradox whereby through the post-war decades British war memory became more exclusive and exclusionary just as the nation itself was in the process of becoming more multicultural.

This leaves slightly open the question of what developments over the last decade or so portend. Gilroy's argument that in Britain war memory serves primarily to block out memory of the Empire suggests that there must be definite limits to the project of incorporating the latter into the former, and certainly in any truly critical form. Many of the recent interventions which have sought to recognise the colonial contribution to Britain's war effort have indeed been criticised for adopting an anodyne, celebratory tone, rather than subjecting the experiences of 'different black and minority ethnic groups' to genuine critical analysis (Ugolini 2014: 104). While making hitherto neglected groups more visible is a positive move, it does not necessarily entail any fundamental restructuring of dominant national narratives: so, the 'good war' myth remains largely in place and enables continued delusion about Britain's status in the world.[13] Moreover, when it comes to the Empire and war memory, the victory of inclusion is not yet even entirely secure. It is also necessary to reckon with a surprising amount of imperial nostalgia: a January 2016 YouGov poll found 43 per cent of those surveyed regarded empire in positive terms while a third of respondents 'also wished that Britain still had an empire'.[14] All that said, the potential for contemporary fierce debates about the nature and legacy of the Empire to generate a significantly new configuration of memory should not be entirely dismissed. It has been widely observed that Gilroy's conceptualisation of the relationship between the memory of war and empire operates according to a 'zero-sum logic' (Francis 2014: 127); alternative models such as Michael Rothberg's 'multidirectional memory' are more open to the possibility of productive interaction between the remembrance of different pasts (Rothberg 2009).

Future imponderables aside, these debates demonstrate how bringing empire into conversation with the memory of the Second World War highlights the imperative to supplement national with transnational considerations. The notion that memory functions as a technology of national identity is, of course, no longer novel, but for the former imperial powers this has particular implications: war remembrance is not simply a means to come to terms with the traumas that it specifically represents and negotiates, it is also a way of grappling with post-war decolonisation. It is therefore important to attend not merely to what is said (or what fails to be said) about the war, but also to the larger terrain on which discourses on different aspects of the past interlock, overlap and interact, and at the subtle workings of mnemonic suppression, displacement and indirect mediation. In the British case, memories of the Second World War have been foundational for hegemonic discourses of national identity, and yet they have also been interpenetrated and co-produced by the larger transnational forces and processes surrounding decolonisation.

Similarly, if the argument is that war memory functions to provide cohesion to a national community, it is vital to attend to the changing composition of that community over time in these post-imperial cases. It is, again, now widely recognised that putatively national memories are always cross-cut by competing affiliations such as gender, class and religion. Yet the large-scale transnational movement of peoples from former colonies to metropoles raises slightly different questions about diachronic changes in the remembering community; how, for example, are incomers stitched into the political and mnemonic fabric of the host, or how far are they in fact excluded and if so, by what mechanisms? (As David Cesarani noted twenty years ago, the war as traditionally represented 'helps construct a sense of nation and nationality that excludes the bulk of post-1945 immigrants' (Travers and Ward 2016: 85)). What, indeed, do incomers bring with them, and how does their engagement with their host change both? Migration, as Michael Rothberg has recently argued, thickens memory and establishes new networks of affiliation, solidarity and contestation. It

> transforms the conditions of social, communicative, and cultural memory; it brings disparate histories into contact with each other, reconfigures individual and collective subjects, and produces novel constellations of remembrance and commemoration in which heterogeneous pasts jostle each other in an unsettled present.
>
> *(Rothberg 2014: 125)*

The implications of these conceptual ideas need to be worked through further in relation to the intersection of Second World War memory and the legacy of empire. This is certainly not a parochial British matter, since these issues have lately become pertinent in other post-imperial European cases as well. In France, for example, much consideration has recently been given to the intertwined memories of Second World War occupation and the Holocaust, on the one hand, and slavery and colonialism, on the other (Michel 2010); in 2006 a hugely successful film about North African combat troops fighting to liberate France – *Indigènes* – also served to bring the imperial dimensions of France's war and the ongoing problems faced by immigrants from the former colonies into sharp focus (Hargreaves 2007). Similarly in the Netherlands, there have been shocking recent revelations about the commission of atrocities by Dutch troops during the struggle to re-establish colonial control in the Dutch East Indies in the later 1940s. These have not only engendered debates about supposed 'active amnesia' regarding Dutch imperial violence, they have also challenged self-understandings about national virtue – embodied in the twin tropes of resistance and victimhood – deriving from the Second World War past.[15]

The 'Empire of memory'

Reconceiving the British war as an imperial one opens up a further transnational mnemonic perspective by bringing into focus the multiplicity of competing narratives that have emerged on the wartime past across the former imperial space. For if, as just discussed, British memory at home was in part a transnational – and 'multidirectional' – product, so in the wider world British memories were in transnational conversation with a host of others generated in the former colonies and Dominions. Of course, it is not possible to offer a comprehensive accounting of the myriad stories of the collectives and individuals who were caught up in the mobilisation of millions across the Empire as a result of the war. But even if we restrict our analysis to the domain of national and official memory – to the most prominent, would-be dominant, narratives in the public sphere – we are confronted with a host of divergent perspectives, shaped by diverse pre-war histories, wartime experiences and post-war circumstances, and often, indeed, forged in opposition to metropolitan memories. Constraints of space preclude discussion of more than a handful of examples even from this tightly delimited category, but these can nonetheless serve to demonstrate the potential fruitfulness of this reconceptualisation. As historians have begun to change our understanding of the Second World War by bringing into focus the 'Empire at war', so there is significant scope for shifting our sense of its mnemonic legacy by trying to get the measure of the 'Empire of memory'.

The case of Singapore – the scene, in 1942, of the Empire's most catastrophic defeat – is particularly revealing. It is scarcely surprising that as colonies gradually became former colonies and negotiated the challenges of nation-building, the stories they elaborated about the wartime past differed greatly from those circulating in Britain; after all both their experiences of the war and the requirements of post-war mnemonic engineering were quite different from those of the metropole. Yet, in the immediate post-war period as the British returned to power in Singapore they did make signal efforts to manage how the defeat and subsequent Japanese occupation were remembered, in order to help restore their credibility, prestige and political control (Blackburn and Hack 2012: 53–95). This involved a range of strategies including the screening of films about the war embodying stirring stories of British victories and heroism: the first film shown when cinemas re-opened in September 1945 was Roy Boulting's 1943 *Desert Victory* about El Alamein; Noel Coward and David Lean's 1942 classic *In Which We Serve* was also given prominence. Films were complemented by travelling photographic exhibitions and various parades and pageants designed to emphasise how the local struggle had been part of a larger integrated imperial effort. Crucially, the colonial establishment also invested great effort in portraying British and European prisoners of war and internees as heroic victims: 'their captivity was portrayed as part of a wider, moral drama, as a sacrifice which enabled victory in a global war against evil' and 'it was presented as an opportunity to display imperial characteristics, and through that fitness to rule' (Blackburn and Hack 2012: 71). Exemplary personal stories were propagated through war crimes trials and pageantry, and also through the careful development of Changi prison as a tourist and memorial site.

Of course, these efforts proved unavailing as the attempt to reconstruct the British position in the Malay peninsula had clearly failed by the mid-1950s, leading to decolonisation. Following its independence in 1965, Singapore soon dedicated a major Civilian War Memorial, honouring civilian war dead from each of the state's main ethnic groups, which became the focal point for official commemorations every 15 February, the anniversary of the 1942 surrender to the Japanese. At the dedication ceremony, Prime Minister Lee Kuan Yew underlined how the experience of war and occupation was being transformed into a foundational myth: 'We suffered together. It told us that we share a common destiny. And it is through sharing such common experiences that the feeling of living and being one community is established' (Blackburn and Hack 2012: 169–70). There was a certain amount of soft-pedalling over the war in the 1960s and 1970s when the city-state's leaders were actively courting Japanese investment, but from the 1980s a more economically secure and confident Singapore joined the ranks of regional critics of Japan's allegedly evasive and unrepentant attitude over its wartime actions.

At the same time Singapore also began more actively to instrumentalise war commemoration for nation-building purposes, in school textbooks, films and television programming, new memorial sites and ceremonies and via heritage tourism and re-enactments. The redesignation of 15 February as Total Defence Day in 1998 was telling: the memory of wartime suffering was still supposed to unite Singaporeans, but commemoration was also freighted with a series of lessons about the need for discipline, preparedness (including compulsory military service) and vigilance against external threats (Blackburn and Hack 2012: 292–333). This was also memory defined in opposition to that of Britain, which had always passed lightly over the humiliating loss of Singapore. The consequences of British failure to prepare the defence of the city adequately were here centre stage, to drive home the need for self-reliance: the British were castigated both for indifference to the fate of their colonial subjects and for their military weakness (Wong 2000: 232–4).

In other South-East Asian former colonies that had experienced Japanese occupation there was considerable variation in how far this history was utilised for nation-building purposes (Blackburn 2010). This was also done quite stridently in Burma throughout the post-war period, with the military uprising against the Japanese from 27 March 1945 being commemorated as the founding of an independent nation. After the military took effective control of government in the early 1960s regime-building intertwined with nation-building: commemoration focused on the role of the army as 'the vanguard of the modern Burmese nationalist movement' and stressed (again) 'the importance of defence and military preparedness' (Blackburn 2010: 21–2). If these instances echo the centrality accorded to the war in the metropole, elsewhere it had a much lower profile. In Malaysia, for example, the war unleashed divisive tensions among the major ethnic groups – Malays, Chinese and Indians – which also led to significant inter-communal violence after the Japanese surrender. These divisions made it highly problematic to use the war experience for unifying, nation-building purposes. To the chagrin of the Chinese community which had suffered most from wartime massacres at the hands of the Japanese, the government under Prime Minister Mahathir Mohamad from 1981 pursued a so-called 'Look East Policy' which entailed cultivating good relations with Japan in order to win capital investment and technical assistance. This too militated against prioritising war remembrance: in 1994 Mahathir – quite unlike most other leaders in the region – even urged his Japanese counterpart to stop apologising for wartime crimes from the distant past. Amongst Malays there were even some positive attitudes towards the occupation period, as 'a time of heightened political consciousness and developing Malay nationalism', but this view was not generalisable and war memories remain sectionalised (Blackburn and Hack 2012: 260; Blackburn 2010: 28–30).

If the nature of war experience is one key variable shaping memory, much also depends on post-war circumstances and the vicissitudes of the road to independence. The war was, for example, absolutely transformative for India. Two and a half million men were mobilised into the Indian Army and served all across the globe from Italy to Iraq to Hong Kong. India made a huge material and financial contribution to the war effort and emerged 'as one of the largest creditors to the imperial power'. By 1946 Japan was defeated and China was falling into civil war, while India stood 'as a potent Asian power'. Yet India's role in this conflict 'is dimly registered in historiography and popular memory'; around the seventieth anniversary of the end of the war in 2015 there was an almost total absence of 'any commemoration in India'. The key reason is that the post-war attainment of independence overshadowed the war. Indian historians prioritising anti-colonial nationalism and subaltern resistance saw the war as 'little more than mood music in the drama of the advance towards independence and partition'; the exploits of the vast Indian Army across the globe did not appeal as an object of study to historians uncomfortable with 'subalterns who collaborated with the Raj' (Delury *et al.* 2015: 815–18). Partition and the emergence of Indian–Pakistani rivalry was a reinforcing factor. The newly minted nation states of India and Pakistan 'needed new histories for self-legitimization': 'neither country wanted much to recall' the war, and so 'they sought to gloss over the war years of common mobilization and sacrifice' (Raghavan 2016: 461). Doubtless there are 'multidirectional' connections to be teased out amongst these different histories and memories, but in some cases – and former Dutch and French colonies such as Indonesia and Vietnam might also be adduced here (Blackburn 2010) – wars and other processes of decolonisation seem to have demonstrably either crowded out or been decisively selected over the Second World War in national remembering.

While some of these memories have evolved in opposition to British remembering, there is also scope for exploring mutual affinities across the Empire. Often these are sectional as well as national, as with the transnational memory work of RAF Bomber Command veterans. The Allied bombing war has always been controversial owing to the civilian casualties inflicted during the area bombing of German cities and doubts about its military necessity and efficacy; thus it has always sat slightly uneasily within the British 'good war' mythology. Bomber Command veterans long felt slighted by a lack of official recognition for their sacrifice, especially given the tremendous crew losses the campaign incurred; worse, they have been aghast to be accused by critics of having perpetrated a mass slaughter of innocent women and children for little strategic gain. This resentment was only partially and belatedly assuaged by the dedication of the Bomber Command Memorial in London in June 2012 (Houghton 2014). The RAF's bombing war was not, however, an entirely British affair, for many thousands of airmen from the Dominions of Canada, Australia and New Zealand also served, and suffered severe losses: over 10,000 of Bomber Command's 55,000 fatalities, for example, were Canadian. Across these former imperial territories the surviving veterans have waged linked and parallel battles through the decades to defend Bomber Command's reputation and to secure a more prominent and hospitable place for themselves within national memory cultures.

In Canada, one notable dispute broke out in spring 1992 when the Canadian Broadcasting Corporation screened a series of documentaries – entitled *The Valour and the Horror* – about key battles in the Second World War. The general tone was critical and revisionist, and aimed to unsettle Canada's own 'good war' myth: 'the battles were presented as catastrophic blunders and fiascoes, or travesties of justice in which Canadians were sent into the whirlwind of war unknowing and ill-prepared' (Taras 1995: 725). The second programme dealt with the strategic bombing offensive and, while aiming to be sympathetic to individual rank and file servicemen, it indicted their commanders for lack of candour about crew survival rates and argued that area bombing entailed the deliberate and illegitimate targeting of civilians. Veterans' organisations responded with fury and triggered a high-level political investigation of the claims which a Senate sub-committee found to be unwarranted in several key respects; in 1993 veterans even launched a libel suit against the films' producers though this was dismissed by the courts. Here the Bomber Command veterans were aligned with the Canadian political establishment in trying to maintain a positive image of the Canadian war effort as justified and virtuous (Taras 1995). In 1993 the programmes were also broadcast in Britain and generated a slightly less high-level controversy in which the same issues were nonetheless centrally at stake, with veterans in the two countries offering each other mutual support (Houghton 2014: 160).

Another furore broke out in 2007 when veterans protested about a display in the Canadian War Museum – reopened in a lavish new building in 2005 on the sixtieth anniversary of the end of the war – which drew attention to the debate over the morality and military value of the bombing campaign. After pressure from veterans (and not just those of Bomber Command), vigorous discussion between leading historians and another Senate sub-committee investigation, the museum amended the display to meet the objections (Dean 2009). As well as their own sectional interest, what the veterans were vigorously defending here was 'a powerful narrative of sacrifice, honour and nationhood' (Dean 2009: 10). This illustrates how elsewhere in the former Empire there was investment in the same kind of broad 'good war' myth as was entrenched in Britain. (There are also obvious parallels to be drawn with public controversies further afield that have pitted veterans and politicians against museum professionals, such as the 'Enola Gay' episode at the Smithsonian in 1994–95.) Bomber Command veterans were here carrying out sectional memory work which also sought to preserve a particular dominant national narrative (and their place in it); yet these episodes also offered intriguing evidence of transnational solidarities between Canadian and British veterans. Taking the imperial nature of Britain's war and post-war more seriously will reveal many other such connections.

That said, what may be most instructive in thinking about war memory in the former Dominions is how it has been used to forge a distinctive sense of national identity, separate or opposed to that of Britain. The prime example here is Australia, and specifically the conscious efforts of Paul Keating as prime minister in the early 1990s to reorient the nation's Second World War history – and even the larger narrative of its national identity – around the Kokoda campaign, the Australian defence of Papua New Guinea from the Japanese in 1942. This was a desperate battle in which Australian troops fought a ferocious defence in harsh jungle and mountain terrain to repulse a Japanese invasion; while it would be an exaggeration to say that their success meant a decisive turning of the tide in the war, it was nonetheless very significant in securing the defence of the Australian mainland. Keating visited Kokoda on Anzac Day in 1992, the year of the fiftieth anniversary of the battle. In a carefully crafted speech he paid familiar tribute to those who died at Gallipoli and elsewhere in the First World War, but more forcefully insisted that, as 'the world moves on', Australia must pay more heed to the dead of the later conflict. The fallen of Kokoda died not on behalf of the British Empire but 'in defence of Australia and the civilisation and values which had grown up there': 'for Australians, the battles in Papua New Guinea were the most important ever fought', ones fought 'not in the defence of the old world, but the new world. Their world.'[16]

This speech, and associated actions – Keating also fell to his knees and kissed the ground in a carefully choreographed gesture before the Kokoda memorial – was controversial given the sacred status of the Anzac myth, in which First World War sacrifice was construed as the formative moment in the birth of an independent Australian nation. It was also a quite conscious act of mnemonic engineering: Keating's speechwriter candidly stated that the aim was to 'mark Kokoda in Australia's collective memory, as perhaps Gettysburg was marked in the American mind by Lincoln'.[17] In part, the lionisation of Kokoda was designed to underpin the foreign policy reorientation of the 'turn to Asia' in which close relations with Japan were to be central. Yet it was also a fundamentally anti-British move, meant to instantiate a more total separation from the mother country. For Keating, a battle in defence of the Australian homeland was far more resonant than battles fought in distant lands on behalf of the British Empire, and offered a far more suitable mnemonic foundation for the republican nation, deeply engaged strategically, economically and culturally with Asia, which he wished to create.[18]

Keating's actions were successful in so far as Australia's connection to Asia has deepened and widened, even as inevitable tensions have lingered within the project to found good contemporary relations with Japan upon more intense remembrance of past hostilities (Curran 2010). The first Wednesday in September has since 2008 been designated Battle for Australia Day, commemorating the service of all who participated in the various battles – including Kokoda – to defend the homeland in 1942 and 1943. Moreover, Kokoda itself is certainly now far more prominent in Australian consciousness. Apart from pilgrimages by descendants of the soldiers who fought and died there, the extreme physical experience of walking the Kokoda trail has become a staple of corporate team-building exercises and youth group field trips, as well as a favourite activity for celebrities in search of authenticity, self-discovery and publicity (Scates 2013: 230–53). The new Australian myth of Kokoda is certainly very different from the war myths of the mother country even as it was in part produced in dialogue with them – witness Keating's ambivalent relationship in his speeches with the deeds and ideas of Churchill.[19] The importance of both –

and their mutual entwinement – will be better understood if we locate them on the larger terrain that constitutes the 'Empire of memory'.

Conclusion

There is a burgeoning literature exploring the memory of empire, and how colonial legacies continue to shape global politics and our frames of reference for apprehending them (Nicolaïdis, Sèbe and Maas 2015). The postcolonial perspectives deployed in it have also been fruitfully brought to bear in work on the interconnections between memories of the Second World War, the Holocaust and the diverse traumas of decolonisation (Craps and Buelens 2008; Rothberg 2009). This chapter argues that extending this work will bring diverse empirical and conceptual benefits for our thinking about processes of Second World War remembrance in the former imperial powers, and has sought to prove the point through a discussion of the case of the British Empire. Writing on the British Empire at war is significantly enriching our understanding of the history of that conflict, and applying similar perspectives to the study of its memory will prove equally productive. On the one hand, this involves thinking more widely and deeply about British war memory as a product of transnational forces, generated in relation to the negotiation of the legacy of ongoing decolonisation. On the other hand, it means exploring how an imperial war effort engendered diverse war memories across the former Empire, memories which have been shaped both by wartime experiences and post-war exigencies but which have also been in transnational conversation with each other. These reframings have the potential to open up whole new perspectives on war memory in Britain and the other former imperial powers; they can also contribute powerfully to the larger project of moving beyond the national in our thinking about Second World War remembrance.

Notes

1 'Isaac Fadoyebo', *The Telegraph*, 28 November 2012, www.telegraph.co.uk/news/obituaries/9709639/Isaac-Fadoyebo.html; David Killingray, 'Isaac Fadoyebo Obituary', *The Guardian*, 21 November 2012, www.theguardian.com/theguardian/2012/nov/21/isaac-fadoyebo-obituary; Monica Mark, 'From Nigeria to Burma's Jungle: Courage and Compassion in the War with Japan', *The Guardian*, 16 August 2015, www.theguardian.com/world/2015/aug/16/from-nigeria-to-burma-jungle-courage-and-compassion-in-war-with-japan-vj-day.

2 Martin Plaut, 'The Africans who Fought in WWII', *BBC News*, 9 November 2009, http://news.bbc.co.uk/1/hi/world/africa/8344170.stm.

3 David Smith, 'They Fought for Britain. In Return They Were Given £10', *The Observer*, 3 September 2006, www.theguardian.com/uk/2006/sep/03/world.secondworldwar.

4 'Aging, Forgotten but still Loyal to Britain, WWII has Never Ended for Fabled Burma Fighters', *Fox News*, 1 August 2010, www.foxnews.com/world/2010/08/01/aging-forgotten-loyal-britain-wwii-ended-fabled-burma-fighters.html.

5 Sally Tomlinson and Danny Dorling, 'Brexit has its Roots in the British Empire, So How Do We Explain it to the Young', *New Statesman*, 9 May 2016, www.newstatesman.com/politics/staggers/2016/05/brexit-has-its-roots-british-empire-so-how-do-we-explain-it-young;

Amit Chaudhuri, 'The Real Meaning of Rhodes Must Fall', *The Guardian*, 16 March 2016, www.theguardian.com/uk-news/2016/mar/16/the-real-meaning-of-rhodes-must-fall.

6 William Dalrymple, 'Violence, Victors and Victims: How to Look at the Art of the British Empire', *The Guardian*, 21 November 2015, www.theguardian.com/artanddesign/2015/nov/20/how-to-look-at-the-art-of-the-british-empire.

7 Santanu Das, 'The First World War and the Colour of Memory', *The Guardian*, 22 July 1914, www.theguardian.com/commentisfree/2014/jul/22/first-world-war-whitewashed-eurocentric.

8 For further details, see the IWMN website at www.iwm.org.uk/exhibitions/iwm-north/mixing-it-the-changing-faces-of-wartime-britain.

9 For further details, see the IWM website at www.iwm.org.uk/collections-research/research-programmes/whose-remembrance.

10 Francis' larger point, however, is that at least some films from this genre, when read against the grain, do in fact offer provocative interlinked meditations on the demise of empire and the Second World War.

11 Anthony Beevor, 'Tommy and Jerry', *The Guardian*, 16 February 1999, www.theguardian.com/theguardian/1999/feb/16/features11.g22.

12 Matt Mead, 'From War to Windrush: Curating Multiculturalism in the Imperial War Museum, London', *photoCLEC: Photographs, Colonial Legacy and Museums in Contemporary Europe Culture*, no date, http://photoclec.dmu.ac.uk/content/war-windrush-curating-multiculturalism-imperial-war-museum-london. I owe this reference to Ugolini 2014: 90–4.

13 Compare, for example, the similar process of incorporation of 'outsiders' into the dominant 'good war' myth in the United States (Bodnar 2010: 166–99).

14 Deana Heath, 'The Ongoing Effect of Empire – in Britain', *The Conversation*, 21 November 2016, http://theconversation.com/the-ongoing-effect-of-empire-in-britain-67429.

15 Paul Doolan, 'Dutch Imperial Past Returns to Haunt the Netherlands', *Imperial and Global Forum*, 6 April 2014, https://imperialglobalexeter.com/2014/04/06/dutch-imperial-past-returns-to-haunt-the-netherlands/. For in-depth analysis, see Luttikhuis and Moses 2012.

16 For the text of the speech, delivered on 25 April 1992 at Ela Beach, Port Moresby, see Paul Keating's website at www.keating.org.au/shop/item/anzac-day–25-april-1992.

17 Mervyn F. Bendle, 'How Paul Keating Betrayed the Anzacs', *Quadrant Online*, 7 January 2014, https://quadrant.org.au/magazine/2014/01-02/paul-keating-betrayed-anzacs/.

18 These points are made even more dramatically in another speech by Keating, delivered on 7 April 1992 and entitled 'Australia and Asia: Knowing Who We Are', www.keating.org.au/shop/item/australia-and-asia-knowing-who-we-are–7-april-1992.

19 Ibid.

References

Bayly, Christopher and Harper, Tim. 2004. *Forgotten Armies: The Fall of British Asia, 1941–1945*. London: Allen Lane.

Bayly, Christopher and Harper, Tim. 2007. *Forgotten Wars: The End of Britain's Asian Empire*. London: Allen Lane.

Blackburn, Kevin. 2010. 'War Memory and Nation Building in South East Asia'. *South East Asia Research*, 18, 1: 5–31.

Blackburn, Kevin and Hack, Karl. 2012. *War Memory and the Making of Modern Malaysia and Singapore*. Singapore: National University of Singapore Press.

Bodnar, John. 2010. *The 'Good War' in American Memory*. Baltimore, MD: Johns Hopkins University Press.

Bourne, Stephen. 2010. *Mother Country: Britain's Black Community on the Home Front, 1939–1945*. Stroud: History Press.

Bourne, Stephen. 2012. *The Motherland Calls: Britain's Black Servicemen and Women, 1939–1945*. Stroud: History Press.

Byfield, Judith A., Brown, Carolyn A., Parsons, Timothy and Sikaingi, Ahmad Alawad. eds. 2015. *Africa and World War II*. Cambridge: Cambridge University Press.

Cobain, Ian. 2016. *The History Thieves: Secrets, Lies and the Shaping of a Modern Nation*. London: Portobello.

Connelly, Mark. 2004. *We Can Take It! Britain and the Memory of the Second World War*. London: Pearson Longman.

Craps, Stef and Buelens, Gert. eds. 2008. 'Postcolonial Trauma Novels'. *Studies in the Novel*, 40, 1–2: 1–234.

Curran, James. 2010. 'L'Australie, le Japon et l'héritage de la Seconde Guerre mondiale'. *Vingtième Siècle*, 107: 115–29.

Dahl, Roald. 2008 [1986]. *Boy and Going Solo*. London: Penguin.

Dean, David. 2009. 'Museums as Conflict Zones: the Canadian War Museum and Bomber Command'. *Museum and Society*, 7, 1: 1–15.

Delury, John, Smith, Sheila A., Repnikova, Maria and Raghavan, Srinath. 2015. 'Looking Back on the Seventieth Anniversary of Japan's Surrender'. *Journal of Asian Studies*, 74, 4: 797–820.

Eley, Geoff. 2001. 'Finding the People's War: Film, British Collective Memory, and World War II'. *American Historical Review*, 106, 3: 818–38.

Ferguson, Niall. 2003. *Empire: How Britain Made the Modern World*. London: Allen Lane.

Francis, Martin. 2014. 'Remembering War, Forgetting Empire? Representations of the North African Campaign in 1950s British Cinema'. In *British Cultural Memory and the Second World War*, edited by Lucy Noakes and Juliette Pattinson. London: Bloomsbury. 111–32.

Finney, Patrick. 2010. *Remembering the Road to World War Two: International History, National Identity, Collective Memory*. London: Routledge.

Gilroy, Paul. 2004. *After Empire: Melancholia or Convivial Culture?* London: Routledge.

Gott, Richard. 2011. *Britain's Empire: Resistance, Repression and Revolt*. London: Verso.

Hargreaves, Alec G. 2007. '*Indigènes*: A Sign of the Times'. *Research in African Literatures*, 38, 4: 204–16.

Hatherley, Owen. 2016. *The Ministry of Nostalgia*. London: Verso.

Houghton, Frances. 2014. 'The "Missing Chapter": Bomber Command Aircrew Memoirs in the 1990s and 2000s'. In *British Cultural Memory and the Second World War*, edited by Lucy Noakes and Juliette Pattinson. London: Bloomsbury. 155–74.

Jackson, Ashley. 2006. *The British Empire and the Second World War*. London: Continuum.

Jackson, Ashley. 2015. 'The British Empire, 1939–1945'. In *The Cambridge History of the Second World War. Volume II: Politics and Ideology*, edited by Richard J. B. Bosworth and Joseph A. Maiolo. Cambridge: Cambridge University Press. 558–80.

Khan, Yasmin. 2015. *The Raj at War: A People's History of India's Second World War*. London: Bodley Head.

Killingray, David, and Plaut, Martin. 2010. *Fighting for Britain: African Soldiers in the Second World War*. Woodbridge: James Currey.

Kwarteng, Kwasi. 2011. *Ghosts of Empire: Britain's Legacies in the Modern World*. London: Bloomsbury.

Levy, Andrea. 2004. *Small Island*. London: Headline.

Luttikhuis, Bart, and Moses, A. Dirk. eds. 2012. 'Mass Violence and the End of the Dutch Colonial Empire in Indonesia'. *Journal of Genocide Research*, 14, 3–4: 257–502.

Michel, Johann. 2010. *Gouverner les mémoires: Les politiques mémorielles en France*. Paris: Presses Universitaires de France.

Mishra, Pankaj. 2013. *From the Ruins of Empire: The Revolt Against the West and the Remaking of Asia*. London: Penguin.

Mukerjee, Madhusree. 2010. *Churchill's Secret War: The British Empire and the Ravaging of India during World War II*. New York, NY: Basic Books.

Nicolaïdis, Kalypso, Sèbe, Berny and Maas, Gabrielle. eds. 2015. *Echoes of Empire: Memory, Identity and Colonial Legacies*. London: I. B. Tauris.

Noakes, Lucy and Pattinson, Juliette. 2014. 'Introduction: "Keep Calm and Carry On": The Cultural Memory of the Second World War in Britain'. In *British Cultural Memory and the Second World War*, edited by Lucy Noakes and Juliette Pattinson. London: Bloomsbury. 1–24.

Raghavan, Srinath. 2016. *India's War: The Making of Modern South Asia, 1939–1945*. London: Allen Lane.

Ramsden, John. 1998. 'Refocusing "The People's War": British War Films of the 1950s'. *Journal of Contemporary History*, 33, 1: 35–63.

Rose, Sonya O. 2003. *Which People's War? National Identity and Citizenship in Wartime Britain, 1939–1945*. Oxford: Oxford University Press.

Rothberg, Michael. 2009. *Multidirectional Memory: Remembering the Holocaust in the Age of Decolonization*. Stanford, CA: Stanford University Press.

Rothberg, Michael. 2014. 'Multidirectional Memory in Migratory Settings: The Case of Post-Holocaust Germany'. In *Transnational Memory: Circulation, Articulation, Scales*, edited by Chiara De Cesari and Ann Rigney. Berlin: De Gruyter. 123–45.

Scates, Bruce. 2013. *Anzac Journeys: Returning to the Battlefields of World War II*. Cambridge: Cambridge University Press.

Taras, David. 1995. 'The Struggle over *The Valour and the Horror*: Media Power and the Portrayal of War'. *Canadian Journal of Political Science*, 28, 4: 725–48.

Travers, Daniel and Ward, Paul. 2016. 'Narrating Britain's War: A "Four Nations and More" Approach to the People's War'. In *The Long Aftermath: Cultural Legacies of Europe at War, 1936–2016*, edited by Manuel Bragança and Peter Tame. Oxford: Berghahn. 77–95.

Ugolini, Wendy. 2014. '"When are You Going Back?": Memory, Ethnicity and the British Home Front'. In *British Cultural Memory and the Second World War*, edited by Lucy Noakes and Juliette Pattinson. London: Bloomsbury. 89–110.

Watson, Janet. 2014. 'Total War and Total Anniversary: The Material Culture of Second World War Commemoration in Britain'. In *British Cultural Memory and the Second World War*, edited by Lucy Noakes and Juliette Pattinson. London: Bloomsbury. 175–94.

Webster, Wendy. 2007. *Englishness and Empire, 1939–1965*. Oxford: Oxford University Press.

Wilson, Cat. 2014. *Churchill on the Far East in The Second World War: Hiding the History of the 'Special Relationship'*. London: Palgrave.

Wong, Diana. 2000. 'Memory Suppression and Memory Production: The Japanese Occupation of Singapore'. In *Perilous Memories: The Asia-Pacific War(s)*, edited by T. Fujitani, Geoffrey M. White and Lisa Yoneyama. Durham, NC: Duke University Press. 218–38.

5

THE SOVIET WAR MEMORIAL IN VIENNA

Geopolitics of memory and the new Russian diaspora in post-Cold War Europe

Tatiana Zhurzhenko

If you happen to be one of the thousands of tourists visiting the beautiful Austrian capital in late spring, you will most probably be drawn to the open-air symphony concert at Heldenplatz (Heroes' Square) on 8 May. Inaugurated in 2013, this new mode of celebrating the end of the Second World War entices both locals and visitors to participate in a big picnic party at the very heart ofVienna. A Russian tourist, however, may well find herself at a very different party the next day, 9 May, just several hundred metres away, around the Soviet war memorial at Schwarzenbergplatz. This is a Victory Day celebration which once a year draws numerous Russians and Russian speakers to a public performative commemoration of the Great Patriotic War which has been at the core of Soviet and post-Soviet Russian identity. This 'invented tradition' is also rather new, as is the Viennese Russian community itself, which is a product of post-Soviet migration. Neither mass performance refers to the other, thereby strengthening the impression that there is practically no dialogue between these two parallel cultures of memory – Austrian and Russian – coexisting in Vienna's urban space. The Austrians and foreign tourists who gather on Heldenplatz on 8 May and those Russians and people from other former Soviet republics who come to the Soviet war memorial the next morning are two different crowds – it is difficult to believe that these two celebrations are dedicated to the end of the same war.

This simple observation on the duality of memory of the Second World War in Vienna can serve as the starting point for a discussion of several questions central to this chapter: what happened to Soviet memory of the Great Patriotic War after the end of the Cold War era when the old geopolitical order in Europe collapsed, burying Stalin's 'empire of memory' under its ruins? How has the role of Soviet war memorials outside Russia changed since 1991 and, in particular, with Moscow's growing ambition to return to the league of great powers and to influence European politics? How did the affirmative commemorative politics of the

Russian government, and more recently the weaponisation of memory of the war in the conflict with Ukraine, contribute to the crystallisation of Russian diaspora identities in the west?

Taking as its point of departure the changing role of the Soviet war memorial in Vienna, the main site of contemporary Russian memory of the Second World War in Austria, this chapter will, however, go beyond the simple dichotomising of Austrian and Russian national memories. A closer look at the ongoing Austrian debates on Second World War memory and national identity, collective guilt and historical responsibility reveals internal divisions, conflicts and taboos. And yet, even if at a slower pace than Germany, Austria has been making continuous efforts to come to terms with its Nazi past. In recent decades Austrian society has increasingly embraced the transnational European paradigm of Second World War memory based first of all on recognising the Holocaust as a foundation of the new global culture of human rights.

In Russian commemorative culture, however, triumph and heroic sacrifice still prevail. As a successor state of the Soviet Union, Russia claims victory in the Great Patriotic War as its most important symbolic legacy. As Boris Dubin has pointed out, once the October Revolution, socialism and the USSR had lost their symbolic value, the role of the Soviet Union in defeating fascism became its only uncontroversial contribution to world history (Dubin 2005). There is, of course, a geopolitical dimension to this triumphalist narrative: the 'victory over fascism' became the Soviet Union's entry ticket to the club of world powers and legitimised its sphere of influence on the European continent. As the USSR did before it, post-Soviet Russia draws its geopolitical ambitions from the historical outcomes of the Second World War. The still very Soviet narrative of the Great Patriotic War has not only been at the core of Russian national identity, but also constitutes the imagined transnational community of the '*Russkiy mir*' ('Russian world'). Russians and Russian speakers abroad now reproduce and perform the memory of the 'great victory' in urban space even at those places where Soviet commemorative culture has never previously existed. Many of these commemorative actions and projects – such as the mass distribution of Saint George ribbons (a symbol of Russian military glory) or the new Museum of the Liberation of Vienna, a joint Austrian-Russian endeavour – obviously address the local public. Therefore, rather than dealing with Austrian and Russian national memories in simple opposition, this chapter addresses two different modes of transnational memory of the Second World War in Europe and sometimes even the interactions between them.

Soviet war memorials in Russia and abroad have been studied from a number of disciplinary perspectives, from history to anthropology to human geography. The emphasis is usually on representations of the Great Patriotic War in architecture and public art, the transformation of Soviet commemorative culture and the Russian narrative of the Second World War (see Palmer 2009 on Mamaev Kurgan in Volgograd; Forest and Johnson 2002 and Schleifman 2001 on Poklonnaya Gora in Moscow). Interestingly, however, after the Second World War the first Soviet memorials were built not in Russian cities but in European countries liberated from the Nazis by the Soviet army and in the western borderlands of the USSR (Gabowitsch 2015). This suggests that apart from the traditional functions of facilitating collective grief and commemoration, Soviet war memorials served an important geopolitical purpose: they marked the post-war partition of Europe into zones of influence. Accordingly, with the end of the Cold War Soviet war, memorials in Central and Eastern Europe have become barometers of political tensions. Originally erected to represent the official Soviet narrative of the Second World War and to demonstrate – or induce – the loyalty of the Warsaw Pact states and the Soviet republics to Moscow, they turned after 1989–91 into sites of contestation and conflict. New national narratives in East-Central Europe portrayed Communist rule as Soviet occupation and states there developed their own narratives of victimhood and suffering.

In the Baltic states, whose annexation by the USSR as a result of the Molotov–Ribbentrop pact had never been internationally acknowledged during the Cold War era, but where at the same time significant Russian-speaking minorities identified with the Great Patriotic War myth, conflicts around Soviet war memorials were predestined. With these countries moving towards the EU and NATO, Moscow started to use their Russian minorities and the memory of the Second World War as leverage against the new national elites, trying to compromise them as 'fascists' and 'Nazi collaborators'. The conflict in spring 2007 around the 'Bronze Soldier' – the Soviet war memorial in Tallinn – was the most egregious case in these memory wars. The decision of the municipal authorities to relocate the memorial from the city centre to one of Tallinn's outlying cemeteries and the subsequent protest riots by local Russians had profound implications for interethnic relations in Estonia and for Russian–Estonian relations (Astrov 2007; Brüggemann and Kasekamp 2008; Ehala 2009; Lehti, Jutila and Jokisipilä 2008; Smith 2008). Populist politicians and public figures not only in Russia but also in Eastern Ukraine offered asylum to the 'Bronze Soldier'.[1] In a similar way, after the Soviet war memorial in the Georgian city of Kutaisi was demolished by order of President Saakashvili, Vladimir Putin publicly promised to re-erect it in Moscow on Poklonnaya Gora, in the so-called 'Victory Park'.

Poland, like other countries of East-Central Europe, experienced a '"dissociation" from narratives commemorating the Red Army as an ally and liberator' because the legitimation of the new regime was based in large part on a break with the communist past. However, an 'initial stage of radical iconoclasm was followed by a period of relative disinterest in the fate of Soviet monuments', which in most cases were de-ideologised and re-integrated into the local memorial landscape (Ochman 2010: 509). Yet in 2007 the issue of Soviet monuments was used by the Law and Justice party and its supporters 'to debate the need for de-communization, respect for national history and patriotism, and to question the post-1989 attitudes towards the Polish People's Republic' (Ochman 2010: 525). With the return of Law and Justice to power in 2015, the issue of Soviet war memorials was raised again, reflecting a deep internal conflict between the two major political camps, the liberals and the nationalists, rather than simply an anti-Russian attitude. In March

2016, Poland's Institute for National Remembrance urged regional authorities to take down 500 Soviet monuments.[2]

Even if Soviet war memorials survive, they have been stripped of their original ideological meaning, and often of any meaning at all. Formerly integrated in official state rituals of loyalty and gratitude to the Soviet Union, today they serve as a stage for various kinds of activities, from leisure to local political protests. The Soviet war memorial in Sofia has become especially well known as a site for artistic performances. In 2011, the memorial underwent a dramatic makeover: 'Red Army soldiers had been transformed into popular American icons including Superman, The Joker, Captain America, Ronald McDonald and Santa Claus. The flag held aloft by the soldiers had also been adorned with the US stars and stripes. A telling slogan was boldly written in black spray paint below the monument to accompany the statue's makeover: "Moving with the Times".'[3] In August 2013, the monument was painted pink in an 'artistic apology' for Bulgaria's support of the Soviet troops who suppressed Czechoslovakia's Prague Spring in 1968. One year later, after the annexation of Crimea, it was coloured yellow and blue as an expression of solidarity with Ukraine.

Soviet war memorials have often become a stage for performing protests and fighting new political battles. Various social groups – leftists, anti-fascists, anti-globalists – choose these memorials for their gatherings, possibly because they still possess some residual aura of an anti-Western, anti-capitalist alternative. Most importantly, however, Soviet war memorials attract Russian and Russian-speaking minorities and diaspora members, especially on Victory Day, 9 May. In this respect, the results of the recent international research project *Soviet War Memorials and Victory Day* are of special interest for this chapter. Research – in which I took part – was conducted on 9 May 2013 in twenty-three cities in eleven countries – including both former Soviet republics and states which had experienced a Soviet military presence.[4] The idea was to study the Victory Day celebrations as public performances centred around Soviet war memorials and including various practices such as the laying of flowers and wreaths, minutes of silence and reading of the names of the fallen, greeting veterans, singing war and Soviet songs, children's performances and the taking of photos (Gabowitsch 2015). While varying significantly depending on the local context, these practices fit into the same canon.

The Soviet war memorial in Vienna is interesting and special in many respects. Unlike the countries of the Warsaw Pact, Austria quickly overcame its collective occupation trauma as the Soviet Army left the country comparatively early, in 1955.[5] This fact can explain the rather marginal place of the Soviet memorial in the local topography of Second World War memory as well as in Austrian debates on the Nazi past and post-war national identity. The memorial has become an uncontested part of the urban landscape. It is rarely noticed by the Viennese and usually elicits neither positive nor negative emotions. The Austrian case is also different from Germany, where Soviet war memorials were integrated in the ideological system of the German Democratic Republic and thus carried a somewhat different ideological charge in the post-reunification context (even as Berlin evinced a relatively tolerant attitude towards this heritage). From the Russian perspective, Austria's depoliticised treatment of the Soviet memorial as part of Austrian cultural heritage is most welcome and serves as a proof of 'special relations' between Moscow and Vienna (which is unhappy about the current crisis in EU–Russian relations). As the diplomatic capital of Europe, Vienna is an important site for demonstrating Russia's new-old glory, while the growing Russian diaspora is turning Victory Day into a celebration of Soviet nostalgia and new Russian nationalism.

Towards a culture of guilt and responsibility

Whatever the place of the Soviet war memorial at Schwarzenbergplatz in the Viennese commemorative landscape, it is not an arena of conflict over Austrian collective memory and identity. This role has been reserved for Heldenplatz, where on 15 March 1938 Adolf Hitler addressed the masses of Austrians who had gathered to support the Anschluss – the annexation of Austria by Nazi Germany. Austria had become part of the Third Reich and lost its national sovereignty, which was restored only in 1945. With its pompous architecture, meant to represent the military glory and imperial power of the Habsburgs, Heldenplatz is the best illustration of Bernhard Giesen's thesis on the ambivalence of triumph and trauma (Giesen 2004): over the last decades this site has become a symbol of many Austrians' complicity in Nazi crimes and the accompanying historical amnesia about it.

Heldenplatz is historically connected with the traditions of Austrian monarchism and Catholicism. Its central symbolic element, the Heldentor (the Heroes' Gate), was constructed in 1824 to celebrate the victory over Napoleon in the battle of Leipzig. In the second half of the nineteenth century the square was decorated with equestrian statues of Archduke Charles of Austria, the winner over Napoleon in the 1809 battle of Aspern, and Prince Eugene of Savoy, who defeated the Ottomans in a number of decisive battles in the late seventeenth and early eighteenth centuries. A site representing the imperial power and military triumph of the Habsburgs, Heldenplatz was also used to celebrate national heroes during the First World War but the 1918 revolution prevented this tradition from being consolidated: 'Red Vienna' – the post-First World War city government was dominated by social democrats – was pacifist and anti-Habsburg (Hanisch 1998: 138). It was only in 1933–34, with the turn to authoritarianism and the corporate state, that the Heldentor was reconstructed to host a memorial to Austrian soldiers fallen in the First World War, the Heldendenkmal. This included the Hall of Glory under the open sky and the crypt in the right wing of the Heldentor, which still today hosts a recumbent statue of the Unknown Soldier made of red marble. The aesthetics of the memorial designed by Wilhelm Frass were in contrast to the new traditions of Austrian republicanism and clearly referred to the Habsburgs' heroic myths (Hanisch 1998: 138–9).

After the Second World War the Heldendenkmal came to symbolise the memory of all Austrians fallen in both world wars; thirty thousand names, mainly of Wehrmacht soldiers, were added to the memorial books kept in the crypt.

Although post-war Austria drew its national identity from the restoration of the sovereignty that had been stolen by Hitler in 1938, most ordinary Austrians considered themselves defeated rather than liberated. With the beginning of the Cold War the 'glorification of the anti-fascist liberation struggle, which had been used to legitimize the new Austria in the immediate aftermath of the war, was … defamed as Communist and thus unpatriotic' (Uhl 2006: 45). Heidemarie Uhl has deftly demonstrated the gap between the official discourse of the nation as 'the first victim of Hitler's aggression' and everyday commemorative culture, especially in the provinces, which rehabilitated and glorified Austrian soldiers of the Wehrmacht (Uhl 2006: 49–54).

In April 1965, on the twentieth anniversary of the Austrian declaration of independence, a remembrance room dedicated to the 'victims of the struggle for Austria's freedom' was opened in the left wing of the Heldentor. In this way the victims of Nazi terror received state recognition equivalent to that given to fallen soldiers, and the role of the Austrian anti-Nazi resistance in restoring state independence was officially recognised. (Five years later, a museum and documentation centre on the Austrian resistance was opened in the former concentration camp Mauthausen). Uhl writes about the two separate memorials – the crypt and the remembrance room – as symbolising the divergent cultures of remembrance in post-war Austria (Uhl 2006: 57). What Heldenplatz still remains silent about, however, is the 'trauma of the perpetrators' (Giesen 2004: 109–53). The myth of 'Austria as the first victim of Hitler' ignored such aspects of the Austrian past as mass support for the Anschluss, the significant role of Austrians in the state apparatus in charge of terror and Austrian responsibility for the crimes of National Socialism, including the annihilation of the Jewish population.

A radical revision of the 'nation-victim' thesis and the turn to a culture of historical responsibility started in Austria in the 1980s, provoked to a large extent by the Waldheim affair. Kurt Waldheim, an Austrian diplomat and politician and UN Secretary General from 1972 to 1981, was nominated as the candidate from the Austrian People's Party in the 1986 presidential elections. Details of his military service in the Wehrmacht in 1938–45, including in Greece and Yugoslavia, subsequently appeared in the media. Rumours about his possible involvement in war crimes forced the Austrian government to create an international historical commission to investigate this part of his biography. Although the accusations were not proven, the Waldheim case forced Austrian society to critically approach the Nazi past and recognise its co-responsibility for the crimes of the Nazi regime, above all the Holocaust. In 1988, on the occasion of the fiftieth anniversary of the Anschluss, the Burgtheater performance of Thomas Bernhard's *Heldenplatz* addressed the taboo topic of Austrian anti-Semitism and provoked a scandal. In 1995 – in the context of Austria's accession to the EU that same year – the National Fund of the Republic of Austria for Victims of National Socialism was established, and the Austrian state started paying compensation to victims of Nazi crimes. In 1997, 5 May, the day when the US army liberated the concentration camp at Mauthausen in 1945, was designated a commemoration day for the victims of National Socialism.

The new configuration of memory of the 'dark years' of Austrian history (1938–45) is reflected in both the Memorial against War and Fascism on Albertina Platz, created in 1988 by the well-known Austrian sculptor Alfred Hrdlicka, and Rachel Whiteread's 2000 Memorial to the Sixty Five Thousand Murdered Austrian Jews of the Shoah at Judenplatz (Kuttenberg 2007).

In general, therefore, Austrian commemorative culture has in recent decades moved into alignment with the European consensus regarding the memory and lessons of the Second World War, including a critical attitude to the National Socialist past and moral responsibility for the Nazi crimes. The memorial action Night of Silence held in 2008 on the anniversary of the Anschluss became a manifestation of this new commemorative culture. Eighty thousand candles were lit at Heldenplatz in memory of the 80,000 Austrians, including 65,000 Jews, who became victims of the Nazi regime.

Appreciation of this tendency towards a Europeanisation of Austrian national memory aids understanding of the recent series of conflicts around the meaning of 8 May and the end of the Second World War in general. It should be noted that the chief national memorial day in Austria is 27 April, the day of the declaration of Austrian independence and the birth of the Second Republic. 8 May, the last day of the Second World War, was until recently more a part of the European commemorative calendar. In Austria from the 1990s, however, this date began to be appropriated by nationalists and the far right who, reacting against the critical turn in commemorative culture, sought to turn it into a day of mourning for the fallen in the Second World War. A mourning ceremony – or '*Totengedenken*' – was held at Heldenplatz by right-wing students' associations and honoured above all Wehrmacht soldiers and the civilian victims of the Allied bombing war. Allusions to the heroic Habsburg myth and to German nationalism and militarism were obvious in the very form of the commemorative ritual, which included a guard of honour in front of the crypt and a torchlight march. On 8 May 2012, the last year it took place, around 200 members of nationalist students' associations took part in this ceremony.

Austria's accession to the EU, on the one hand, and the growing popularity of the nationalist Freedom Party, on the other, led to a significant politicisation of the 8 May rituals. The liberal part of Austrian society and the centre-left politicians – above all the Social Democrats and Greens – associated this ceremony with the National Socialist past, and some radical opponents criticised it as a sign of dangerous nostalgia. From their perspective, mourning Wehrmacht soldiers in front of the national memorial site on the day of Nazi Germany's capitulation was unacceptable. Even if the students' associations themselves usually denied any sympathy for National Socialism, far-right politicians known for their ambivalent attitude to the Nazi past did take part in this ceremony.

For the Austrian government, representing a pro-European coalition of Social Democrats and conservatives, the '*Totengedenken*' became a growing public embarrassment. Austrian chancellor Werner Faymann commented in 2013 that 'May 8 is a day of liberation and not of defeat'. 8 May 1945 was a 'zero hour' for Europe, he continued, and therefore the unity of Europe was 'the only answer to such a regime as National Socialism'.[6] The Greens, the most outspoken critics of Austria's ambivalent commemorative culture, suggested declaring 8 May as a national holiday in order to raise awareness of its meaning in society. The mourning ceremony organised by the far right usually provoked counteractions from radical left groups and created significant problems for the Viennese police.

In May 2013, the '*Totengedenken*' was prevented for the first time through coordinated actions of the Austrian Ministry of Defence, which organised its own honour guard at Heldenplatz on 8 May, and the Austrian Mauthausen Committee, which organised a Festival of Joy in the evening of the same day, with public speeches and the Vienna Symphonic Orchestra giving a free open air concert. In this way, the space for the far-right groups was blocked and the symbolic meaning of the date was altered. In their speeches Austrian politicians presented the last day of the Second World War as a symbol of all-European liberation from National Socialism and the 'zero hour' for a new Europe. While the victims of Nazism were mentioned, joy was meant to be the dominant emotion of the public celebration. The defeat of National Socialism in 1945 was associated with the triumph of democracy and the European idea in Austria. It seems that since 2013 this new format of celebrating 8 May has become an established tradition, although it remains to be seen whether the growing electoral success of the Freedom Party will lead to a reversal of this in the future.

In any case, the new meaning of 8 May is just one aspect of profound changes in Austria's commemorative culture and symbolic politics. In 2012, at the initiative of the Ministry of Defence, the Heroes' Memorial and the crypt on Heldenplatz were closed for reconstruction, which will turn them into an information and education centre. After heated political discussions, a new Memorial for the Victims of Nazi Military Justice (that is, soldiers who were executed for desertion from the Wehrmacht) was opened in close proximity to the Heroes' Gate, a signal of radical redefinition of such notions as 'heroism' and 'duty'. The symbolic landscape of Heldenplatz which traditionally represented military triumph and state power has been challenged by new commemorative projects and actions that refer instead to such values as tolerance, moral responsibility for the past and European unity.

The changing meaning of the Soviet war memorial in Vienna

In March 1945 the Soviet Army entered the territory of Austria. Addressing the local population, the Soviet military commanders stressed that the aim of their operation was the liberation of Austria from the Nazi regime, not its occupation. The Soviets referred to the Moscow Declaration signed by the foreign ministers of the countries of the anti-Hitler coalition in 1943. In this document the annexation of Austria in 1938 was declared illegitimate and the country was guaranteed the right to state independence after the defeat of Nazi Germany. As early as April 1945, when the Soviet Army was still approaching Vienna, Stalin entrusted Karl Renner, the leader of the Social Democrats and one of the founding fathers of the First Austrian Republic, with the task of forming a provisional government. Immediately after Vienna was taken by Soviet troops, the government formed by the Social Democrats, the Communists and conservatives was introduced to Marshal Tolbukhin, the commander of the Third Ukrainian Front, and on 27 April the restoration of the independent Austrian state was officially declared. The Allied forces that entered Austrian territory from the west when Vienna was already in Soviet hands protested against Stalin's hasty unilateral actions, but to no avail. Seventeen thousand Soviet soldiers died in the battle for Vienna (all in all, around 28,000 are buried on Austrian territory).

The military race for control over Austria explains why the Soviet war memorial in Vienna was erected at such a Stakhanovite tempo. It was opened on 19 August 1945, only three months after the end of the war, thus becoming the first Soviet war memorial in Europe (in contrast, the one in Treptow Park in Berlin was only inaugurated in 1948). This speed and the effort invested in the ambitious project testify to the geopolitical rather than simply commemorative role of the memorial. By means of symbolic politics the Soviets tried to establish an image of the Soviet Union as a liberator of Austria in the mass public consciousness. The Soviet war memorial was supposed to remind the local population of Stalin's military triumph, as well as the price paid by the Soviet army and the Soviet people to defeat Nazi rule in Europe, thereby serving as an argument in the oncoming fight for spheres of influence in post-war Europe. In a way, retrospectively it can be seen as the first memorial of the Cold War, built before that war had even begun.

The Soviet war memorial in Vienna is constructed in socialist realist style. The huge bronze figure of a Soviet Army soldier looms on a 20-metre pedestal against the backdrop of a semi-circular white marble colonnade. The inscription on the colonnade reads: 'Eternal glory to the warriors of the Soviet Army who fell in battle against the German fascist aggressors, fighting for freedom and independence for the nations of Europe!' A soldier with a Shpagin machine gun strapped across his chest holds a flag in his right hand, and in his left a gold-plated shield with the crest of the USSR. Engraved on the forward-facing side of the pedestal is a decree from the Supreme Commander, Stalin, dated 13 April 1945, on the taking of Vienna. Engraved on the rear-facing side of the pedestal is the second verse of the state anthem of the USSR in its 1943 iteration, as well as a further quote from Stalin: 'From now on the great flag of freedom of the nations and peace between nations will wave over Europe'. Moreover, on the rear-facing side of the pedestal one can also read the poetry of Sergei Mikhalkov, addressing the liberators of Vienna. Two sculptural compositions, adorning the wings of the colonnade, depict soldiers in the heat of battle, while the soldier on the pedestal symbolises the end of war and the arrival of peace. The architecture and stylings of the memorial express less a sense of grief for the fallen and more the triumph of victory.[7]

A project of the Soviet occupation authorities, the memorial was created by military sculptors and architects and designed even before the Soviet Army entered Austria. Erich Klein, an Austrian journalist who worked in Moscow in the 1990s, interviewed the still-living creators of the memorial, among them Dmitriy Shepilov,

FIGURE 5.1 The Soviet war memorial in Vienna, 9 May 2015. Photograph © Tatiana Zhurzhenko.

a Soviet general and the main ideologist of the project, who later became a member of the Politburo and the editor of *Pravda*. According to Shepilov, the memorial was a prestige object for the Soviet military authorities which was meant to demonstrate the organisational capacities of the Soviet army to the local population as well as to the Western Allies. This memorial erected on the boundary between the Soviet and British occupation zones and in close proximity to the Allied Commission for Austria situated in the House of Industry at Schwarzenbergplatz – then Stalinplatz – was meant to play an important representative function (Klein 2005: 27).

According to Klein, it was Dmitriy Shepilov who decided upon the location of the memorial, having chosen Schwarzenbergplatz as a site with numerous resonant historical associations.[8] Connected by the Ringstrasse to two other historical squares – Heldenplatz and Rathausplatz – Schwarzenbergplatz, with its equestrian statue of Karl Philipp, Prince of Schwarzenberg, is part of the imperial symbolic landscape representing the military triumph of the Habsburgs. According to Jan Tabor, an Austrian historian of architecture, the location of the memorial points to the similar fates of Napoleon and Hitler, two failed conquerors of Europe, and alludes to the legacy of the Russian–Austrian alliance:

> It is difficult to say whether the decision in favour of Schwarzenbergplatz was the result of profound historical knowledge on the part of immensely skilful

> Soviet monument builders or merely an instinct for the monumentality of the square and the *genius loci* of the military. But they surely knew all too well who Prince Karl Schwarzenberg was, as he looms over the front of the square from high on his horse. The victor in the Battle of the Nations at Leipzig in 1813 was an ally in the Napoleonic Wars, in which the Russians were involved closely, almost as brothers, with the Austrians. They latched onto this ideologically. Napoleon's campaign against Russia in 1812, which ended in a fiasco and led to his downfall, exhibited numerous parallels to Hitler's war of conquest against the Soviet Union, which could be boiled down to the idea that the Battle of Borodino in winter 1812 meant the same thing for Napoleon that the Battle of Stalingrad did in winter 1942–43 for Hitler.
> *(Tabor 2005: 115).*

The opening of the Soviet memorial (the first monumental project of the Second Republic) on 19 August 1945 was attended by representatives of the Western Allies and the ministers of the Austrian temporary government. The celebration was organised in keeping with the familiar symbolic repertoire of Soviet mass events, including a military parade and a concluding firework display. Turning on city residents' beloved fountain, which dated back to 1873, was meant to demonstrate a desire for normalisation and the city's return to peaceful life. The speeches of Austrian politicians at the opening ceremony for the Soviet memorial were full of words of thanks to the Soviet army and assertions of the firm determination of the Austrian nation to resurrect an independent democratic state. At the same time, their speeches also contained meaningful nuances – depending on the political affiliations of the speaker. Thus, state secretary Leopold Figl, a representative of the Christian conservative People's Party, in contrast to the Social Democratic chancellor Karl Renner, spoke not of a monument to the heroes of the Red Army, but of a memorial to the 'liberation of Austria'; he was the only speaker to refrain from expressing gratitude to Stalin personally. Entirely different emphases were evident in the speech made by the leader of the Communists, Ernst Fischer, who spoke of the friendship between Austrians and the 'great Russian nation' (Spitaler 2005).

The Communists possessed significant influence in post-war Austria and enjoyed the unconditional support of the Soviet occupying forces. The Soviet military command's strategy, even before the battles for Vienna were over, was to create organs of local self-government comprised of representatives of the anti-fascist resistance, predominantly Communists, and to turn a variety of practical questions regarding the organisation of civilian life over to them. Schwarzenbergplatz, the southern part of which bore the name Stalinplatz until 1956, was home not only to the Allied Commission for Austria, but also the Central Committee of the Communist Party of Austria – its party functionaries could see the Soviet war memorial from their windows. From this point of view, Stalinplatz can be seen as the embryo of a new, Communist Austria, which could have become a reality, as did happen in other countries of East-Central Europe.

Austria, however, did not become part of the Soviet bloc. In 1955 the State Treaty was signed between Austria and the four Allied countries confirming its state sovereignty. The neutral status of Austria, which is written into its constitution, was a condition imposed by Moscow. During the Cold War era, Austria thus took on the special status of a neutral zone between the NATO bloc and the countries of the Warsaw Pact. The Soviet war memorial (which the Austrian government took responsibility for guarding and caring for following the departure of Soviet troops) can be seen as a symbol of sorts of the post-war reconstruction of Europe, the foremost outpost of the Soviet geopolitical frontier. When Soviet forces left Austria, they left behind a bronze soldier, raised above the city on a 20-metre pedestal – in exchange for the State Treaty, the original of which, as recently came to light, has been kept in Moscow all these years.

In everyday life, the ambivalent attitude of Austrians towards the Soviet war memorial found expression in the multitude of names for it. Officially named the Heroes Monument of the Red Army, or sometimes Liberation Monument, it was colloquially called the 'memorial to the unknown looter' (or even 'to the unknown father'), referring to the mass lootings (and rape of Austrian women) by Soviet troops in the first weeks of occupation. One more exotic name for the memorial, '*Erbsendenkmal*' or 'pea monument', associated it with the food relief given to Austrians by the Soviet military command in May 1945, as this famously included 1,000 tons of peas. Most often, however, the Soviet memorial is simply called the 'Russians' monument'.

This ethnicisation is a testament to the cultural alienation of the Soviet monument, the discursive exclusion of the events that it symbolises from the core of Austrian history and the drive to externalise the ambivalent experience of liberation / occupation. This is not primarily because it is reminiscent of the historical period when Austria was more the object of external geopolitical strategies than an independent state subject. Rather, just as the 'totalitarian' Soviet war memorial in the style of socialist realism stands out from the visual ensemble of Viennese imperial architecture, so the figure of a Russian (Soviet) soldier embodies the Other, something foreign (if not inimical) to European civilisation and Austrian culture. This understanding of the USSR/Russia in mass consciousness was founded on historical stereotypes of Russia as an Asiatic, despotic state and Russians as barbarians that were deeply rooted in Austrian culture; it had also, of course, been sedulously inculcated by many years of Nazi anti-Bolshevik propaganda and in the post-war years it was reinforced by the tales of former Wehrmacht soldiers returning from Siberian captivity.

On the whole, however, in the post-war decades the memorial quickly lost its political significance and became largely invisible in the urban landscape. As Wolfgang Müller has shown there was little interest in Austria in thematising the crimes of the Soviet Army and Soviet occupation authorities (Müller 2009). The Soviet war memorial thus can also be seen as a site of amnesia and of the absence of will to deal with the crimes of Stalinism from both sides of the Iron Curtain. The memorial returned to Austrian political discourse only after 1989, when its possible removal was mooted in the media. This partial re-politicisation was a side effect of the 1989 revolutions in the neighbouring countries of East-Central Europe, where Soviet memorials were often vandalised, demolished or relocated. Debates about the future of Soviet memorials in Hungary, Poland and Czechoslovakia sensitised Austrian society in this respect. Moreover, the dissolution of the Soviet Union to which Austria had a special relationship as a neutral, non-bloc country deprived the memorial of its former geopolitical meaning. The idea of dismantling the memorial was propagated mainly by some right-wing politicians who began to reproduce in Austria the discourses on the 'Soviet occupation' that were flourishing in the former Warsaw Pact countries. According to Jörg Haider, for example, 'There were not many who had reason to rejoice in 1945. ... The liberation from Hitler was still far from freedom for us. It was the freedom of the Soviets, the freedom of rapes, the freedom of Stalin. ... It was not our freedom' (Liebhart 2005: 149). From this point of view, the Soviet Army's liberation ofVienna in May 1945 resembles a myth elevated to the level of state ideology, while the Soviet war memorial serves as a reminder of the decade of Soviet occupation. However, this sort of political instrumentalisation – delayed by several decades – of the trauma of the Soviet occupation was not met with particular support from Austrian society. The dismantling of the memorial was not seriously considered and even Stalin's quotes were not removed, in deference to the terms of the State Treaty.

If we look at the Soviet war memorial as a symbol of the Cold War, in which Austria ended up on the side of the liberal Western victors, the Viennese 'Bronze Soldier' most resembles an architectural-historical curiosity. At one time a symbol of the geopolitical triumph of Stalin, today it calls to mind the USSR's defeat in the Cold War and the downfall of a superpower that had controlled half of Europe. As Matthias Marschik has written, 'today we describe it in the language of victors ... We articulate it from the perspective of Austria, which was spared from the (real or fabricated) danger of Communism just as it had successfully countered the "Turkish menace" hundreds of years earlier' (Marschik 2005: 121).

In the jubilee year of 2005 (marking the sixtieth anniversary of the Second Republic, fifty years since the Austrian State Treaty and ten years of EU membership) the Soviet war memorial and the square on which it stands were the stage for a variety of informational and art installations and projects. For example, on Schwarzenbergplatz and Heldenplatz the Austrian Film Archive organised screenings of documentary films about recent Austrian history; soldiers dressed up in Allied uniforms rode around in an American military Jeep demarcating the borders of the occupation zones in white paint; and walking tours were organised around various historical locations.

Among the recent art projects connected with the Soviet memorial on Schwarzenbergplatz, one that deserves particular mention is a project by the Czech artistic group *Pode Bal*, connected with the putative relocation of the Monument to the Suffering of the 6th Army to Schwarzenbergplatz. In 1996, this somewhat controversial memorial to the Wehrmacht 6th Army was erected at Austrian initiative near Volgograd (formerly Stalingrad). The monument, in the form of a 20-metre corroded iron thorn, was initially meant to be erected in the centre of Volgograd but it was relocated to the city's distant outskirts after the protests of Russian war veterans. In 2004 *Pode Bal* then proposed returning the monument to the heart of Vienna. An urban development project was created including architectural plans and a visualisation of how the memorial would look at a new location on Schwarzenbergplatz. This installation was displayed in the Künstlerhaus as part of the collective exhibition 'No Man's Land'. The hypothetical initiative was also communicated through the website of a fictitious development company, where visitors could vote for or against the return of the monument. A member of *Pode Bal*, Petr Motycka, explained: 'The location is very suitable for our intentions. The proximity of the Soviet monument establishes a visual platform for a dialogue about recent Austrian history.' The project succeeded in its aim to provoke debate about the representation of the Nazi past and Austrian responsibility for Nazi crimes (as well as the appropriateness of particular forms of transnational memorialisation) and the installation was subsequently also shown in Berlin in 2005.[9]

In May–June 2014 the Russian art collective *Chto Delat* ('*What is to be done?*') tried, under the auspices of the 'Into the City' programme of the annual Vienna Festival, to engage the Soviet war memorial in a different kind of dialogue about the future of commemoration. In a newspaper produced on the occasion of its intervention in this urban space in May 2014, the collective wrote: 'It seems that the concept of monumentality is entirely obsolete in this day and age. The history of monuments has fallen into the past.' The idea of the project, entitled 'Face to Face with the Monument', was to put a replica of the famous Tatlin Tower – a never-built constructivist behemoth planned to house the headquarters of the Comintern in Petrograd – over the pedestal and statue of the Red Army soldier that forms the main part of the memorial, and to allow visitors to ascend to confront the monumental figure – 'a ghost from the past' – close up. The Russian embassy, however, vetoed this proposal. As a compromise the collective built an installation opposite the memorial consisting of a paper replica of the soldier, a 'red wall' presenting works of various artists, a tent and a stage hosting performances, exhibitions, lectures and workshops, partly broadcast live.[10]

From a Soviet to a Russian memorial

The Russian Federation sees itself as the successor state to the USSR, and thus acts as the protector of all Soviet war memorials. From the 2000s on, the protection and maintenance of Soviet war memorials in the countries of East-Central Europe, especially in those where the Soviet historical narrative has been dismissed or radically questioned, has become a political priority of the Russian state. Seeking to regain the status of a great power and reclaim its voice in European politics, Russia points to its contribution to the defeat of Nazi Germany as a prime source of symbolic capital. This historical achievement provides Russia with a link to the Soviet past because for the USSR the liberation of Europe from the Nazi yoke had served as an entrance ticket to the post-war club of world powers and legitimised

Moscow's new sphere of influence on the European continent. It is this symbolic position as the country that liberated Europe from fascism that the Kremlin has been defending in its political battles against 'historical revisionism' in East-Central Europe. The victory in the Second World War appears to the Russian political elites and society as the moment of ultimate geopolitical triumph, recently often placed in opposition to the so-called 'geopolitical catastrophe' of 1991. Soviet war memorials in Europe testify to this triumph, and any failure to protect them from revisionist politics and provocations serves as a reminder of the recent humiliation and weakness of post-Soviet Russia.[11]

The symbolic capital of Russia's contribution to the defeat of Nazism in Europe (and the Soviet war memorials which represent it) can be seen as part of Russia's soft power. In opposition to the USSR's soft power, which was based on communist ideology and offered an alternative to capitalism, 'Russia's soft power looks to the past, mobilising the memories and legacies of an imagined and real common history'.[12] During the last decade Moscow sought to strengthen its influence abroad by means of cultural and information policy. In addition to the network of cultural centres and 'societies of friendship' inherited from the USSR, new institutions were created such as the Russia Today TV channel and the Russian World Foundation, with the mission of promoting the Russian language and culture abroad. The Association of Compatriots was founded in 2007 as an instrument for the consolidation of the Russian diaspora abroad. One of the tasks of these institutions is the promotion of the official Russian version of the history of the Second World War, debunking 'historical revisionism' and fighting against 'falsifications' of history, especially in the former Soviet republics and satellite states. The Historical Memory Foundation, sponsored by the Russian government, is especially active in this regard.

Moscow's conflict with Tallinn over the 'Bronze Soldier' in 2007 further politicised the issue of Soviet military graves and memorials abroad. In May 2007 the Russian government announced a special programme aimed at the protection and improved maintenance of Soviet war memorials abroad; in 2008 a special department in charge of the memorialisation of the 'fallen in defence of the Fatherland' was created in the Ministry of Defence. The latter, together with the Russian Foreign Ministry, takes care of Soviet war graves and memorials abroad. Commenting on the possibility of a transfer of Soviet soldiers' remains to Russia, General Aleksandr Kirillin from the Ministry of Defence argued that

> the price of Europe's freedom is more than one million of our soldiers. To move ten thousand military graves [to Russia] is not only technically difficult, it is also morally wrong and harmful from a historical perspective. Because in ten years we will not be able to prove that our soldiers were there. Now our graves prove that we liberated Europe. Not the Americans, not the British.[13]

It is in this new post-Cold War geopolitical context and against the background of the ongoing 'memorial wars' in East-Central Europe that the role of the Soviet war memorial in Vienna should be considered. From Moscow's perspective, the respectful (even if indifferent) treatment of the memorial by Austrian authorities is an indicator of the traditionally good relations between the two countries. Not by accident, Vladimir Putin's visit to Austria in 2007 ended with an official wreath-laying ceremony at Schwarzenbergplatz. In the context of the conflict with Estonia, Putin explicitly thanked the Austrians for treating the Soviet war memorial with respect. In 2008 the memorial was closed for reconstruction, which cost the city of Vienna €828,000.[14] During its re-inauguration ceremony, the Russian foreign minister Sergey Lavrov stressed that 'this is our common monument' and expressed his hope that 'the Austrian government will do everything to keep it in proper form so that it reminds us of the fallen, and of the necessity to be watchful not to allow the horrors of war to be repeated'.[15] The Soviet war memorial was also on the agenda of President Putin's visit to Austria in June 2014, his first official visit to the West after the annexation of Crimea and the imposition of international sanctions on Russia. The Russian media presented this visit as a diplomatic breakthrough and a demonstration of the special relations between Russia and neutral and pragmatic Austria. It should be mentioned that the plaque with the explanatory text in front of the memorial had been painted over in yellow and blue, the colours of the Ukrainian flag, in the wake of Victory Day and just some weeks before Putin's visit – a manifestation of the political polarisation between (and within) the Ukrainian and Russian communities in Vienna. The Russian embassy denounced this action as an anti-Russian provocation and an act of vandalism.[16]

The Soviet war memorial is not the only commemorative site in Austria re-appropriated by Russia after the collapse of the USSR. In the last decade the Russian state – together with a number of private sponsors – has invested significant efforts in preserving the memory of the Second World War in Austria. With the support of the Russian embassy, one of the barracks in Mauthausen where Soviet prisoners of war had been kept was restored. In 2011 a memorial plaque was inaugurated commemorating Soviet paratroopers who saved one of Vienna's historic bridges from destruction by the Nazis. Finally, in 2015, on the occasion of the seventieth anniversary of the end of the Second World War, the Museum of the Liberation of Vienna, a joint Austrian-Russian project supported by the city of Vienna and the Austrian Cultural Foundation, opened in a former bunker in Alsergrund, in North-Central Vienna. This project, though a modest communal initiative, is especially interesting and perhaps unique. While similar museums in Eastern Europe originating from the Cold War era have been closed or refurbished as Soviet 'liberation' turned into 'occupation', the new Museum of the Liberation of Vienna presenting the Russian narrative is supported by the Austrian authorities and thus demonstrates at least a partial consensus in terms of how the outcomes and lessons of the Second World War are understood by Austrians and Russians. In Austria, the Russian national narrative of Russia as a 'liberator of Europe' is widely accepted and legitimised, not least due to the deep gratitude of the Austrians – not so much for the liberation itself as for the withdrawal of Soviet troops ten years later.[17]

The Soviet war memorial at Schwarzenbergplatz serves as the main site of commemorative actions related to Second World War history orchestrated by the Russian embassy; these include the official wreath-laying ceremony on 12 April, the day the Soviet Army's Vienna offensive successfully ended in 1945, and, of course, Victory Day on 9 May, which has become the most important memorial day in post-Soviet Russia.[18] The official Victory Day ceremony now generally starts in the morning with the laying of wreaths and flowers, first on the Soviet military graves at Vienna's Central Cemetery and then at the Soviet war memorial at Schwarzenbergplatz. Military attachés and ambassadors from other European countries take part in the commemoration, which concludes with an official reception at the nearby Russian embassy. Vienna, as a European diplomatic capital, and Schwarzenbergplatz, situated at the heart of Vienna's diplomatic quarter, offer a perfect stage for this annual performance of Russia's new identity as a great power. Like the official Victory Day celebration in Moscow, this also serves as a demonstration of loyalty and political sympathies and can be seen as an indicator of the twists and turns in Kremlin foreign policy. In Vienna, a tradition of a joint commemoration of Victory Day that includes former Soviet republics and refers to the Soviet narrative of a 'common victory' started in the mid-2000s – though without Ukraine and Georgia whose diplomatic relations with Russia were strained at the time. Ukraine later joined in, but then since 2014 Ukrainian diplomats in Vienna have again commemorated 9 May separately from Russia, and since 2015 with a different official symbol – a poppy flower as opposed to the Russian Saint George ribbon.[19]

Over a period of years, these official commemorative rituals have come to be complemented with mass public celebrations of Victory Day, with the memorial serving as a stage where once a year the new Russian identity is performed. For the two days of 8 and 9 May, the memorial becomes a point of crystallisation for the Russian-speaking diaspora which is otherwise barely present in the Austrian public space, let alone in Austrian politics. On 9 May people begin coming in the morning, very often with flowers – individuals, couples, extended families with children and the elderly. These are mainly Russians and Russian speakers from the former Soviet republics who live in Austria. Many of them are students, contract workers employed by Russian or joint companies in Austria, and Russian tourists who happen to be in Vienna that day. While many of them lay flowers at the memorial, take photos and leave, others stay longer to socialise; some even bring food and vodka to have a picnic in the cosy shadow provided by the colonnade.

According to a tradition that has now existed for years, the key element of the public celebration is an improvised concert organised by the Russian cultural centre, diaspora activists, the high school at the Russian embassy and the Russian private lyceum in Vienna, together with children's and adult music groups. The programme mainly consists of old Soviet songs nostalgically performed in front of the memorial. There is something intrinsically Soviet in the very organisation of the public space: a fountain in the centre of the square, benches around it occupied by families and elderly people and the Stalin-style colonnade create the proper background for a spectacle of Soviet nostalgia. The raised platform in front of the

FIGURE 5.2 Musical performance in front of the memorial, 9 May 2013. Photograph © Tatiana Zhurzhenko.

monument is used as a stage for the artists and speakers, and the steps along the colonnade behind the monument offer seats for the public. The memorial creates a special nostalgic space in the very centre of the Austrian capital where Soviet symbols, Soviet military decorations and Soviet songs are allowed to flourish. Certain eye-catching sights in the crowd – a young man wrapped in a Soviet flag, children and adults dressed in ethnic costumes, a mixture of Russian and Soviet symbolism – give the feeling of a carnival, but in fact this is a well-structured event which reproduces the Victory Day rituals existing in Russia itself. For one or two days, the Soviet war memorial becomes an exclave of post-Soviet Russian commemorative culture in the middle of Vienna. To apply the notion of the 'territorialisation' of memory one could say that with the Victory Day celebration, the Russian speaking diaspora appropriates – or rather borrows – a fragment of Viennese urban space. In this way, the Russian diaspora creates a link to Vienna and Austria, positioning itself in the complex local multicultural landscape.

However, unlike Russians in the Baltic states, the Russian diaspora in Austria is a new phenomenon. People who come to the Soviet war memorial in Vienna have no personal memory of the liberation of Vienna, no biographical connection to this myth and thus, unlike Russians in the Baltic states, cannot so easily draw their sense of group rights from it. Most of them came to Vienna in recent years or are just short-term visitors, and as a rule they know next to nothing about the

FIGURE 5.3 Russian folk music group in front of the memorial, 9 May 2013. Photograph © Tatiana Zhurzhenko.

battle for Vienna and Austria's post-war history. To put it bluntly, they come to Schwarzenbergplatz to commemorate not so much the Great Patriotic War, but their own past, to be reminded of similar celebrations in the 'good old days' in Russia or the Soviet Union, to share these memories with their children or grandchildren and to experience and re-establish bonds of family and friendship. The memorial thus turns into a mnemonic object – it refers not so much to the historical event as such but to the cultural memory of this event, while the orchestration of emotions prevails over commemoration (Oushakine 2013).

In the conflict with Ukraine the memory of the Great Patriotic War was weaponised by the Russian state, as anti-fascist discourse was used to incite a pro-Russian insurgency on Ukrainian territory. Since the annexation of Crimea in March 2014, Russia has emerged as a revisionist power under the banner of the 'fight against fascism', this time against the new Kyiv leadership, which is depicted as a reincarnation of fascism. In Russian propaganda, the conflict in and around Ukraine has thus become a re-embodiment of the Great Patriotic War and Russia has once again turned to its eternal historical mission of preventing the return of fascism. This has led to a palpable politicisation and instrumentalisation of Victory Day which, since 2014, has become a manifestation of the 'post-Crimean' pro-Putin consensus in Russian society and of the new Russian nationalism. The Victory Day celebrations in Vienna have changed, too: the relaxed atmosphere of informal mass

FIGURE 5.4 Improvised collective singing of Soviet songs, 9 May 2013. Photograph © Tatiana Zhurzhenko.

festivity has been somewhat muted and the celebration seems to have become more official and choreographed. There are more political speeches and they are now translated into German – the organisers want the local Austrian population to get their message. Russian state symbolism and of course Saint George ribbons have become omnipresent, children and young people are often dressed in Soviet military uniforms, and the event has almost turned into a pure manifestation of Russian state patriotism, leaving little space for more private and apolitical forms of commemoration. Clear indicators of political agitation and radical polarisation – symbols of Novorossiya, political posters with slogans such as 'Stop Russophobia' and donation boxes for Donetsk and Luhansk Soviet veterans – could be seen at Schwarzenbergplatz on 9 May in 2015 and 2016. Since 2015, the Night Wolves, a radical nationalist biker club from Sevastopol which enthusiastically supported Putin's annexation of Crimea, have organised a memorial tour to Berlin dedicated to Victory Day, with intermediate stops in other European cities. Although only a few of the Night Wolves made it to Vienna in 2015 and 2016, their commemorative action at Schwarzenbergplatz has been given considerable media attention, not least because of the participation of the Russian ambassador.

New commemorative innovations from Russia arrive in Vienna almost instantaneously, with great regularity. Since 2015, the all-Russian commemorative action The Immortal Regiment has also taken place in Vienna. This is a public initiative

FIGURE 5.5 Russian family posing for a photo in front of the memorial, 9 May 2015. Photograph © Tatiana Zhurzhenko.

in which ordinary people join a street procession carrying photos of their relatives fallen in the Second World War. Born as a grassroots initiative in the Russian provincial city of Tomsk in 2012, it is now supported and co-organised by the Russian authorities after Putin himself joined The Immortal Regiment in May 2015. Like other rituals and symbols of the Victory Day celebration, The Immortal Regiment

FIGURE 5.6 A Russian activist protesting against alleged Russophobia in the West and another one holding a Novorossiya flag, 8 May 2015. Photograph © Tatiana Zhurzhenko.

has become part of the new Russian patriotic discourse, alienating those who oppose Putin's identity politics – not only Ukrainians but some Russians as well.

Conclusion

Soviet war memorials in Europe provide an excellent standpoint for reflecting upon changing national identities and collective memories of the Second World War in post-Cold War Europe. Far beyond their traditional function of commemorating and mourning fallen soldiers, they symbolise past military triumphs and recent political defeats, visualise new conflicts in European societies and help to consolidate Russian minorities, both old and new. The Soviet war memorial in Vienna, erected in summer 1945, not only tells the story of Russian–Austrian relations during and after the Cold War; it can be seen as a meeting point of two commemorative cultures, both currently in flux. In Austria, the growing willingness to embrace the European culture of guilt and responsibility and a new critical distance from the post-war national myth of 'the first victim of Hitler's aggression' has been reflected in the recent changes in Vienna's commemorative landscape, with Heldenplatz and the Heldendenkmal being at the centre of these transformations. This transition is, however, open-ended, and with the rise of the far right in Austria and of populist

FIGURE 5.7 Soviet war veteran addresses the public in front of the memorial, 9 May 2015. Photograph © Tatiana Zhurzhenko.

FIGURE 5.8 'Immortal Regiment' at Schwarzenbergplatz, 9 May 2015. Photograph © Tatiana Zhurzhenko.

forces in many European countries a new wave of re-nationalisation of the history of the Second World War can be observed.

With the end of the Cold War and the advance of EU integration, 8 May has been increasingly seen as a 'zero hour' and the origin of a new united Europe; meanwhile, in post-Soviet Russia 9 May as Victory Day has also become a new founding myth to replace the October Revolution. As the changing character of the Victory Day celebration at Schwarzenbergplatz demonstrates, the Soviet narrative of the Great Patriotic War has been nationalised and turned into a myth of imperial military glory and national exceptionalism, especially after the annexation of Crimea. At the same time, even while positioning itself in opposition to the EU, Russia lays claim to a leading role in European politics and draws its identity as a European great power from its historical contribution to the defeat of the Nazi Germany and the liberation of Europe. Post-Soviet Russian memory politics, not unlike those of the Soviet Union, have an important geopolitical and thus transnational dimension, which has often been overlooked in the ongoing debates over European memory of the Second World War.

Notes

Unless otherwise indicated, all translations are my own.

1 Mikhail Dobkin, then mayor of Kharkiv (in Ukraine), known for his negative attitude to then president Viktor Yushchenko's anti-Soviet memory politics, offered asylum to the 'Bronze Soldier' to demonstrate his 'anti-fascist' stance.

2 'Poland Set to Demolish 500 Soviet Monuments', *The Moscow Times*, 31 March 2016, www.themoscowtimes.com/news/article/poland-set-to-demolish-500-soviet-monuments/564120.html.

3 Kelly Hignett, 'Monumental Makeover in Bulgaria Illustrates the Contested Status of Soviet-Era War Memorials', *The View East*, 4 July 2011, https://thevieweast.wordpress.com/2011/07/04/monumental-makeover-in-bulgaria-illustrates-the-contested-status-of-soviet-era-war-memorials/.

4 The project was initiated and coordinated by Mischa Gabowitsch (Berlin) and Elena Nikiforova (St. Petersburg). Further details can be found in a 2015 themed collection of essays, '9 maja: pochti 70 let spustja', *Neprikosnovennyi Zapas*, 3,101, http://magazines.russ.ru/nz/2015/3. A collaborative volume entitled *Pamiatnik i Prazdnik* will be published in Moscow by Novoe Literaturnoe Obozrenie in 2017. In 2015 a new project was launched focussing on Russia, Belarus, Ukraine and Moldova as well as Germany (Gabowitsch, Gdaniec and Makhotina 2016).

5 I am very grateful to Wolfgang Müller, Austrian Academy of Sciences, for sharing his knowledge of Austrian post-war history.

6 See 'Mahnwache: "Heldenplatz von Ewiggestrigen befreit"', *Die Presse*, 8 May 2013, http://diepresse.com/home/politik/innenpolitik/1399759/Mahnwache_Heldenplatz-von-Ewiggestrigen-befreit.

7 Grief and the pain of loss are expressed to a much greater extent in a sculptural composition at the Soviet military burial ground in Vienna's Central Cemetery. Here we see a soldier holding military insignia, lowered as a sign of mourning, with his head bared and his helmet pressed to his chest.

8 Unverifiable legend says that it was Stalin himself who decided upon the location of the memorial; he knew the city as he had lived in Vienna in exile in 1913.

9 For further details see the *Pode Bal* website at www.podebal.com/content/projects/leiden.

10 For full details see the *Chto Delat* website at https://chtodelat.org/category/b7-art-projects/a_1/.
11 Tatiana Zhurzhenko, 'The Geopolitics of Memory', *Eurozine*. 10 May 2007, www.eurozine.com/articles/2007-05-10-zhurzhenko-en.html.
12 'Soft Power? The Means and Ends of Russian Influence', REP Seminar Summary, Chatham House, 31 March 2011, quoted in Tatiana Zhurzhenko, 'Russia's Never Ending War against Fascism', *Eurozine*, 8 May 2015, www.eurozine.com/articles/2015-05-08-zhurzhenko-en.html.
13 'Polnaya mogilizatsiya', *Kommersant-Vlast'*, 14 May 2007, www.kommersant.ru/doc/764743?themeid=116&fp.
14 '"Russendenkmal": Erster Bau der Zweiten Republik wird saniert', *Vienna Online*, 25 November 2008, www.vienna.at/russendenkmal-erster-bau-der-zweiten-republik-wird-saniert/news-20081125-10123226.
15 'Restavracija pamjatnika sovetskomu voinu-osvoboditelju oboshlas' Vene pochti v million evro', *Russkiy Mir*, 24 June 2009, www.russkiymir.ru/russkiymir/ru/news/common/news2495.html.
16 'Neizvestnye oskvernili pamjatnik sovetskomu Voinu-osvoboditelju v Vene', *RIA Novosti*, 8 May 2014, https://ria.ru/world/20140508/1006993695.html.
17 'Russian Ambassador Attends Opening Ceremony for Museum on Liberation of Vienna', *Russkiy Mir*, 10 April 2015, www.russkiymir.ru/en/news/188651/.
18 Victory Day is sometimes observed on 8 May, depending on the contingencies of the calendar.
19 This section – and others in the chapter – is informed by my personal observations of the ceremony from 2013 to 2016.

References

Astrov, Alexander. 2007. 'Liturgija po Bronzovomu soldatu: Pamjat' i istorija v formirovanii krizisa'. *Ab Imperio*, 3: 427–47.

Brüggemann, Karsten and Kasekamp, Andres. 2008. 'The Politics of History and the "War of Monuments" in Estonia'. *Nationalities Papers*, 36, 3: 425–48.

Dubin, Boris. 2005. 'Goldene Zeiten des Krieges. Erinnerung als Sehnsucht nach der Breznev-Ära'. *Osteuropa*, 4–6: 219–33.

Ehala, Martin. 2009. 'The Bronze Soldier: Identity Threat and Maintenance in Estonia'. *Journal of Baltic Studies*, 40, 1: 139–58.

Forest, Benjamin and Johnson, Juliet. 2002. 'Unravelling the Threads of History: Soviet-Era Monuments and Post-Soviet National Identity in Moscow'. *Annals of the Association of American Geographers*, 92, 3: 524–47.

Gabowitsch, Mischa. 2015. 'Pamiatnik i prazdnik: etnografiia Dnia Pobedy'. *Neprikosnovennyi Zapas*, 3, 101, http://magazines.russ.ru/nz/2015/3/9g.html.

Gabowitsch, Mischa, Gdaniec, Cordula and Makhotina, Ekaterina. eds. 2016. *Kriegsgedenken als Event. Der 9. Mai 2015 im postsozialistischen Europa*. Paderborn: Ferdinand Schöningh.

Giesen, Bernhard. 2004. *Triumph and Trauma*. Boulder, CO: Paradigm.

Hanisch, Ernst. 1998. 'Wien: Heldenplatz'. *Transit: Europäische Revue*, 15: 122–40.

Klein, Erich. 2005. 'Drei Monate statt ein Jahr. Die Autoren des Russendenkmals'. In *Das Wiener Russendenkmal. Architektur, Geschichte, Konflikte*, edited by Matthias Marschik and Georg Spitaler. Wien: Turia and Kant. 21–33.

Kuttenberg, Eva. 2007. 'Austria's Topography of Memory: Heldenplatz, Albertinaplatz, Judenplatz and Beyond'. *The German Quarterly*, 80, 4: 468–91.

Lehti, Marko, Jutila, Matti and Jokisipilä, Markku. 2008. 'Never-Ending Second World War. Public Performances of National Dignity and the Drama of the Bronze Soldier'. *Journal of Baltic Studies*. 39, 4: 393–418.

Liebhart, Karin. 2005. 'Vom Wiener Schwarzenbergplatz nach Wolgograd'. In *Das Wiener Russendenkmal. Architektur, Geschichte, Konflikte*, edited by Matthias Marschik and Georg Spitaler. Wien: Turia and Kant. 147–54.

Marschik, Matthias. 2005. 'Russenbilder. Die Visualisierung des Heldendenkmals am Schwarzenbergplatz'. In *Das Wiener Russendenkmal. Architektur, Geschichte, Konflikte*, edited by Matthias Marschik and Georg Spitaler. Wien: Turia and Kant. 121–33.

Müller, Wolfgang. 2009. 'Stalinismus und gesamteuropäisches Gedächtnis. Überlegungen am Beispiel Österreichs'. *Transit*, 38: 96–109.

Ochman, Ewa. 2010. 'Soviet War Memorials and the Re-Construction of National and Local Identities in Post-Communist Poland'. *Nationalities Papers*, 38, 4: 509–30.

Oushakine, Serguei. 2013. 'Remembering in Public: On the Affective Management of History'. *Ab Imperio*, 1: 269–302.

Palmer, Scott W. 2009. 'How Memory was Made: The Construction of the Memorial to the Heroes of the Battle of Stalingrad'. *The Russian Review*, 68, 3: 373–407.

Schleifman, Nurit. 2001. 'Moscow's Victory Park: A Monumental Change'. *History and Memory*, 13, 2: 5–34

Smith, David J. 2008. '"Woe from Stones": Commemoration, Identity Politics and Estonia's "War of Monuments"'. *Journal of Baltic Studies*, 39, 4: 419–30.

Spitaler, Georg. 2005. '"Dank für dieses Befreiungswerk!" Die Reden österreichische Politiker zur Eröffnung des Heldendenkmals am 19.8.1945'. In *Das Wiener Russendenkmal. Architektur, Geschichte, Konflikte*, edited by Matthias Marschik and Georg Spitaler. Wien: Turia and Kant. 34–45.

Tabor, Jan. 2005. 'Entblößt das Haupt! Zum politischen Urbanismus des Schwarzenbergplatzes'. In *Das Wiener Russendenkmal. Architektur, Geschichte, Konflikte*, edited by Matthias Marschik and Georg Spitaler. Wien: Turia and Kant. 111–20.

Uhl, Heidemarie. 2006. 'From Victim Myth to Co-Responsibility Thesis: Nazi Rule, World War II, and the Holocaust in Austrian Memory'. In *The Politics of Memory in Postwar Europe*, edited by Richard Ned Lebow, Wulf Kansteiner and Claudio Fogu. Durham, NC: Duke University Press. 40–72.

6

ABOLITIONISM IN THE HISTORY OF THE TRANSNATIONAL 'JUSTICE FOR COMFORT WOMEN' MOVEMENT IN JAPAN AND SOUTH KOREA

Caroline Norma

The transnational 'justice for comfort women' movement in North-East Asia that has been operative since 1990 is seen as an unprecedented success in the history of international women's organising.[1] Katharine Moon writes that 'South Korean survivors of Japanese military sexual slavery … and activists on their behalf have been noted as some of the most persuasive and omnipresent advocates of women's human rights at international meetings and conferences' (Moon 2010: 125). The movement's origins are well documented (even in English, for example, see Chou 2003; Lee 2006; Yun 2007; Kern and Nam 2009; Moon 2010; Yoon 2010): the Japanese military sexually enslaved hundreds of thousands of Asian and Pacific Islander women (as well as some women from Western colonial settlements) during the China and Pacific wars between 1937 and 1945, but the movement in support of recognition and reparation for these victims did not emerge until 1990. The first half of this chapter recalls the rest of this story.

This standard recollection of the history of transnational activism in support of the so-called 'comfort women' is not at issue here. However, in its second half this chapter describes a parallel history of individual and women's group campaigning against prostitution in South Korea and Japan going back to the 1970s. It suggests this abolitionist campaigning intersects with the history of the 'comfort women' justice movement in terms of timing, perspective and participants. The argument of the chapter is that, contra the oft-repeated view that the justice movement originated in the early 1990s, its origins can actually be traced back to the 1970s, and that these earlier origins are significant because they indicate abolitionist tendencies in the movement's emergence and development. While these tendencies were still discernible in the 1990s this fact is mostly unacknowledged in histories of the justice movement. These histories tend instead to highlight the liberal political hues of early justice campaigning in both South Korea and Japan (Szczepanska 2014), and almost wholly overlook abolitionist activism by either radical feminists or

Christians. The understated abolitionist contribution to the 'comfort women' justice movement in South Korea and Japan in both the 1970s and 1990s is explored here; recognising the transnational movement's early and sustained abolitionist history also has important implications for its future sustainability.

Abolitionism involves a view of prostitution as a form of male violence against women, and one that persists by virtue of the ideological protection afforded to those who pimp and prostitute women either by liberal notions of work and contract or conservative notions of male and female sexuality. Its divergence from liberal or conservative views of prostitution makes feminist abolitionism recognisable politically as a distinctive alternative approach, as described in clear terms by Janice Raymond:

> In the liberal view, prostitution is a woman's choice; in the conservative view, prostitution is her determined behavior. In the liberal view, prostitution is a woman's economic necessity; in the conservative view, prostitution is a man's natural need. In the liberal view, prostitution is female sexual liberation; in the conservative view, prostitution is female sexual perversion. In the liberal view, prostitution is a woman's basic human right; in the conservative view, prostitution is her essential moral failing. In ... [the] feminist abolitionist view, prostitution is one of the final strongholds of sexualized male dominance.
>
> *(Raymond 2013: xvii)*

The feminist abolitionist view holds that prostitution is sexual slavery regardless of its wartime or peacetime context. So Catharine MacKinnon writes that military sexual slavery 'is at once both mass rape and serial rape in a way that is indistinguishable from prostitution', and that 'prostitution is that part of everyday non-war life that is closest to what we see done to women in ... war' (MacKinnon 1994: 191). The feminist abolitionist project, therefore, seeks to abolish systems organising the prostitution of women in peacetime as a matter of sex class justice and as a means of discouraging the emergence of military sexual slavery schemes in contexts of war. This latter aim of feminist abolitionism was tacitly flagged in 1999 by Morita Seiya:

> No matter how oppressive the Japanese military was compared to other militaries in the world at the time, and no matter how debased soldiers became within the violence of the military machine, the extremity of the sexual violence inflicted on women in the warzone, and on comfort women, and the fact these crimes were accepted with such tolerance at the time, is testament only to the nature of the surrounding environment that gave rise to them.
>
> *(Morita 1999: 115)*

In spite of the years that have elapsed since Morita's work was published, an anti-prostitution perspective, whether historical or political, continues today to be mostly prohibited within the transnational movement that advocates on behalf of the former 'comfort women'. An 'e-museum' run by South Korea's Ministry of Gender Equality and Family broadcasts the currently mandated position that 'comfort women were not the same as licensed prostitutes, but were victims of a state-run system of sexual violence', as shown in the purported fact that 'the women had no free choice of where to live or freedom of movement', '[n]or did they have the liberty of quitting', which is 'a key point of differentiation from licensed prostitutes'.[2] Feminist abolitionists, in contrast, would see no lesser harm accruing to 'licensed prostitutes' than to any other women enslaved in comfort stations. Muta Kazue brings out the double standard in play here, criticising the fact that survivors of military prostitution trafficked into comfort stations from peacetime brothels are seen today as '"dirty" women by definition' and as somehow not 'entitled to human rights and dignity'. Muta observes that 'this way of thinking has kept most Japanese comfort women from going public', because 'many Japanese ex-comfort women had been recruited to warfront comfort stations from various kinds of sex-related businesses' (Muta 2016: 627).

To be fair, contemporary rejection of an abolitionist perspective in the 'justice for comfort women' movement is largely reactive: it is a response to provocations from defenders of the Japanese military's wartime record advanced since the 1990s. These Japanese nationalists assert that victims of Japanese military sexual enslavement were 'merely' prostitutes who freely chose to enter comfort stations on a money-making basis, and so their existence comprises no historical evidence of wrongdoing by the Japanese military. In reaction to this kind of rhetoric, distancing comfort station survivors from any association with prostitution – either before, during or after their military sexual enslavement – has been a concerted task of advocates since the early 1990s. Even now, the justice movement works hard to persuade the public that discounting the historical experience of survivors on the basis that their experience included commercially mediated prostitution is unjust, because the latter claim is untrue. It is notable that in the campaigning of advocates, the injustice arises as a product of factual inaccuracy rather than flawed logic.

These vexed politics inhabiting the transnational women's movement in support of the former 'comfort women', which are still evident today even in its feminist strand, mostly disallow the telling of an abolitionist version of the movement's history. This chapter attempts to construct such a version. Recalling this history is important for the future of the 'justice for comfort women' movement, as highlighted by the historian Katharine Moon:

> Understandably, the focus is on getting Japan to respond favorably. But there [i]s no sense of what might or should come after. What comes after, though, is a pressing question, given the momentum of attention to women's human rights issues and the voicing, after generations of silence, of women's victimization through militarization.
>
> *(Moon 2010: 141)*

Answering Moon's questions, this chapter highlights the historically persistent and continuing international abolitionist links of the South Korean- and Japan-based justice movements, and suggests these links are key to the international movement's future sustainability. It suggests sustainability is afforded by an abolitionist perspective because, beyond the confines of the 'justice for comfort women' transnational movement in countries like South Korea and Japan, feminist abolitionism is politically ascendant globally today. This ascendance is evident most clearly in the abolitionist policy-making of a growing number of governments since the turn of the twenty-first century, including those of Sweden, South Korea, Iceland, Norway, Canada, Northern Ireland and France.

The history of the military 'comfort women' has featured in feminist abolitionist theorising and activism since the 1990s, and continues to do so today (Hughes, Chon and Ellerman 2007; Raymond 2013; Norma 2016). Janice Raymond, the co-founder of the world's largest abolitionist group, the US-based Coalition Against Trafficking in Women (CATW), remarked in 2015 that 'we can honour the "comfort women" by opposing the contemporary comfort systems of today'.[3] Raymond's comment is loyal in its sentiment to the history of the 'justice for comfort women' movement which in its origins has significant transnational abolitionist hues. Emphasising these hues aids the future viability of the movement because, as I have argued elsewhere:

> While surviving victims of the military system may be dwindling in number as each year passes, there is now a globally organized movement of survivors of civilian sexual slavery who can assume the mantle of their struggle for public recognition and government redress of human right harms, both for prostitution systems operating now and in the past.
>
> *(Norma 2016: 16)*

Moon's query about the future sustainability of the justice movement and 'what might or should come after' any concessions are extracted from Japan can be answered through looking at contemporary feminist abolitionist incorporation of the history of the 'comfort women' into its campaigns. This movement has held a candle for the 'comfort women' since the 1990s, but not in the way the mainstream justice movement has done in Japan and South Korea. In contrast to the justice movement's view of comfort station survivors primarily as victims of colonialism, war and Japanese military brutality, the history of the 'comfort women' features within the feminist abolitionist movement as an example of prostitution organised on a global scale by militaries with institutional backing and at the behest of states that are still today recalcitrant about the harms sexual slavery inflicts on women and girls. For abolitionists, military sexual slavery vividly exemplifies the problem with prostitution, in contrast to the contemporary justice movement for which it does not exemplify anything about prostitution. The divergence of perspective between liberal and abolitionist approaches to campaigning over the history of military sexual slavery entails different possibilities for the movement's future; this future can be more clearly and positively understood through adopting an abolitionist view of the movement's history.

Abolitionism has to date not been popular as a frame for historical analyses of twentieth-century transnational feminist social movements and, indeed, is rarely mentioned in them. Moreover, when it is mentioned the tone is often disparaging, as in the 2015 *Oxford Handbook of Transnational Feminist Movements* in which Thanh-Dam Truong suggests that

> those who have been rescued and placed in government-sponsored shelter have to bear with the antisex industry attitude of the rescuers, who not only infantalize their opting to migrate but pathologize them and classify their entry into prostitution as deviant behavior.
>
> *(Truong 2015: 299)*

This kind of characterisation of abolitionists as 'rescuers' who consider prostitution a deviant behaviour of women, rather than an abusive behaviour of men, is common in even the feminist literature and leads feminist abolitionism to be left out of accounts of women's international activist history in favour of liberal accounts of networked groups purportedly organising in support of 'sex worker rights' (Jeffreys 1997).

Nonetheless, however surprising the fact might be to contemporary feminist activists, abolitionism has long been a mainstay of women's transnational political organising, even of that organising occurring before the Second World War, and in Japan. It was central, for example, to the transnational suffrage movement (Martz 2005), the social reform movement (Jordan and Sharp 2003) including that operating through the League of Nations (Rodríguez García 2012), within Christian women's international organising (Nolland 2004), and even within some female socialist organising (Murray 1979). In recent literature, however, this historical facet of feminist transnationalism is mostly erased, and this tendency is particularly noticeable in histories of the 'justice for comfort women' movement because of the aforementioned concern that referring to prostitution might give succour to the position of right-wing sexual slavery deniers in Japan who accuse comfort station survivors of having profited from their experience as 'prostitutes'. Putting this tactical consideration aside, this chapter now proceeds to demonstrate that the recent history of the 'comfort women' justice movement, on the South Korean side at least, does not warrant such erasure.

The 1990s' history of the 'Justice for Comfort Women' movement in South Korea

The 'justice for comfort women' movement in its current guise emerged in South Korea (henceforth, 'Korea') in the early 1990s, and at its heart was a new organisation, the Korean Council for Women Drafted for Military Sexual Slavery by Japan (henceforth, 'the Council'). In May 1990, a coalition of Korean women's groups issued a press release calling on President Roh Taewoo to raise the history of the 'comfort women' during a visit to Japan planned for that month. He did so, but the response was one of denial – Japanese parliamentarians claimed civilian traffickers rather than the Japanese military or state had been responsible for the women's fate – and his government's follow-up was timid. Reacting to this, in October 1990, thirty-seven women's groups held a press conference in Seoul calling on both the Japanese and Korean governments to release historical documents about wartime events (Yun 2011: 119). The press conference attracted significant public attention, and the groups then coalesced to form the Council in November 1990, initially on a shoestring budget. On its inaugural executive committee was the head of the Korean Women's Associations United (KWAU, established in 1987 with twenty-one participating women's organisations), academics from Ewha Womans University, as well as representatives from the Korean Women's Hotline (a nationwide domestic violence service established in 1983 that is still running today), the Buddhist Human Rights Committee, the Korea Church Women United (KCWU) (founded in 1967) and the Korean Council of University Women (Kim 1992; Song and Moon 1998; Kern and Nam 2009; Yun 2011).

The Council launched a telephone hotline via a radio and newspaper publicity campaign in late 1990, appealing for information about Japanese military wartime labour mobilisation, including the trafficking of Korean women and girls for labour and, indirectly, sexual enslavement. This appeal attracted a strong response, and 20 per cent of respondents disclosed information about, specifically, the wartime history of military sexual slavery (Pak 1992: 50). In August 1991, a military prostitution survivor who had previously responded to the hotline campaign, Kim Haksun, met face-to-face with Council members, and her story was subsequently reported in Korean television and print media. In December, she led a group of three survivors linked to the Council in launching a joint civil action in Japan with a group of Korean forced labour survivors, and in the following year undertook a major speaking tour in Japan (Song and Moon 1998).

If Kim was a visible figurehead for the new 'justice movement', the inaugural head of the Council, Yun Chungok, was a driving force behind the scenes. Yun had recently retired as a professor of English literature at Seoul's prestigious Ewha Womans University – in 1977 the first university in Korea to offer a women's studies programme, before any university in Japan had done so (Kim 1992: 186). The 'comfort women' issue resonated with Yun on a personal level:

> In 1943 I was seventeen and in my first year at Ewha Girls' High School in Seoul ... I remember the students in our class being summoned to the school art room. You could have cut the air with a knife. We were sitting in silence, scarcely daring to breathe, when a man in uniform entered the room with several subordinates. He distributed pieces of paper the same size as a page from our exercise books. There were tiny blue characters on the white paper. Without having time to read this, we were given red stamping ink to put our thumbprints in a rectangle at the edge of the document. The papers were

> collected in again immediately with the thumbprint. That night I told my parents what had happened and I was not allowed to go back … [At the end of the war] the men returned to Korea. However, we did not hear anything from the women who had joined the 'volunteer corps' … This surprised me and I searched for different ways to find out what had happened to them.
>
> *(Yun 2007: 234–5).*

In the late 1970s, Yun came across a book on the history of the 'comfort women' that included a translated contribution by Japanese journalist Senda Kakou which spurred her on to further research (Yun 2007: 235). She travelled to Thailand, Papua New Guinea, Japan and Okinawa to meet with former Korean 'comfort women' rumoured to be still living in wartime trafficking destinations. Her first trip was to meet a woman living in Okinawa in 1979 and, on the basis of that meeting, Yun wrote a newspaper piece that was published in 1980 in a Korean daily. It attracted little attention, but she persisted in her research (Yun 1992).

Through the 1980s, that research drew strength from a burgeoning Korean feminist movement. Feminist organising there began in earnest from 1987, according to Yun, in step with the democratisation movement that emerged after the end of Chun Doo Hwan's dictatorship, and with a particular focus on campaigning against issues of violence against women. Feminists associated with the newly founded KWAU developed skills in political activism and theorising, and some of its original members, such as Cho Youngsook and Chon Mirye, continue today as recognised leaders of the anti-prostitution movement. The founders of the women's studies programme at Ewha, Lee Hyojae, Chung Jinsung and Lee Hyunsook, also became significant figures in the women's movement from the 1980s, later becoming executive members of the Council. Although Yun did not teach in the women's studies programme at Ewha, she worked with these feminist scholars and their students. Ewha students played a key role in lobbying the KWAU to take up the cause of the former 'comfort women' and were instrumental in forming the coalition that persuaded President Roh to raise the issue with Japan in 1990 (Kim 1992). Yun's sustained research was crucial in encouraging these kinds of progressive activists to respond to the historical plight of the 'comfort women'. In January 1990 she had a series of four articles published in Korea's leftist newspaper, the *Hangyoreh Shinmun*, reporting on her decade-long research and describing the history of the military sexual slavery system from the point of view of its victims (Yun 1992). In contrast to her efforts in the 1980s, this work finally found a receptive audience.

From its founding in November 1990, the Council not only agitated to raise the profile of the 'comfort women' in Korea, but also mounted sustained international advocacy efforts which were crucial to the justice movement's later success. In early 1992, the Council wrote to women's movement organisations across Asia asking for cooperation in investigating the historical details of wartime sexual slavery in each country (Yoon 2007: 254). After undertaking their requested fact-finding activities, representatives from each country reported back to an inaugural Asian Solidarity Conference held in Seoul in August 1992, which included over 100 women's group representatives from the Philippines, Hong Kong, Thailand, Taiwan and more than thirty participants from Japan.

From early on, the Council also worked internationally through the United Nations (UN), and here historical overlap with abolitionist groups is evident. Action at the UN was led mostly by Shin Heisoo, holder of a Master's degree in international relations from Ewha and a PhD from Rutgers University. Her Rutgers dissertation focused on the prostitution tourism of Japanese men to Korea that began in the 1970s; it was awarded in 1991 and published in Japanese translation in 1997. With links to both Christian and feminist groups, Shin had abolitionist views: she became subsequently involved with the Centre for Women's Human Rights (later renamed the Women's Human Rights Commission of Korea) which had a mandate after 2004 to implement Korea's ground-breaking anti-prostitution legislation (Farley and Seo 2005; Norma 2011), and later she became director of the National Movement for Eradication of Sex Trafficking. In the early 1990s Shin undertook diplomatic work in Geneva on behalf of the Council (taking advantage of the fact that the Republic of Korea had just joined the UN in 1991).

The ground had been prepared for Council action at the UN by Ewha professors Lee Hyunsook and Chung, who travelled to Geneva and New York to take advice on how best to put the 'comfort women' on the organisation's agenda. Subsequently, the Council's first step was to write to the UN Secretary General explaining the issue, describing individual victim cases and enclosing translations of documents used in the litigation in Japan that commenced in late 1991. Following this, in August 1992, four representatives of the Council, including one survivor and Shin, travelled to Geneva to approach the Sub-Commission on Prevention of Discrimination and Protection of Minorities. Prior to this, the Council had contacted the CATW, which – according to Shin – had already raised the 'comfort women' 'as an issue of trafficking and forced prostitution with the [UN] Working Group on Contemporary Forms of Slavery'. So, when the Council later approached the Sub-Commission, 'the base for the discussion had been laid soundly' (Shin 2011: 22). Accordingly, the lobbying efforts proved successful: in 1993 Shin was able to prompt the Commission on Human Rights to launch an official UN investigation of Japanese military sexual slavery (Shin 2011: 15–16).

This engagement with CATW in the Council's early steps towards having the international community recognise the wartime history of the 'comfort women' is significant: CATW had been founded only shortly before, in 1988, and this was one of the first campaigns it engaged in, and one it pursued consistently thereafter. As Janice Raymond recalled, the CATW

> partner[ed] with WHISPER, the earliest [civilian sex industry] survivor-led organization in the US, to support their collaborative protest with the Korean community in Minneapolis-St.Paul against Japan's refusal to officially apologize and compensate the victims of the 'comfort woman system'. Those protests took place in front of the Mitsubishi bank in Minneapolis … CATW

> also worked closely with Matsui Yayori [a prominent Japanese journalist, women's rights activist and 'comfort women' campaigner].[4]

Raymond is still actively involved with the CATW, and in her campaigning continues to link the history of the 'comfort women' with the contemporary anti-prostitution struggle:

> The history of the 'comfort women' system is timely because it reverberates with lessons about state-sponsored prostitution today. For some, it may be easier to comprehend that meaningful consent does not exist within a military context where women of another country are used in prostitution by the dominant power than in a modern democratic government, which legalizes or decriminalizes the sex industry. Because these countries draw a line in the sand between voluntary and forced prostitution, and base their systems of sexual exploitation on women's right to choose, people are not so ready to understand the harm to women of modern state-sponsored prostitution regimes.[5]

The Korea-based justice movement of the 1990s did not explicitly draw such connections between military sexual slavery of the past and prostitution of the present, and nor does it do so much today. It nonetheless benefited in its development from contact with an organisation that did. Moreover, the abolitionist transnational links of the Korean justice movement in the 1990s were not restricted to US-based organisations like CATW. Korean activists engaged concurrently with similarly oriented women's groups in Japan.

The 1990s' history of the 'Justice for Comfort Women' movement in Japan

In the forging of links between Japanese and Korean activists in the 1990s, certain individuals played crucial roles. Yamashita Yeongae was a critical conduit of information between women's groups in Korea and Japan during the important period of the early 1990s (Kinoshita 2011). Yamashita had travelled to Ewha as an exchange student in 1988, the daughter of a Japanese mother and Japan-resident Korean (*zainichi*) father. As such, her decision to study in Korea had some grounding in a desire to explore familial origins, but the reputation of the Ewha women's studies programme was also a major attraction. She had met the programme's director Lee Hyojae on one occasion in Japan, and Lee became her Master's degree supervisor from 1988. Upon arriving at the university, she quickly found herself immersed in researching and campaigning around the history of the 'comfort women' (Yamashita 2008: 4).

Unusually for a student in Japan in the late 1980s, Yamashita was already familiar with this history after having read Yun Chungok's work in Japanese newspapers. Moreover, on the basis of connections she had within the Japan-resident Korean community, she had been invited to accompany feminist historian Suzuki Yuuko on trips to Chiba to visit Japanese comfort station survivor Shirota Suzuko in the facility where she lived with other survivors of prostitution. Shirota was the only publicly identified survivor of military prostitution of Japanese nationality at this time (Shirota 1971). She spoke about this history on Japanese radio in 1986 to raise funds to build a memorial shrine to former 'comfort women', a shrine that still stands in Chiba today near where Shirota lived before passing away in 1993. Yamashita's early knowledge of the history of the 'comfort women' appears to have come from these meetings with Shirota who was, notably in terms of the present discussion, a comfort station survivor who had been trafficked from Japan's civilian sex industry.

Yamashita's unusual biography, extensive network of contacts and Japanese-Korean bilingualism, made her a pivotal figure in the transfer of information between women's groups in the two countries in the early 1990s. She mediated important connections between individual academics and activists, such as facilitating Suzuki Yuuko's visit to Seoul in March 1990 where she was introduced to Yun Chungok, and setting up a meeting between Yun and Shirota in Japan. These connections had far-reaching effects: Yun and Suzuki collaborated in research and activism over two subsequent decades (Yun 2007: 243), and Yamashita went on to study for a decade in Korea. Collaboration between her, Yun and Suzuki was vital to the transfer of information between Japan and Korea in the early years of the justice campaign. Soon after President Roh's visit to Tokyo in May 1990, for example, Yamashita travelled back to Japan from Seoul for a visit and was asked to speak at a public workshop in Tokyo (Yamashita 2008: 40). Yamashita and Yun then worked together in writing the parallel texts in Japanese and Korean for the October 1990 press release calling on the Japanese and Korean governments to release documents about the history of military sexual slavery.

Christian-based abolitionists kept pace with this transnational feminist advocacy on behalf of the 'comfort women', and, in the same month of October 1990, Christian *zainichi* women's groups from Japan and Korea held a joint memorial service on Tokashiki Island (in Okinawa prefecture) for deceased 'comfort women' that was attended by thirty delegates (Kim 2011: 198). Collaborative campaigning between feminists and Christian campaigners occurred during the same period, moreover: in December 1990, Takahashi Kikue's Japan Anti-Prostitution Association invited Yun to Tokyo to speak at a workshop entitled 'Human Rights and War: The Korean Comfort Women' (Seo 2005: 93), an invitation that was mediated by Yamashita (Yamashita 2008: 198). Takahashi's group had been active since the 1970s in campaigning against prostitution tourism, and Takahashi herself had been a persistent voice in progressive circles in Japan in the 1980s in encouraging a focus on the history of the 'comfort women' that was informed by an anti-prostitution perspective (Takahashi 2004).

This activity preceded the Korean survivor litigation in Tokyo in late 1991 that is often cited as having prompted Japan-based women's groups to begin organising in support of the 'comfort women' (Kim 1992: 169; Kim 2011: 198). The litigation did prompt the formation of significant groups, such as the *zainichi* Comfort

Women Problem Women's Network in November 1991, but their formation relied heavily on work already undertaken in support of 'comfort women', such as Yun's scholarship, which the group translated into Japanese in late 1991 (Seo 2005: 94). Following the Korean precedent, the group then collaborated with three other women's groups in Tokyo in January 1992 to operate a three-day hotline that solicited disclosures about wartime military prostitution from 235 callers in Tokyo (Juugun Ianfu 110-ban Henshuu Iinkai 1992). These callers were mostly war veterans who described with surprising candour their wartime experience of observing, recruiting and prostituting 'comfort women'. By this stage, the justice movement had attracted worldwide attention, and transnational links between campaigners in Japan and Korea had developed to the point where, in December 1992, survivor Kim Haksun embarked on a two-week speaking tour of Japan (Song and Moon 1998).

Despite Yamashita's centrality to these outcomes arising from collaboration between Korean and Japanese women's groups, she had nonetheless been uncomfortable since her move to Ewha in the late 1980s with the distinction drawn by local feminists between 'Korean comfort women' and 'Japanese prostitutes', defined respectively by their 'enslavement' and supposed 'volunteer service' during the war (Yamashita 2011). This was perhaps unsurprising given Yamashita's earlier meetings in Japan with Shirota Suzuko. Her subsequent body of scholarship suggests these early feelings of unease at distinctions drawn between different groups of prostituted women continued, and her work as a whole reflects an abolitionist view of prostitution as sexual slavery regardless of its military or civilian form. This is unusual, particularly for a historian writing in the early years of the justice movement. That said, it was a view shared in the early 1990s by a small number of Japanese feminists, including journalist Matsui Yayori who wrote and campaigned against Japanese men's prostitution tourism in South-East Asia. Matsui founded the Asian Women's Association in 1977 in reaction to this tourism, and that organisation endures today as the Asia Japan Women's Resource Centre.

It was mainly through the Asian Women's Association that Japanese feminists engaged internationally in the 1980s and early 1990s around prostitution, including military sexual slavery, with Takahashi Kikue's Japan Anti-Prostitution Association comprising a second hub for abolitionist women of Christian background. There were other women's groups that campaigned domestically against prostitution and pornography in Japan in the 1980s (Tanaka 2010), but these groups did not mobilise in a substantial way in relation to the history of the 'comfort women'. Unlike Takahashi's Anti-Prostitution Association or Matsui's Asian Women's Association, their abolitionism did not take on an internationalist orientation, and so their opposition to prostitution and pornography manifested in local (but important) campaigns against egregious examples of female exploitation arising in Japanese media and society.

Japan-based abolitionist groups that did adopt an internationalist orientation, on the other hand, developed overseas links in the 1980s through international gatherings held in the lead-up to the formation of the CATW in 1988. Asian Women's

Association member Uri Kondou attended one such meeting held in Copenhagen in 1980 that was organised as part of an NGO forum taking place at the UN mid-decade conference on women (Barry 1984: 9). Soon after, in 1983, Takazato Suzuyo travelled to Rotterdam as an Asian Women's Association representative at a second meeting of international anti-prostitution organisers, one which is often cited as another precursor to the formation of the CATW (Barry 1995: 4). Matsui Yayori was supposed to have attended the Rotterdam meeting but had to cancel at the last minute, though she nonetheless submitted a chapter on Japanese prostitution tourism to the conference's published proceedings (Matsui 1984). Takazato's subsequent biography is revealing of the political perspective she brought to these activities in the 1980s. She later formed the Okinawa Women Act against Military Sexual Violence group in 1995, and wrote a number of pieces in the 1990s that included critical comment on prostitution by US military men in Okinawa (Takazato 1994, 1996). She also had the history of the 'comfort women' on her agenda from early on: Pak Yunnam recalls that Takazato visited the offices of the Korean Council on 31 January 1992 when, by chance, a survivor was scheduled to visit the office to give personal testimony. Apparently the survivor allowed Takazato to remain in the room while she gave testimony to Council members (Pak 1992: 57).

While, therefore, the 1990s history of Japanese women mobilising in support of the former 'comfort women' shows early, autonomous and sustained engagement with the issue, it was nonetheless the case that international links, and particularly those with Korean feminists, were important stimuli, even for abolitionist groups. Further, the activity of Japanese women's groups in the early 1990s was heavily reliant upon achievements by Korean women decades prior, and especially in the 1970s.

The 1970s' history of the 'Justice for Comfort Women' movement in South Korea

While the abolitionist connections of the 'justice for comfort women' movement in Korea in the 1990s are perhaps only weakly visible – in the biographies of individuals like Shin Heisoo and in some early interaction between Japanese and Korean feminists and the CATW – they are much more evident in the 1970s. These 1970s' origins are, however, mostly not included in histories of the movement which contributes to an overall underestimation of its abolitionist dimensions.

That said, the 1970s' origins of the Korean 'comfort women' justice movement that are henceforth described are traceable in only an indirect way because Korean women's groups in this era campaigned primarily against sex tourism and local US military prostitution, rather than directly in relation to the history of military sexual slavery. It was not until a conference held in Korea in 1988 that the history of Japanese military enslavement of Korean women came to be identified as a campaign target. However, bringing a lens of abolition to this 1970s' history reveals indirect but nonetheless palpable origins of 'comfort women' justice campaigning in Korea arising from early action against sex tourism. Recalling these origins is important to understanding that the justice movement developed in the country on the basis of shared goals of abolitionism between different groups of women, and recognising this fact permits better acknowledgement of the full scope of collaboration that women activists of diverse political stripes achieved in the early days of globally important transnational movements like that in support of the 'comfort women'.

Collaboration between women activists of different political backgrounds in the same era as the justice movement is visible in campaigning launched against US military prostitution in Korea that began after 1987. This concurrent anti-US prostitution movement, according to Lee Na Young, involved in the late 1980s' 'revolutionary period' 'two different groups of women, both active in [the] resistance movement, [who] came together to form a *kijich'on* [camptown prostitution] movement. The first group was involved with Christian women's organizations; the second was involved with the students' democratic movement' (Lee 2006: 156). While the two groups of women operated from different constituent bases, their political positioning was not too dissimilar. Lee explains the history of this convergence in terms of the fact that

> in the 1970s and 1980s, progressive Christian women's groups helped generate a more explicit focus on gender inequalities and served as an important breeding ground for future feminist activists ...The Korean Church Women United ... was one of the core organizations for progressive women at the time....Korea's civil society [then] consisted of various groups of people including students and intellectuals, religious groupings, labor unions, *chaeya* groups (progressive people outside political parties), and politicians ... Similarly, Christian women, intellectuals including college students, and labor workers were the main components of organizations in the women's movements. In particular, Christian women's groups have played major roles in the labor movement, the anti-war/peace movement, the anti-prostitution movement, and the reunification movement, as well as raising issues regarding comfort women ... [Japanese sex tourism] was first challenged by these Christian women's groups.
>
> *(Lee 2006: 156)*

Lee's view of the political hues of women's organising in 1970s and 1980s Korea, both in its anti-prostitution stance and the collaboration taking place between faith-oriented and feminist women, sheds light on the political configuration of the justice movement of the time, which we might expect to have been similarly organised.

The particular progressivism of Korean women's anti-prostitution campaigning in the post-war period (regardless of the background of the participants) is described by Kim Puja. She wrote in 1992 that a women's association established just two days after Korea's liberation from Japan began campaigning for female equality in the country on a number of fronts, but with prostitution and trafficking as its core concerns. While the organisation disbanded after the country's division, one of its final actions was to lobby American administrators to outlaw prostitution in the country, which was achieved in March 1946 (reversing its legalisation by the former Japanese colonial administration). Notably, and as an important indication of the abolitionist priorities of this early movement, subsequent groups did not think the policy change comprehensive enough, and so continued campaigning against the sex trade. They lobbied the ruling party of the time, and in August 1946 formed a coalition against prostitution that was eventually successful in achieving the passing of a stronger law in Korea in 1947 (Kim 1992: 173–4).

Before the war, too, there had been activism by Korean women on the same issue. Lee describes the example of a colonial women's association that was 'formed by a coalition of Christian and socialist women in 1927', and which had an explicitly anti-prostitution platform. The group saw women's inequality as 'caused by both Confucian patriarchy and the contradictions of modern capitalism', and so advocated for women's rights with a particular 'sensitiv[ity] to gender inequality and class injustice' (Lee 2006: 69). In light of this history of women's campaigning both before and after the war, it is unsurprising that the women's movement that ultimately arose in South Korea against the wartime sexual slavery imposed by Japanese men is traceable, albeit in an indirect way, to a Korea-Japan National Council of Christian Churches conference in Seoul in July 1973. This conference was part of efforts to raise support in Japan for the Korean democracy movement of the time:

> Many Korean Christians had studied at Japanese theological seminaries during the 1950s and the 1960s and had met Japanese Christians in other countries where they had gone for study or for international conferences and workshops. These networks linking Japanese and Korean Christians, especially progressive Christians, were strengthened in the context of the world ecumenical movement. In the early 1970s, the National Council of Churches in Korea (NCCK) and the National Council of Churches in Japan (NCCJ) institutionalized annual meetings; the first was held in Seoul on July 2–5, 1973. The participants discussed (1) Japan's economic advance, (2) the legal status of Zainichi, (3) Koreans in Sakhalin, (4) Japan's immigration law, (5) Korean victims of the atomic bombing, (6) the Yasukuni Shrine, (7) sex tourism, and (8) history textbooks. The meeting produced a resolution calling for further cooperation.[6]

It was the Korea Church Women United who put the seventh item, sex tourism, on the conference agenda because of the prostitution tourism of Japanese men that had been proliferating in the country since the early 1970s in spite of the legislative ban on prostitution. The resolution was duly passed, and in December 1973 the KCWU convened a sub-group to organise action on it. An occasion to act presented itself six months later in the lead-up to the scheduled convening on 25 December of the Japan-Korea Joint Ministerial Meeting, a bilateral forum created by the two governments after diplomatic relations resumed in 1965. The group recruited more than twenty Ewha students on 19 December 1973 to greet inbound Japanese male tour groups flying into the country. The students held up posters 'exposing the Japanese sexual invasion' (Willoughby 2007: 117–18). Staged at the height of military rule in Korea, this protest involved a significant risk of arrest and ill-treatment in detention and shows how strongly the issue resonated among young Korean women at the time.

The protest also attracted attention in Japan and generated transnational support from Japanese feminists. Matsui Yayori recalled how 'campaigners demonstrated against Japanese arriving on [so-called] *kisaeng* tours at Seoul's Kimpo airport … Almost simultaneously, the proceedings of the "Citizens Committee to Abolish *Kisaeng* Tours" held in Seoul was broadcast on Japanese television' (Matsui 1984: 70). The movement's campaigning repertoire also extended beyond this kind of skilful publicity stunt. KCWU members soon after commenced a fieldwork-based investigation of prostitution tourism in four major Korean cities. The resultant research report, which was compiled in 1983 and translated into English and Japanese soon after, eventually influenced the Korean government to change its tourism policies (Korea Church Women United 1984).

A second outcome of the research project was a conference convened in April 1988 by the KCWU on the southern Korean island of Cheju. Entitled 'Women and the Culture of Tourism', it was attended by around 120 women from countries including Japan (with Takahashi Kikue among the delegates), the US and the UK, as well as members of the KWAU, and was timed to precede the opening of the Seoul summer Olympics. The mood of the conference – according to Yun who was a keynote speaker – was one of outrage at Japanese men's prostitution tourism taking place just a few decades after the end of the war, a mood that was heightened by the carefully chosen venue. Cheju was a major centre for the sex tourism industry and had been one of the sites included in the KCWU research project: out of the 75,000 tourist visitors to Cheju in 1985, 43,000 were sex tourists and roughly 60 per cent of these were Japanese men (Korea Church Women United 1984). The spirited anti-prostitution activity of local feminist campaigners on Cheju led directly to the convening of the conference there (Kim 1992).

The feminist contours of the anti-prostitution movement in Korea had sharpened considerably by the time of the conference. Women's groups had begun to campaign more vigorously against the escalation in sexual violence they identified as a consequence of intensified urbanisation. They pointed to statistics that showed rising incidents of rape and also rising rates of domestic trafficking of women. Reported incidents of trafficking rose from 196 in 1987 to 249 in 1988, and feminists attributed this to the expansion of the sex industry in major cities. Between 1983 and 1990, the number of registered prostitution businesses (technically, in statutory regulation, 'entertainment industry' venues) in Korea rose from 277,000 to 415,000. In total, 650,000 women were entangled in Korea's sex industry in 1990, which equated to one prostituted woman for every thirteen women between the ages of fifteen and forty-five in the country (Norma 2014). Simultaneously, as previously discussed, feminist and faith-based female campaigners were beginning to organise against US military camptown prostitution,

By her own admission, Yun saw herself as having a personal connection to the history of the 'comfort women' through her experience in wartime at high school rather than an activist connection to it; she recalled that she had not really been politically active before attending the Cheju conference. Her participation in that conference arose through her colleague Lee at Ewha liaising with conference organisers to have Yun speak on the history of the 'comfort women'. Yun had returned in February from a research trip (together with two women from the KCWU) investigating the history of the 'comfort women' in places like Fukuoka and Okinawa in Japan.[7] While the conference was held to address the problem of sex tourism in Korea by Japanese men around the time, Yoon Bang-Soon notes that it produced 'limited but somewhat positive political rewards to the comfort women survivors'. This resulted from Yun's presentation as well as Lee Hyun-sook's declaration at the conference that 'Japanese tourists join[ing] with the *gisaeng gwangwang* [i.e. *kisaeng* tourism] for sex are descendants of the colonial era militarists who hunted for *jungshindae* ["comfort women"]' (Yoon 2010: 28).

It might appear odd that recognition of the history of the 'comfort women' in Korea prior to the 1990s was forged at a conference against prostitution tourism. From an abolitionist perspective, however, this convergence is relatively unremarkable. The sex tourism of Japanese men in Korea in the 1970s allowed activists to understand the sexual slavery of the war not as an isolated aberration arising from military endeavour but as a continuing pattern of Japanese male sexual exploitation of Korean women. Recognising the crime of wartime military prostitution as a problem of contemporary North-East Asia in the 1970s required, critically, that the past be re-enacted in the present. Japanese men travelling in droves to prostitute women in Korea was, in the eyes of both the Korean and Japanese women's movements, a jarringly realistic simulation of male wartime behaviour. Significantly, the comparison pointed in both historical directions: outrage at the prostitution tourism of the present and at the crimes of the past was mutually intensifying. Without this recognition, which was crucially reliant upon an abolitionist perspective adopted by activists, organised opposition to the two phenomena would likely not have emerged.

The 1970s' history of the 'Justice for Comfort Women' movement in Japan

Japanese women's groups are generally regarded as having been – in comparison to their Korean sisters – slow in mobilising over the history of the 'comfort women'. This mobilisation began, it is suggested, only in the 1990s, and only in a reactive, rather than proactive, way. Vera Mackie, for example, writes that 'feminist analysis [in Japan] of military prostitution only became possible after a series of developments in the women's movement in Japan … and parallel developments in women's movements in the countries which shared this history' (Mackie

2003: 219). Specifically, the emergence of the justice movement in Japan in the early 1990s was made possible only by, on the one hand, the agitation by Korean women such as Kim Haksun and, on the other, research by (male) Japanese historians such as Yoshimi Yoshiaki who uncovered archival evidence of the complicity of the military in the 'comfort women' system. In this telling of history, the Japanese women's movement of the early 1990s was historically not well-placed to autonomously mobilise on behalf of former 'comfort women'. Some Japanese feminist veterans of the 1970s express such regrets. Yoshitake Teruko, for example, who was one of the founders in 1975 of the Tokyo-based Group of Activist Women, noted how the presence of a military regime in Korea made it difficult for information about the 'comfort women' to be transmitted to Japan; simultaneously, feminist campaigning was preoccupied with opposing other issues of sexism within Japan, which retarded the growth of a justice movement there (Koudou suru Onnatachi No Kai 1999: 237).

These explanations imply that the wartime history of military sexual enslavement was a phenomenon primarily relevant to Korean women and external to the lives of Japanese women, and that little connection existed between it and problems of sex discrimination afflicting women in Japanese society; hence it required an external impetus for the issue to be taken up by feminists there. But this interpretation overlooks the fact that the movement was able to swing into action so quickly in the early 1990s precisely because there had already been considerable ferment over the 'comfort women' issue in the Japanese women's movement in the 1970s, albeit that it was somewhat unfocused and problematic in character.

On the face of it, the political climate in which the Japanese women's movement in the 1970s emerged was propitious for the growth of consciousness on the 'comfort women'. Setsu Shigematsu characterises the women's liberation movement in Japan as approximating 'what has been characterized and designated as radical feminism in other contexts' (Shigematsu 2012: xix). Its members comprised, for example, female defectors of the hard left, its political approach was to reject 'equality' as a goal in favour of political class liberation and it aimed to overhaul the political, economic and social system instead of renovating or reforming existing institutions. When this movement did engage with the history of the 'comfort women', however, it did so in an unfortunately distorted way.

On 21 October 1970 a women's liberation protest rally was held in Mizutani Park involving 200 women carrying placards bearing a number of different protest slogans. One of these, according to a report in the *Asahi Shinbun*, was an anti-war message that included the sentence 'prostitutes and comfort women facilitate military invasion'.[8] The placard criticised women as having historically collaborated with Japanese men in military adventurism through offering support to them in the form of sexual service. A month or so after the rally, a statement from one of the groups attached to the radical feminist hub Liberation Shinjuku Centre apologised for the group having composed this placard. On reflection, the group now believed, it should have read: 'prostitutes, as prostitutes, support militarism, and are responsible for forcing Korean women to become sullied with the ejaculate of their own Japanese men'. The group explained that they now understood that Korean women had merely been

> the ones who followed behind the [Japanese] prostitutes but were nonetheless sent to the front lines of battle to act as receptacles of male bodily evacuation (as public toilets) so that men would be kept in order under the Japanese military through the control of their sexuality.

The placard was a mistake because

> we can't talk of prostitutes and comfort women in equal terms: we don't have the right to do that as Japanese women and as members of the ruling ethnic group. We don't have that right because the great majority of comfort women were Korean wives and daughters who were abducted.
>
> *(Ribu Shinjuku Sentaa Shiryou Hozonkai 2008: 92)*

In the short space of a month, therefore, the group revised its analysis of the history of the 'comfort women' from one of blame laid at the feet of all women prostituted by Japanese men in war, as having been collaborators, to one of blame attributed to Japanese women in general for having pushed innocent Korean women in their stead to sexually service Japanese men in the course of their military ventures. While this protest message, and the group that broadcast it, were marginal to any kind of organised civic activity by Japanese women in the early 1970s, the incident is notable for the radical political stripe of the group involved. The radicalism of the group prompts the expectation that its political formulation of the 'comfort women' issue would have been the most progressive of all Japanese women's groups.

Instead, this trope of Japanese women bearing responsibility for the victimisation of Korean women became well established in the movement in the 1970s. Three years later, the same group published a newsletter protesting against the prostitution tourism of Japanese men in Korea. Again, the group evinced a great deal of sympathy for Korean women prostituted in conditions of poverty. They also successfully drew a parallel between the prostitution of the past and that of the present when stating that 'instead of military boot leather, it is the sound of *geta* sandals that grows louder in Korea', referring to the footwear commonly worn during trips to hot spring resorts where Japanese men carried out a lot of their prostitution activity (Ribu Shinjuku Sentaa Shiryou Hozonkai 2008: 546). In another publication, the group characterised the contemporary plight of Korean women as manifesting a revival of the 'nightmarish vision of the Greater East Asian Co-Prosperity Sphere', given the influx of Japanese men into Korea as economic and sexual 'animals'. However, as previously, there was a sting in the tail of the group's analysis: Japanese women, and Japanese wives in particular, through their dutiful 'keeping of the home fires burning' as spouses, were facilitating the overseas crimes of their husbands (Ribu Shinjuku Sentaa Shiryou Hozonkai 2008: 545). While Japanese feminists in the early 1970s thereby recognised the prostitution activity of

Japanese men as perpetrating a wrong against Korean women, they did not extend this recognition to similar harms accruing to Japanese women. In blaming wives, rather than their perpetrator husbands, Japanese feminists lost an opportunity to reflect on the military sexual slavery that was enforced for women of their own nationality by their countrymen, and therefore to comprehend the historical wrong of the military 'comfort women' system as relevant to themselves and as one that connected them in solidarity with Asian women abroad. This failure meant the justice movement on the Japanese side developed only weakly in the 1970s and 1980s.

Despite these contrasts between developments in Japan and Korea, events in Japan a few years later in the 1970s brought its justice movement into closer parallel to that of Korea, even if for just a short time. Takahashi Kikue founded the Japan Anti-Prostitution Association in January 1973, and on 9 March 1974 – International Women's Day – she facilitated an alliance in Tokyo of fifteen women's groups (comprising 300 members in total) to form Women against Prostitution Tourism to support the efforts of Korean women to protest at tour groups of Japanese men. A joint conference was then held between Korean and Japanese women's groups in November 1974. True, on the Japanese side, movement towards this outcome had taken some time to gain momentum: Takahashi had called for activists to hand out pamphlets at Haneda airport on 8 December 1973 in support of a planned action by Korean feminists, but attracted a response from only three volunteers. Support subsequently grew among Japanese feminists, however, as a result of news about the activism of Korean women: specifically, the news that Korean female students and their supporters had protested at Kimpo airport led a large group of Japanese women to gather at Haneda airport on Christmas Day 1973 for a parallel action (Mizoguchi, Saeki and Miki 1992: 252).

After this spike of activism, however, the issue of the 'comfort women' fell down the agenda of the broader feminist movement. Matsui Yayori's Asian Women's Association, founded in 1977, did press the issue, and consistently drew parallels between contemporary sex tourism and wartime sexual slavery. But other wings of the feminist movement 'shifted their attention to other issues and practically dropped it'(Muto 1997: 159). Matsui has argued that the chief obstacle to greater enhanced consciousness of the 'comfort women' issue was lack of information and the absence of the voice of the victims in the public domain. Historian Kinoshita Naoko has, however, challenged the notion that the victims were not speaking out, pointing to the 1971 publication of Shirota Suzuko's autobiography and other Japanese and Korean victim testimony (Kinoshita 2011: 99). Kinoshita argues that it was not an absence of testimony that stopped Japanese feminists organising around the issue, but rather their inability to recognise their fellow countrywomen as victims of wartime military sexual slavery (rather than as 'mere' prostitutes). Feminists were inevitably influenced by the culture of denial and hostility around the former 'comfort women' that had developed in the Japanese media, and which was often directed specifically at local survivors. In contrast to South Korea, information and public comment about the comfort station system and its victims circulated relatively plentifully in Japan in the 1970s. But most media reports, academic books, novels and biographies that emerged in the 1970s and 1980s were unsympathetic to local victims (Kinoshita 2011). Hence, despite the persistent activism of groups like Takahashi Kikue's Japan Anti-Prostitution Association, it was only in the early 1990s, with the civil action launched in Tokyo by Korean survivors, that feminist groups in Japan really began to mobilise in support of justice for the victims of military sexual slavery.

Even this campaigning, however, as before, focused on Korean and other Asian victims, rather than local Japanese women. In this respect, while some of the historical origins of the justice movement in Japan might be seen as abolitionist in nature, the extent of this abolitionism was constrained by the limited extent to which advocates were able to see Japanese victims – who were most often trafficked into comfort stations from civilian sex industry venues – as equal victims of sexual enslavement, and as equally deserving of historical redress as survivors. There is, however, a shift underway in the justice movement in Japan today towards full recognition of such Japanese women as equal victims and this fact reflects the development of an increasingly robust abolitionist perspective among its members (Norma 2016).

Conclusion

The history of the transnational Japan-Korea women's movement in support of the former 'comfort women' reaches as far back as the 1970s. While the feminism of the movement in these early decades may not have been strong, the movement's historical origins can be characterised as abolitionist. Anti-sex tourism campaigning by women's groups in both Korea and Japan was integral to the historical emergence of a critique of the wartime military sexual slavery system, even if this critique was not translated into sustained action in either country over the subsequent decade. Important nonetheless is the fact that the original transnational critique of military sexual slavery developed historically in the context of condemnation of the prostitution activity of Japanese men. Their sexual exploitation of women in wartime came to be condemned in the 1970s as having occurred on a continuum with their subsequent sexual exploitation of women in peacetime tourism. Crucial to this recognition of a pattern in the behaviour of Japanese men were abolitionist views held among female activists and academics that prostitution was worthy of condemnation irrespective of whether it occurred in wartime or peacetime.

However, in recognising this pattern, Korean women came to be identified strongly with the historical crime of military sexual slavery. This association of Korean women with the crimes of sexual exploitation by Japanese men meant that, in Japan, feminist groups did not sustain action on the issue of the 'comfort women' into the 1980s. The existence of comfort station survivors of Japanese nationality, and indeed survivors of other nationalities who continued to reside in Japan in the post-war period, did not serve as an impetus to action for Japanese feminist groups. This was both because of the strong association of the issue with Korean women, but also because of long-standing misogynistic ideas circulating in

Japan about women of Japanese nationality who had been victimised in comfort stations after being trafficked out of the civilian sex industry. On the Korean side, government repression in the 1970s and 1980s was a major barrier to political organising and the lack of campaigning stimulus from Korean women's groups in the era accordingly left Japanese feminist activism mostly at a standstill until the early 1990s.

When the movement in both countries revived in the early 1990s, the anti-prostitution perspective that had been at the foundation of the critique of military sexual slavery in earlier decades had weakened. Sensitivity to arguments by right-wing defenders of the Japanese military that defamed prostituted victims of comfort stations as undeserving was one cause of this. These right-wing groups emerged quickly after the 1990s' revival of justice campaigning, and their ascendance created a barrier to the revival of an abolitionist perspective, which continues to some extent today. On the Korean side, too, as personally observed by Yamashita Yeongae in the late 1980s, there circulated from early on misogynistic ideas about the relative victimisation of Japanese compared to Korean women.

However, the strength and historical depth of the abolitionist perspective on the Korean side should not be underestimated. As is well known, feminists in that country were successful in 2004 in lobbying for a policy approach to prostitution that is the preferred legislative model of abolitionists globally today. The legislation resulted from many decades of work by both feminist and Christian groups in the country against prostitution. According to Kim Seung-kyung and Kim Kyounghee,

> the two most important achievements produced by the women's movements' alliance with the government were the Act to Prevent Prostitution in 2004 and the abolition of the Family-Head System in 2005. These two legal changes abolished two systems that were supporting unequal gender relationships and show that the government was taking charge of fundamental social change, and had embraced progressive feminist ideology as its policy. Both abolishing the Family-Head System and preventing prostitution had been on the women's movements' agendas for several decades.
>
> *(Kim and Kim 2010: 201)*

This contemporary achievement is significant for the support it offers to a clear future direction and path of sustainability for the 'comfort women' justice movement. Highlighting the abolitionist historical connections of this movement is important for understanding the movement as not merely a single-issue campaign that will persist only as long as survivors are with us, or until concessions are extracted from the Japanese government. The justice campaign did not arise in a vacuum without historical context or links to existing social movements. On the contrary, the campaign is understood by feminist abolitionists today as not only the 'first and strongest survivor movement in history', but also one that that serves as an historical beacon of abolitionist activism and philosophy.[9] In Korea at least, its strength is bolstered by the success of a strong coalition of feminist and faith-based abolitionists who achieved the 2004 law and continue today to lobby for its strengthening. Remembering the abolitionist historical context of the justice movement, and connecting it with this activity in the present, will only strengthen its future prospects. A way forward for the sustained struggle for justice for survivors can be seen in the transnational activism that continues in the form of feminist abolitionist campaigning in Korea, and to a limited extent in Japan. This activism is waged on behalf of all victims of sexual slavery, whether they have survived prostitution in war or in peace, and whether in the past or the present. The ascendance of transnational feminist abolitionism in the world today has, fortunately, come just in time for the elderly survivors of the wartime crimes of Japanese military men.

Notes

Unless otherwise indicated, all translations are my own.

1 I gratefully acknowledge funding from the School of Global, Urban and Social Studies at RMIT University for two months' writing sabbatical at the National Library of Australia in Canberra to complete this chapter. Thanks to Shinozaki Mayumi for her boundless assistance and hospitality during my time in the Asian Collections Reading Room.
2 See the Ministry of Gender Equality and Family website, *'I'm the Evidence': E-Museum of the Japanese Military Sexual Slavery*, http://actionforpeace.net/sub.asp?pid=226.
3 Janice Raymond, 'Honoring the "Comfort Women" Drafted into Military Sexual Slavery', RadFems Resist, London, 13 September 2015, www.youtube.com/watch?v=XvSYaIamzlo.
4 Email communication, Janice Raymond to author, 12 January 2016.
5 Raymond, 'Honoring the "Comfort Women"'.
6 Lee Misook, 'The Japan-Korea Solidarity Movement in the 1970s and 1980s: From Solidarity to Reflexive Democracy', *The Asia-Pacific Journal*, 21 September 2014, http://japanfocus.org/-Misook-Lee/4187/article.html#sthash.6Kf9ACi3.dpuf.
7 Kwon Hee-Soon, 'The Military Sexual Slavery Issue and Asian Peace', conference paper delivered at 'The First East Asian Women's Forum', 20–22 October 1994, Japan, www.macalester.edu/~tam/HIST194%20War%20Crimes/documents/comfort%20women/KoreanWomen.htm.
8 'Kyoubashi Mizutani Kouen de josei 200 nin, josei kaihou shuukai, hageshii demo (uuman ribu)', *Asahi Shinbun*, 22 October 1970.
9 Raymond, 'Honoring the "Comfort Women"'.

References

Barry, Kathleen. 1984. *Female Sexual Slavery*. New York, NY: New York University Press.

Barry, Kathleen. 1995. *The Prostitution of Sexuality*. New York, NY: New York University Press.

Chou, Chih-Chieh. 2003. 'An Emerging Transnational Movement in Women's Human Rights: Campaign of Nongovernmental Organizations on "Comfort Women" Issue in East Asia'. *Journal of Economic and Social Research*, 5, 1: 153–81.

Farley, Melissa and Seo, Sungjean. 2005. 'Prostitution and Trafficking in Asia'. *Harvard Asia Pacific Review*, 8, 2: 9–12.

Hughes, Donna M., Chon, Katherine Y. and Ellerman, Derek P. 2007. 'Modern-Day Comfort Women: The U.S. Military, Transnational Crime, and the Trafficking of Women'. *Violence Against Women*, 13, 9: 901–22.

Jeffreys, Sheila. 1997. *The Idea of Prostitution*. North Melbourne: Spinifex.

Jordan, Jane and Sharp, Ingrid. eds. 2003. *Josephine Butler and the Prostitution Campaigns: Diseases of the Body Politic*. 5 vols. London: Routledge.

Juugun Ianfu 110-ban Henshuu Iinkai. eds. 1992. *Juugun ianfu 110-ban: Denwa no mukou kara rekishi no koe ga*. Tokyo: Akashi Shoten.

Kern, Thomas and Nam, Sang-hui. 2009. 'The Korean Comfort Women Movement and the Formation of a Public Sphere in East Asia'. In *Korea Yearbook: Politics, Economy and Society*, edited by Rüdiger Frank, Jim Hoare, Patrick Kölner and Susan Pares. Leiden: Brill. 227–55.

Kim, Puja. 1992. 'Kankoku josei undou kara mita Chousen jin ianfu mondai'. In *Chousenjin josei ga mita "ianfu mondai": Asu o tomo ni tsukuru tame ni*, edited by Yun Chungok. Tokyo: San'ichi Shobou. 168–206.

Kim, Puja. 2011. *Keizokusuru shokuminchi shugi to jendaa: "kokumin" gainen, josei no shintai, kioku to sekinin*. Yokohama-shi: Seori Shoboou.

Kim, Seung-kyung and Kim, Kyounghee. 2010. 'Mapping a Hundred Years of Activism: Women's Movements in Korea'. In *Women's Movements in Asia: Feminisms and Transnational Activism*, edited by Mina Roces and Louise Edwards. London: Routledge. 189–206.

Kinoshita, Naoko. 2011. 'Nihonjin "ianfu" no higaisha sei: 1990 nen shotou no gensetsu, undou o furikaette'. *Tokai Gender Research Journal*, 14: 89–113.

Korea Church Women United. 1984. *Kisaeng Tourism: A Nation-wide Survey Report on Conditions in Four Areas; Seoul, Pusan, Cheju, Kyongju*. Seoul: Catholic Publishing House.

Koudou Suru Onnatachi No Kai. ed. 1999. *Koudou suru onnatachi ga hiraita michi*. Tokyo: Miraisha.

Lee, Na Young. 2006. 'The Construction of US Camptown Prostitution in South Korea: Trans/formation and Resistance'. PhD dissertation, University of Maryland, http://drum.lib.umd.edu/bitstream/handle/1903/4162/umi-umd-3959.pdf;jsessionid=5F60C222B3156C0B022FA900FEB7F2D5?sequence=1.

Mackie, Vera C. (2003). *Feminism in Modern Japan: Citizenship, Embodiment, and Sexuality*. Cambridge: Cambridge University Press.

MacKinnon, Catharine. 1994. 'Rape, Genocide, and Women's Human Rights'. In *Mass Rape: The War against Women in Bosnia-Herzegovina*, edited by Alexandra Stiglmayer. Lincoln, NE: University of Nebraska Press. 183–96.

Martz, Linda. 2005. 'An AIDS-Era Reassessment of Christabel Pankhurst's *The Great Scourge and How to End It*'. *Women's History Review*, 14, 3–4: 435–46.

Matsui, Yayori, 1984. 'Why I Oppose the *Kisaeng* Tours'. In *International Feminism: Networking against Female Sexual Slavery*, edited by Kathleen Barry, Charlotte Bunch and Shirley Castley. New York, NY: International Women's Tribune Center. 64–72.

Mizoguchi, Akiyo, Saeki, Youko and Miki, Souko. eds. 1992. *Shiryoou Nihon uuman ribu-shi*. Vol. 1. Tokyo: Shoukadou.

Moon, Katharine H. S. 2010. 'South Korean Movements against Militarized Sexual Labor'. In *Militarized Currents: Toward a Decolonized Future in Asia and the Pacific*, edited by Setsu Shigematsu and Keith Camacho. Minneapolis, MN: University of Minnesota Press. 125–45.

Morita, Seiya. 1999, 'Senji no sei bouryoku heiji no sei bouryoku'. *Yuibutsuron Kenkyuu Nenshi*, 4: 113–40.

Murray, Nicola. 1979. 'Socialism and Feminism: Women and the Cuban Revolution, Part I'. *Feminist Review*, 2, 2: 57–73.

Muta, Kazue. 2016. 'The "Comfort Women" Issue and the Embedded Culture of Sexual Violence in Contemporary Japan'. *Current Sociology*, 64: 620–36.

Muto, Ichiyo. 1997. 'The Birth of the Women's Liberation Movement in the 1970s'. In *The Other Japan: Conflict, Compromise, and Resistance since 1945*, edited by Joe Moore. Armonk, NY: M. E. Sharpe. 147–71.

Nolland, Lisa S. 2004. *A Victorian Feminist Christian: Josephine Butler, the Prostitutes and God*. Carlisle: Paternoster.

Norma, Caroline. 2011. 'The Koreanization of the Australian Sex Industry: A Policy and Legislative Challenge'. *The Korean Journal of Policy Studies*, 26, 3: 13–36.

Norma, Caroline. 2014. 'Demand from Abroad: Japanese Involvement in the 1970s' Development of South Korea's Sex Industry'. *Journal of Korean Studies*, 19, 2: 399–428.

Norma, Caroline. 2016. *The Japanese Comfort Women and Sexual Slavery during the China and Pacific Wars*. London: Bloomsbury.

Pak, Yunnam. 1992. 'Kouhen'. In *Chousenjin josei ga mita "ianfu mondai": Asu o tomo ni tsukuru tame ni* by Yun Chungok. Tokyo: San'ichi Shobou. 49–69.

Raymond, Janice. 2013. *Not a Choice, Not a Job: Exposing the Myths about Prostitution and the Global Sex Trade*. North Melbourne: Spinifex.

Ribu Shinjuku Sentaa Shiryou Hozonkai. eds. 2008. *Ribu Shinjuku Sentaa shiryou shuusei*. Vol. 2. Tokyo: Inpakuto Shuppankai.

Rodríguez García, Magaly. 2012. 'The League of Nations and the Moral Recruitment of Women'. *International Review of Social History*, 57, S20: 97–128.

Seo, Akwi. 2005. 'The Emergence of a New Subject for Korean Women in Japan: A Case Study of "Comfort Women" Redress Movement in 1990s'. *F-Gens Journal*, 4: 93–101.

Shigematsu, Setsu. 2012. *Scream from the Shadows: The Women's Liberation Movement in Japan*. Minneapolis, MN: University of Minnesota Press.

Shin, Heisoo. 2011. 'Seeking Justice, Honour and Dignity: Movement for the Victims of Japanese Military Sexual Slavery'. In *Global Civil Society 2011: Globality and the Absence of Justice*, edited by H. Seckinelgin and Billy Wong. London: Palgrave Macmillan. 14–28.

Shirota, Suzuko. 1971. *Mariya no sanka*. Tokyo: Nihon Kirisuto Kyoudan Shuppan Kyoku.

Song, Young I. and Moon, Ailee. eds. 1998. *Korean American Women: From Tradition to Modern Feminism*. Westport, CT: Praeger.

Szczepanska, Kamila. 2014. *The Politics of War Memory in Japan: Progressive Civil Society Groups and Contestation of Memory of the Asia-Pacific War*. London: Routledge.

Takahashi, Kikue. 2004. *Baibaishun mondai ni torikumu: Sei sakushu to Nihon shakai*. Tokyo: Akashi Shoten.

Takazato, Suzuyo. 1994. 'Trials of Okinawa: A Feminist Perspective'. *Race, Poverty and the Environment*, 4–5, 4–1: 10.

Takazato, Suzuyo. 1996. *Okinawa no onnatachi: Josei no jinken to kichi, guntai*. Tokyo: Akashi Shoten.

Tanaka, Mitsu. 2010. *Inochi no onnatachi e: torimidashi uuman ribu ron*. Tokyo: Pandora.

Truong, Thanh-Dam. 2015. 'Human Trafficking, Globalization and Transnational Feminist Responses'. In *The Oxford Handbook of Transnational Feminist Movements*, edited by Rawwida Baksh and Wendy Harcourt. Oxford: Oxford University Press. 295–320.

Willoughby, Heather A. ed. 2007. *Footsteps across the Frontier: 120 Years of Globalization at Ewha Womans University*. Seoul: Ewha Womans University Press.

Yamashita, Yeongae. 2008. *Nashonarizumu no hazama kara: 'Ianfu' mondai e no mou hitotsu no shiza*. Tokyo: Akashi Shoten.

Yamashita, Yeongae. 2011. 'Revisiting the "Comfort Women": Moving Beyond Nationalism'. In *Transforming Japan: How Feminism and Diversity are Making a Difference*, edited by Kumiko Fujimura-Fanselow. New York, NY: The Feminist Press. 366–89.

Yoon, Bang-Soon L. 2010. 'Imperial Japan's Comfort Women from Korea: History and Politics of Silence-Breaking'. *Journal of Northeast Asian History*, 7, 1: 5–39.

Yoon, Mee-hyang. 2007. 'Fifteen Years of the Asian Solidarity Conference: Upcoming Issues and Further Solidarity for Resolving the Issue of Japan's Military Sexual Slavery'. In *Forced Prostitution in Times of War and Peace: Sexual Violence against Women and Girls*, edited by Barbara Drinck and Chung-Noh Gross. Bielefeld: Kleine. 253–60.

Yun, Choung-ok. 1992. *Chousenjin josei ga mita "ianfu mondai": Asu o tomo ni tsukuru tame ni*. Tokyo: San'ichi Shobou.

Yun, Chungok. 2007. 'Findings from 50 Years of Research on the "Comfort Women" Issue'. In *Forced Prostitution in Times of War and Peace: Sexual Violence against Women and Girls*, edited by Barbara Drinck and Chung-Noh Gross. Bielefeld: Kleine. 231–46.

Yun, Mihyang. 2011. *20-nenkan no suiyoubi: Nihongun "ianfu" harumoni ga sakebu yuruginai kibou*. Osaka-shi: Touhou Shuppan.

PART III

Local and sectional memories

7

THE TREACHERY OF MEMORIALS

Beyond war remembrance in contemporary Okinawa

Gerald Figal

With over 300 war-related monuments strewn across its 1,200 square kilometres of land, Okinawa Island in all likelihood holds the dubious distinction of possessing the highest density of Second World War memorial sites in the world. As location of one of the bloodiest battles of that war – claiming the lives of over 200,000 Japanese and Okinawan combatants, local non-combatants and American combatants combined over a span of three months from late March 1945 – the vast number of physical markers memorialising the war dead, concentrated largely in the southern half of the island, is not surprising. The battle of Okinawa had scarcely ended before makeshift graves and ossuaries dotted the landscape, marked as 'spirit consolation pillar' ('*ireitō*'), the most common designation for a marker of the war dead in Okinawa. Within a year of the battle's end, three major war memorial sites were established and still stand as major stops on war commemoration pilgrimages and general tourism on the island: Kenji-no-tō, commemorating the local boys who perished in the Imperial Blood and Iron Youth Corps (a locally raised, notionally volunteer, unit of boys aged 14 and over); Himeyuri-no-tō, for the local girls who died in the Himeyuri Student Nurses Corps; and Konpaku-no-tō, for over 35,000 unidentified dead, a mixture of combatants and civilians. The Himeyuri-no-tō in particular, enshrining the tragic fates of the young battlefield nurses who died in action, has grown with the addition of a popular memorial museum and significant archive. It has come to dominate and (narrowly) define the mainland Japanese public image of local Okinawan war experience as hundreds, then thousands, and then hundreds of thousands visited the site that was the showcase for the war memorial tours that began in the 1950s and have continued to this day.

Today's southern battle sites tour – although no longer the dominant form of tourism on Okinawa as the wider leisure tourism industry has boomed – still generally traces the route first established in the 1950s. Since the dedication of the impressive Cornerstone of Peace monument in 1995 and the opening of the adjacent upgraded Okinawa Prefectural Peace Memorial Museum in 2000, however, the majority of visitors tend to gravitate to just that pair before or after a stop at the Himeyuri Peace Memorial Museum, short-circuiting the full original battle sites loop (Figal 2012: 25–45). But even in such a, more streamlined, tour-packaged form, the extent of discursive and physical space dedicated to historical explanation and public memorialisation of the battle of Okinawa and the Asia-Pacific War on this small island does not fail to impress. Yet despite this vigorous history and the physically conspicuous presence of war memorials, I argue that the abundance of war remembrance in these typical forms – the stone monuments, the solemn ceremonies – is not what renders the case of Okinawa noteworthy; rather, the more important forms of Okinawan war remembrance are those that overcome the temptation to relieve the burdens of war history and memory at the base of a war memorial. Local unwillingness to commemorate the war in order to forget it is at the heart of what puts Okinawa at odds with the central government of Japan on just about anything connected with war legacies, from what is covered in school textbooks and museum displays to the issue of US bases on the island.

Public monuments run the risk of ironically lulling one into forgetting that which they were designed to keep in mind. 'The most important [thing about monuments],' Robert Musil wryly observed, 'is somewhat contradictory: what strikes one most about monuments is that one doesn't notice them. There is nothing in the world as invisible as monuments' (Levinson 1998: 7). Even if one in fact physically notices them, it is safe to surmise that instances of deep reflection and historical reckoning in response to them are not common. In the case of memorials to the war dead, physically manifesting a marker onto which memory is deposited can serve to liberate the living from the burden of actively and continually remembering the dead – the act of remembrance is always already done with, neatly taken care of by the physical monument and perhaps a ritual event (public or private) surrounding it. It is there, a concrete testament. Official state-sponsored commemorative events also tend to induce this effect, as they follow expected forms, scripts and choreography, all of which can work to distract from, and dull one's attention to, the past, as one becomes fixed on the spectacle and preoccupied by the politicised protocol – which officials attended, which individual groups were invited (and who declined), in what order did they appear or speak, what was said (and not said), and so on.

Present sight – to see and to be seen – dominates as video rolls and cameras click, framing the memorial in media terms and technologies to produce a handful of representative images, visual public proof that government officials, vested interest groups and common citizens were not remiss in honouring and remembering the war dead. But images so taken, spanning columns of the next day's newspaper or, more commonly nowadays, light-speeding in virtual real-time across electronic news and social media networks, can, like mini digital memorials, aid and abet forgetfulness. American photographer Sally Mann knows this phenomenon:

> Photography would seem to preserve our past and make it invulnerable to the distortions of repeated memorial superimpositions, but I think that is

> a fallacy: photographs supplant and corrupt the past, all the while creating their own memories. As I held my childhood pictures in my hands, in the tenderness of my 'remembering', I also knew that with each photograph I was forgetting.
>
> *(Mann 2015: xiii)*

Mann refers to this tendency of photographs to eclipse the memory of all else around them as 'the treachery of photography'. There is an analogous 'treachery of memorials' as well, and it is against such treachery that much of the energies of local Okinawan efforts to activate – rather than simply remember – the wartime past have been relentlessly directed. In this sense, then, there is no war remembrance in Okinawa. What has gone on and will continue to go on there in the foreseeable future – so sharply divergent from mainland Japan and the source of much friction with it – goes beyond simple war remembrance as made manifest in monuments and recited in rituals. Rather, it is remembrance that forgets the memorial to make space for action.

International style, localised

Before discussing the forms and practices of Okinawa's 'activated war memory', the more traditional – and yet innovative – form of war memorial embodied in the Cornerstone of Peace warrants brief examination for the ways it signals local difference even as it reflects a style of war commemoration site that has become internationally popular. The innovations, tensions and contradictions that the Cornerstone of Peace embraces speak to the complicated and messy position that Okinawa occupied within the Japanese Empire until war's end and has occupied between Japan and the United States ever since. Annexed as the last Japanese prefecture in 1879 after the forced dissolution of the Ryukyu Kingdom (the seat of which was on Okinawa Island) and the severing of trading and diplomatic ties with Qing China, Okinawa existed as a domestic quasi-colony and Okinawans as second-class subjects compelled to assimilate to mainstream Japanese language and culture. In the wake of the Battle of Okinawa and end of war, Okinawa's second-class status continued in the form of a bargaining chip to end the occupation of mainland Japan in exchange for prolonged US military occupation of Okinawa, which resulted in the maintenance of military bases even after Japan regained sovereignty over Okinawa in 1972. It is this conflicted modern history with mainland Japan and between Tokyo and Washington, in addition to hosting the war's only major land battle in the Japanese home islands, that positions Okinawans' relationship to war and memory differently from that of the mainland. The most striking and most advertised feature of the Cornerstone of Peace – composed of 117 marble walls radiating at about a 120-degree angle from a Peace Flame overlooking the Pacific Ocean on a cliff at the southern tip of Okinawa Island – is the inclusion of the engraved names of combatants from both sides of the conflict and of local Okinawan non-combatants. Rarely does one see non-combatants included equally alongside combatants in war memorials, nor does one usually see enemy war dead recognised with one's own. This unprecedented effort to produce a transnational and ecumenical monument to serve as a 'global message of everlasting peace' garnered much praise and critical scrutiny (including my own) upon its unveiling. While promotion at the dedication ceremony on 23 June 1995 highlighted that the commemorated dead were included 'regardless of nationality' and that the monument transcended ethnicity, within the monument site itself there are clear classifications and implied hierarchies based on national and ethnic affiliations. The northern 'upper' half of the layout bisected by a main east–west pathway drawn from the Peace Flame to the central entry point comprises the war dead from Okinawa Prefecture (combatants and non-combatants) and has rest shelters and information booths along its perimeter; the southern 'lower' half, in contrast, contains mainland Japanese and foreign war dead and has only restrooms on its perimeter, privileging the locals and casting the mainland Japanese as quasi-foreign (as if in response to having been treated as a quasi-colony), located between the Okinawan and foreign sections (Figal 1997: 747–64). The foreign section is subdivided into American, British, Korean (South and North in separate areas) and Taiwanese, further reflecting anachronistic national and political divides as well as marking former Japanese colonies (Taiwan and Korea) from where labourers, soldiers, and '*ianfu*' ('comfort women') were conscripted and found themselves in Okinawa during the war.

The locals are additionally privileged by a wider qualification for inclusion: while the non-Okinawan dead are war casualties of operations related to the battle of Okinawa from the deployment of Japanese forces on Okinawa Island a year in advance of it on 22 March 1944 until a year after the official surrender on 7 September 1945 that marked the battle's final end, the commemorated Okinawans encompass, as the official guidelines state:

1. Okinawan people who died inside or outside the prefecture as a result of the 15 years' conflict beginning with the Manchurian Incident.
2. Okinawan people who died inside or outside the prefecture within the year following September 7th, 1945 (however the names of Okinawan people who died of the atomic bombs radiation in the following years are inscribed notwithstanding the period stated above).[1]

In other words, the memorial honours all Okinawan dead – combatants and non-combatants – of any war-related operation from the 1931 Japanese incursion in North-Eastern China until 7 September 1946, with no time limit at all on Okinawan radiation victims from the atomic bombings in Hiroshima and Nagasaki. The Cornerstone of Peace thus goes beyond being a Battle of Okinawa memorial and raises all kinds of thorny issues even as it strives to smooth over nationalistic divides and unequal treatment of the war dead.

Despite the good intentions and the progressive concept behind the design, the very idea of (theoretically) equal treatment of the war dead within this commemorative space drew some of the strongest criticism. Critics pointed out that this kind of communal commemoration renders war responsibility ambiguous. In effect, the culpability of those responsible for the killing is diluted by the innocence of those outside of it. The military personnel responsible for giving orders and the emperor in whose name they were carried out are not explicitly identified. There is no effort to distinguish truly innocent bystanders or degrees of willing participation among Okinawans. And the monument's much-lauded international inclusiveness, so it is argued, risks premature reconciliation without full reckoning of Japan's colonial domination and war of aggression. Still, even with these shortcomings, the Cornerstone of Peace signals a willingness – even boldness – among Okinawans to insist on a fuller accounting of the war than anything imaginable at a public memorial on mainland Japan and almost anywhere else in the world.

That it does not fully realise its latent historical critique of Japan's wartime actions – including oppression against colonial subjects and Okinawans themselves – as sharply as some commentators would like is probably a tactical decision to keep the rhetoric of this public site within reasonable bounds of public decorum so as not to offend any parties with vested interests. The primary groups who are, nonetheless, offended comprise strident anti-war activists, on the one hand, who view the Cornerstone of Peace as a sell-out, and staunch Japanese nationalists, on the other, who view it as an affront even in its muted form. Every year since its unveiling on Okinawa's Memorial Day (23 June) in 1995, the former have boycotted the official memorial ceremonies at the Cornerstone of Peace, which involve the kind of predictable orchestration and commonplace peace rhetoric from public officials, veterans and bereaved family members that tends to dull rather than sharpen critical historical awareness. To counter this tendency, anti-war activists stage an alternative free-form gathering at the 'original' battle of Okinawa memorial, Konpaku-no-tō, a few kilometres away. Here a hodgepodge of groups and individuals, young and old, make plain the connections between the war that is being commemorated and the one that is still being fought against the continued militarised state of the island that Article 3 of the San Francisco Peace Treaty (leaving the Ryukyu Islands under US trusteeship) and the US–Japan Security Treaty (ensuring US bases in Japan) have wrought. Gathering around the simple mass tomb of the unknown war dead while demonstrating with signs, songs and speeches against the continued presence of US military bases on the island drives home the relationship between war past and political present. They lay bare a chain of causation that holds the Japanese national government culpable for not only wartime devastation brought about by sacrificing Okinawa in a war of attrition to buy time to fortify the main islands for a final defence of the homeland, but also for the postwar sacrifice of Okinawa to prolonged US occupation (until 1972) and significant US military presence that continues to this day. This is only one concrete way that Okinawans keep war memory hot and active.

Activated war memory

Okinawa's history of invasion, defeat and occupation by American forces from 1945 to 1972 and the continued presence of US bases there have guaranteed a direct and active link between remembrance of the wartime past and activism in the postwar present. This immediate historical context and Okinawa's longer quasi-colonial history after being forcibly subsumed by Imperial Japan in 1879 have nurtured a degree of historical awareness coupled with political action that sets Okinawa dramatically apart from mainland Japan and is reflected in the forms of active and embodied war remembrance there. These include not only the counter-memorial gatherings seen at Konpaku-no-tō on 23 June, but also 'peace tours' – variously official and private – conducted in Okinawa all year round. Upon the unveiling of the Cornerstone of Peace in 1995, a newly established Peace Promotion Division of the prefectural government cultivated a cadre of 'peace guides' to give educational tours that encompassed battlefields, memorials and US bases. This initiative was supported by the governor, Ōta Masahide – an Imperial Blood and Iron Youth Corps survivor, battle of Okinawa scholar and anti-base activist – who also spearheaded the creation of the Cornerstone of Peace, the Peace Memorial Museum renovation and the building of the new Okinawa Prefectural Archives. Ōta's efforts on the war/peace education front were particularly galvanised by the fiftieth anniversary of the end of the Second World War and the high-profile case of a rape of a local 12-year-old girl by three Okinawa-based US Marines in September 1995. Nowhere else in Japan does one see such energy put into grassroots efforts to teach war history and its abiding impact in the present in direct and hands-on ways. The memorial function in such practices is secondary to the present action they aim to cultivate; it serves as a perpetual opening to action, not an annual closure to memory.

The 'peace tours' initiative served to counter a long history of southern battle site tours conducted by tour bus companies whose popular female guides had typically merely narrated tragic tales of wartime hardship and heroism wrapped in routine appeals to peace in the future. To their credit, the tour bus guides who were responsible for establishing and extending the practice of battle site tourism from the 1950s, have over the years enhanced the critical elements in their narratives in the wake of constructive criticism from activists and academics. Yet the increasingly high volume of tour groups, and the commercial incentive to deliver a pleasing product to paying customers, limits what can be done on the educational front. These limitations are manifest in the experience of the tens of thousands of school field trip groups that come annually from mainland Japan and are routinely processed *en masse* on treks that encompass beaches, cultural sites, shopping, war memorials and glimpses of US bases. The pace is quick and attention spans short among chattering student groups (whom I extensively shadowed and occasionally interacted with during my own fieldwork on several occasions between 1995 and 2009). The advent of high-quality smartphone cameras has also noticeably transformed the nature of the traditional commemorative group photo. Formal tour group photos for both general and student groups that are taken by professional photographers at the Peace Flame Plaza of the Cornerstone of Peace with the Peace Memorial Museum in the background strike one as a quaint throwback from another age, as for a few moments their staging stills the near-non-stop taking of selfies and small-group shots via smartphone. A double layer of Mann's 'treachery of photography' is happening here, the treachery made even more extreme by centring on the self as subject at the site rather than on the site itself and what it intends to signify.

Whatever the virtues of an alternative approach, the Okinawa Prefecture's Peace Promotion Division and the 'peace guides' associated with it lasted only as long as Ōta's term of office. After his election defeat in 1998, his conservative Liberal Democratic Party (LDP)-backed successor, Inamine Keiichi, initiated a retrenchment of many of Ōta's projects and dissolved the Peace Promotion Division, which was reorganised in diluted (and underfunded) form as the still existing Peace and Gender Equality Promotion Division. While annual official war memorial events centred on the Cornerstone of Peace remain intact whichever way political winds are blowing, the stability and the level of direct government support for peace education initiatives that have sprung from Okinawa's war history and experience are thus prone to ebb and flow. Yet there is a persistent grassroots commitment to keep war and peace issues alive and meaningful. The election in 2014 of the current anti-base governor, Onaga Takeshi, after sixteen years of governors compliant to Tokyo, manifests this commitment and underscores the particularly close and deep connection between war memory and everyday life and politics in Okinawa. That Onaga is a conservative life-long member of the LDP and is yet unwaveringly anti-base and has not flinched in the face of threats from Tokyo is testament to the depth and power of a historically informed anti-base position in trumping natural political alliances.

Regardless of the vagaries of official support, peace education and tourism initiatives among private, largely volunteer, groups have a long and steady postwar history that predates Ōta's initiatives and show no signs of abating. Not only were private groups and individuals responsible for battlefield-clearing (bone collecting and burial) and the establishment and maintenance of the first battle of Okinawa memorials in the late 1940s and 1950s; they have also been at the forefront of organising war-related tourism of the island that goes well beyond standard war memorial pilgrimages and general tourism that includes war sites. This 'activated war memory' in Okinawa encompasses independent groups and individuals who publish field guides to war remains, lead study tours, conduct excavations of battle sites and refugee caves, organise critical interventions on the base issue and more. As volunteer groups – albeit ones that might occasionally receive some government support, depending on the administration – they are not constrained by the need for political compromises. Independent 'peace tours' offer perhaps the most concrete example of countering the complacency that routine war memorial practices can induce. These devote as much energy to teaching about Okinawa's militarised present as they do to teaching about its wartime past; the two go hand-in-hand. Disillusionment among the majority of Okinawans with the terms of reversion to Japanese sovereignty in 1972 – specifically the continued maintenance of a high concentration of US military bases on the island – has cemented the connection between war remembrance and present-day anti-base action. While memorialisation of the war elsewhere in Japan and across the globe almost invariably comes with anodyne appeals for peace, such appeals in Okinawa – despite risking hollowness through repetition – are grounded in a concrete everyday reality of an unwanted postwar militarisation of the island that is the direct result of the war that produced the dead being memorialised.

Apart from peace tours independent of formal institutions, this situation is underscored in the 'peace study tours', together with supporting materials, organised by public schools and volunteer citizens' groups in Okinawa. Serious efforts here coalesced in the 1980s from grassroots initiatives to educate Okinawan schoolchildren about the war and its legacies in a more systematic way. Living amid those legacies, students had ample opportunities for active hands-on fieldwork, which is another hallmark of Okinawan relations with the wartime past. Whether in the form of oral interviews with surviving Himeyuri women or street surveys of the base town of Kōza bordering Kadena air base, the guide books published in the early 1980s by the Okinawa High School Teachers' Union Educational and Cultural Materials Centre focused on active engagement that brought past and present together. Haebaru High School in particular became a centre for such fieldwork activities when a teacher there began organising students to conduct door-to-door surveys to compile statistics about wartime households. Such examples spread to other communities throughout Okinawa and eventually served as the foundation for the Haebaru Culture Centre, which has since greatly expanded into a significant museum, archive and resource centre for wartime experience and local history in general. It is also the institution that has overseen the excavation of the nearby Haebaru Army Field Hospital Cave, which was officially designated an 'Important Cultural Property' by the Japanese Agency for Cultural Affairs in 1990, the first battle site in Japan to receive this distinction. The Haebaru Culture Centre now conducts guided tours through the part of the cave that was opened to the public with much fanfare on 17 June 2007, joining other caves on the island which have become highlights of 'peace study tours' (Figal 2012: 80–2).

It is significant that such caves have become key sites of active engagement with war memory in Okinawa, since this symbolises the need to dig below the surface monuments to get at messier and dirtier truths beneath. Given the Japanese command's defensive strategy of hunkering down in the dozens and dozens of natural caves that riddle Okinawa Island, the subterranean focus is in one sense unsurprising. What is remarkable is the way in which refugee caves have risen to become the fulcrum for critique of Japan's conduct of the battle, of its portrayal in history textbooks and of the continuing presence of US bases in Okinawa. Caves where both combatants and non-combatants sought shelter created volatile situations in which civilians found themselves subjected not only to enemy grenades and flamethrowers, but also to threats and physical violence at the hands of Japanese military personnel – most infamously in the cases of compulsory group suicides that historians and activists have documented and popularised as the *cause célèbre* of the battle of Okinawa.

What had been buried in silence for years among the bereaved saw the full light of day – most notably in research and publications by grocery store owner and political activist Chibana Shoichi concerning the eighty-four civilians who, just after the American invasion of Okinawa in April 1945, killed themselves in Chibichiri cave on the coast near his hometown of Yomitan. Chibana explicitly connected such wartime oppression of civilian refugees with present-day US–Japan agreements for the maintenance of US bases in Okinawa and with longstanding second-class treatment of Okinawans within Japan. Such grievances famously climaxed when he burned the *de facto* Japanese national flag, the Hinomaru, at the Okinawa National Athletic Meet held in Yomitan on 26 October 1987 and was put on trial for trespassing, damaging property and obstructing business. In his testimony, Chibana turned the trial into a public indictment of Japanese violence against Okinawans during the war and the postwar militarisation of Okinawa Island:

> The cause of my action of pulling down the 'Hinomaru' and burning it is that I had learned of the tragic experience and misery suffered in Okinawa during World War II, and I am concerned with the current leanings towards war.
> *(Chibana 1992: 125)*

The notoriety that Chibana attracted through his flag-burning and anti-base activism raised local, national and international public awareness of Japanese conduct toward the local population during the battle of Okinawa and dovetailed with other private efforts to document civilian war experience, excavate refugee caves, organise peace education tours and press for fuller historical accounts in textbooks, memorial sites and museums.

Chibana developed guided tours of Chibichiri cave, and tours of other refugee caves also grew in numbers and sophistication. The Haebaru Army Field Hospital Cave mentioned above offers one example of how years of local efforts led to the clearance of a rough and dangerous site and its transformation into an alternative tourist destination managed by the nearby Haebaru Culture Centre. The same kind of transformation, but on a larger scale, occurred at Itokazu cave, also known locally as Abuchiragama, about eight kilometres south of Haebaru, in the thick of the former battleground area. This was first featured as an alternative tourist destination alongside other caves and memorial sites in 1983 in the first of many editions of *The Okinawa not on Tourism Routes: Battle Sites, Bases, Industry, Culture* (*Kankō kōsu de nai Okinawa: senseki, kichi, sangyō, bunka*). This book series, edited by a group of eight local historians and journalists identified with progressive politics against the US–Japan security arrangement in Okinawa, was the first and most prominent to introduce the 'underside' of Okinawa's war history and its impact on the present. As it relates in text and figures, the 80-metre-long natural cave was originally conceived as an army encampment but was converted into a hospital annexe a month into the battle of Okinawa and served as a refugee cave, complete with medical rooms, food storage, pit stoves, a well and gear lockers (Arasaki *et al.* 1998: 85–90). Nearly a thousand wounded soldiers and refugees inhabited the cave. The remains of a Korean 'comfort woman' were also discovered inside upon excavation. Once the cave was cleared of debris and paths were marked, occasional informal tours began, led by peace guides and schoolteachers. Explorations by unguided individuals (such as myself) also took place. Until the early 2000s the cave existed unattended and open to the public. It was then gradually improved with the installation of handrails along paths and central lighting for large groups, although flashlights and headlamps are the norm for this kind of battlefield spelunking. To simulate and reflect upon the experience of wartime refugees, it was general practice on guided tours of school groups to cut all the lights at one point and remain in pitch black darkness for a few minutes. The experience, I can attest, was unsettling, especially given the accompanying sounds of dripping water and chirping bats, not to mention the possible presence of snakes in the cave.

On my last visit to Abuchiragama in November 2009, the further transformation of the site was apparent as I encountered a wholly different apparatus for entry into the cave. The frequency and volume of visitors had reached such a level that out of concerns for safety and maintenance visitors, whether in groups or individually, were now required to rent helmets and flashlights at the nearby community centre which oversaw traffic into the cave and served as a gathering point for group tours. The entrance to the cave itself, a short walk away, was formerly an unmarked opening down uneven stone steps obscured on the edge of a sugar cane field; now, it was clearly signposted and gated with an attendant. Along with the Haebaru Army Field Hospital Cave, Abuchiragama had been transformed into a fully fledged off-the-beaten-path tourist destination designed to engage war memory viscerally and actively.

As school field trips and 'peace study tours' that include these sites are physically (in paths taken) and discursively (in guides written and read) linked to the Cornerstone of Peace, the Himeyuri Peace Museum, the Okinawa Prefectural Peace Memorial Museum and active US military bases, war remembrance as such transforms into something that is very concretely connected to the lived present. It serves as catalyst to education about the origins and structures of contemporary everyday life on Okinawa as pawn within the US–Japan Security Treaty, which then can and does lead to direct political action for many who participate in this kind of tourism on the island. The three-decade-old series of editions of *The Okinawa not on Tourism Routes* and field guides put out by the Okinawa Peace Education and Research Association since the 1980s provide the historical contexts, critical commentary, maps, routes and photos to cement the connections between past and present, always with a sense of urgency for action. The editions of *The Okinawa not on Tourism Routes* since the mid-2000s have also notably added a section on the ongoing controversy over moving the functions of Marine Corps Air Station Futenma from the densely populated town of Ginowan to the less populated site of Henoko in the north, where locals have objected to the proposed development. As recently as 21 September 2015, Okinawa governor Takeshi Onaga enunciated the connection between the wartime past and the political present in an address to the United Nations Human Rights Council, pleading for help in blocking the base construction in Henoko and citing the persistent neglect by the governments of Japan and the United States of local self-determination in Okinawa: 'After World

War II, the US military took our land by force and constructed military bases in Okinawa. We have never provided our land willingly' (Wanklyn 2015). In such articulations, American bases themselves become war memorials insofar as they perpetually invoke Okinawa's war history by their genealogy and their physical presence. The long and very active history of peace education aiming to activate rather than merely enshrine war memory sharply distinguishes Okinawa's relationship to the wartime past from that of mainland Japan.

The battle with Okinawa tourism

The increase in war-related educational and political activities from the mid-1980s also coincided with a nascent 'Okinawa boom' that exploded after the 1987 Resort Law went into effect. This pro-development legislation encouraged the growth of vacation resorts throughout Japan by offering developers tax breaks and fast-track approval of construction permits. The subsequent acceleration of leisure tourism in Okinawa and enhanced prominence of Okinawa in popular media (including music, television dramas, movies and news documentaries) throughout the 1990s and into the twenty-first century paralleled and complicated the active forms of war-related tourism, local education and political critique of US bases happening during the same time. The intensifying touristification of Okinawa – in particular, the active branding of the Ryukyu Islands as tropical resort paradise – presented another challenge for the active memorialising of war for present politics. While vacationing on smaller outlying islands in the Ryukyu chain might allow the effective bypassing of war legacies, there is no hiding reminders of war on the main Okinawa Island where war memorials and American bases are thickly concentrated and where US military air space allowances – aerial easements, if you will – force abnormal flight paths for commercial air traffic in and out of Naha International Airport. And, of course, daily US Marine Corps and Air Force air traffic generates high levels of noise pollution and potential for accidents. It is not unusual to be lost in reveries on an Okinawa Island beach or in the embrace of a tropical garden only to be returned to the realities of nearby bases by the roar of an F-15 taking off or landing at Kadena.

One can, however, with proper planning and a little luck, conduct oneself as if moving through a parallel 'tropical resort world' divorced from Okinawa's war experience and militarised present. Mainstream leisure tourism promotion, tour routes, landscaping and resort locations do their best to produce this result, containing if not erasing war history and the military presence. The key iconic war tourism sites – such as the Cornerstone of Peace or the Himeyuri Peace Museum – are all located conveniently in the southern half of the island, away from the airport, resorts, shopping districts, tropical parks and cultural attractions in the centre and north, which makes it possible to marginalise them. (The one notable exception here is the Okinawa World cultural theme park, centred on its main attraction of Gyokusendo, an impressive 5,000-metre long cave full of stalagmites and stalactites. It is not far from Abuchirigama, the war refugee cave that has become a main attraction of war/peace tourism. The physical proximity of these two emotionally distant sites is ironic.) Tour packages and guidebooks often relegate war tourism sites to the status of optional extras. Amazingly, all of the suggested itineraries on the current (as of October 2015) Okinawa Convention and Visitors Bureau website – even the one focused on the southern half of the island – lack any mention of *any* war memorial site. One must dig deep through the 'Okinawa Database' section of the website to find any sign of war-related sites, and those five listed are predictable: the Japanese Navy Underground Headquarters, Okinawa Prefectural Peace Memorial Museum, the Cornerstone of Peace, the Okinawa Peace Memorial Hall, and the Himeyuri Peace Museum.[2] It is against this kind of active suppression of war history by public and private promoters of leisure tourism that active war memory in Okinawa also battles.

In the long run of tourism development in postwar Okinawa, the gradual backgrounding of the war-related sightseeing that defined early tourism to the island unsurprisingly parallels growing temporal distance from the war. Economic imperatives have guided decisions in the prefecture to aspire to becoming 'Japan's Hawai'i', a 'South Seas Island Paradise' and 'Japan's Tourism Prefecture' for leisure-seeking visitors, a goal that is difficult to reconcile with the conspicuous reminders of war throughout the island. This separation of war memorial tourism from leisure tourism received its first big catalyst from the hosting of Marine Expo '75, three years after Okinawa's political reversion to Japan after being under American control for twenty-seven years. The Japanese government and mainland private investors provided virtually the entire financial outlay for the construction of venues, accommodation and supporting infrastructure, with the promise of raising Okinawan standard of living to mainland levels. War history and legacies did not feature in the official plan led by these mainland Japanese. 'Blue Sea Okinawa' was the official theme of Marine Expo '75, which was sited along the west coast in the far north of the island in order to realise the planning committee's goal to 'put the focus of the place on the sea as much as possible, to have the visitor subjectively experience the sea' (Tada 2004: 69–70). Marine Expo '75 was largely successful in promoting and planting in the minds of mainland Japanese visitors the notion of 'Blue Sea Okinawa' and laid the foundation for the serious cultivation of Okinawa as a tropical destination, an aim that had existed before reversion but realisation of which had been frustrated by lack of capital and anxieties over the lingering scars of war and the US military presence. By the time the Resort Law was in place twelve years later, however, Okinawa was primed and ready for the construction of high-end resorts that took advantage of the tropical trope and obviously clashed with ongoing local efforts to keep war memory not only alive but 'activated'.

And yet the 'activated war memory' outlined above saw its first major post-reversion catalyst coinciding with Marine Expo '75, when the original Okinawa Prefectural Peace Memorial Museum opened in the Peace Park at the southern tip of the island where the final fighting in the battle had taken place. The opening of this museum was consciously planned to take advantage of the 1,500,000 visitors who would come to the Expo that year, and it did see strong attendance during its inaugural year before this dropped off in the immediately subsequent ones. What this revealed was that it would not suffice simply to build sites for war remembrance and education; strong grassroots efforts to build a counter-narrative of Okinawan postwar development – one that highlighted the politics of the postwar settlement – were also vital. The Peace Memorial Museum served as a physical anchor for this counter-narrative with its frank and often grisly depictions of local suffering during the battle of Okinawa and Japanese violence against Okinawan civilians. Although many Okinawans were actively complicit in Japan's war effort and a minority have benefited economically from postwar US bases, a narrative of Okinawa as 'sacrificial pawn' between Japan and the United States was not difficult to produce given Japanese treatment of Okinawans as second-class citizens throughout the modern period, from annexation in 1879, through the Second World War, Okinawa's prolonged occupation, and a reversion agreement that allowed the continued stationing of high numbers of US military personnel. Rather than rest on a form of simple victimhood, however, accounts of Okinawa's modern tragedies at the hands of more powerful states have served as impetus for grassroots activities that work to agitate if not change the *status quo* by vigilantly maintaining the connections between past and present. That has been the thrust of locally organised alternative 'off-the-beaten-path' tourism motivated to set the historical record straight and tie it into present day political action. The rapid rise of leisure tourism since the late 1980s has complicated this activity because the market forces driving it have no interest in promoting anything war-related as part of the Okinawa brand, with the dubious exception of merchandising US Army-Navy surplus clothing and accessories as part of local chic.

The ambivalent relationship between local culture and the foreign military presence (which, in my opinion, includes those Japanese Self-Defense Force personnel sharing base space and conducting joint exercises with the US military) parallels tourism promoters' ambivalent relationship with Okinawa's war history and war memory. True, the US military – its personnel and its gear – has been an object of mainland Japanese tourist curiosity since the 1950s, effectively becoming an unacknowledged tourist attraction, while underground Japanese guidebooks to bases and adjacent base town entertainment districts (meaning, bars and brothels) have been in circulation for years. Strong annual attendance by locals and tourists at Kadena air base's mid-summer open base weekend festival also testifies to the bases' status as spectacle sites. (These open base events were suspended for several years post-9/11 before being fully re-established in 2007.) Despite their appeal as exotic spectacle, however, military equipment, personnel and the bases that house them could never be openly promoted because of the political sensitivity of the continued US presence. Efforts, for example, to include brief rides on bases during guided bus tours had to overcome resistance and red tape, and when finally put in place they were abruptly abandoned in the wake of 9/11. Past invitations to the US Air Force marching band to participate in annual parades in downtown Naha met with political protests from Okinawan activists and went nowhere. And, similarly to the case of war-related sites, US bases are mentioned nowhere on the Okinawa

Convention and Visitors Bureau website and are scarcely mentioned in mainstream tour guides. Typically, the nearest thing to a mention will be a reference to the shopping area in Chatan, sandwiched between Kadena air base and Camp Foster, which caters to American military personnel and their families and is themed as an 'American Village' for locals and tourists.

The efforts of leisure tourism to camouflage the war and its legacies have arguably served to energise – not to erase – the practices of 'activated war memory' in Okinawa as I have tried to define and briefly describe them here in this chapter. The contemporary result is the creation of two very different public media images and popular understandings of Okinawa: one characterised by hibiscus blossoms, tropical fish, well-groomed resorts, water sports and a distinct eco-healthy Okinawa product brand; and one characterised by tales of wartime tragedy, prominent war remembrance rituals, war history archives and museums, active peace education tours and cutting-edge battlefield archaeology – all of which become implicitly and explicitly tied to current anti-base protests. Within the second image, there exists too an uneasy relationship between official war remembrance practices, with their more polished and packaged representations and routine state rituals, and the 'activated war memory' of grassroots groups composed of a mix of educators, students, activists and common citizens who emphasise the causal connections between war history and present politics. It is the latter that dramatically distinguishes war remembrance in Okinawa from that of mainland Japan, even that which is seen annually in August at Hiroshima and Nagasaki where people are passionately activated for anti-nuclear and anti-war causes, but in a generalised and abstract way that lacks the palpable political immediacy and urgency that one sees and feels in Okinawa's acts of war remembrance. There, it is war remembrance that goes beyond an act of memorialisation that risks falling into forgetfulness once it is ritually completed; indeed, it goes beyond war remembrance itself as the war past which it remembers manifests itself daily in the militarised space the war has wrought and against which many Okinawans ceaselessly struggle as a part of everyday life.

Notes

Unless otherwise indicated, all translations from Japanese are my own.

1 See the website of the Okinawa Prefecture, 'The Cornerstone of Peace, Names to be Inscribed', at www.pref.okinawa.jp/site/kodomo/heiwadanjo/heiwa/7797.html.
2 See the Okinawa Convention and Visitors Bureau website, *Be. Okinawa*, at http://en.okinawastory.jp/itineraries/ and http://en.okinawastory.jp/facilities/see/se-history/ respectively.

References

Arasaki, M., Nakasone M., Maezato T., Nakaoji K., Ōshiro M., Yamakado K., Kinjō A., *et al.* 1998. *Kankō kōsu de nai Okinawa: senseki, kichi, sangyō, bunka.* Tokyo: Kōbunken.

Chibana, S. 1992. *Burning the Rising Sun: From Yomitan Village, Okinawa: Islands of U.S. Bases.* Kyoto: South Wind.

Figal, G. 1997. 'Historical Sense and Commemorative Sensibility at Okinawa's Cornerstone of Peace'. *Positions: East Asia Cultures Critique*, 5, 3: 745–78.

Figal, G. 2012. *Beachheads: War, Peace, and Tourism in Postwar Okinawa*. Lanham, MD: Rowman and Littlefield.

Levinson, N. S. 1998. *Written in Stone: Public Monuments in Changing Societies*. Durham, NC: Duke University Press.

Mann, S. 2015. *Hold Still: A Memoir with Photographs*. New York, NY: Little, Brown.

Tada, O. 2004. *Okinawa imēji no tanjō*. Tokyo: Tōyō keizai shuppansha.

Wanklyn, A. 2015. 'Onaga Takes Base Argument to U.N. Human Rights Panel'. *The Japan Times*. 22 September. www.japantimes.co.jp/news/2015/09/22/national/politics-diplomacy/onaga-takes-base-argument-u-n-human-rights-panel/.

8

THE YOKOHAMA WAR CEMETERY, JAPAN

Imperial, national and local remembrance

Joan Beaumont

The burial grounds of the dead of the First and Second World Wars have played a central role in the 'memory boom' of recent decades. These *lieux de mémoire*, to use Pierre Nora's now classic term, provide the stage on which politicians perform 'memorial diplomacy': that is, those 'carefully choreographed public ceremonies [held] on the anniversaries of historic occasions at selected sites of memory … typically on the margins of international summits or intergovernmental forums' (Graves 2014: 170). War cemeteries also provide the focal point of the countless 'pilgrimages' now undertaken by veterans, families and battlefield tourists. Here, individuals, engaged in memory making at the sub-national level, are able to position their own family history within 'wider, at times universal, narratives of war' (Winter 2006: 40).

This capacity of cemeteries to allow the memory of war to be individualised owes much to the vision of the Imperial (from 1960, Commonwealth) War Graves Commission (IWGC/ CWGC). In the cemeteries it created, each 'British' soldier of the two world wars was honoured, individually if possible, with his own headstone listing his name, age and a personal message from his family. Where a soldier's remains were unidentifiable, his name was listed on vast memorials to the missing, the most famous of which is the Menin Gate at Ypres. These honour rolls and individual tombstones have allowed later generations of visitors to engage with the specificity of death in a way that mass graves do not permit. Yet, even though the aesthetics of CWGC cemeteries are universally affecting, not all have become 'active' sites of memory, in the sense of attracting significant and ongoing commemorative activity by governments and other collectives. Today's practices of remembrance suggest – to paraphrase George Orwell – that while all cemeteries are equal, some are 'more equal than others'. The mnemonic prominence of a particular cemetery seems to be contingent upon a number of variables: its location and accessibility; its association with memories of significance in national narratives of war; and its capacity to engage multiple agents of memory making, ranging from national governments to individuals. Where these variables are absent, a cemetery can slip to a lower place in the hierarchy of sites of war memory. This chapter examines one such site, the Yokohama War Cemetery in Japan. Created after the Second World War according to the impeccable IWGC template, for at least one group of national stakeholders, the Australians, this failed to become a dynamic site of memory in the decades that followed.

The imperial vision of burial

The Yokohama War Cemetery came into being because the bodies of the British Empire and Dominion Second World War dead were buried overseas rather than being repatriated when the war ended. This practice was a continuation of the policy developed by the IWGC after the First World War when, after considerable public debate, the vision of the initial IWGC director, Fabian Ware, prevailed over those who advocated the repatriation of bodies: the dead of 1914–18 were interred in garden-like cemeteries, located close to the battlefields or the hospitals in which they had died (Longworth 2003; Summers 2007).

When the British Empire again went to war in 1939, the question arose as to whether this practice would be continued. The IWGC, on which were represented the British government, the Dominions and India, turned its attention to this question as soon as the war began.[1] Its concern at this stage was to prohibit the removal and transport of bodies while hostilities were continuing; but as the war neared its end, the question arose as to whether to allow the repatriation of bodies. By September 1945 the IWGC had received some 2,000 requests for repatriation from families, the bulk of them from within the United Kingdom but some from Australia and New Zealand.[2] The Australian government also received similar requests. On 9 June 1945, for example, the caretaker of the local cemetery in the country town of Waikerie, South Australia, wrote to the acting prime minister Frank Forde, saying:

> There will be many sad hearts when the war is over, & the soldiers return home, for those whose loved ones will not return, & if their bodies could be brought back it might help to comfort them somewhat. … There have been about 30 boys from Waikerie killed in this war, & I would consider it a sacred duty to be able to attend to their graves.[3]

Questions were also asked in the federal parliament as to whether the Australian government would follow the United States' example and repatriate bodies.[4]

Such requests gained no traction with Ware, who was still holding the position of vice chairman of the IWGC. With his lifetime achievement seemingly under challenge, he claimed that there were 'overwhelming' reasons against any change in established practice. As he said to an IWGC meeting on 17 May 1945:

> For the Governments of the Empire to undertake to repatriate all our dead (or even all those whose relatives desired it) would be a task of even greater magnitude than it would have been in 1918; for, though the numbers involved are happily fewer, the graves are far more widely scattered and shipping facilities practically non-existent. To allow private repatriation by a few individuals (of necessity only those who could afford the cost) would be contrary to that equality of treatment which is the underlying principle of the Commission's work and has appealed so strongly to the deepest sentiments of our peoples.[5]

Ware's position was supported other members of the Commission. It was, after all, 'a Commonwealth organisation in the very fullest sense',[6] and, in the case of Australia, its representative was a long-time advocate of imperial unity, the high commissioner and former prime minister, Stanley Bruce. Perhaps more surprisingly, the Dominion governments, to whom the matter was referred in early June 1945, expressed no objection to the perpetuation of the First World War policy.[7] The *modus operandi* of the IWGC seems to have been to use the consent of one government to pressure others.[8] But it seems also that the Australian authorities accepted the emotional and pragmatic logic of the IWGC argument.[9] As the secretary of the department of the army, F. R. Sinclair, put it: even though his own son was buried 'in a lonely part of Kenya in Africa', he was satisfied that the grave would be tended by the IWGC. Any change of the established policy in favour of repatriation would bring 'extreme pressure … in practically every instance, particularly on the part of mothers and wives of deceased members, and thus old wounds would be re-opened'.[10]

Hence by mid-1945 the governments of the IWGC had reached consensus against repatriation of bodies. Initially this did not take into account the sensitive issue of graves in enemy countries but the end of the war against Japan in August 1945 soon put this on the agenda. Bruce now argued – with some prescience – that public opinion in Australia would be 'strongly against leaving bodies in Japan, though no doubt it was a feeling that might die down later'. The New Zealand government, meanwhile, expressed a preference for its soldiers' remains to be exhumed and reinterred in British- or Allied-controlled territory. However, after some extended discussion it was decided that the remains of Empire and Dominion dead who had been buried or cremated in Japan should be treated no differently from those elsewhere. They should be concentrated in one suitable cemetery in Japan.[11]

The site ultimately chosen was a pre-war children's park in the Hodogaya-ku district of Yokohama. This was where the greatest number of burials of Allied prisoners had occurred during the war, and the land was able to be requisitioned during the Allied occupation of Japan. There was no guarantee, at this stage, that this land would be granted 'in perpetuity', as were the First World War cemeteries in Europe and the former Ottoman Empire, but it was assumed that such tenure would be bestowed in the peace treaty with Japan – just as Articles 128 and 129 of the Treaty of Lausanne had granted in perpetuity the land on which the graves and memorials of Allied personnel were situated in Turkey.[12]

Burying the Australian dead in Japan

As the only IWGC cemetery in Japan, Yokohama would become a large and transnational war cemetery. Divided into a number of national sections, about two-thirds of its 1,517 burials were British. Most of the remainder were from Australia, Canada, New Zealand and pre-independence India. The dead were largely prisoners of war, many of whom had been transported to work in Japan from South-East and East Asia where they had been captured.

However, a significant proportion of the 278 Australians had not died in Japan, but on Hainan Island. These men had been part of Gull Force, a battalion-sized unit of 1,131 men, most of whom were captured defending the island of Ambon in the Netherlands East Indies in January-February 1942. Initially the prisoners were all interned on Ambon but in October 1942 some 263 of them had been taken to Hainan Island, where over the next three years some eighty-two died of malnutrition and other causes (Beaumont 1988: 200). In early 1946 most of these dead (some were missing) were exhumed by an Australian war graves unit and shipped to Hong Kong, where they were reburied between 17 March and 2 April 1946.[13] As it happened, there were significant problems with the development of war graves on Hong Kong, in the form of competition for scarce land, steep terrain that required terracing and unanticipated construction difficulties.[14] Hence, military authorities in Melbourne decided on 4 April 1946 to exhume the bodies of Gull Force once more and rebury them in Yokohama, a cemetery within the jurisdiction of the newly created Anzac Agency of the IWGC. This transfer took place in mid-1946.[15]

Three months later the matter hit the Australian press. On 28 September the Melbourne *Argus* published a letter from the former commanding officer of Gull Force, Lieutenant-Colonel W. R. J. (Jack) Scott. In this he condemned as 'an incredible insult' the burial in Japan of men who had died as a result of 'incredible and fiendish brutality and bestiality, inhuman conduct and deliberate murder' by Japanese officers, medical officers and other ranks. The decision to move the remains to Hong Kong was understandable, given the problems of access and upkeep on Hainan but, Scott said, 'No words of mine can describe the horror I feel' at the proposed transfer to Japan:

> To move these graves deliberately to Japan itself, to ask relatives to visit Japan and all that that country conjures up, to visit the grave of a loved one in such surroundings so far removed from peace and quiet thought, must not be allowed. ... The burial ground of Australian soldiers murdered by Japanese, by whatever means, should be found and cared for in any other place in the world, but not Japan.[16]

Scott's motives can only be guessed at. He had been a deeply unpopular leader of the Australian prisoners on Hainan, losing their respect and loyalty by withdrawing into himself and imposing a draconian disciplinary regime which involved men being handed over to the Japanese for punishment for even minor offences within the camp (Beaumont 1988: 179–85). Scott may also have been trying to rebuild his reputation because, as a senior staff officer at the time of Gull Force's despatch to Ambon, he had been deeply implicated in its reckless deployment. In his letter to the *Argus* Scott took pains to claim that Gull Force was not 'ill-fated', but had been given 'the honour of being selected to attempt the delay of the enemy, and in doing so increase the possibility of our homes and people being saved from a Japanese invasion'.

Whatever Scott's motives, his comments resonated with the families of Gull Force, who took to lobbying their members of parliament.[17] One W. S. Farrell wrote on behalf of his sister-in-law:

> I am quite sure that many other wives and mothers feel that this action is an insult to the memories of their dear ones. On looking at the map of the Pacific it is not such a great distance from Hainan to Australia where they should have been interred.[18]

The wider ex-prisoner of war community also spoke out against the Yokohama burials. Lieutenant-Colonel Edward 'Weary' Dunlop, a surgeon on the Thai–Burma railway and now president of the Australian Prisoners of War Relatives' Association, wrote to Prime Minister Chifley on 11 October 1946:

> We do not regard the Japanese as an honourable foe, and the action contemplated … would be most distasteful to the feelings of relatives and friends, and, I venture to submit to the majority of Australians generally. … the distance from Australia to Japan is so great as to make it impossible for many relatives to ever visit the graves of their men.[19]

A few weeks later the Returned Sailors', Soldiers' & Airmen's Imperial League of Australia (later the Returned and Services League) took up the cause, advising the minister for the army that

> After the treatment received from a vile enemy while in their hands, we feel it is repugnant to think that their last resting place should be in Japan, particularly when it needs two movements over long distances to achieve it. These brave boys did their best for Australia, and as a result gave their lives, and we feel Australia should do its best for them.

If bodies did need to moved, then they should be moved 'to the soil for which they fought and died, i.e. Australia, or taken and placed with their pals at Ambon where they were captured'.[20]

These protests seem to have caught the Australian authorities by surprise. Their initial response was to stress the functional reasons for transferring the remains to Yokohama: namely, that it was IWGC policy to concentrate graves in such a way as to make them accessible to relatives and to provide 'economy in beautification and maintenance'; that the Australian War Graves Service had responsibility for Yokohama and not for the Hong Kong burial site; and that it was desirable that all remains of Australians in the area should 'rest together'.[21] The government also argued that it was a relatively common practice for Australian dead to be buried in enemy territory – as indeed it was. Over 1,600 Australians killed in the Second World War would ultimately be buried or commemorated in the former enemy countries, including nearly 1,400 in Germany. Even more (nearly 2,300) had been buried or commemorated in Turkey after the First World War.[22]

However, this missed the point. For many Australians, Japan was not just any enemy. It was – to quote the ex-prisoners – a dishonourable foe, 'inhuman', 'fiendish' and 'vile'. There was good cause for this hatred. As a captor, the Japanese had violated much of the 1929 Geneva Convention Relative to the Treatment of Prisoners of War. Nearly 36 per cent of Australian prisoners of the Japanese had died.[23] In the case of Gull Force, the death toll had been around 31 per cent of the men transferred to Hainan in October 1942, and a staggering 77 per cent of the prisoners left on Ambon for the duration of the war (Beaumont 1988: 4). Moreover, more than 200 of the Australians lost on Ambon had been callously executed by the Japanese, being bayoneted and beheaded shortly after capture in February 1942.

That said, the visceral dislike of the Japanese also owed much to the racism of 'White Australia'. Since the Russo-Japanese war of 1904–05, Australians had entertained almost hysterical fears of invasion by the Japanese, a people who were depicted in popular culture as an anthropoid 'other' (Tanner 1980; Walker 1999). When this threat finally materialised in 1941, Australian propaganda depicted the Japanese as 'little yellow stinkers'; or, to quote the wartime commander-in-chief General Thomas Blamey, 'a subhuman beast', 'a cross between a human and an ape'. Some Australians found this discourse excessive, but reports from the battle front in Papua and New Guinea spoke of Japanese suicidal charges, desecration of the bodies of Australian dead and – the ultimate taboo – cannibalism (Johnston 2000: 85–7, 89–102). We now know that at least some of this savagery was mutual. In the 'war without mercy' in the Pacific (Dower 1986), Australian soldiers too showed a disdain for Japanese bodies. But at the time the Australian press represented the Japanese as 'the guilty', and failed to differentiate between the Japanese government and military and the ordinary Japanese soldier or civilian (Grant 2014: 81–2, 169).

With such a cultural chasm, it was almost inevitable that Japan would be seen as a 'repugnant' place for the burial of Australian war dead. Burial sites are political and strategic spaces (Lefebvre 1977: 341). Intimately connected with grief, they are 'emotionally highly-charged site[s], not only for the families concerned, but also at times for the ethnic and cultural group concerned' (Christopher 1995: 43). In particular, when cemeteries house those who died defending the nation, they are 'transformed into sacred landscapes' (Tan and Yeoh 2002: 1). Burial in the culturally alien Japan, then, entailed the transgression of a powerful norm and generated a sense of unease about the improper burial of war dead. As Heonik Kwon has argued in relationship to Vietnam, where many casualties of the 'American war' are interred far from the dead person's familial location: 'it is only when the deceased's body is properly entombed in the socially recognized domain … that the dead is understood to be genuinely dead, that is, settled in the other world'(Kwon 2008: 58).

So too in the First World War, Australians had had 'an abiding anxiety' about leaving the graves of their dead at the culturally alien Gallipoli. While French and Belgian territory was seen as 'friendly Christian soil', Turkey was viewed as a 'heathen, hostile country'. Only the symbolic taming of the Gallipoli landscape by IWGC cemeteries, replete with Australian flora and, more importantly, the construction in the inter-war years of a new identity for the Turk, as an honourable foe, had reassured Australians that their dead were, to quote Kemal Atatürk's' famous words of 1934, 'lying in the soil of a friendly country' (Ziino 2007: 59–81).

While the Australian military authorities had not initially grasped the political sensitivities involved in the Yokohama burials, by October 1946 they had escalated the matter to Cabinet for consideration. The minister for the army, Francis Forde, conceded that the transfer of Australian dead from Hainan to Yokohama was 'naturally repugnant to Australian national feeling … [and] offensive to the relatives and next of kin of the servicemen concerned'. He recommended that the remains should be returned to Hong Kong, even though this would raise the problematic issue of what to do with the ashes of Australian prisoners who had died while in camps in Japan and whose remains had been mixed with those of the dead of other nationalities.[24] However, the Cabinet decided on 5 November to leave the dead of Gull Force in Yokohama.[25] It acknowledged that the incident was most regrettable, but concluded it was not in the best interests of the prisoners' relatives that the remains of 'these unfortunate men' be further disturbed. Instead, they should remain in Yokohama sharing this space with the Australian dead of the British Commonwealth Occupation Force who were being interred in a nearby 'post-war' cemetery.[26]

It is a testament to how much the politics of memory have changed in recent decades that this ended the public debate in 1946. No such decision would be acceptable today. Not only is there an acute sensitivity on the part of Australian governments to public sentiment about the treatment of the war dead, but the option of burying war dead overseas has been excluded since the Vietnam War when policy shifted in favour of repatriation. In 1946, however, the Australian press did not have the interest which it has today in being a populist custodian of war commemoration. Only a few newspapers reported, without editorial comment, the Cabinet decision to leave the remains in Yokohama.[27] The families of Gull Force meanwhile seem to have lacked the sense of agency which Australians exhibit today when they demand of government that newly discovered remains from earlier wars be reinterred with great ceremony (for Fromelles, see Lindsay 2008: for Vietnam, see Ekins 2003). As Pat Jalland has suggested, the Second World War generation had inherited from the Great War the belief that mass bereavement rendered insignificant the grief of individual parents: 'What was the sorrow of any one parent among the vast suffering of so many? … [T]he more damaging consequence of this line of thought was the assumption that the individual must be strong and suffer in silence' (Jalland 2006: 144–5). This, too, was a generation which seemed ambiguous about commemoration. In contrast to the First World War, when war memorials had sprung up across Australia, 20 per cent of Australians, when polled in the aftermath of the Second World War, voted against any sort of commemoration. If there were to be commemoration, earlier polls showed, it should take 'useful' forms in preference to monuments, cenotaphs or shrines (Inglis 1998: 352). Finally, ex-prisoners of war and the families of Gull Force may have been persuaded by the assurances of their government that in future the next-of-kin of deceased servicemen would be consulted about such decisions; that, if the opportunity arose, the remains of all Australians buried in Japan would be reinterred;[28] and that access to the cemetery land would be guaranteed in the forthcoming peace treaty with Japan.

In the event, none of the Australian bodies in Japan were ever relocated. Nor did the 1951 San Francisco peace treaty with Japan include guarantees about war graves, although it did commit the Japanese government to further negotiations on this subject.[29] These discussions dragged on until late 1955.[30] The Yokohama City Council seems to have driven a hard bargain about leasing the land and there was 'considerable sentiment' in the city against the cession of the Allied cemetery.[31] When finally concluded, the agreement granted a lease on the Yokohama land for thirty years, renewable so long as it continued to be used as a war cemetery. This was hardly 'in perpetuity' but, the Japanese claimed, it was the only solution permissible under Japanese law.[32]

Yokohama as an Australian site of memory

When completed, the Yokohama War Cemetery was judged to have a particularly powerful aesthetic. With discrete sections for the various national groups, it was landscaped with gullies, a Japanese bridge and foliage chosen to conform to an IWGC template. Near the large British section was an urn containing the ashes of the 335 servicemen who had been cremated while prisoners of war.[33] Yokohama soon came to be renowned as one of the 'most outstanding of the IWGC cemeteries in the Asia-Pacific region'.[34] Its aesthetics were, of course, consciously imperial. As a regional director visiting in 1960 said:

> It is very pleasing to report that the 'Japanese' character of the cemetery is rapidly being replaced by the development of the cemetery more along 'Commonwealth' lines. This change will, however, not be completed until such time as the essentially Japanese trees in the areas between the various sections have been replaced.[35]

The beauty of the Yokohama cemetery was appropriated by the Australian government to reassure the families of the dead buried there. A brochure depicting the cemetery was produced in the early 1950s to allow next of kin 'to visualize the care and attention which is being afforded to the graves and cemetery as whole'.[36] The Australian press also reported as early as 1949 that Yokohama was 'one of the most beautiful war cemeteries in the world' which made it 'a fitting resting place for the

Empire's dead'.[37] In later years newspapers carried the occasional report by a visitor to the cemetery, such as the following from July 1952:

> The head gardener told me to tell the people of Australia that they would always look after them with loving care. He spoke very good English and, you could see, tended every grave as though it was a child and loved every blade of grass there. It's just like a lovely garden and a fitting resting place for heroes.[38]

Yet it seems clear, six decades later, that Yokohama War Cemetery never fully shed the ambiguity of its origins. At neither the national nor sub-national level did it assume a central place in practices of remembrance of the Second World War. There was none of that dynamic interaction between government officials, collectives and individuals that has been evident in other memory-making processes, and which has ensured that other sites of the Pacific War – notably Hellfire Pass on the Burma–Thailand railway, Changi Prison in Singapore and the Kokoda Track in Papua New Guinea – have secured a prominent and continuing place in national remembrance (Beaumont 2009; 2012; 2016).

In the early post-war decades Australian commemoration at Yokohama was largely at the diplomatic or official governmental level. Regular ceremonies were held on Remembrance Day (11 November), Memorial Day (the last Monday in May) – to honour the remains of US personnel contained in the urn of ashes – and Australia's premier day of remembrance, Anzac Day (25 April). These were international events, with a combined ceremony at the larger British section and then national commemorations at specific national sections. At other times Australian politicians in Japan for official business made a point of visiting Yokohama and laying wreaths.[39] If available, defence personnel, such as sailors from the HMAS *Sydney* or Korean War veterans, were incorporated into Anzac Day ceremonies.[40] In 1955 Wilfred Kent Hughes, a minister in the Robert Menzies government, also made a visit to Yokohama as part of a two-week inspection of Australian war graves in the Asian region. A former prisoner of the Japanese himself, he was received warmly and was granted a private audience with the emperor and empress.[41] Possibly this courtesy was granted because only a few months earlier Kent Hughes had publicly defended a Japanese mission to the Pacific searching for the remains of their dead: 'nothing' he claimed then

> could be built on hate except more hate. He hoped the Japanese would continue to treat the Australian cemetery at Yokohama as a sacred spot and he could see no reason why we should not do the same for the Japanese.[42]

Yet this commemoration at the national level seems not to have been matched by remembrance activities of the sub-national level. Part of the explanation for this may be functional. As Bruce Scates has noted, the cemeteries of the Asia-Pacific War were not regularly visited by Australians in the immediate aftermath of the conflict (Scates 2013: 56–65). This was in marked contrast to the situation after the First World War when the battlefields of the Western Front attracted perhaps 10,000 visitors from Australia in the 1920s. Families seemed 'disinclined' to visit the Pacific War cemeteries, dispersed, as they were, across the much wider geographical area of Asia with its difficult climates and non-Western cultures. The prohibitively expensive air fares of the 1950s and 1960s may also have acted as a deterrent (especially as the government refused to provide any financial assistance for travel in the immediate post-war years).[43] Possibly, too, the long time it took to complete some cemeteries and memorials, notably in Sandakan and Labuan, may have dampened family interest in them.

Yet Yokohama was a stable site, dedicated in 1951. The failure of Australian veterans and families to visit it therefore was presumably attributable to the distance from Japan, both physically and culturally. The Japanese may have been quickly rehabilitated as a Western ally and an Australian trading partner in the post-war world, and some Australians, such as Kent Hughes, were open to reconciliation. But for many others the memories of the war remained vivid and resentment of Japan continued for decades (Hadju 2005: 152–4). Emotionally, they had 'lost their avenue to the graves' (Ziino 2007: 59).

Beyond this, Yokohama struggled to become a focus for sub-national remembrance because it had no inherent significance in the Australian narrative of the Second World War. Sites of remembrance are, after all, generally spaces on which the events of the past have already imprinted an intrinsic significance, even before the processes of formal commemoration are shaped. Yokohama was not a place where Gull Force – or any other Australians – had fought in battle, suffered as prisoners of war or even died. Rather, the dead had simply been transported there as a function of the IWGC policy of concentration of graves. Menzies said in the official brochure about Yokohama cemetery: 'Here they lie in comradeship on their field of honour, Australia will not forget them';[44] but it was *not* their field of honour in any literal sense. Rather, the place where these soldiers had 'fallen', and the soil on which their blood had been spilled, was far away, and the link between the place of death and of burial which had provided the original and emotionally powerful justification for IWGC policy had been broken.

The remembrance activities initiated by the Gull Force Association in the post-war years reflected this sense of disconnection with Yokohama. A particularly active veterans' collective, it organised pilgrimages from 1967 on, but these were to Ambon, not Hainan or Yokohama. This was not because of ease of access. Ambon is geographically closer to Australia, but even today it is not on any major international air route (Gull Force 'pilgrims' initially relied on the Royal Australian Air Force to provide flights). Nor was Ambon politically stable in the immediate post-war years when there was political unrest in the Malukus and nearby Sulawesi. Rather, Ambon was privileged in memory formation because of its place in the Gull Force story. It was here that the Australians fought the short battle which might justify their claim to a place, as warriors, in the foundational national narrative, the Anzac legend. It was here, too, that the experience of captivity was its most extreme. At 77 per cent, the death toll on Ambon was the second highest (after Sandakan) of any group of Australian prisoners of war. Hence, it was the Tan Tui cemetery, the site of the former prison camp in Ambon, which became, and remains, the site of memory for Gull Force veterans and their families. Similarly, it was Ambon rather than Hainan which was the beneficiary of aid and development programmes initiated by Gull Force veterans in the post-war years when they wanted to manifest their gratitude to the local peoples who supported them in captivity.

This marginalisation of Yokohama continued even when the memory boom in the late twentieth century spawned a virtual orgy of state-sanctioned memorialisation and elevated prisoners of war, as victims of trauma, to a more privileged position within Australian national memory (Twomey 2014). While new rituals of remembrance and memorials proliferated at home and overseas – at Gallipoli, on the Western Front, in London, Israel, Thailand, Papua New Guinea and Malaysia – Yokohama failed to attract much attention. The exception was in May 1995, when the Labor prime minister Paul Keating (1991–96) visited Japan. As Keating's biographer has said, the Second World War 'washed through Keating's prime ministership like reflux' (Watson 2003: 182). Not only had his own uncle died as a prisoner-of-war at Sandakan; the Pacific War represented, for Keating, a radical nationalist of Irish-Catholic extraction, a time when the bankruptcy of British imperial power had been vividly exposed (Holbrook 2014: 179–83). As he famously said to the Australian parliament in February 1992, not for him 'some cultural cringe to a country which decided not to defend the Malayan peninsula, not to worry about Singapore and not to give us our troops back to keep ourselves free from Japanese domination'.[45] On his many trips to Asia, Keating was drawn to the 'indescribable places of sadness' (Watson 2003: 182) associated with the dead of the Pacific War. At Yokohama in 1995 he both honoured the dead and called for greater Japanese contrition for their maltreatment of prisoners of war:

> we believe it is important that Japan should not allow these events to be forgotten. We believe that our friendship will be stronger if the truth about these events is known to the Japanese people – and we are pleased that the Japanese Government has taken steps to make it known.[46]

This was a well-publicised intervention – Japanese prime minister Murayama Tomiichi was then trying to persuade the Diet to apologise for Japan's aggression and atrocities in the Second World War – but after this Yokohama reverted to a low-key place in the calendar of remembrance: prime ministerial wreath-laying; a delegation of the Returned and Services League; and an unknown number of individual 'pilgrims'. Anzac Day continued to be observed by the diplomatic corps, as did Remembrance Day and US Veterans Day.[47] Much of this commemoration probably had the emotional sterility of such official remembrance. Meanwhile, the families of Gull Force, as exemplars of 'postmemory' (Hirsch 2008), maintained a strong affective engagement with the memory of captivity but they continued to look not to Yokohama but to Ambon where in 2013 they installed a large plaque listing all who had been interned there and on Hainan.

Yokohama War Cemetery and the Japanese

Yokohama War Cemetery, therefore, attests to the importance of national and sub-national impulses intersecting in processes of remembrance and of links between places and past events of some inherent significance. But Yokohama also speaks, albeit to a lesser degree, to the capacity of such cemeteries to acquire significance beyond that intended by their creators or those who claim to 'own' them. We know nothing about the local reception of this cemetery, which was imposed upon the citizens of Yokohama in the aftermath of their devastating defeat. It was, literally, a physical footprint of the victorious powers. The IWGC reported in the 1950s that there was some 'unseemly conduct by visitors' which was 'not in keeping with the dignity of the war cemetery'.[48] But with the passage of time the cemetery, like so many others around the world, seems to have become part of the local cultural landscape. By the early 1970s the cemetery had become so popular with Japanese tourists that the CWGC had to restrict the hours of entry.[49] These visitors, who outnumbered the foreigners, came from across Japan, as individuals and in organised groups, and included school children. Their motives are unknown. A local resident suggests that the visit of Queen Elizabeth II in 1975 simulated interest in the cemetery, as did a later visit by Prime Minister Margaret Thatcher.[50] Meanwhile visitor books at the cemetery indicated that the Japanese showed respect for the graves. There were no problems of theft, vandalism or littering,[51] unlike in other Asian cities where the CWGC confronted 'the most acute problems of damage from the visiting public' who stole or vandalised plants and flowers.[52]

At the official level also, the Japanese authorities manifested a cooperation which went beyond the merely diplomatic. When in the late 1960s it was decided to construct a motorway nearby, the Japanese did 'everything possible to preserve the peaceful and beautiful character of the cemetery'. One CWGC official engaged in the negotiations could not speak 'too highly of the generosity exhibited by the Japanese Highway Corporation in their approach to this matter'.[53] A representative of the Japanese Ministry of Foreign Affairs on the joint Commonwealth–Japanese committee which had oversight of the cemetery meanwhile stated in 1957 that his government was 'most anxious to honour the war dead of the Commonwealth countries … By doing so, he felt sure that in some small way we would be contributing to a future peaceful world.'[54]

With the passage of time Yokohama cemetery also became a site of remembrance for small groups of Japanese intent on promoting peace and reconciliation between the former enemies of the Second World War. Pre-eminent among these was Nagase Takashi, who had witnessed the suffering of prisoners of war on the Burma–Thailand railway. He had served as an interpreter first for the feared Japanese military police during the war and then for the Allied war graves units who had exhumed remains of the dead along the railway in 1945–46. Seeking to atone for the crimes of his countrymen, Nagase devoted the rest of his life to reconciliation with ex-prisoners of war and to education of his compatriots about Japan's role in the war (Nagase and Watase 1990). He initiated reunions with ex-prisoners of war in Japan, including, famously, Eric Lomax, *The Railway Man* (Lomax 1995). He also made some 135 pilgrimages to Kanchanaburi, at the southern end of the railway in Thailand, funded the construction of peace temples in Kanchanaburi province and introduced education programmes for local Thai children (Nemoto 2011). Nagase's activism was complemented, from 2002 on, by another progressive initiative, the Prisoner of War Research Network Japan. This, too, sought to educate the Japanese public about prisoner-of-war issues and to organise open meetings with ex-prisoners, including an Australian, visiting the Yokohama War Cemetery (Szczepanska 2014: 36, 68–70). In such encounters, it is perhaps possible to see an embryonic form of transnational memory being shaped around an agenda of peace.

Conclusion

The scale of these initiatives has, however, been small and, on balance, the Yokohama War Cemetery seems not to be invested with any special significance and meaning for either the community within which it resides or the foreigners for whom it was created. Its contested origins and its irrelevance in the national narratives of the Second World War have rendered it almost invisible within Australia, even during the current centenary commemorations that have sought to explore 'A Century of Service' rather than just the First World War. Whether the same can be said for Britain, whose nationals occupy the bulk of the graves at Yokohama, is beyond the scope of this research. But given that the Pacific War and prisoners of the Japanese have long struggled to find a place in British national memory to rival that occupied by Dunkirk, the Battle of Britain and escape from Colditz (Flower 2013; Mackenzie 2006), it is probable that Yokohama occupies an even lower place in the British hierarchy of sites of Second World War memory.

Yokohama War Cemetery, it needs to be said, is not alone in having such a status. Across the globe there are CWGC war cemeteries, from both world wars, that struggle to attract significant attention from politicians, battlefield tourists or individual pilgrims. Impeccably manicured by local curators, they sit quietly in the fields of France, Belgium and elsewhere and in urban environments that have encroached upon them over the years. Many seem almost frozen in the moment of their creation. How long they will remain in this state is impossible to tell. Perhaps, as the world wars recede even further into the past, the memory boom will lose some of its current emotional power and some of these cemeteries will be closed. The phrase 'in perpetuity', after all, is surely not intended to be taken literally. At some time in the future the CWGC, an institution of a Commonwealth that is of declining relevance to its constituent governments, may lack the resources to maintain the thousands of cemeteries in its care across 159 countries. Possibly it may need to establish a hierarchy of cemeteries. However uneasily a demand-driven model of economics would sit with remembrance, the CWGC governments might choose to privilege those cemeteries that have been 'reinvented' by members of national and local communities and have high levels of usage.

However, at the time of writing, this scenario seems improbable. Even though the imperial vision that created the CWGC cemeteries may be anachronistic, and the sub-national engagement with cemeteries such as Yokohama limited, the political message that these sites enshrine has lost none of its utility. Each CWGC cemetery speaks to an implied contract between the state and its military forces: namely, that the nation will never forget anyone who dies in its defence. It would be an unusual government that chose to risk opening this value to critique by closing a war cemetery, no matter how marginal it might be to national commemoration.

Notes

1 230th meeting, Imperial War Graves Commission (IWGC), 25 September 1939, Commonwealth War Graves Commission Archives (CWGCA).
2 273rd meeting, IWGC, 29 September 1945, CWGCA.
3 S. Rainey to Acting Prime Minister (J. B. Chifley), 9 June 1945, MP 742/1 132/1/496, National Archives Australia (NAA).
4 Parliament of Australia, House of Representatives, Question, Arthur Fadden, 7 June 1945, parlinfo.aph.gov.au.
5 269th meeting, IWGC, 17 May 1945, CWGCA. This wording became something of a mantra, repeated widely: for example, High Commissioner's Office, London, no. 6005 to Prime Minister's Department, 1 June 1945, A461/7, B337/1/9 pt 2, NAA.
6 Minutes of the first meeting of the Japanese–Commonwealth Joint Committee, 17 September 1957, ADD 1/41/1, CWGCA.
7 Stanley Bruce, High Commissioner, London, to Acting Prime Minister (Chifley), tel. 88, 1 June 1945, cablegram to London, 25 August 1945, A461/7, B337/1/9 pt2, NAA.
8 High Commissioner (Bruce), London, tel. no. 7256, 3 July 1945, MP 742/1 132/1/496, NAA.
9 H.V. Johnson, Minister for Interior, to Prime Minister, 20 August 1945, A461/7 B337/1/9 pt 2, NAA.
10 F. R. Sinclair to Prime Minister, 13 July 1945, MP 742/1 132/1/496, NAA.
11 273rd, 274th, 275th and 278th meetings, IWGC, 27 September 1945, 18 October 1945, 15 November 1945, 21 February 1946, CWGCA.
12 H.V. Johnson, 'Burial Place of Australian Service Personnel who Died in Japan', 13 January 1947, A2700 1261A, NAA.
13 Adjutant-General, 'Transfer of Australian Remains from Hainan to Yokohama', 8 October 1946, MP 742/ 132/1/496, NAA.
14 GHQ SEALF, Quarterly Historical Report, Graves, 1 Oct – 31 Dec 1946, WO 268/109, National Archives, London (TNA).
15 Adjutant General, 'Transfer of Australian Remains from Hainan'.
16 'Gull Force played epic part in delaying Jap advance', *Argus*, 28 September 1946.
17 Parliament of Australia, House of Representatives, Question. Thomas White, 8 November 1946, parlinfo.aph.gov.au.
18 W. G. Farrell to Colonel R.S. Ryan, Parliament House, 1 November 1946, MP 742/1 132/1/496, NAA.
19 E. E. Dunlop, President, Australian Prisoners of War Relatives' Association, to Prime Minister (Chifley), 11 October 1946, MP 742/1 132/1/496, NAA.
20 Roland A. Newton, Honorary Secretary RSS & AILA, to Minister for Army, 18 October 1946, 132/1/461, MP 742/1 132/1/496, NAA.

21 Cyril Chambers, Minister for the Army, to Colonel R. S. Ryan, Parliament House, no date; Cyril Chambers, Minister for the Army to Prime Minister Chifley, no date, MP 742/1 132/1/496, NAA.
22 'List of Names of Cemeteries in which Australian Service Personnel are Commemorated 1914–1918 and 1949–1945 Wars', Office of Australian War Graves, Canberra, 1995.
23 For details, see the Australian War Memorial website at www.awm.gov.au/encyclopedia/pow/general_info/.
24 F. M. Forde, Minister for the Army, to Prime Minister Chifley, 30 October 1946, A705/2 95/1/29, NAA.
25 F. Strahan, Secretary to Cabinet to Cyril Chambers, Minister for the Army, 7 November 1946, A705/2 95/1/29.
26 Parliament of Australia, House of Representatives, Question, Cyril Chambers, 8 November 1946, parlinfo.aph.gov.au.
27 'War graves in Japan', *Sydney Morning Herald*, 9 November 1946; 'Burial of soldiers in Japan deplored', *Canberra Times*, 9 November 1946; 'Australian war graves to remain in Japan', *Argus*, 24 December 1946.
28 Parliament of Australia, House of Representatives, Question, Cyril Chambers, 8 November 1946, parlinfo.aph.gov.au. This was reported in the press: for example, 'Probe into Aust [sic] burials in Japan', *Townsville Daily Bulletin*, 9 November 1946.
29 Appendix to draft letter from W. R. Hodgson, Australian mission, Tokyo to Mr Yoshida, April 1952, A5105 8/7 pt 1, NAA.
30 Details of the agreement negotiations, which Australia led on behalf of the Commonwealth, are in A2909/2, AGS4/2/2 pt 52, AGS2/2/65 pts 2, 3, NAA.
31 H. A. H. Cortazzi, British embassy, to N. S. Currie, Australian embassy, 11 Feb. 1953, A5105/8/7, NAA; Headquarters, British Commonwealth Forces, Korea, to Joint Secretaries, Chiefs of Staff Committee, Melbourne, 'Cemeteries in Japan and Korea', 18 January 1955, WO32 16045, TNA.
32 Australian embassy, Tokyo, to Secretary, Department of Veterans' Affairs, Canberra, 9 November 1976, ADD 1/41/14, CWGCA.
33 For descriptive details, see the Commonwealth War Graves Commission website at www.cwgc.org/find-a-cemetery/cemetery/49433/YOKOHAMA%20WAR%20CEMETERY.
34 'Hodogaya Park: Beautiful war cemetery', *Cairns Post*, 30 June 1949. This is repeated in other regional presses.
35 'Report by the Regional Director covering a visit to the Yokohama British Commonwealth War Cemetery, Japan', June/July 1960, RA 41562 pt 3, CWGCA.
36 A. E. Brown, IWGC, to W. H. Bunning, Australian High Commission, London, 28 August 1952, AGS2/2/65, pt 2, A2902/2, NAA; 'Report by the Regional Director covering a visit to the Yokohama British Commonwealth War Cemetery, Japan'.
37 'Hodogaya Park: Beautiful war cemetery', *Cairns Post*, 30 June 1949; 'Hodogaya, Japan: Well kept area', *Goulburn Evening Post*, 15 July 1949. These reports appear to draw on an official press release.
38 'Cemetery at Yokohama well tended', *West Australian*, 7 July 1952.
39 'Mr. Francis ends Japanese visit', Adelaide *Advertiser*, 8 January 1952; 'War cemetery visit', *Newcastle Sun*, 24 November 1952; Minister for Health, Brisbane, to A. I. Allan. Secretary-General, Anzac Agency, 21 September 1972, RA 41562, pt 5, CWGCA.
40 'The Sydney arrives in Yokohama', *West Australian*, 24 April 1954; 'Services in Korea and Japan', *Canberra Times*, 26 April 1954; 'Remembrance Day in Yokohama', *Newcastle Sun*, 17 November 1954.
41 Ambassador, Tokyo (E. Ronald Walker) to Secretary, Department of External Affairs (Arthur Tange), 2 March 1955, A1838 532/6/4, NAA.
42 'Jap Mission to Collect Dead', *Barrier Miner*, 24 December 1954.
43 E. V. Britnell, Australian Prisoners of War Relatives' Association, to Prime Minister Chifley, 11 January 1946; F. Strahan, Secretary to Cabinet, to Britnell, 8 February 1946, A431 1946/380, NAA.

44 'Report by the Regional Director covering a visit to the Yokohama British Commonwealth War Cemetery, Japan'.
45 For the text of Keating's speech see 'Keating Blasts the Old Fogies of The Liberal Party and the Cultural Cringe of the 1950s', *Australian Politics*, 27 February 1992, http://australianpolitics.com/1992/02/27/keating-blasts-liberal-party-fogies.html.
46 'Japan's evil role in WWII cannot be forgotten', *Canberra Times*, 28 May 1995.
47 Personal communication from Colonel Tim Gellel (formerly of the Australian embassy, Tokyo), 11 September 2013. Gellel escorted Prime Ministers Kevin Rudd and Tony Abbott to the cemetery in 2008 and 2010.
48 Minutes of the second meeting of the Japanese–Commonwealth Joint Committee, 27 May 1958, ADD 1/41/1, CWGCA.
49 Extracts from Japanese–Commonwealth Joint Committee minutes, 28 February 1974, RA 41562 pt 5, CWGCA.
50 I am grateful to Keiko Tamura of the Australian National University for this information.
51 Draft introduction to Cemetery report, 28 October 1976, ADD 1/41/14, CWGCA.
52 Extracts from Japanese–Commonwealth Joint Committee minutes, 28 February 1974.
53 Extracts from fourteenth meeting of Japanese–Commonwealth Joint Committee minutes, 15 December 1970, RA 41562, pt 4, CWGCA.
54 Minutes of the first meeting of the Japanese–Commonwealth Joint Committee, 17 September 1957, ADD 1/41/2, CWGCA.

References

Beaumont, Joan. 1988. *Gull Force: Survival and Leadership in Captivity 1941–1945.* Sydney: Allen and Unwin.

Beaumont, Joan. 2009. 'Contested Transnational Heritage: the Demolition of Changi Prison, Singapore'. *International Journal of Heritage Studies*, 15, 4: 298–316.

Beaumont, Joan. 2012. 'Hellfire Pass Memorial Museum, Thai-Burma Railway'. In *The Heritage of War*, edited by Martin Gegner and Bart Ziino. New York, NY: Routledge. 19–40.

Beaumont, Joan. 2016. 'The Diplomacy of Extra-Territorial Heritage: the Kokoda Track, Papua New Guinea'. *International Journal of Heritage Studies*, 22, 5: 355–67.

Christopher, A. J. 1995. 'Segregation and Cemeteries in Port Elizabeth, South Africa'. *The Geographical Journal*, 161, 43: 38–46.

Dower, John. 1986. *War without Mercy: Race and Power in the Pacific War.* New York, NY: Pantheon Books.

Ekins, Ashley. 2003. 'Australian MIAs of the Vietnam War – "Missing in Action" or "No Known Grave"?' *Wartime*. 23: 14–18.

Flower, Sibylla Jane. 2013. 'Memory and the Prisoner of War Experience'. In *Forgotten Captives in Japanese-Occupied Asia*, edited by Karl Hack and Kevin Blackburn. London: Routledge. 57–72.

Grant, Lachlan. 2014. *Australian Soldiers in Asia-Pacific in World War II.* Sydney: NewSouth Publishing.

Graves, Matthew. 2014. 'Memorial Diplomacy in Franco–Australian Relations'. In *Nation, Memory and Great War Commemoration*, edited by Shanti Sumartojo and Ben Wellings. Bern: Peter Lang. 169–87.

Hadju, Joe. 2005. *Samurai in the Surf: The Arrival of the Japanese on the Gold Coast in the 1980s.* Canberra: Pandanus Press.

Hirsch, Marianne. 2008. 'The Generation of Postmemory'. *Poetics*, 29, 1: 103–28.

Holbrook, Carolyn. 2014. *Anzac: The Unauthorised Biography*. Sydney: NewSouth Publishing.

Inglis, K.S. 1998. *Sacred Places: War Memorials in the Australian Landscape*. Melbourne: Melbourne University Press.

Jalland, Pat. 2006. *Changing Ways of Death in Twentieth-Century Australia: War, Medicine and the Funeral Business*. Sydney: University of New South Wales Press.

Johnston, Mark. 2000. *Fighting the Enemy: Australian Soldiers and their Adversaries in World War II*. Cambridge: Cambridge University Press.

Kwon, Heonik. 2008. *Ghosts of War in Vietnam*. Cambridge: Cambridge University Press.

Lefebvre, Henri. 1977. 'Reflections on the Politics of Space'. In *Radical Geography: Alternative Viewpoints on Contemporary Social Issues*, edited by Richard Peet. Chicago, IL: Maaroufa Press. 339–52.

Lindsay, Patrick. 2008. *Fromelles*. Victoria: Hardie Grant Books.

Lomax, Eric. 1995. *The Railway Man*. London: Jonathan Cape.

Longworth, Philip. 2003. *The Unending Vigil: The History of the Commonwealth War Graves Commission*. Rev. edn. Barnsley: Leo Cooper.

Mackenzie, S. P. 2006. *The Colditz Myth: British and Commonwealth Prisoners of War in Nazi Germany*. Oxford: Oxford University Press.

Nagase, Takashi and Watase, Marasu. 1990. *Crosses and Tigers*. Bangkok: no publisher.

Nemoto, Kei. 2011. 'A Life of Reconciliation: Mr Takashi Nagase and the Thai–Burma Railway'. Unpublished conference paper delivered at '*Rekishi to Wakai*: War Memory, War History and Reconciliation – The Experiences of Japan, China, Korea and the UK', White Rose East Asia Centre, University of Leeds.

Scates, Bruce. 2013. *Anzac Memories: Returning to the Battlefields of World War II*. Melbourne: Cambridge University Press.

Summers, Julie. 2007. *Remembered: The History of the Commonwealth War Graves Commission*. London: Merrell Publishers.

Szczepanska, Kamila. 2014. *The Politics of War Memory in Japan: Progressive Civil Society Groups and Contestation of Memory of the Asia–Pacific War*. London: Routledge.

Tan, Boon Hui and Yeoh, Brenda S. A. 2002. 'The "Remains of the Dead": Spatial Politics of Nation-Building in Post-War Singapore'. *Human Ecology Review*, 9, 1: 1–13.

Tanner, Thomas W. 1980. *Compulsory Citizen Soldiers*. Sydney: Alternative Publishing Co-operative.

Twomey, Christina. 2014. 'POWs of the Japanese: Race and Trauma in Australia, 1970–2005'. *Journal of War and Culture Studies*, 3, 3: 191–205.

Walker, David. 1999. *Anxious Nation: Australia and the Rise and Fall of Asia 1850–1939*. St Lucia, Queensland: University of Queensland Press.

Watson, Don. 2003. *Recollections of a Bleeding Heart: A Portrait of Paul Keating PM*. Sydney: Vintage.

Winter, Jay M. 2006. *Remembering War: The Great War between Memory and History in the Twentieth Century*. New Haven, CT: Yale University Press.

Ziino, Bart. 2007. *A Distant Grief: Australians, War Graves and the Great War*. Nedlands: University of Western Australia Press.

9

THE MEMORY OF THE JOOP WESTERWEEL RESISTANCE MOVEMENT IN ISRAEL AND THE NETHERLANDS

Joyce van de Bildt

As part of the activities of the Zionist movement in Europe in the early 1900s, special educational centres were established in different countries in order to physically and mentally prepare Jewish youth to settle in Palestine. This programme was called '*hachshara*', literally meaning 'preparation', which involved professional training in agricultural and other skills for the ultimate goal of emigration to *Eretz Israel*. In the Netherlands, the popularity of this Zionist youth *Hechalutz* or Pioneers movement was initially minimal. The first Pioneers movement had been founded in 1918 by Rudolf Cohen in Deventer, a town in the east of the Netherlands. Its pupils lived and worked at farms throughout the country, and a Pioneers House was founded in Deventer for courses and cultural activities. During the 1930s, the appeal of emigration to Palestine increased due to the rise of anti-Semitism in the Netherlands. At the same time, a large number of German Jewish refugees arrived in the Netherlands as a result of Adolf Hitler's rise to power; the Pioneers' sentiment had been more widespread among the German Jewish youth than in the Netherlands, and this gave the movement a further boost (Pinkhof and Brasz 1997: 13). Most of them intended to stay in the Netherlands only for a limited period of time, in order to receive the necessary training on their way to Palestine. As a result of the presence of the German Jewish refugees, additional work centres and *hachshara* farms were established. Among the most famous were a large farming village in Wieringermeer and the Pavilion *Loosdrechtse Rade* in the North Holland province.

After the occupation of the Netherlands by Nazi Germany in 1940, the *hachshara* movement was forced to be more careful in its activities until its farms were eventually banned in 1942. As Jews became persecuted in the Netherlands, several young Zionist Pioneers (*Halutzim*) engaged in underground activities. One of them, German Jewish refugee Joachim Simon ('Shushu'), established an extensive network to hide fugitives and organise escape routes. He was assisted in this effort by a Dutch Christian teacher and pacifist from Rotterdam, Johan Gerard (Joop)

Westerweel and his wife Wilhelmina Dora (Wil) Bosdries. Both Jews and non-Jews formed part of their resistance movement, which came to be called the Westerweel *Hechalutz* Underground Movement, or later simply the Westerweel group.[1] The majority of the Jewish members of this underground movement were Zionist Pioneers, most of them of German origin in their teenage years or early twenties.

Due to the efforts of the Westerweel group, about 400 young Jews were saved during the Second World War. Many of them succeeded in escaping with forged identity papers through secret routes via Spain and Switzerland, and arrived in Mandate Palestine by boat during the 1940s. Once in Palestine they were divided between several *kibbutzim*, among them the so-called 'Dutch' *kibbutzim* Chulioth, Sde Nehemia and Hazorea. A larger group of Westerweel survivors came to live in *kibbutz* Even Yitzhak (later called *kibbutz* Gal'ed), which was at the time largely inhabited by German Jews. The Dutch leader of the underground movement, Joop Westerweel, was arrested in 1944 and assassinated in Camp Vught in the Netherlands shortly after. His partner Joachim Simon was caught during one of his missions in the south of the country and committed suicide in prison.

Described by the Netherlands Institute for War Documentation as embodying 'nonconformist resistance', the Westerweel group was unique in two respects: it did not make use of weapons, and it was comprised of both Jews and non-Jews. In fact, the Westerweel underground chose to work with an established Pioneers movement, which makes it an even rarer phenomenon. Hans Schippers argued that all members of the Westerweel movement were somehow marginalised in Dutch society (Schippers 2015: 35, 77). On one side were the young East European and German Jews who were fervent socialists and engaged in only minimal interaction with the Dutch Jewish community; on the other side were the leftist, pacifist Dutchmen whose idealism led them to risk their lives for the sake of others. Schippers added that the nonconformist nature of this particular resistance movement was further apparent in the unconventionally equal position of women within it. The Westerweel group was also distinctive in the sense that it was actively working for the sake of Jews, instead of against the Germans. There were certainly many types of passive and active resistance during the Second World War but only a small fraction of it was immediately directed against the persecution of the Jews.

The unique position of the Westerweel movement in the Dutch history of the Second World War is reflected in the survivors' continuous efforts to commemorate their own distinctive, shared past through private memory initiatives. In the commemoration of their past, they put special emphasis on the non-conformist nature of their resistance as described above, and clearly attempt to establish it as a symbol for humanity. The practice of using a person or event as a reference point to commemorate a larger phenomenon is common: after all 'the power of collective memory does not lie in its accurate, systematic, or sophisticated mapping of the past, but in establishing basic images that articulate and reinforce a particular ideological stance' (Zerubavel 1995: 8). In this case, the Westerweel commemorations are not strictly connected to the personality of its leader but are meant to commemorate and legitimise the ideals he embodied. The following examination of the commemorative practices of the Westerweel group in Israel serves to demonstrate the wider meaning its members sought to attach to their memories.

The Joop Westerweel forest in Israel

Efforts to commemorate Joop Westerweel started as early as 1945. In December 1945, six months after the liberation from the Nazis, a new commissioner was appointed to the Dutch branch of the Jewish National Fund (JNF) as part of the first steps towards the resumption of its functions. One of the first campaigns it organised was the 'Westerweel-campaign', which aimed to raise 36,000 guilders to plant 10,000 trees in a forest in Israel to be dedicated in his name.[2] During a meeting of the Amsterdam Zionist Organisation in January 1946, its chair J. Soetendorp officially announced the decision to create the Joop Westerweel forest to honour the non-Jews who helped Jews escape from the Nazis during the war.[3] The JNF invited all Dutch Jews to donate and plant a tree in the name of their non-Jewish helpers. On 25 January 1946, the Dutch Jewish weekly *Nieuw Israëlitisch Weekblad* featured an article about the commemoration of Joop Westerweel on its front page, and called on its readers to help plant a forest in his name.[4] Donations arrived from people throughout the Netherlands and the JNF was able to officially inaugurate the forest in March 1947. The forest was established in the Menashe hills in Israel near *kibbutz* Gal'ed, which had recently become home to many of the Dutch and German Pioneers saved by the Westerweel movement.

Considering that afforestation was one of the key tools of the Zionist settlement effort, it was a highly symbolic choice to commemorate the rescue of Dutch and German Zionist youth through the establishment of a forest in what became their safe haven, *Eretz Israel*. Irus Braverman argued that the act of planting trees was central 'in transforming the Diaspora Jew into a *halutz* [pioneer], and in redeeming the land from its perceived desolation' (Braverman 2009: 319). Afforestation of the land of Israel had been one of the JNF's main objectives since 1908, a few years after its founding. Since many of the donations to plant trees came from Jews outside of Israel, its campaigns enhanced the Diaspora Jews' connection to Israel while at the same time contributing to the development of the land. As a contributor to *Nieuw Israëlitisch Weekblad* put it:

> While other nations award medals and decorations, the Jewish people chooses to connect its friends' names to developing their country and planting trees in their honour. [...] is there any greater honour thinkable than to be connected forever to the growth of this country, in which a nation was able to settle down after wandering and suffering as no other nation?[5]

Donations to the Joop Westerweel forest continued in the 1950s, 1960s and 1970s. Trees were commonly donated in someone's name to mark a special occasion in their life, such as a birthday, *bar mitzvah*, wedding, graduation or wedding anniversary. Others donated a tree to this forest in special memory of a particular individual or to express gratitude to the resistance. The names of the donors were published by the JNF, and every donor received a special certificate, indicating the name of the donor and the name of the person to whom the tree was dedicated. This blue and white certificate was adorned with the following verse from the Book of Psalms, in Hebrew and in Dutch: 'The righteous one flourishes like the palm; as a cedar in Lebanon he grows.'[6]

Former members of the Westerweel movement encouraged the donations of trees through personal initiatives. One such was E. E. Meursing, who had been the local doctor of the city of Dordrecht for forty years and had been active in helping Jewish patients during the war, thereby risking his own life. During a local event marking his retirement in March 1963, the community suggested offering the doctor and his wife a trip to Israel to thank him for his services.[7] However, Meursing responded that a donation of trees in the Joop Westerweel forest would be a much more desirable gift. Two months later, he was presented with a certificate for 800 trees on behalf of the people of his town. In return, Meursing published a brochure called *The Joop Westerweel Forest in Israel* to provide everyone who donated with information about Westerweel's deeds, and he called on people to continue the campaign.[8]

In 1973 members of the Dutch Youth Workers Central (AJC), the socialist youth movement of the Social Democratic Workers Party, offered to plant trees in the Joop Westerweel forest to mark the twenty-fifth anniversary of the state of Israel. Joop was once a member of the party and it used to have many Jewish members. A group of 240 alumni planned to visit Israel and the organisers offered to plant two trees on behalf of each of them in the Westerweel forest. However, the various campaigns for the donation of trees to the forest had been so successful by the early 1970s that the JNF had to inform them that there was insufficient space for that many more trees in the Westerweel forest.[9] Instead, the JNF suggested an alternative location.[10] During a ceremony on 10 May 1973, the AJC members visiting Israel accordingly buried a lead tube between the trees of the Westerweel forest, containing inside a list of names of AJC members who were killed in the Second World War. Twenty more trees were also planted.[11]

Joop Westerweel: a symbol of humanity

The first trees in the Westerweel forest were planted during an inauguration ceremony on 3 March 1947, which was attended by officials from the Dutch embassy in Israel and representatives of the Dutch immigrant and youth movements. Although some came from as far as Haifa and Jerusalem, turnout was affected by the siege that had just been imposed by the British and Arabs which hindered representatives of various institutions from attending the planting. JNF representative Shlomo Levy stressed during his speech that he personally had decided to undertake the journey despite the siege because 'it is exactly in times like this that we should raise the memory of those who were among the righteous of the nations, and whose love for the people of Israel was not limited to mere words and statements'. Pioneers from Holland who immigrated to Israel during the war expressed gratitude for the help they received from Joop Westerweel, 'hero of the Dutch underground, who sacrificed his soul to save Jewish children in the war years'. Mirjam de Leeuw, who spoke on behalf of the organisation for Dutch immigrants in Israel, recalled the words Westerweel had spoken as he bid farewell to those refugees whom he accompanied all the way on their escape route to Spain: 'Don't forget the actions of those who enabled you to obtain freedom; those who gave their lives, in order for you to reach your goal.'[12] These words were often repeated during commemorations in the following years.

In September 1954, the Westerweel group marked ten years since Joop's death with a ceremony in the Westerweel forest, where his widow Wil Westerweel unveiled a monument for him. It is located in a small open space surrounded by trees and greenery, and reads in Dutch and Hebrew that he was 'an inspiring force in the underground activities during the German occupation of the Netherlands, and [...] gave his life to save the Jewish youth'. A sign at the entrance to the site also indicates the centrality of Joop Westerweel as the leader of the movement:

> Joop Westerweel, born in Holland (1899–1944) to Christian parents, was a great educator and a pursuer of peace. He was a central figure in the underground movement of Jewish Pioneers (Halutzim). He and his friends bound their own fate with that of the Halutzim and founded a non-violent underground group in accordance with Joop's views. His energy and great inspiration roused his friends to action.

However, despite the dedication of the forest to the leader of the Westerweel movement and the centrality of his figure in the memory of the group, it can be argued that the memorial and the commemorations had a wider function than just remembering Joop and his colleagues. In fact, many *Halutzim* who were saved by the Westerweel movement had never known Joop in person. One survivor, Hanan Florsheim, said that the monument is a general expression of gratitude to everyone who risked their lives to save Jews during the Second World War, and that the place is meant to symbolise the heroism of the entire Dutch resistance.[13]

During a commemoration ceremony for Joop's colleagues Joachim Simon and Kurt Hanneman in March 1963, Wil Westerweel said it was important to remember the past for the sake of the future:

> There is only one thing we can do to keep Shushu's name alive, and that is to carry on his struggle for justice, uprightness and freedom. This is the value of this memorial for us and our descendants, rather than to bury the spirit of the resistance underneath a pile of stones.[14]

During the same event, reference was made to a biblical verse from the Book of Joshua, according to which Joshua ordered the Israelites to take twelve stones from the Jordan River, one for each tribe, and place them in the encampment near the river as a memorial for the children of Israel until the end of days.[15] One of the speakers remarked that in this biblical story the point was not to commemorate the great deeds of the personality of Joshua, but rather the significant events that had happened. Exactly the same point applied to the memorial for the Westerweel group:

> If descendants will ask, what is the meaning of these names? It does not suffice to tell them just about the actions of these two friends; it is only possible to understand this memorial stone if presented in the context of the life of the Pioneers in the Netherlands before and after the occupation, and the spirit of the resistance.[16]

Wil Westerweel often said that she preferred not to describe Joop as a hero because that placed him at a certain distance from the common people, while his deeds should function as an example for others of how to act. She believed that the main way to keep Westerweel's memory alive was to strive to live one's life as he did.[17] Despite Westerweel's reluctance to use the characterisation, Yael Zerubavel's argument about heroes nonetheless seems to apply here: 'heroes that figure in myths are often supposed to serve as models for the new situation. Their centrality is not as an individual but rather as a collective representation' (Zerubavel 1995: 44). In the representation of the past, 'heroes' come to embody a change and provide a new paradigm of action that sometimes assumes mythical dimensions.

Remembering the 'Righteous among the Nations'

Aside from providing an example for future action, the immediate establishment of the Westerweel monument after the war and the glorification of Joop Westerweel and his friends served an important purpose in dealing with a traumatic past. Irena Steinfeldt has argued that after the Holocaust, 'the Jewish people and the survivors needed to hang on to some hope for mankind, something that would enable them to maintain their faith in human values and rebuild their lives after having witnessed an unprecedented moral collapse'. She noted how the commemoration of so-called 'righteous gentiles' suited this effort.[18] Indeed, the monument in the Westerweel forest seems to emphasise the immense sacrifice that was made by both Jewish and non-Jewish activists in their effort to save Jews, as its text reads:

> Many members of the underground movement, Jews and gentiles, sacrificed their lives in the struggle against the Nazis. Joop Westerweel was captured and put to death at the Vught concentration camp in Holland on August 11, 1944. [...] The memorial stones in the forest commemorate all those activists, Jews and gentiles, who sacrificed their lives in order to rescue the Halutzim.

Throughout the text, there is a double emphasis on the background of the activists; that is, they were both Jews and gentiles. The appreciation for the participation of non-Jews in the Joop Westerweel movement was also highlighted in a personal interview with Hanan Florsheim, who said:

> I always say, [...] what a courage they had! I don't know if I would have done what they did for me. Risking the entire family to save a Jewish child ... to take in a boy or a girl and to host it in secret, not for days or weeks but sometimes for months! You had to be careful with family members who were with the NSB,[19] who consorted with the Germans [...]. Yes, the people who helped hiding Jews took upon themselves an incredible risk.[20]

A similar sentiment was expressed on 21 August 1957 during a large reunion of members of the Westerweel movement held in Moshav Beit Yitzhak in Israel in honour of a visit of the Dutch couple Bauke and Vrouwkje de Koning who had saved many Jews during the war. Jewish resistance fighter Menachem Pinkhof expressed his appreciation on behalf of the survivors and said that they often wonder if they would have acted in the same way in their circumstances.[21]

The state of Israel merged the commemoration of righteous gentiles into commemorations of the *Shoah* from an early stage. In 1953 Yad Vashem was established with the chief task of commemorating the six million Jews who had perished during the *Shoah*; the commemoration of the 'Righteous among the Nations' (non-Jews who had put their lives at risk to save Jews during the Holocaust) was defined as another key task of the museum from its very inception. Since 1962, the Commission for the Designation of the Righteous has been in charge of awarding the honorary title which, among other things, consists of an honorary certificate, mention in Yad Vashem and even citizenship rights. Joop Westerweel has long been recognised as a worthy member of the 'Righteous among the Nations', and his work has been acknowledged in key historical works on the Holocaust in the Netherlands. Some have, however, claimed that he deserved much more attention. A 1964 book review published in the Israeli newspaper *Maariv* addressed the Hebrew book *His Inner Light* (*Oro Ha-Ganoz*) about Westerweel's life and death. The reviewer wondered why this book had not aroused the same interest as Anne Frank's diary. He believed that

> it should be among the first ranks of Holocaust literature, and be translated to all languages, and be mandatory reading in schools. Especially in this time of extreme cynicism and scorn for ideals, it shows the meaning of courage, sacrifice and noble personality.[22]

Some specifically highlighted the fact that Joop was Christian, in order to underline a certain bond between Jews and non-Jews. An Israeli author wrote once that Joop Westerweel 'sacrificed his life for the sake of love for men and for Israel', since he recognised that 'it was the duty of each nation and that of every righteous Christian to help the Jewish people to arrive alive and free and safe to their historic homeland'.[23] In 1963, the Dutch Jewish weekly *Nieuw Israëlitisch Weekblad* expressed its appreciation for Wil Westerweel who had enrolled in Hebrew classes and since then only spoke in Hebrew at commemoration ceremonies: 'This is the most pure way of honouring the movement, since from this resistance, a bond was forged between Christians and Jews, a bridge was built to a free life on this soil [of *Eretz Israel*]'.[24]

In contrast, others sought to deemphasise the difference between Jews and non-Jews and sought to highlight the human aspect of the resistance movement. For example, in January 1967 a group of about forty Dutchmen received an award from the Dutch ambassador in Israel, Dr. D. Lewin, on behalf of Yad Vashem. The ambassador remarked that the award was intended to preserve the memory of the many Dutchmen who helped their fellow Jewish countrymen, 'not because they were Jews, but because they were people'.[25] Moreover, in 1994, Wil Westerweel protested against one of the captions accompanying her husband's photos in the Ghetto Fighters' House Museum in Northern Israel, which mentioned that he was Christian. She urged the museum not to focus on Joop's religion, but on the fact that he was a combatant against injustice and suppression.[26]

While the survivors saved by the Westerweel movement had an interest in preserving their particular shared memory of the past, their activities also drew the interest of the Dutch and Israeli governments. The 1964 memorial gathering marking the twentieth anniversary of Joop's death was celebrated in extensive fashion as a group of Dutch underground members from the Westerweel movement was invited by the Israeli government to visit Israel. As part of the visit a ceremony was organised in Yad Vashem where certificates of honour were distributed to the resistance fighters and Wil Westerweel planted a tree in the museum's Garden of the Righteous. She herself was awarded the title 'Righteous among the Nations' and received a posthumous recognition on behalf of her late husband. That night Israeli foreign minister Golda Meir received the group in her house, where she told them: 'Your words and acts of protest formed the foundation stone for a better world'. The next day, the group was invited to visit Israeli president Zalman Shazar who expressed his gratitude on behalf of the Israeli nation. He added that the Dutch tradition of tolerance and understanding for the Jewish people dated as far back as the period of Spinoza and Rembrandt.[27] Menachem Pinkhof then presented Shazar with a book about Joop's life. A few days later, on 11 August 1964, on the anniversary of Joop's death, the JNF and Dutch survivors in Israel organised a commemoration service in the Westerweel forest on the occasion of the visit.[28] It was attended by Westerweel's family, representatives of the Dutch Jewish survivors and Dutch Foreign Ministry officials.[29] A representative of the embassy of the Netherlands planted a tree in Joop's name, and at the end of the ceremony, members of the Westerweel group planted trees near the memorial stones. Finally, the group visited the Ghetto Fighters' House Museum where the archives of the Westerweel group were stored.

On the level of bilateral relations, the actions of the Joop Westerweel movement were sometimes presented as a reflection of the sympathetic attitude of the Dutch nation towards the young state of Israel.[30] In the Netherlands, a street in Rotterdam

FIGURE 9.1 The son and daughter of Joop Westerweel at a memorial gathering marking the 20th anniversary of his murder. Courtesy of the Ghetto Fighters' House Online Archives.

FIGURE 9.2 A representative of the Netherlands embassy in Israel, planting a tree in a forest planted in memory of the Zionist Pioneer underground in the Netherlands. Courtesy of the Ghetto Fighters' House Online Archives.

was named after Joop in September 1974.[31] In the years that followed, several other streets in the Netherlands were named after him, including in the municipalities of Heemskerk, Montfoort and Vlaardingen. In Amsterdam, a public elementary school was named after him. Moreover, the work of the group is acknowledged in the Amsterdam Resistance Museum and the National Monument in former Camp Vught, where Westerweel was killed.

However, it has been argued that 'recognition for the Westerweel group in the Netherlands was considerably less than in Israel' (Schippers 2015: 210). Moreover, conflicting narratives about the movement's legacy caused tension at times. For example, in April 1984 a documentary was broadcast on Dutch television entitled *To Never Forget*, telling the story of the Westerweel group. The documentary was produced by Jan Grijpink, Jan Pieter Visser and Loes van Egmond in cooperation with Israeli television. However, the Dutch public broadcasting services believed that the original documentary represented the events 'too much from an Israeli perspective' and requested that the makers adjust the documentary and add new materials highlighting the Dutch role.[32] Similarly, Schippers pointed out an additional controversy when another documentary about the movement was broadcast on Dutch television in the mid-1990s. According to some of the Dutch members of the movement, the documentary did not do enough justice to the share of the non-Jewish participants and had exaggerated the role of the Jewish Palestine Pioneers (Schippers 2015: 8).

A critical narrative in the Ghetto Fighters' Museum

A few years after the Second World War had ended, the Ghetto Fighters' House Museum in northern Israel started archiving documents and other materials that the *Halutzim* had brought to Israel and that testified of their experiences. This came at the initiative of Mirjam Pinkhof, one of the members of the Westerweel group. Pinkhof worked with the museum's archival staff to collect testimonies from more than one hundred individuals related to the Westerweel group and to create a comprehensive archive of its history. In order to translate the material from Dutch into Hebrew, the German-speaking Mirjam requested the help of Tanya Ronen, the daughter of German-born parents, who spent part of their lives in hiding in the Dutch border town of Nieuwlande. With the help of the Westerweel group, Tanya's parents managed to reach Israel. Ronen was born and grew up in *kibbutz* Gal'ed, where she met Mirjam. The two women worked on the preservation of the Westerweel movement for years. The Ghetto Fighters' House Museum housed the archives of the Westerweel group until they were moved to the Netherlands Institute for War Documentation in Amsterdam in 2011.

Their efforts also culminated in a unique permanent exhibition in the Ghetto Fighters' House Museum in Israel, focusing exclusively on the Jews in Holland and the Dutch resistance during the Second World War, which was inaugurated in 1996 in the presence of the Dutch ambassador to Israel. An organisation called Dutch Friends of the Holland Department of the Ghetto Fighters' House Israel had been founded to support and subsidise the exhibition which, according to Miriam Pinkhof, was intended to underline the positive aspects of the Dutch resistance against the Germans. However, it was also intended to debunk the myth that the Dutch were generally good to the Jews during the war. Pinkhof emphasised that, unfortunately, the large majority of the Dutch people had not demonstrated the courage to take action.[33]

The message of the Joop Westerweel forest discussed above, as well as the narratives of Dutch *Halutzim* such as Hanan Florsheim, contributed to the positive image of Dutch behaviour during the Second World War which was widespread in Israel and the Netherlands, especially in the first decades after 1945. Based on personal experiences, the Dutch *Halutzim* told about the exceptional endeavours by people risking their own lives and those of their families for their sake. However, this positive portrayal of the Dutch resistance overlooked the fact that many Dutchmen had collaborated with the Germans during the war, while others remained on the sidelines as Jewish neighbours and acquaintances were rounded up. The former Dutch ambassador in Israel, Gideon W. Boissevain, recognised exactly this fact during the inauguration ceremony of the Westerweel forest in September 1954, saying that among the Dutch a feeling of guilt remained for having witnessed the injustice committed against their Jewish counterparts. 'If we are able to look ourselves in the mirror again, this is only due to men like Joop Westerweel', he said.[34]

Still, it took years for a nuanced narrative to gain some ground in both Israeli and Dutch society. In the Netherlands in the 1950s, only Jewish historians wrote about the *Shoah*, and their writing, according to Brasz

> did not bring about a genuine recognition of these events [while] the negative involvement of Dutch non-Jews in the Shoah was rarely discussed. The Jews seemed to deal with the subject of the persecutions only within the isolation of their own community.
>
> *(Brasz 2001: 156)*

In the 1960s, 'non-Jews began to recognize Jewish suffering, but the Jews' fate was discussed mainly by psychiatrists, as an issue of individual psychic trauma. [...] They were perceived as victims' (Brasz 2001: 157). Only towards the end of the 1960s did the recognition of Jewish traumas give rise to a campaign for social benefits for the victims of Nazi persecution. In the 1980s a critical discourse gained pace as the Dutch role in the persecution of the Jews became highlighted and historical inaccuracies were revised. However, the process of demystification was slow and did not completely alter the dominant narrative of the war in the Netherlands, which focused on the German occupation of the country and portrayed the Dutch as victims of the Nazi regime. In this commemorative narrative, heroic stories of the resistance

> helped shape what Dienke Hondius has termed 'the resistance norm' [...] which had the effect of creating a standard for evaluating conduct during

> the war in terms of 'goodness' and 'wrongness'. Although some Dutch individuals were singled out as wrongdoers, these people were immediately condemned by society and viewed as exceptions to the general standard of resistance that placed the Netherlands as a nation on the right side of the war, fighting for the good of all its citizens. Acts of individual heroism and resistance were not only celebrated, but also taken to be emblematic of the Dutch nation as a whole.[35]

Considering this, the exhibition in the Ghetto Fighters' House Museum may be understood as an attempt to contribute a critical narrative about the Dutch position in the Second World War. This is clear from the description of the exhibition on the museum website, where it is introduced as follows:

> The conquest of the Netherlands rather resembled an annexation, for the Germans were met with cooperation from the Dutch population, including its Jewish community. The deviously mild occupation policies, coupled with the Dutch people's trusting belief in the rule of law, enabled the Nazis to essentially do as they liked with Dutch Jewry.[36]

The exhibition starts with a brief history of the Jews in the Netherlands and then follows their gradual marginalisation and eventual persecution and deportation in the war. Equal attention is paid to the German Nazi presence in the Netherlands and the role of Dutch Nazi political parties such as the NSB. And while the activities of the Dutch resistance are highlighted, the exhibition also demonstrates the role of Dutch collaborators and the *Joodsche Raad* (the Jewish Council). Moreover, the exhibition touches on several elements that are not widely known in the Netherlands when it comes to the pre-war years, such as the story of the arrival of German Jewish refugees throughout the 1930s and the activities of the Zionist Pioneer movement in the Netherlands. For example, the exhibition highlights the fact that the Dutch work camp Westerbork, which later became a notorious transit camp during the occupation, was built by the Dutch government in 1939 in order to house German Jewish refugees who had entered the Netherlands. The camp was built after the Dutch government had already closed its borders to German refugees in December 1938, shortly after *Kristallnacht*, after which the flow of refugees had increased.

According to Tanya Ronen, one of the curators of the exhibition, these controversial aspects of Dutch pre-occupation history are rarely presented in the Netherlands. In an interview with the author she emphasised that the narrative as it is told in this exhibition is not presented anywhere else in such a complete manner, which is precisely why her team invested so much effort in creating it. Ronen claimed that the exhibition made a huge impact on Israeli visitors. However, according to her, a similar recognition by the general Dutch public or the Dutch government was still 'far away'.[37] This too may be changing, however. At the time of the interview, the Jewish Historical Museum in Amsterdam had not yet announced its plans to establish a National Holocaust Museum in 2016. Yet this planned museum will present the history of the Holocaust in a broad international context and use it as a starting point to address timely issues such as genocide, integration of minorities, religious intolerance, anti-Semitism and the violation of human rights and international law. The museum will seek to complement the commemorative function of an existing war monument and museum that is located across the street in Amsterdam, *De Hollandsche Schouwburg* (The Dutch Theatre), which used to function as the Nazis' assembly place for Jews awaiting deportation.

As pointed out earlier, for the Dutch *Halutzim* in Israel who were saved by the Westerweel group, the fact that only a minority of Dutchmen actually participated in the resistance was hard to grasp. Hanan Florsheim admitted that even in his mind the legend of the benignity of the Dutch people only started to change in the last twenty years. Hanan acknowledges that with their stories he and his friends contributed to the positive image of the Netherlands during the war. Although he knows that in retrospect the heroes were only few, he continued to reiterate how difficult it was for Dutchmen to stand up against the Germans and the Dutch collaborators:

> You cannot resent most Dutchmen. They hated the Germans, but had to continue their lives. They went through a lot too, the famine,[38] the horrors in Amsterdam *etcetera*. The people in the resistance were the bravest and were also the minority. It was very dangerous. But the real fighters are always the minority, and in the Netherlands it really was very dangerous.[39]

Shared memories, group identity and future generations

The relations between the surviving members of the Westerweel group now living in Israel and its non-Jewish members living in the Netherlands have remained exceptionally good. Florsheim emphasises that the contact with these families, for example those who helped to hide Jews, remained enduring and special after the war. The Jewish members of the movement regularly hosted Joop's widow Wil in Israel, and the *Halutzim* would receive similar hospitality and visit Wil while in the Netherlands. Other Dutch rescuers, such as Bauke and Vrouwkje de Koning, were invited to Israel as the guests of the survivors.

As is demonstrated from the above, the commemoration of the Westerweel group served to maintain a sense of group identity amongst its members. Those Pioneers cherished the shared experience of surviving the war due to the help of the Westerweel group. Halbwachs argued that memory is a social construct and is shaped in interaction with and *vis-à-vis* others: reconstructed images of the past provide a group with an account of its origin and development and allow the group to recognise itself through time (Halbwachs 1992: 38). As summarised by Aleida Assmann, memory 'provides a repository for group affinities, loyalties, and identity formations' (Assmann 2010: 39). Since one usually belongs to multiple groups in

FIGURE 9.3 Young Jews from the Netherlands whose rescue was aided by members of the Zionist Pioneer underground, hosting Wil Westerweel. Courtesy of the Ghetto Fighters' House Online Archives.

society, it is possible to identify with multiple collective memories at the same time, ranging from those as small as the memory of the family to as large as the memory of the nation. On the one hand, collective memory is instrumental in expressing or proving one's belonging to a group. At the same time, it is crucial for distinguishing this group from other groups. The members of the Westerweel group adhere to multiple collective identities, among them that of the Israeli Pioneer movement and that of the Westerweel group.

The memory of the Westerweel *Hechalutz* Underground is a two-fold memory of survivors of the Second World War who were saved with the help of non-Jews and became Pioneers in *Eretz Israel*. On the one hand, these Dutch Pioneers fulfilled the Zionist dream in which Jews assumed 'an active role in changing the course of their own history', by 'liberating themselves from centuries of exile' and 'revitalizing Jewish national culture' (Zerubavel 1995: 14–15). Their emigration to *Eretz Israel* and their contributions to the settlement of the land are highly praised in the Zionist reconstruction of the past. The story of the Jewish survivors who reached Palestine due to the clandestine efforts of the Westerweel group complies with this narrative as they became Pioneers and were fully absorbed into Israeli society. On the other hand, the way these Dutch Pioneers arrived in Israel does not entirely fit the Zionist representation of the past. They were forced to flee their home countries because of anti-Semitism, went into hiding in the Netherlands and were eventually able to escape to *Eretz Israel* with the help of non-Jews. Their departure from Europe was not always an ideological move. For example Hanan Florsheim, who was among those saved by the Westerweel group, wrote in his memoirs:

> Thus I returned to the land of my ancestors. However, I cannot pretend that a dream had been fulfilled. Although I had been a member of *Maccabi Hazair*, the Zionist youth organization in Amsterdam, and had lived in the Zionist living quarters of Wieringen, all of that did not mean very much to me. To be honest, today I still explain my arrival in Palestine as the result of the kick in the butt that the Nazis gave me. Without it, I would be living today in Germany, my country of birth, without devoting a single thought to immigration. However, owing to the stormy times in which I had become trapped, I was lucky enough to end up in a circle of friends led by comrades of the resistance who had set the goal of reaching Palestine.
>
> *(Florsheim 2007: 119).*

Since their arrival in Palestine, the Jewish members of the Westerweel group have made various efforts to preserve their history and to create a legacy out of their experiences in Europe and the bravery of the Westerweel resistance movement. They continued to pay tribute to their rescuers and preserved their particular history locally through the establishment of a memorial forest, annual commemoration services, reunions, archiving and the publication of memoirs.

The survivors of *Hechalutz* Westerweel living in Israel have stayed in touch and organise commemorative initiatives within the community. The Association of the Pioneers Underground in Holland consists of former members of the Westerweel group and meets once a year. Its meetings are usually held in *kibbutz* Gal'ed, which seems to function as the base of the group. This is despite the fact that most former activists have left Gal'ed and have helped to establish other *kibbutzim* such as Yakum or have moved to cities in the centre of Israel such as Ramat Gan. The annual meeting of the Association generally starts with a ceremony in the Joop Westerweel forest, where a '*yizkor*' ('memorial prayer') verse is read, and wreaths are laid on the monuments in the forest. After that, the group convenes in the clubhouse of *kibbutz* Gal'ed where they are hosted by Rolf Rozenthal and his son Amir.

Nevertheless, the members of the Westerweel group have aged greatly and fewer and fewer people attend the annual meetings. In the past, it was very common for them to bring their children and involve them in commemorative events or to introduce them to their rescuers from the Netherlands when they visited Israel. By the same token, Joop's own children had not known their father very well but supposedly came to know him through the preservation of his memory by those he rescued. Joop's son Leo said that for a long time he had been unable to really connect to the past: 'As the son of the man who gave his life in the battle against injustice, I most of all missed having a father.'[40] One of his children, Marta, settled in Israel, where she met many of those whom her father had saved. She testified: 'I was three-and-a-half years old when my father was arrested and five years old when he was executed. I never really knew him. In the Netherlands I was a fatherless

FIGURE 9.4 Paved area. Joop Westerweel forest, Israel. Photograph © Joyce van de Bildt.

child; here in Israel I became my father's daughter'.[41] It was from the survivors that she learned stories about her father. After the war, Wil regularly visited Israel with her four children, one of whom was later married there.[42]

Besides these interactions, there is a question mark over whether the second and third generation of survivors will continue the commemorative initiatives. Marianne Hirsch introduced the concept of 'postmemory', which she defines as 'the relationship of the second generation to powerful, often traumatic, experiences that preceded their births but that were nevertheless transmitted to them so deeply as to seem to constitute memories in their own right' (Hirsch 2008: 103). Hirsch notes that although memory can be transmitted, the 'received' memory will be distinct from the recall of contemporary witnesses and participants. This contradiction is inherent to the phenomenon of postmemory, which is not identical to memory but approximates memory in its affective force (Hirsch 2008: 109). In the case of the Westerweel group, its memory has been transferred to the second generation but to different extents. While some descendants, such as Tanya Ronen, are actively engaged in preserving historical material related to the group, others have limited their involvement to joining their parents on 'roots tours' to Europe. One member of the second generation, Yoram Goren, is a good example of the former. His mother Lori Durlacher was rescued by the Westerweel group and Yoram has taken upon himself the task of founding and managing the website of the group.[43]

FIGURE 9.5 Monument in the Joop Westerweel forest, Israel, with names of key actors in the underground movement, and the Hebrew phrase '*Nizkor*' ('We will remember'). Photograph © Joyce van de Bildt.

The Israeli-born Yoram has designed the website entirely in Hebrew, which makes it available mainly to the Israeli public. There is no comparable endeavour in Dutch, German or English. Another member of the second generation, Amir Rozenthal, has started to help his ageing father with taking care of the surroundings of the Westerweel forest, and hosting the group in *kibbutz* Gal'ed once a year. However, according to Hanan Florsheim, there are only a few who are attracted by the Westerweel history to the extent that they are actively involved in the preservation of its legacy.

Conclusion

The Westerweel case serves as an example of a sectional community memory. Its meaning is limited to a particular group and does not completely fit into the memory of other groups. This case study has attempted to show that individual consciousness of the past is linked to group identity, not only on the national level but also on the level of communal groups that perceive their past as distinct. Indeed, although the survivors of the Westerweel group form an integral part of Israeli society, they seek to distinguish themselves through the memory of their group's past.

The sectional nature of this memory is first of all evident in the nature of the group's commemorative initiatives, such as its intimate reunions and remembrance services. Moreover, the location of the Joop Westerweel monument in the forest that became the group's main commemorative site is exemplary of the local nature of this memory. In general, monuments or memorial stones are likely to be established inside a populated area, where their exposure is most guaranteed. They help sustain a group memory and its presence in the public space functions as a constant reminder of the past. However, in this case of sectional community memory, the memorial was placed in nature, close to *kibbutz* Gal'ed where a large part of the survivors had found a new home. When passing through this rather remote area in Israel, the memorial area is easily overlooked. This underlines the fact that the memorial served most of all to sustain a group memory particular to the residents of the area and others who share it.

Since afforestation was one of the key tools of the Zionist settlement effort, and it was common to plant trees in someone's name, the establishment of the Joop Westerweel forest was a highly symbolic form of commemoration for those European Jews saved by Westerweel who became Pioneers in Palestine. Viewed from the Israeli state level, it could be said that the forest's establishment in 1947 came relatively fast, since, during those years, the nascent Israeli state had not yet started dealing with the trauma of the Holocaust. This observation again reiterates the fact that the initiative was private and belonged to a select group of people.

Moreover, the local memory of the Westerweel group does not precisely map onto dominant national discourses in Israel and the Netherlands. In the Netherlands, resistance is an important element of the narrative of the Second World War, but the Joop Westerweel movement was exceptional in many ways and has been marginalised in this narrative. The uncommon combination of its members, as well as the group's aim to save Jews and help them escape to *Eretz Israel*, were unique in the history of the Dutch resistance. The various Joop Westerweel commemorative activities emphasise the exceptional nature of the Westerweel group. In the private memory initiatives dedicated to the Westerweel group, the nonconformist nature of the group is presented as an example for future generations. It should be noted that at the same time, others chose to emphasise the movement's acts of humanity, and not so much the unique cooperation between its Jewish and non-Jewish counterparts. For them, commemorations held by the Westerweel group are not necessarily about its leader Joop Westerweel, but to honour all those who risked their lives to save Jews. Hence, they sought to attach a wider meaning to the legacy of the Westerweel movement. Finally, the Ghetto Fighters' House Museum in Israel took the story of Joop Westerweel as a starting point to contribute a critical narrative to the story of the Second World War in the Netherlands. A special exhibition on the Jews of Holland highlighted the heroic acts of the Westerweel movement and the ultimate price paid by some of its members. At the same time, this exhibition sought to balance both the Dutch and the Israeli perception that the position of the Dutch during the Second World War was largely benign, as the exhibition paid ample attention to the role of collaborators and bystanders.

Notes

Unless otherwise indicated, all translations are my own.

1 The term 'Westerweel group' was first introduced in the 1960s. In fact, as Hans Schippers pointed out, the activities of Westerweel and the Pioneers took place in three different frameworks that interacted with each other: that of Westerweel and his non-Jewish colleagues, the Pioneers organised in the *Hechalutz* and another group led by Frans Gerritsen (Schippers 2015: 8). In this article, the term 'Westerweel group' is used to refer to all this activity.
2 'Het J.N.F. na 1945', *Nieuw Israëlitisch Weekblad*, 4 September 1953, 6.
3 'Een "Westerweel-woud" in Palestina', *De Waarheid*, 18 January 1946, 2.
4 'Joden in Nederland geven uiting aan hun dankbaarheid', *Nieuw Israëlitisch Weekblad*, 25 January 1946, 1–2.
5 'Joop Westerweelwoud'. *Nieuw Israëlitisch Weekblad*, 21 January 1966, 2.
6 Psalms (*Tehillim*) 92:13.
7 'Een bijzondere geste', *Nieuw Israëlitisch Weekblad*, 22 March 1963, 5.
8 'Joop Westerweel-Woud', *Nieuw Israëlitisch Weekblad*, 12 July 1963, 8.
9 'Israël krijgt van oud-AJC-ers 2000 bomen', *Het Vrije Volk*, 20 March 1973, 13.
10 The AJC subsequently planned to establish a '*Paasheuvelbos*' in Israel, named after their famous meeting place in Holland. The forest was to be called Tel Pesach, consisting of 500 trees. See 'Paasheuvel in Westerweel-Woud', *Nieuw Israëlitisch Weekblad*, 1 December 1972, 2.
11 'Oud-AJC'ers schonken Israël Paasheuvel', *Nieuw Israëlitisch Weekblad*, 25 May 1973, 3.
12 'Le-zecher Joop Westerweel', *Davar*, 27 March 1947, 11; 'Ya'ar Westerweel nita be-harei Menashe', *Hatsofe*, 12 March 1947, 3.
13 Interview with Hanan Florsheim, 31 January 2013.
14 'Verzetsstrijder Shushu in Israël herdacht', *Nieuw Israëlitisch Weekblad*, 31 May 1963, 4.
15 Book of Joshua, 4:9
16 'Verzetsstrijder Shushu in Israël herdacht'.
17 'Gedenksteen in Westerweel-woud', *Nieuw Israëlitisch Weekblad*, 3–8 October 1954, 3.
18 Irena Steinfeldt, 'Paying the Ultimate Price', *Jerusalem Post*, 4 August 2009, www.jpost.com/Opinion/Columnists/Essay-Paying-the-ultimate-price.
19 The National-Socialist Movement (NSB) was a Dutch fascist political party and remained the only legal political party in the Netherlands during the Second World War, functioning as a collaborationist party.
20 Interview with Hanan Florsheim, 31 January 2013.
21 'Bauke Koning en zijn vrouw door hun "kinderen" in Israël ontvangen', *Nieuw Israëlitisch Weekblad*, 29 September 1957, 4.
22 'Oro haganuz', *Maariv*, 11 December 1964, 14.
23 'Le-zecher Joop Westerweel'.
24 'Verzetsstrijder Shushu in Israël herdacht'.
25 'Ambassadeur reikt certificaten uit aan verzetsstrijders', *Nieuw Israëlitisch Weekblad*, 3 February 1967, 1; 'Veertig Nederlanders onderscheiden', *Algemeen Handelsblad*, 25 January 1967, 9.
26 'Westerweel', *Nieuw Israëlitisch Weekblad*, 29 April 1994, 6.
27 'Verzetsstrijder Joop Westerweel in Israël herdacht', *Limburgsch Dagblad*, 6 August 1964, 5; 'Atzeret le-zichram shel chavrei makhteret Holandim ba-Ya'ar Joop Westerweel'. *Herut*, 12 August 1964, 6.
28 'Westerweelgroep bezoekt Israël', *Nieuw Israëlitisch Weekblad*, 14 August 1964, 3.
29 'Atzeret le-zecher chavrei ha-makhteret ha-Holandit', *Davar*, 12 August 1964, 3.
30 'Ambassadeur reikt certificaten uit aan verzetsstrijders'.
31 'Verzetsstrijders met straatnamen geëerd', *Het Vrije Volk*, 9 September 1974, 7.
32 'Verzetsgroep', *Nieuwe Leidsche Courant*, 2 April 1984, 10.
33 'Israël herdenkt verzet', *Nieuw Israëlitisch Weekblad*, 11 September 1992, 7.

34 'Gedenksteen in Westerweel-woud'.
35 M. Kronemeijer and D. Teshima, 'A Founding Myth for the Netherlands: The Second World War and the Victimization of Dutch Jews', *Humanity in Action*, 2000, available at www.humanityinaction.org/knowledgebase/293-a-founding-myth-for-the-netherlands-the-second-world-war-and-the-victimization-of-dutch-jews.
36 See 'The Jews of Holland during the Holocaust' on the website of the Ghetto Fighters' House Museum at www.gfh.org.il/Eng/?CategoryID=61&ArticleID=452.
37 Interview with Tanya Ronen, 20 February 2013.
38 The famine of 1944 is known as the 'hunger winter' in the Netherlands and took place in the German-occupied part of the country, especially in the densely populated western provinces. A German blockade cut off food and fuel shipments from farm areas to punish the reluctance of the Dutch to aid the Nazi war effort. Some four and a half million individuals were affected and only survived because of soup kitchens; around 22,000 are believed to have died.
39 Interview with Hanan Florsheim, 31 January 2013.
40 'Westerweel'.
41 See 'The Westerweel Network: Johan Gerard & Wilhelmina Dora Westerweel. The Netherlands' on the Yad Vashem website at www.yadvashem.org/yv/en/righteous/stories/westerweel.asp.
42 'Verzetsstrijder Joop Westerweel in Israël herdacht'.
43 See *Ha-Makhteret ha-khalutzit ba-Holland ve-kvutzat Westerweel*, www.westerweel-hechaluz-group.com/.

References

Assmann, A. 2010. 'Re-framing Memory. Between Individual and Collective Forms of Constructing the Past'. In *Performing the Past: Memory, History, and Identity in Modern Europe*, edited by K. Tilmans, F. van Vree and J. Winter. Amsterdam: Amsterdam University Press. 35–50.

Brasz, C. 2001. 'After the Shoah: Continuity and Change in the Postwar Jewish Community of the Netherlands'. *Jewish History*, 15: 149–68.

Braverman, I. 2009. 'Planting the Promised Landscape: Zionism, Nature, and Resistance in Israel/Palestine'. *Natural Resources Journal*, 49, 2: 317–61.

Florsheim, H. 2007. *He Who Dares Wins: Across the Pyrenees to Freedom. Diary of Chanan (Hans) Flörsheim 1923–1944.* Translated by Dieter Heymann. Konstanz: Hartung-Gorre.

Halbwachs, M. 1992. *On Collective Memory*. Translated by Lewis A. Coser. Chicago, IL: Chicago University Press.

Hirsch, M. 2008. 'The Generation of Postmemory'. *Poetics Today*, 29, 1: 103–28.

Pinkhof, M. and Brasz, I. 1997. *De Jeugdalijah van het Paviljoen Loosdrechtsche Rade, 1939–1945.* 2nd edn. Hilversum: Uitgeverij Verloren.

Schippers, H. 2015. *De Westerweelgroep en de Palestinapioniers: Non-conformistisch verzet in de Tweede Wereldoorlog*. Hilversum: Uitgeverij Verloren.

Zerubavel, Y. 1995. *Recovered Roots: Collective Memory and the Making of Israeli National Tradition*. Chicago, IL: University of Chicago Press.

PART IV

Practices of remembrance

10

A HOLY RELIC OF WAR: THE SOVIET VICTORY BANNER AS ARTEFACT

Jeremy Hicks

Since 1965 the centrepiece of the 9 May Victory Day celebrations in Moscow has been a parade on Red Square in which the Victory Banner raised over the Reichstag on 30 April 1945 is ceremonially displayed by a guard of honour before the watching public. The Banner is a red Soviet flag bearing the hammer and sickle emblem, with the name of the unit that raised it added in white.[1] Newsreel and still photographic images of the raising of the Victory Banner over the Reichstag became a central symbol in the 1960s birth of what has been called a Soviet 'war cult' (Tumarkin 1994: 137). More recently, the actual banner and – since its adoption as an official state symbol in 2007 – replicas of it have played an increasingly important role in articulating and disseminating the Soviet and post-Soviet Russian view of victory in the Second World War, the Soviet dimension of which has long been referred to as the Great Patriotic War.

This chapter is an attempt to understand how this flag came to acquire such symbolic resonance and to trace its place within the practices of Second World War commemoration that have evolved since May 1945. The introductory section adumbrates a theoretical approach premised on the notion that national understanding of the past is constructed in part through the selection and mediation of symbols. I then trace the fate of the Victory Banner from its initial journey to Moscow in May 1945, examining its installation in what is now known as the Central Museum of the Armed Forces and how changing approaches to displaying it in the years since have variously constructed this symbol's meaning amidst changing societal attitudes to the war. I then explore the use of the Banner in parades, both formal and informal, since the revival of war commemoration in the 1960s; the debates around the Victory Banner's second revival in the 1990s and early 2000s, when it became a central symbol of the post-Soviet Russian state; and its recent appropriation as a political symbol across the post-Soviet space in political demonstrations. While sketching out the broad historical and political context, I will also analyse in detail how the Banner's incorporation in specific museum sites, parades, performances and re-enactments has reinflected and reshaped both its meaning and the broader memory of the war.

Understanding 'invented traditions'

In her influential study of what she called the 'cult' of the war in the Soviet Union, Nina Tumarkin discusses the Victory Banner as a holy relic:

> By 1975, the war cult had so deepened and its accompanying language had become so sentimental that the Victory Banner had gained the epithet 'holy of holies' and had been turned into its single most exalted relic, an embodiment of the collective virtue implied in the official remembrance of the victory.
>
> *(Tumarkin 1994: 137)*

For Tumarkin, this was evidently ridiculous and she quoted a sceptical 1970s teenager's lack of interest in the Victory Banner, implicitly dismissing any claim as to its auratic power as nothing but hollow rhetoric. This dismissive attitude seems erroneous, and it is not unrelated to her book's profoundly mistaken assumption that the practice of commemoration of the Great Patriotic War was in terminal decline and would disappear in post-Soviet Russia.

One factor informing Tumarkin's study, and her condescension towards the sacred status conferred by the Soviets upon the symbol of the Victory Banner, was an assumption that Soviet inconsistencies and silences about the war constituted a fatal flaw in the 'war cult' and that the post-Soviet period would therefore witness a move from collective to individual grieving as the 'cult' withered (Tumarkin 1994: 226).[2] This approach stems from a tradition in historical scholarship that sees its task as distinguishing between mythical elements, including what we have come to term 'memory', and the factual elements of history, which are deemed not only primary but ultimately pivotal in shaping societal understanding. Implicit in this approach, as with Eric Hobsbawm's attempts to show how 'invented traditions', associated, for example, with the British royal family, were actually symbolic practices invented fairly recently with the aim of constructing a spurious continuity, was wishful thinking masquerading as scholarly method: an assumption that exposing the constructed nature of memory would lead to it becoming less influential (Hobsbawm 1983). Working within a different tradition, the paradigm of memory studies, Aleida Assmann has criticised this approach:

> By showing that some traditions are a fake, such categories as 'true' and 'authentic' were affirmed and reinstated *ex negativo*. It was the trust of enlightenment shared by these historians writing on the presuppositions of Marxist and modernization theory that by the very act of exposure, by merely

> pointing to the inventedness, manufacturedness, and hence to the 'falseness' of the tradition, its spell would be broken and automatically dissolved.
>
> *(Assmann 2008: 66).*

Assmann argues that this is a misunderstanding of the way in which traditions function in the context of collective memory:

> Memory constructs that inform commemorative practices and traditions are therefore not necessarily false because they are constructed – of course they are! The questions to be asked should not only focus on empirical evidence and the substance of the narrative or tradition alone but ought to take the wider context into account: Why and how do memory constructs work? Why do they succeed to mobilize? Why do they find or fail to raise mass support and resonance? As they are necessarily selective, the question is: By which norms and bias are they chosen? What is included and what is excluded from the constructions of collective memory? And what are the political consequences of such choices in the present and for future?
>
> *(Assmann 2008: 67)*

It is this perspective, which sees the Victory Banner as a mobilising symbol within an 'affectively charged … narrative', that informs the present study: it as an attempt to understand how the symbol functions, how it acquired the power it now wields and what effects this particular 'memory construct' has in the societies where it has become prominent.

Assmann sees this kind of collective memory as 'social, political, national, and cultural memory' and argues that it works through a range of forms which are vehicles for a range of representations. These include:

- emplotment of events in an affectively charged and mobilizing narrative;
- visual and verbal signs that serve as aids of memory;
- institutions of learning and the dissemination of mass media;
- sites and monuments that present palpable relics;
- commemoration rites that periodically reactivate the memory and enhance collective participation.

(Assmann 2008: 55–6).

The distinctive and privileged nature of the Victory Banner as a Soviet and Russian symbol of the Second World War becomes apparent from a consideration of its relation to these categories. Effectively, one might say that it relates to all of them. Evidently it is a symbol aiding memory, but since it represents the final, most triumphant, moment of the Soviet victory, it also serves to articulate an 'affectively charged' narrative. As a museum object, it is a 'palpable relic', housed in a museum with an ostensive educational function. And, finally, it has played and continues to play a role in 'commemoration rites' with an increasingly wide dimension of 'collective participation'. First and foremost, however, the Victory Banner is an object that functions as an artefact and a relic.

The Victory Banner as artefact: the power of objects

There is an extensive literature devoted to the discussion of museum objects, the overwhelming tendency of which is to see them as central to museums' claims to authority and truth: 'objects play a crucial role as material evidence supporting a particular version of the world and events in it'. However, as Naomi Stead characterises it, there has been a historic tension between those who see the museum object as inherently meaningful, bearing a trace of its original context and use, on the one hand, and those, on the other, who see it as acquiring meaning when placed in a 'network of interpretation' (Stead 2007: 38). In this instance, the Victory Banner might be seen as an inherently meaningful symbol of victory, or rather an indexical proof of it, because it is the actual flag raised over the Reichstag to signify victory. However, the situation is in fact far less straightforward, for several reasons. First, the actual Victory Banner was neither the first nor the only flag raised over the Reichstag during and immediately following its capture on 30 April-2 May 1945: each of the Red Army units attacking the Reichstag from different directions raised a red flag on the building, from various points including a window, a balcony, a column, an equestrian statue on the roof and the building's cupola. The official Victory Banner appears only to have been raised later (Pospelov *et al.* 1963: 282–5). Second, the capture of the Reichstag was not the most strategically or politically significant moment in the battle for Berlin, or the fall of the Nazi regime, given that it was not a centre or symbol of Nazi power and the German act of capitulation was signed days after its capture. Third, the singularity of the Victory Banner as a museum object is a paradox, since it is essentially just a red flag bearing the hammer and sickle emblem of the Soviet Union: its ubiquitous state flag. Fourth, as an index of the event it is rivalled by photographic and filmic images purporting to record the capture of the Reichstag. All of this suggests that the fact that this particular flag has come to serve as a unique signifier of victory is the product of a discourse, a conventionalised narrative, which is the subject of our investigation.

This discourse has conferred upon the Victory Banner a perceived special power, an originality and authority that might be conceptualised in terms of Walter Benjamin's notion of 'aura', originally coined to describe works of art, but also adapted to apply to museum objects (Walsh 1992: 35). Benjamin saw aura as relating to the cultic and ritual value of the object (Benjamin 1992 [1936]: 237) and it is this fetishistic (Belting 1998: 19), or implicitly sacred, quality possessed by the museum object that is particularly relevant to an understanding of the ways in which the Victory Banner has come to be seen and used in Russia and the former Soviet Union since 1945. Also relevant here is Emile Durkheim's division of objects into the sacred and profane as a feature of religious belief, and his argument that what makes an object sacred is not an intrinsic property but rather attitudes and social rituals attached to it and the setting of it apart from the profane sphere

(Durkheim 1995 [1912]: 37). Rituals of consecration are key to transmitting the sacred qualities of an object, due to the 'extraordinary contagiousness' of the sacred (Durkheim 1995 [1912]: 322). As we shall see this also relates to the way in which the Victory Banner was presented as sacred and contrasted with profane objects through its use in Victory Day parades and the narrative constructed around it in its museum home.

The Victory Banner as museum object: the evolution of a relic

The Victory Banner did not actually take part in the 24 June 1945 Victory Parade on Red Square, after the frontline troops who had initially raised the flag and were due to carry it performed poorly at the dress rehearsal on the previous day (Neustroev 1990: 144). Instead, Marshal Georgii Zhukov, who was to be the central figure in the parade, sent the Banner to what was then called the Central Museum of the Red Army (now the Central Museum of the Armed Forces). Nevertheless, despite the Victory Banner's absence, other banners played a key role. The voice-over for the commemorative documentary film, entitled *Victory Parade*, identified the representatives of the various 'fronts' as they marched past the mausoleum podium, and as the 1st Belorussian Front filed past the commentary stated that they were carrying thirty-six battle banners: 'They took the Reichstag and raised the Victory Banner over Berlin'.[3]

Banners were once again to the fore in the original parade's most dramatic moment, when to the stirring rhythm of eighty drummers, 200 captured Nazi banners were cast down before Lenin's mausoleum. This performance reworked the contest of symbols, the old versus new, which had been key to pre-war Soviet parades, only now it was not the church or internal opponents but the Nazis who were associated with the profane (Rolf 2013: 41). Their vanquished symbols were contrasted with Lenin's mausoleum and the leaders, including Stalin, standing upon it. Later, when placed in a museum, the Victory Banner would similarly be contrasted with Nazi banners, taking on a sacred status from its differential opposition to them.

In the first year after the war the Central Museum of the Red Army was almost entirely devoted to the Great Patriotic War and contained an enormous number of artefacts, but the Victory Banner was not yet presented as an exceptional object. Rather it was just one among many physical artefacts of the war including a sniper's rifle that killed more than 1,000 Germans, mounted on red velvet, and the effects of fallen heroes, such as Zoia Kosmodem´ianskaia the 18-year-old schoolgirl dropped behind enemy lines during the Battle of Moscow, captured, tortured and killed by the Nazis, who was the subject of a number of propaganda narratives across many media. Not only was the Victory Banner initially one among many other artefacts of the war, it was also overshadowed by the museum's emphasis upon Stalin as the central figure in wartime victory. As the official museum guidebook put it:

> In the Museum's rooms the visitor sees orders issued by Supreme Commander Marshal Stalin during the Great Patriotic War, letters from Red Army

> soldiers, officers and workers of our Motherland to comrade Stalin and other documents testifying to the uniting of the Soviet people around the Party of Lenin-Stalin and the government to resist the enemy. Battle plans, genuine relief maps and documents show the realisation of the genius of Stalin's strategic plans for the defeat of the German-Fascist invaders.[4]

The description of how the Victory Banner was displayed also underlined the overriding importance of this Stalin-centric narrative:

> The Museum display concludes with the Hall of Banners. Here one can find the military banners of the Red Army units who have distinguished themselves in battles for the Motherland. Soviet medals received by the divisions and regiments are attached to the banners, with their medal ribbons. On a high pedestal, lit up by projectors, burns the red flame of the Victory Banner raised on the German Reichstag on 30 April 1945. In the centre of the Hall, is a bust of the Great Leader, the commander of genius, comrade Stalin, under whose leadership the Soviet people and their armed forces won historical victories in the Great Patriotic War.[5]

Alongside the bust of Stalin, the Victory Banner is already the culminating point of the museum and it is presented dramatically, in a glass case, lit with projectors, so as to underline its importance and auratic power. Yet, the Hall of Banners does not only contain flags relating to the Second World War and to the Victory Parade, but also ones relating to the defence of the Soviet state in previous conflicts such as the Civil War. The Victory Banner did yet play the central political role it would later assume.

By the final year of Stalin's life, the museum had been remodelled so that ten of its fifteen rooms were devoted to the Great Patriotic War, with three on the Civil War, one on the inter-war period and one on the post-war years (Arsenin 1953: 115–18). There were now sculpted portraits of the soldiers credited with raising the flag, Mikhail Egorov and Meliton Kantariia, a model of the burning Reichstag, photographs and other materials about the last days of the war all alongside the Victory Banner, now displayed with other materials representing the battle for Berlin rather than in the Hall of Banners. For the first time the guidebook stressed its sacred character: 'Here is the holy relic of the Great Patriotic War – the modest red flag with the names of the unit that captured the Reichstag – the Victory Banner' (Arsenin 1953: 80).

Even though the Victory Banner itself was no longer in the Hall of Banners, references to 9 May 1945 as Victory Day and also, for the first time, to the 24 June 1945 Victory Parade were now very prominent in this room. Moreover, while even before Stalin's death his bust had been removed from the Hall of Banners, evidently visitors were still supposed to think of him when visiting it, as the guidebook makes clear:

> Before leaving the Museum, visitors proceed to the Hall of Banners, the contents of which seem to sum up the whole collection. In the centre of the

> Hall hangs the painting 'Victory Salute'. On the 9 May 1945 Muscovites celebrate Victory Day. And all their thoughts and cogitations are for the architect of the greatest military triumph of our Motherland, comrade Stalin.
>
> *(Arsenin 1953: 86)*

In this organisation of the room, the banners of the conquered German armies lay on the ground before the triumphant Soviet ones as they had in the June 1945 Victory Parade, yet they mingled with other symbols of triumph including flags of Civil War White guards and interventionists as well as those of the Japanese in the Second World War. Thus, despite acquiring stronger associations with the sacred, implicitly underscored by the contrast to profane Nazi banners, the Victory Banner's singularity and the unique importance of the Second World War were not yet so apparent. Rather, it was integrated into and subordinated within a system of Soviet symbols in which Stalin was still key and which stressed a longer revolutionary history.

Following Stalin's death in 1953, the Victory Banner, still in its glass case on a tall pedestal, remained at the centre of a room devoted to the storming of Berlin. As explained by the guidebook, this was now the penultimate room of the museum, followed only by a room that spelled out the importance of the Soviet Army (as the Red Army had been renamed in 1946) for the maintenance of peace in the contemporary world.[6] As the now dead Stalin receded from view within official Soviet symbolism, the Victory Banner's indexical significance connoting the pinnacle and culminating point of Soviet martial achievement meant that it was becoming more prominent. It now had to perform some of the symbolic function once carried out by the image of Stalin, as a kind of widely recognised shorthand for the Communist cause and the Soviet state.

The 1963 fifth volume of the official six-volume history of the Great Patriotic War had encountered such difficulties in getting to the bottom of the eyewitness accounts of who actually put up the Victory Banner that it had instead stressed the multiplicity of flags raised over the Reichstag and the fact that the official Victory Banner was raised later than the others (Pospelov *et al.* 1963: 282–5). However, such potentially iconoclastic disclosures were quickly drowned out by the triumphalist fanfare of commemoration unleashed following the deposing of Nikita Khrushchev and Leonid Brezhnev's October 1964 ascent to the post of first secretary of the Party. This included the decision to mark Victory Day with a parade in Moscow, the first of which, on 9 May 1965, was so hastily organised that it entailed the last minute cancellation of the traditional 1 May military parade. The Victory Banner was at the heart of proceedings, as its entry onto Red Square, held aloft by Egorov and Kantariia, was the signal for the start of the parade. While it is unclear who took the decision to include the flag in the reinvented parade, the mobilising of its symbolic significance was illustrative of the wider approach to the war in the Brezhnev period. The same year, the now renamed Central Museum of the Armed Forces of the USSR moved to a new building, opened on the eve of Victory Day, where the Victory Banner was prominently displayed in its own special Victory Hall, where it was elevated and sealed in glass above a photograph of the June 1945 Victory Parade showing the lowered profane Nazi banners (Pisareva and Poplyko 1969). True, symbolism around the war was still in flux in the 1960s, and one guidebook to the museum published in 1965 emphasising photographs of exhibits did not include an image of the Victory Banner.[7] Yet the general trend was clear: it was assuming ever greater auratic power.

The fact that the Victory Banner was not in fact a part of the 1945 Victory Parade, as opposed to the post-1965 Victory Day parades, was not made clear in the museum; indeed, the displays seemed to imply that it was present. As the Victory Banner came to serve after 1965 as the ultimate symbol of victory, so a number of accounts erroneously reinserted it into descriptions of the 1945 parade (Svoichakov 1973: 222). One eyewitness account called the parade unforgettable, but on the same page referred to the Victory Banner as being there, and as having been transferred to the museum after the parade (Drozdovskii *et al.* 2000: 50). Yet another eyewitness was quoted describing how the Banner appeared on Red Square that day:

> On the day of the parade the Victory Banner was fixed to a specially adapted open-topped automobile above which a large globe was suspended. The Victory Banner was fixed to it on a spot marked with the word 'Berlin'.
>
> I shall never forget that day in Moscow.
>
> *(Tiurin 2000: 32)*

The proliferation of such false memories underlines the incredible combined myth-creating power of the Victory Banner itself, the museum and the post-1965 Victory Day parades. The symbolic, sacralised power of the Victory Banner continued to grow throughout this late Soviet period, so much so that by 1985, not only did the Victory Banner occupy its own special Victory Hall, but this was so much the most important part of the museum that one could buy a guidebook devoted to it alone.[8] Before the collapse of the Soviet Union, work was already under way on a project to build a grandiose museum and memorial complex to victory in the Great Patriotic War – a Victory Park – at the Hill of Prostrations in Moscow (Schleifman 2001). The Victory Banner was scheduled to be moved to the new museum, and housed in a new Hall of Glory, while a dedicated memorial to it was also to be constructed. The project was frozen in 1987, and only completed in 1995, though then without the Victory Banner itself or the monumental sculpture to it. This is a result of the timing of its completion at the height of the Yeltsin years when, as we shall see, there was a concerted attempt to rethink memory of the war so as to cleanse it of all Communist symbolism.

The basic format of the room devoted to the Victory Banner, the storming of Berlin and the Moscow Victory Parade of 24 June 1945 seems to have continued unchanged to this day, even if since 1965 the actual flag has been kept in a sealed capsule so as to arrest its decay.[9] Yet this surface image of timeless continuity obscures the remarkable fact that the Victory Banner only grew to acquire its special, or independent, auratic power in the post-Stalin years, when it came to take the place of the charismatic leader cult. The overall continuity of the flag's place in the museum and its use in the Red Square Victory Day parade also masks the more profound contradiction that what is in essence the state flag of the Soviet Union has survived that state's disappearance to become a state and national symbol in a post-Soviet Russia that is largely hostile to the Communist project. This brief sketch of the changing ways in which the Victory Banner has been presented in Soviet museums gives us a sense of its evolution as a key symbol for Soviet and Russian commemoration of the war. However, it is only by also considering the rituals associated with the Victory Banner that one can truly grasp its sacred power.

Rituals of the flag

From the moment of the Victory Banner's first arrival in the Central Museum of the Red Army in 1945, it was common for members of the Pioneers, the official Soviet youth organisation, to swear their oath by it (Arsenin 1953: 94). Invoking Durkheim, we might describe these as rituals of consecration that enabled the participants to partake of the Victory Banner's sacred power. Such power was even more in demand following Stalin's death: in the wake of the 1956 decision to permit the forming of Union-wide veterans' organisations (Edele 2008: 162), Victory Day became a focus for their activity and veterans began to gather together annually in Moscow in the period between 15 April and 10 May. The Central Museum of the Armed Forces' Victory Hall became packed in this period, as thousands of people, especially participants in the storming of the Reichstag, came to pay their respects to the dead and to reminisce (Shatilov 1988: 188). The choice of the Victory Hall, dominated by the Victory Banner, was symbolic.

Emboldened by their discovery of their power to organise, veterans strove to seize greater control over the narrative of the war in general and of the Victory Banner. The flag itself began to leave the premises of the museum to take part in their gatherings. A 1962 guidebook describes this phenomenon:

> Participants in the Battle of Berlin often come to the Museum, to the Victory Banner. On numerous occasions, heroes of the Soviet Union Egorov, Kantariia, Neustroev, S´ianov and other veterans of the Great Patriotic War have spoken in the Museum about their memories of the raising of the Victory Banner. On occasion the Victory Banner, accompanied by a guard of honour, has been ceremonially displayed at meetings devoted to notable events in the history of the Soviet Army.[10]

The use of the flag in commemorative political meetings, such as the enormous gathering in the Lenin stadium in Moscow on 9 May 1960, commemorating the fifteenth anniversary of the end of the war, embodied the growing grassroots pressure from veterans for whom the war was the central event of their lives and of the Soviet Union's history. Seen in this light, the decision to declare Victory Day a public holiday, and to stage the enormous 1965 parade – the first since 1946 – was not solely a myth imposed from above, or a manipulation through guilt (Tumarkin 1994: 133); it was also part of a bid by the state to assert control over a powerful grassroots impulse to intensify commemoration of the war (Weiner 2001). As Russian historian Boris Dubin has argued, the state mobilised every possible institutional means including parades, medals, monuments, film and literature to ensure that it retained 'the monopoly as keeper of memory and constructor of history' as part of a 'symbolic politics' (Dubin 2008).

Although the Victory Banner does not figure in Dubin's list, it too was a crucial part of the resurgent cult of the war. Effectively, the Victory Day parade controlled and regimented uses of the flag, incorporating it into a solemn state-endorsed ceremony and removing it from the unpredictable and harder to manage sphere of spontaneous, veteran-dominated, political meetings. Possession of this artefact, and the power to shape its symbolic meaning, was a key part of this battle, the struggle to determine the meaning of victory in the war for Soviet society.

It is in this period of change, when the fully fledged 'war cult' first starts to coalesce, that the Victory Banner artefact comes to play a particularly important role. One way of understanding this is through the need for new symbols for the state in the vacuum left by the critique and collapse of the Stalin cult. As Malte Rolf argues: 'Power needs symbols and it needs to be conveyed symbolically.' This symbolic dimension is particularly important in difficult times and times of transition owing to the power of symbols to confer stability through repetition (Rolf 2013: 41). This need for symbols and repetition fuelled the creation of the various Victory Day rituals. The holy associations of the Victory Banner are particularly important here, since a mystical dimension is an important factor in both rituals and the most effective flags (Pastoreau 2004: 296). Thus, in the 1965 parade, the Victory Banner is almost the main star: there are many close ups of it in the footage of the official newsreel *20th Anniversary of the Great Feat*, and it is referred to as a 'holy relic of war' in the voice-over commentary.[11] The cultivation of this holy aura around the Victory Banner was not only a way of generating symbolic capital in the absence of the Stalin cult or a new leader cult, but it was also an attempt to ensure the occasion was imbued with a sense of mystique and tradition. In 1945 the Soviet generals rode into Red Square on horseback, but in 1965 Minister of Defence Rodion Marinovskii inspected the parade from a limousine, an approach repeatedly taken in all the subsequent Soviet Victory Day parades. This motorised arrival paralleled the focus on powerful new military technologies such as rockets. The deployment of the Banner ensured this emphasis on vigorous and robust modernity was leavened with a sense of the authentic antique.

The fact that the Victory Banner came to play so important a role in post-Stalin war commemoration culture is also indicative of the Brezhnev era's implicit rehabilitation of Stalin. The original Banner had been firmly associated with Stalin, who had personally ordered a Victory Banner to be raised over Berlin, and newsreel depictions of its raising emphasised that this was the carrying out of Stalin's order; similarly, the initial post-war presentation of the Banner in the Central Museum of the Red Army suggested a close association with Stalin. It might therefore *prima facie* seem a little odd that the Banner had such a central place in this new phase of war commemoration, which incarnated the state's response to post-Stalin-era independent civic initiative. The new social agency of veterans in commemoration opened the floodgates for a chaotic flux of competing and contradictory memories, with an enormous expansion of serious historical scholarship drawing on archives as well as myriad first person accounts and popular historical narratives (Pyzhikov 1998: 76).

Polly Jones traces some of the responses in this turbulent context to Konstantin Simonov's 1959 novel *The Living and the Dead* (Jones 2013: 187–98), and describes the differences between the Stalin era and post-Stalin visions of the war:

> This emphasis on the visual, the corporeal, the personally witnessed and experienced, enacted a break with the spectacular and hierarchical structure of Stalinism.
>
> *(Jones 2013: 189)*

As a physical artefact, the Victory Banner in fact had the capacity to bridge these different kinds of visions of the war: it was a concrete, visually striking object that could be situated within a network of personal testimony in memoirs, as well as photographs and newsreel film records of it supposedly being raised and flying over the Reichstag (Barbat 2014). But at the same time its singularity and display at Moscow's Central Museum of the Armed Forces and on Red Square gave it a spectacular and hierarchical charge that was redolent of and still residually associated with the leader cult. It was, therefore, perfectly suited for the state's purpose as it could be mobilised to prevent the war cult becoming too horizontal and democratic.

Under Khrushchev, there had been a perceptible effort to de-Stalinise official memory of the war. At two specially convened conferences attended by the participants in the storming of the Reichstag, it had been established that the raising of the flag was a process in which a large number of individuals took part. Accordingly, it was concluded that the elevation of Egorov and Kantariia to the status of the sole raisers of the flag was an error connected to the 'cult of personality', that is, of the Stalin cult, which needed to be reassessed in favour of a notion of 'mass heroism'.[12] This version did not in fact make it in full-blooded form into the official six-volume Khrushchev-era history of the Great Patriotic War, published between 1960 and 1965, but in any event such complexities were decisively banished by the 1965 Victory Day parade, and the reappearance of Egorov and Kantariia as flag bearers. Henceforth, access to archives was more strictly controlled for fear documents might be found that would support an alternative view (Maksimenkov 2015: 381), and memoirs were tightly controlled, subject to compulsory vetting by the author's comrades and commanders to ensure undesirable themes were edited out (Kudryashov 2010: 104–5). Without returning to the hagiography of the immediate post-war period, official memory under Brezhnev was much more hospitable to Stalin than it had been under Khrushchev, and the emphasis placed on the Banner was conducive to that.

During the post-Khrushchev Soviet era full Victory Day military parades on Red Square were not held every year, but only on significant round dates: 1970, 1975, 1980, 1985 and 1990. On each occasion the Victory Banner was central. The most lavish and monumental was the 1985 commemoration of the fortieth anniversary of the end of the war when the parade was conducted on a larger scale than ever before. However, by 1990 the parade had lost much of its grandeur and pomp, and with the collapse of the Soviet Union the following year the disappearance of the state that had secured the victory also led to a questioning of the need for such parades and widespread uncertainty as to the appropriate symbols with which to commemorate it.

The post-Soviet fate of the Victory Banner

In 1986, under Mikhail Gorbachev, the Soviet public were allowed to vote on whether a monument inspired by the Victory Banner would be the appropriate symbol with which to commemorate the war at the new Victory Park war memorial complex. They rejected this project (Tumarkin 1994: 149). While the precise reasons are a matter of speculation, it seems likely that they were a product of the growing popular scepticism about the official cult of the Second World War as Soviet legitimacy waned, and also fuelled by a certain anti-military tone. How and whether to commemorate the war had become a divisive and complex issue in the era of *glasnost*. Formerly sensitive issues such as the Soviet retreat in 1941, the signing of the Nazi–Soviet pact, the annexation and occupation of parts of Eastern Europe and the murder of Polish officers at Katyn were being openly discussed to the detriment of the traditional patriotic narrative of the Soviet Union as anti-fascist saviour. The 1990 parade reflected this uncertainty: Tumarkin describes it as brief, small in scale and lacking in the 'swagger' of previous years as a result of the crisis facing the country, and the widely held perception that its social system and ideology were not after all superior to those of the West (Tumarkin 1994: 200). Nevertheless, the Victory Banner and the other traditional trappings of the parade still featured.

Under the post-Soviet Russian Federation's first president Boris Yeltsin there was a conscious effort to break with the symbolism of the Soviet Union and emphasise a new democratic identity. From 9 May 1992 there was a very low-key marking of Victory Day, with no parade and an emphasis on a victory being achieved despite, rather than because of, Stalin and the Communist system. However, Yeltsin's Communist opponents began to gather and mobilise at the Victory Park memorial complex every 9 May to preserve the Soviet-era myth and, in order not to let the fiftieth anniversary events fall into their hands, he was forced to sponsor more elaborate Victory Day events in 1995, including a parade, and to permit Soviet-era red flags to co-exist with the new tricolour of the Russian state (Smith 2002: 89). The 1995 parade occurred in two distinct parts. In the historical part, veterans assembled on Red Square where they were inspected by generals in limousines, following the model established in 1965, and there was also a march by of troops in Second World

War-era uniforms bearing period submachine guns. The parade of contemporary military hardware, however, took place at Victory Park. There was also an enormous image of a Soviet and an American soldier displayed on the Historical Museum facing Red Square. Together these changes symbolised a Yeltsin-era break with the narrative of the victory as exclusively Soviet and with an overtly instrumentalising, militaristic message. Despite these changes, however, the fact that the parades had even taken place was effectively a recognition that Yeltsin's democrats had not succeeded in creating their own novel rituals and symbols, and were instead forced to reconcile themselves to and resurrect the rituals of commemoration invented in the Stalin and Brezhnev periods (Smith 2002: 85–91).

Whilst being forced to acknowledge the power of inherited symbols, Yeltsin – who had banned the Communist Party of the Russian Soviet Federal Socialist Republic in 1991 – was still anxious to control and restrict the circulation of Soviet-era imagery. In the 1996 Victory Day parade the Victory Banner itself once more featured, and Yeltsin's speech invoked the importance of 'the continuity of times contained in our symbols' (Smith 2002: 89–90). He also introduced a law in April 1996 which permitted exact facsimile copies of the Victory Banner to be displayed. But this permission was strictly circumscribed: it only applied to official state ceremonies on Victory Day and Defender of the Motherland Day (23 February, formerly Red Army Day), and the facsimiles could only be displayed in conjunction with the new Russian national flag. Moreover, in all other cases, instead of exact copies organisers of local parades were to use the so-called 'Symbol of the Victory Banner', which was a red flag with a five-pointed star on it and no hammer and sickle.[13] This need to manage and restrain the use of so powerful a symbol is interesting and a further indication of the Yeltsin government's ineffective attempts to break with the Communist heritage and failure to find an alternative symbol with comparable resonance. The Communists ridiculed the 'Symbol of the Victory Banner' as a cross between the Chinese and Vietnamese flags and a contemptible sign of the embarrassment which Yeltsin had brought upon Russia's greatest historical achievement.[14]

Even before he was inaugurated as president on 7 May 2000, Vladimir Putin had evoked the memory of the Second World War and associated himself with Russia's victory (Wood 2011). This remembrance of the war has been a central part of the Putin project to restore national pride and project Russian power globally. The association of the war with Stalin has not concerned Putin's administration, since this association too is one of which they make positive use. Since 2000, 9 May has become Russia's most important national holiday and day of commemoration, and since 2005 it has involved a full military parade with rockets, tanks and pomp equal to that evident in the Soviet parades prior to 1990. In each case, the Victory Banner has been central. Then, in 2007, the Communists proposed to replace the whole notion of the 'Symbol of the Victory Banner' with exact replicas of the original flag, bearing both the hammer and sickle and the name of the unit. Ceding to pressure from the Communists and at the same time stealing their thunder, President Putin passed a law on 7 May 2007 that overturned the Yeltsin-era statute and abolished the notion of the 'Symbol of the Victory Banner'.[15] Now, exact facsimile copies of the Victory Banner could be used by any organisation or anyone honouring the memory of the war (Kruglov 2007). By this point the Victory Parade had become an annual fixture with the Victory Banner at its centre and the cult of the war was once again in full swing.

Re-enactments and demonstrations in the post-Soviet space

The 2007 change in the law has fuelled a rise in the use of facsimiles of the Victory Banner, which has been paralleled by the growing popularity of military re-enactment – termed 'reconstruction' in Russian – since the 1990s. As Jenny Thompson has noted, for re-enactors genuine and replica artefacts play a key role in authenticating the bearer's right to own or control history (Thompson 2004: 135). In addition to replica uniforms and weapons, copies of the Victory Banner have been increasingly used in public re-enactments, thus confirming its potency as a symbol authenticating the dominant Russian account of the Great Patriotic War as glorious victory. The fact that the re-enactment movement began following the collapse of the Soviet Union in the early 1990s, when official military parades on Red Square had ceased, meant that 'reconstruction', by virtue of employing banned Communist symbols, immediately possessed a more intense political charge than was the case in places like the United States, where the politics of the practice, if present, are implicit and not central (Thompson 2004: 125–34). Moreover, while American re-enactors rarely re-stage particular historic events, being more oriented towards recreating and reliving the experience of the common soldier, in the Russian and Ukrainian context such a practice is commonplace: the liberation of specific towns and cities and the storming of the Reichstag are amongst the more popular scenarios.

One significant expression of this political dimension in the growth of military re-enactment, and practices close to it, is the use of auratic objects of veneration normally housed in museums, or at least replicas of them, as with the Victory Banner. Moreover, the crossover between practices of re-enactment and politics is evident most acutely in the events surrounding the tensions and armed conflict in Eastern Ukraine. It is probably no coincidence that Igor Strelkov (aka Igor Girkin), the one-time prominent insurgent leader in Eastern Ukraine, had long been an ardent military re-enactor. Following the Victory Banner's 2007 reinstatement as an officially sanctioned symbol of Russian and Soviet victory in the war, the flag also became a symbol of pro-Russian identity in Ukraine. Following his 2010 election, Ukraine's Party of the Regions president, Viktor Ianukovich, began to actively promote it: in April 2011, in the run up to Victory Day, Ianukovich's government passed a law requiring Ukrainian national and regional governments to fly facsimiles of the Victory Banner on 9 May and to use it in remembrance ceremonies.[16] The symbol had not formerly played an important role in post-Soviet Ukraine and this was a highly provocative and divisive move, which flew in the face of local authorities in the Ukrainian-speaking west of the country banning the use of the red flag in all its guises. In Russian-speaking cities such as Kharkiv and Odessa, however, Ianukovich's new law was enthusiastically obeyed on Victory Day 2011 with the parading of a copy of the Victory Banner, in imitation of the practice in Moscow, albeit alongside the Ukrainian flag. This was preceded by dancing and a parade by re-enactors in Second World War period uniforms. In Kyiv itself, there was a historic parade, featuring people in uniforms and with period weapons.

As in Russia in the early 1990s the Communists, especially in Russian-speaking regions, attempted to seize the initiative, and organised their own demonstrations with an enormous copy of the Victory Banner.[17] In Odessa in 2012 there was an actual reconstruction of the storming of the Reichstag, before a festive crowd in bright sunshine on the beach, in which a copy of the Victory Banner was carried into battle and raised to signify the Soviet triumph.[18] The spectacle was organised by the Odessan chapter of Ianukovich's Party of the Regions. The following year, on 22 June 2013, a reconstruction of the battle for Kyiv was followed by the hoisting of a copy of the Victory Banner by the local authorities.[19] In each case, the events were photographed and filmed for subsequent dissemination on the internet. Predictably, in the west of the country there was a hostile reaction to the revival of this Soviet-era symbol. On 9 May 2011 in L´viv copies of the Victory Banner were publicly defiled, repeatedly driven over by a motor cavalcade, before they were burnt to the sound of the chant 'hammer and sickle – death and famine'.[20] Since Ianukovich's 2014 toppling from power, copies of the Victory Banner have been widely used a symbol by pro-Russian demonstrators and forces in Ukraine but they are now effectively banned in, for example, Odessa.[21]

In Russia, the Victory Banner has in parallel become an even more important and widely disseminated symbol, especially for the state-sponsored anti-Maidan movement, agitating in favour of the pro-Russian elements in Ukraine. So in March 2015 a giant 200-square-metre copy of the Victory Banner began a 25,000-kilometre journey starting in Sevastopol through ninety towns and cities and ending up on Victory Day in Novorosiisk, one of the Soviet 'hero cities'. It was transported as part of a supposedly long-running 'international' project, a motor race entitled 'Our Great Victory'. The report of the Kuban regional site of the Rossiia news channel explained the symbolism:

> In the three years that the project 'Our Great Victory' has been running, thousands of hands of people from various ethnicities, generations and social groups have already touched it. The ritual symbolised the unity of the peoples who fought the German-Fascist invaders in the years of the Great Patriotic War for the freedom of our multi-ethnic Motherland.[22]

The emphasis here on the international dimension of war memory is significant. The Victory Banner is not just a symbol with resonance in the Russian Federation, as we have seen with regard to Ukraine: rather, it symbolises precisely the international claims of Russian nationalism and the pretensions of Russia to exert influence beyond its borders, especially in the former countries of the Soviet Union (the race also passed through Belorussia and Kazakhstan), and especially, but not exclusively, among Russian-speaking populations. At the same time, this campaign was a way of underlining that Crimea is part of Russia, as is implied by the fact that the flag began its journey in Sevastopol, on the anniversary of Crimea's unification with Russia, and was evidently intended to link that event with victory in the Great Patriotic War and the symbolism of the 9 May Victory Day parade.

Conclusion

In the years since 1945, the Victory Banner has been repeatedly recuperated for symbolic usage to bolster the Soviet and Russian narratives of the war as a triumphant enterprise inspiring national pride and attachment to the Russian state. It came to the fore most of all at the beginning of the Brezhnev era, and under Putin's and Dmitrii Medvedev's presidencies: in both cases periods of retrenchment in which collective memory of the war was relentlessly mobilised as a stabilising and unifying force. The notion of the flag as sacred was built up and widely disseminated in each case. In order to achieve this – and somewhat paradoxically – since the 1960s the Banner has been widely represented and reproduced in film and photographs and, since 2007, through commercially available exact copies. The Banner has thus escaped from its fixed position in the Central Museum of the Armed Forces to appear on the streets, brandished by crowds of demonstrators in parades around Russia and Ukraine, and reviled and desecrated whenever possible by Ukrainian nationalists. The fact that the object of reverence and revulsion, in each case, is a copy of the flag, albeit an exact copy, rather than the original auratic object is curious: its power as an object is sustained even through the many copies.

The purpose of all this is evidently to galvanise group identity, which we might also understand in Durkheimian terms as the sanctifying of a whole group who have contact with the totemic, sacred object, and the rituals associated with it. This functions at the same time to underscore the increasingly widespread notion that the Great Patriotic War was sanctified as a holy and just war, and therefore should not be subject to discussion or debate. We may see this as a Putin government-orchestrated bid to endow memory of the war with a sacred aura so as to legitimise the political order in the post-Communist period, in contrast to Yeltsin's failures to articulate a new mythology of the state.

Yet seeing the exploitation of this symbol entirely in terms of government manipulation is to overlook the palpable power of the Victory Banner as an artefact, one that has a genuine resonance with people that does not depend solely on state sponsorship. As an object that can be experienced directly, or vicariously through a replica, it has been employed in grassroots insurgencies for commemoration of the war in the 1960s, the 1990s and more recently. Its power is such that by attending a parade where a copy of the Banner is carried, or by bearing it or waving it themselves, people feel they can overcome the distance that characterises history as represented by remote museums and feel its direct presence, or even exert control over it. It is in this sense that we can understand the influence of and analogy to re-enactments, and to living history. This is perhaps the true danger of such a mobilisation of so potent a sign – it suggests the immanence of the past, the palpability of the wartime experience, potentially enhancing its allure.

This might be contrasted to the epistemological uncertainty about the war that emerged in the late Soviet and early post-Soviet years, where eyewitnesses, including those who had raised the Victory Banner over the Reichstag (Neustroev 1990), came forward to contest accepted accounts of all manner of official versions of history, and where the photographic record of events such as the raising of the Victory Banner was subject to critique. The incontrovertible physicality of the artefact of the Victory Banner was attractive for its literal solidity. In this regard, the Victory Banner shares its 'tactile and visual specificity' with the widely adopted black on gold Saint George ribbon, worn on 9 May (Oushakine 2013: 291). This materiality facilitates a more personal, affective connection with historical memory than any narrative might.

But for all its grassroots resonance, what distinguishes the Victory Banner from the Soviet flag is the fact that it bears the name of the unit who raised it written in Cyrillic. This insists on its Russianness, its unique resonance in a Russian-speaking space, and on its association with Soviet martial glory and military feats of arms. The rituals the flag is displayed in further cement this sense that this is not an internationalist, but a specifically Russian, symbol. With its recent use in the anti-Maidan activities, it has become a nationalist symbol, the very opposite of a symbol of world revolution and of socialism.

Since the medieval world, flags have very rarely been changed, because those with mythical origins function best. To change a flag is to mark a profound break, it is a very strong symbolic act, and it is rarely done (Pastoreau 2004: 291). The Yeltsin government's attempt to get rid of this symbol was symptomatic of their desire to create and signal a break with the past but, as with the attempts to ditch the Soviet national anthem, the fact that ultimately this failed is indicative of a wider difficulty in moving on, in symbolic terms – but not only those – from the Soviet era.

The Victory Banner delivers on its promise of continuity and resolutely stands for and evokes Soviet victory in the Second World War as an exclusively Soviet achievement, focusing attention on the moment of triumph, on victory, and distracting gazes and thoughts from the price paid and less glorious moments. The version of history this narrative entails may be simplistic, and the Victory Banner and the whole commemoration of it may seem ridiculous to rationally minded outsiders, but the strange power it exerts is incontrovertible and enduring. Pointing out that it is part of an invented tradition will do nothing to diminish its force.

Notes

Unless otherwise indicated, all translations from Russian are my own.

1 The 150th Idritskaia Division, order of Kutuzov 2nd class, 79th Rifle Corps, 3rd Strike Army, 1st Belorussian Front ('150 стр. ордена Кутузова II ст. идрицк. див.

79 С.К. 3 У. А. 1 Б. Ф.'). There is a number '5' on the reverse side, indicating that it was the fifth of the nine banners issued to combat divisions before the storming of the Reichstag.

2 Tumarkin acknowledged this miscalculation in a later revision of her thesis written at the beginning of the Putin era: Tumarkin 2002.

3 The film *Parad pobedy 1945* is available at www.youtube.com/watch?v=c2DqWGY1QHM.

4 Izdanie Tsentral´nogo Muzeia Krasnoi Armii, *Tsentral'nyi muzei Krasnoi Armii. Kratkii putevoditel'po zalam ekspozitsii. V pomoshch posetiteliu*. 1946. 1–2.

5 Ibid. 3–4.

6 Voennoe izdatel´stvo Ministerstva Oborony Soiuza SSR, *Tsentral'nyi muzei sovetskoi armii. Kratkii putevoditel'*. 1955. 21.

7 Voennoe izdatel´stvo Ministerstva Oborony SSSR, *Tsentral'nyi muzei vooruzhennykh sil SSSR. Putevoditel'*. 1965.

8 Entitled *Zal Pobedy*, this guidebook was published in Moscow in 1985 by Planeta.

9 'Dmitrii Medvedev otkryl zal "Znamia Pobedy" v Tsentral´nom muzee Vooruzhennykh sil', *Rossiiskaia gazeta*, 8 May 2011. https://rg.ru/2011/05/08/znamya-anons.html; see also the entry for the Victory Hall on the website of the Central Museum of the Armed Forces, 'Tsentral´nyi muzei Vooruzhennykh sil: Ofitsial´nyi sait. Zal 18, Zal Pobedy', at http://cmaf.ru/ekspo/inside/129.

10 Voennoe izdatel´stvo Ministerstva oborony SSSR. *Relikvii boevoi slavy*. 1962. 151–2.

11 The film *20-letie velikogo podviga* is available at www.youtube.com/watch?v=zZDqtQ6Ry3Y.

12 Stenogramma soveshchaniia otdela istorii velikoi otechestvennoi voiny na temu 'Shturm Reikhstaga'. In *Institut Marksizma-Leninizma pri TsK KPSS, otdel istorii velikoi otechestvennoi voiny*, November 1961, Russian State Archive of Social and Political History 71/22/102.

13 'Ukaz Prezidenta Rossiiskoi Federatsii ot 15 aprelia 1996 "O znameni Pobedy"' ('Decree of the President of the Russian Federation 15 April 1996, "On the Victory Banner"'). http://sbornik-zakonov.ru/215419.html.

14 See the discussion in the article on the website of the Communist Party of the Russian Federation by Stanislav Slivko, 'Kommunisty vernuli Khabarovskomu kraiu Znamia Pobedy', 26 January 2014. https://kprf.ru/party-live/regnews/127563.html.

15 'Federal´nyi zakon Rossiiskoi Federatsii ot 7 maia 2007g. N 68-F3 "O Znameni Pobedy"' ('Federal Law of 7 May 2007 N 68-F3 "On the Victory Banner"'). *Rossiiskaia gazeta*, 8 May 2007. www.rg.ru/2007/05/08/znamya.html.

16 'Rada obiazala podnimat´ krasnoe znamia v Den´ Pobedy', *Zerkalo nedeli*, 21 April 2011. http://zn.ua/SOCIETY/rada_obyazala_podnimat_krasnoe_znamya_v_den_pobedy.html.

17 Some (unidentified) broadcast news footage of such a demonstration from 2011, entitled 'Aktsiia kommunistov "Znamia Pobedy"', can be found at www.youtube.com/watch?v=N7cAAJKRj_o.

18 'Voennaia rekonstruktsiia vziatie Berlina', *Odessit.ua*, 9 May 2012. www.odessit.ua/photo/389-voennaya-rekonstrukciya-vzyatie-reyhstaga.html.

19 Textual description and photographs of this event are available at http://krasna-vest.narod.ru/fakt/dot179_rek.html.

20 Amateur footage of this demonstration is available at www.youtube.com/watch?v=8ERXH1LYx2c.

21 'V Odesse zapretili znamia Pobedy', *lenta.ru*, 23 October 2015. http://lenta.ru/news/2015/10/23/flag/.

22 'B Novorosiisk privezut 200-metrovoe Znamia Pobedy', *Rossiia*, 19 March 2015. http://kubantv.ru/pobeda/91809-gigantskoe-znamia-pobedy-provezut-po-gorodam-kubani/?utm_source=dlvr.it&utm_medium=twitter.

References

Arsenin, A. 1953. *Tsentral'nyi muzei Sovetskoi Armii.* Moscow: Moskovskii rabochii.

Assmann, Aleida. 2008. 'Transformations between History and Memory'. *Social Research*, 75, 1: 49–72.

Barbat, Victor. 2014. 'Bannières et drapeaux, sur quelques manières de les lever et de les représenter: l'exemple du Reichstag, mai 1945'. *1895*, 74: 70–95.

Belting, Hans. 1998. *The Invisible Masterpiece.* Translated by Helen Atkins. London: Farringdon.

Benjamin, Walter. 1992 [1936]. 'The Work of Art in the Age of Mechanical Reproduction'. In *Illuminations*, edited by Hannah Arendt. London: Fontana. 211–44.

Drozdovskii, E. A., Zakharov, N. K., Ionov, M. D., Skok, I. I., Tiulin, Iu. G., Chokhonelidze, N. A. and Iakimanskii, N. A. 2000. *Tverichi na Parade Pobedy.* Tver′: Litera-M.

Dubin, Boris. 2008. 'Pamiat′, voina, pamiat′ o voine. Konstruirovanie proshlogo v sotsial′noi praktike poslednikh desiatiletii'. *Otechestvennye zapiski*, 4, 43. http://strana-oz.ru/2008/4/pamyat-voyna-pamyat-o-voyne-konstruirovanie-proshlogo-v-socialnoy-praktike-poslednih-desyatiletiy.

Durkheim, Emile. 1995 [1912]. *The Elementary Forms of Religious Life.* Translated by Karen E. Fields. New York, NY: Free Press.

Edele, Mark. 2008. *Soviet Veterans of the Second World War: A Popular Movement in an Authoritarian Society 1941–1991.* Oxford: Oxford University Press.

Hobsbawm, Eric. 1983. 'Introduction: Inventing Traditions'. In *The Invention of Tradition*, edited by Eric Hobsbawm and Terence Ranger. Cambridge: Cambridge University Press. 1–14.

Jones, Polly. 2013. *Myth, Memory, Trauma: Rethinking the Stalinist Past in the Soviet Union, 1953–70.* New Haven, CT: Yale University Press.

Kruglov, Sergei. 2007. 'Istoriiu ne perepishesh′'. *Voenno–promyshlennyi kur′er*, 9 May. http://vpk-news.ru/articles/3637.

Kudryashov, Sergei. 2010. 'Remembering and Researching the War: The Soviet and Russian Experience'. In *Exprience and Memory: The Second World War in Europe*, edited by Jörg Echternkamp and Stefan Martens. New York, NY: Berghahn. 86–115.

Maksimenkov, Leonid. 2015. 'Arkhivno-istoricheskoe obespechenie nyneshnego i budui-ushchikh iubileev'. In *Pobeda-70: rekonstruktsiia iubileia*, edited by Genadii Bordiugov. Moscow: AIRO-XXI. 381–448.

Neustroev, Stepan. 1990. 'O reikhstage na sklone let'. *Oktiabr′*, 5: 130–44.

Oushakine, Serguei. 2013. 'Remembering in Public: On the Affective Management of History'. *Ab Imperio*, 1: 269–302.

Pastoreau, Michel. 2004. *Une Histoire symbolique du Moyen Âge occidental.* Paris: Seuil.

Pisareva, I. A. and Poplyko, F. N. 1969. *Tsentral'nyi muzei vooruzhennykh sil SSSR.* Moscow: Voennoe izdatel′stvo Ministerstva oborony SSSR.

Pospelov, P. N., Andreev, V. A., Antonov, A. I., Bagramian, I. Kh., Belov, P. A., Boltin, E. A., Bragin, M. G. *et al.* 1963. *Istoriia Velikoi Otechestvennoi voiny Sovetskogo Soiuza 1941–1945.* Vol. 5. Moscow: Voennoe izdatel′stvo ministerstva oborony SSSR.

Pyzhikov, Aleksandr. 1998. *Opyt modernizatsii sovetskogo obshchestva v 1953–1964 godakh. Obshchestvenno-politicheskii aspekt.* Moscow: Gamma.

Rolf, Malte. 2013. *Soviet Mass Festivals, 1917–1991.* Translated by Cynthia Klohr. Pittsburgh, PA: University of Pittsburgh Press.

Schleifman, Nurit. 2001. 'Moscow's Victory Park: A Monumental Change'. *History and Memory*, 13, 2: 5–34.

Shatilov, Vasilii. 1988. *V boiakh rozhdennoe Znamia.* 2nd edn. Moscow: Sovetskaia Rossiia.

Smith, Kathleen E. 2002. *Mythmaking in the New Russia: Politics and Memory During the Yeltsin Era*. Ithaca, NY: Cornell University Press.

Stead, Naomi. 2007. 'Performing Objecthood; Museums, Architecture and the Play of Artefactuality'. *Performance Research: A Journal of the Performing Arts*, 12, 4: 37–46.

Svoichakov, Maksim. 1973. *Oni brali reikhstag*. Moscow: Voennoe izdatel´stvo.

Thompson, Jenny. 2004. *War Games: Inside the World of Twentieth-Century War Reenactors*. Washington, DC: Smithsonian Institute.

Tiurin, Iurii. 2000. *Dva Parada*. Moscow: Fond Andreia Pervozvannogo.

Tumarkin, Nina. 1994. *The Living and the Dead: The Rise and Fall of the Cult of World War II in Russia*. New York, NY: Basic Books.

Tumarkin, Nina. 2002. 'The Great Patriotic War as Myth and Memory'. *European Review*, 11, 4: 595–611

Walsh, Kevin. 1992. *The Representation of the Past: Museums and Heritage in the Post-Modern World*. London: Routledge.

Weiner, Amir. 2001. *Making Sense of War: The Second World War and the Fate of the Bolshevik Revolution*. Princeton, NJ: Princeton University Press.

Wood, Elizabeth A. 2011. 'Performing Memory: Vladimir Putin and the Celebration of WWII in Russia'. *The Soviet and Post-Soviet Review*, 38, 2: 172–200.

11

EXPERIENCING AND PERFORMING MEMORY

Second World War videogames as a practice of remembrance

Eva Kingsepp

'The past is a foreign country; they do things differently there'. The line from L. P. Hartley's novel *The Go-Between* offers an especially felicitous metaphor when dealing with historical videogames, with their seemingly unlimited technological possibilities for re-creating the world of bygone days – or, more correctly, a version of that world that corresponds to our current concept of it, as represented in cultural memory. Previously film and television have been regarded as especially potent in this regard, but in the last decades historical videogames have achieved a reputation for functioning almost like time-travel machines, offering the player intense feelings of authenticity and realism. Moreover, the videogame industry surpassed the US film industry in size by around 2007, indicating that gaming as a way of handling the past is a field that demands serious study.[1] As media of cultural memory videogames are part of what has recently been called a 'memory boom', the growth of a profound interest in history and heritage visible both in the media and in a range of cultural practices including re-enactment and battlefield tourism (Winter 2006; Samuel 2012; Lowenthal 2015). At the heart of this boom, it has been argued, lies 'the need to attend to, to acknowledge the victims of war and the ravages it causes' (Winter 2006: 1). However, this does not really seem to be the case in videogames using the Second World War as their narrative frame, as they mostly highlight the 'fun' parts of war and neglect the unspectacular and the traumatic (Ramsay 2015). The main question I will address in this chapter is the potential function of Second World War videogames in heritage culture, or, more specifically, how they contribute to the cultural memory of the war on a collective and individual level. Are we talking about 'authentic experiences of the Second World War', as is often claimed in marketing and game reviews, or is something else at stake here?

The conclusion that Second World War-themed videogames are primarily expressions of nostalgia has been particularly highlighted by scholars focusing on US cultural memory (Allison 2010; Campbell 2008).[2] The question one must ask, however, is who is being nostalgic, and in what way? After all, these games are being played all over the world which means that their function in heritage culture must be examined from multiple perspectives. Videogames are part of a global popular culture in which they contribute to an ongoing process of encoding and decoding, negotiation and cognition. They are powerful actors in a transmedia/transnational discourse where issues relating to national identity and identification with cultural role models are ambiguous and demand a multifaceted scope of analysis. In his insightful study on collective memories in contemporary multicultural societies, Michael Rothberg highlights the need to shift a dominant mindset in which cultural memory is viewed as competitive memory, obeying a 'logic of scarcity' according to which the Holocaust and other traumas compete to outrank each other in collective consciousness. Instead, he suggests considering 'memory as multidirectional: as subject to ongoing negotiation, cross-referencing, and borrowing; as productive and not privative' (Rothberg 2009: 2–3). This will be of importance for the discussion in this chapter, as many historical videogames offer 'the potential for thinking about historical relationships in new configurations' (Graeme Davison, quoted in Uricchio 2005: 335). However, different types of Second World War games deal with history in significantly different ways, a fundamental distinction often neglected by scholars writing on the topic. In fact, it can be argued that the most successful Second World War games are not even historical games.

The same critical stance needs to be adopted regarding questions of remembrance. Remembering what? Who remembers, or is supposed or obliged to remember? What is being omitted from the historical narrative? What is subject to forgetting in the games? Benedict Anderson highlights the characteristic role of remembering and forgetting in the construction of national genealogies: citizens are obliged to remember pivotal events in national history such as battles, massacres and civil wars, yet simultaneously they are expected 'already to have forgotten' their disturbing aspects (Anderson 2006: 199–201). Victims and perpetrators are occluded by the naturalised ideology of myth, as the idea of the Event takes over its historical reality. When history becomes myth it has lost its complexity and diversity. That said, it has then acquired the status of an Important Story to be remembered over generations, treasured and shared within one's culture, and never questioned. 'Ignorance about others reinforces pride in our own past' (Lowenthal 2015: 506). The 'others' can be anyone who does not fit the mythical narrative. Anderson refers to English history textbooks that teach children about William the Conqueror as a great national 'Founding Father' but never ask the question 'Conqueror of what?' Anderson concludes that 'the only intelligible modern answer would have to be "Conqueror of the English", which would turn the old Norman predator into a more successful precursor of Napoléon and Hitler' (Anderson 2006: 201).

The seventy years that have passed since the end of the Second World War do not constitute a vast temporal distance. After all, living, informal memory among individuals is said to last for three to four interacting generations (Assmann 2010: 117). However, in popular media culture there is an ongoing mythification process resulting in three kinds of interconnected discourses about the war. On a social level there is the communicative memory discourse of individuals, either those who still have personal memories or, to use Marianne Hirsch's term, the 'generation of postmemory', who have inherited the memories of their parents or others close to them (Hirsch 2012). On a cultural level there is cultural memory discourse, related to 'historical, mythical, cultural time' and to cultural identity. As a kind of institution, cultural memory is 'exteriorized, objectified, and stored away in symbolic forms that … are stable and situation-transcendent: they may be transferred from one situation to another and transmitted from one generation to another' (Assmann 2010: 109–111). Institutions of cultural memory include museums and monuments, as well as the media and the broader cultural industry, with film as one of the most important forms. Popular culture is, I suggest, a necessary third dimension of discourse related to the memory of the Second World War, as its texts consist of much more than just commercial products from the cultural industry. As has been acknowledged, particularly in fan and subculture studies, an important part of popular culture is also situated outside commercial media, in the cultural production taking part within the audience. New media and the internet especially have dramatically increased the opportunities for independent creativity and the production of texts, as well as for distribution outside established channels. Thus, there is today an alternative dimension of global memory culture outside the established institutions of 'official cultural memory' that needs to be taken into consideration.

A comprehensive study of Western popular culture representations of the Second World War, focusing on films (fiction and documentary) and videogames, including an audience perspective, reveals a process of mythification of the war, as well as of Nazi Germany, in popular media. While many texts are not directly part of the mythification process, others can be regarded as promoting a mythical mode of discourse through, for example, the frequent repetition of certain familiar tropes, symbols and archetypes within a traditional narrative framework based on a Manichean battle between Good and Evil. The intertextual transmedia character of this process entails the fixation of certain codes and signifiers in this semiotic tissue, and while it would be misleading to say that there is one grand narrative about the war in Western popular culture, there are a number of specific elements used repeatedly and in different contexts which thereby contribute to a mediated transnational 'mainstream memory' about the Second World War (Kingsepp 2008).[3] The same kinds of tropes and symbols are often found in other contexts where they function to communicate societal values and to create bonds between members of imagined social, ethnic and national communities (Moscovici 2000). As Astrid Erll notes, 'cultural memory is constituted by a host of different media, operating within various symbolic systems. … Each of these media has its specific way of remembering and will leave its trace on the memory it creates'. Asking what it is 'that turns *some* media (and not *others*) into powerful "media of cultural memory", meaning media which create and mold collective images of the past', Erll offers a three-part model for the analysis of memory texts. This entails examining in turn: their '*intra*-medial "rhetoric of collective memory"'; their '*inter*-medial dynamics', which means 'the interplay with earlier and later representations', with a special focus on remediation and premediation; and 'the *pluri*-medial contexts in which memory-making films and novels appear and exert their influence' (Erll 2010: 389–90; italics in original). I find this highly relevant for the study of videogames, given that a) the field itself is very heterogeneous with different rhetorical possibilities, b) many games rely to a high degree on trans-medial intertextuality and remediation and c) their full meaning can only be assessed by contextualising them within gaming culture.

Digital Second World War games: a basic introduction

There is a wide range of digital games using the Second World War as their narrative framework, with multiple subgenres and hybrid forms that make categorisation difficult. However, a distinction can be made between the following basic types, according to the character of the gameplay: First-Person Shooters (FPS), 'shoot-'em-up' games where action and killing are the main objectives; games primarily based on real-time simulation of battlefield tactics and/or strategy, a group for which I here use the synthetic term Real-Time Tactics/Strategy (RTT/S); and simulators, where the player is, for example, flying a bomber. Here I will only deal with the first two categories. FPS are set in a first person perspective, while RTT/S can be set in first or third person or 'god' perspective, or a combination of these.[4] Second, in both these categories there are single-player and multi-player options, sometimes within the same game. In single-player mode the game is designed for one gamer who is interacting solely with the game's artificial intelligence. Multi-player games are designed for several gamers who, often in the form of teams, interact with each other, preferably over the internet. The attractiveness of this kind of gameplay, combined with the demand for innovation within the Second World War genre, has led to games such as *Red Orchestra: Ostfront 41–45*, a multiplayer tactical FPS where you play either on the German or Soviet side, and *World War II Online*, reputedly the first massively multiplayer online FPS, in which German, British, French and US forces are continuously clashing in a virtual battlefield set in Europe during the Second World War. Moreover, there are further distinctions between the games that need to be considered. While most Second World War FPS and all RTT/S are military-themed, there is also a FPS subgenre where fantastic adventure *à la* Indiana Jones is mixed with top-secret missions behind enemy lines. Accordingly, an FPS can be set in basically any narrative framework, realistic or fantastic, often including intertextual elements from genres like science fiction and gothic horror, while RTT/S are elaborated remediations of classical table-top military strategy board games (Atkins 2003; Vorhees 2012).

This brings us to the broader question of genre. MacCallum-Stewart and Parsler offer a useful definition: a historical game 'has to begin at a clear point in real world history and that history has to have a manifest effect on the nature of the game experience' (MacCallum-Stewart and Parsler 2007: 204). One of the most significant differences between the two categories is that while real history is foundational in Second World War RTT/S, in FPS it may contribute to, but is not essential for, the actual gaming experience. In a rough classification following Caillois' classic typology of games (Caillois 2001 [1958]), both categories are more or less based on *agôn*, competition, while FPS also include intense moments of *ilinx*, feelings of vertigo and disorder, especially when you are close to death, or actually 'dying'. In comparison, RTT/S relies more on *mimicry*, simulation, and the feeling of actually 'being' the squad leader, general, field marshal and so on. (This contrast has implications regarding immersion, which will be discussed later.) Therefore not all Second World War games are historical games, especially not those in the FPS category. In Elliott and Kapell's words, 'history is designed with the goal of knowledge, understanding, and enlightenment in mind; video games are designed to be played. As a result, playability can be seen to overpower historicity' (Elliott and Kapell 2013: 13).

Scholars have focused considerable attention on the best-selling military-themed FPS *Medal of Honor* (*MoH*) and, especially, *Call of Duty* (*CoD*), and have analysed them primarily as texts (Allison 2010; Gish, 2010). However, while their textual dimensions are certainly important, understanding videogames as carriers of cultural meaning requires attention to their hybrid character as both text and game (Atkins 2003; Frasca 2003). Although the distinction between the narrative and the ludic has been highlighted since the early days of game studies, it is not always a familiar one outside this comparatively new research discipline. The ludic aspects influence how in-game time and space are perceived by the player. In one of the first scholarly analyses of videogames as a fictional form Barry Atkins introduces the term 'game-fictions', using the classic RTT/S *Close Combat* as a representative example of 'games that offer a fictional intersection with historical events in the creation of a species of historical fiction' (Atkins 2003: 22–3). The game-fiction dimension is crucial for understanding how videogames work in the creation of a narrative experience. In single-player FPS the game's storyline is often programmed as a fixed chain of events that can be altered by the player only to a limited extent (or not at all). There are missions that are to be fulfilled, with objectives that need to be accomplished in order for the game to continue. Further, the gamer is 'living' the story through a preset point of view – that of the avatar – who is, in single-play, usually a US GI (or, less frequently, another Allied soldier). This means that the possible identification with the avatar, and thereby the potential for immersion, is influenced by the gamer's personal background. Not all gamers are happy to identify with what several of my own (Swedish) interviewees believed was an exaggerated US patriotism (Kingsepp 2010; cf. Malliet, Thysen and Poels 2011; Penney 2010).

Traditionally, a narrative contains the unfolding of events in a logical temporal sequence from beginning to end (or, a sequence that it is afterwards possible to interpret as logical). In another early text Patrick Crogan describes the concept 'gametime' as 'the transformation of events (in an "event space") into potential resources for the execution of a controlling procedure or algorithm' (Crogan 2003: 291). This means, in short, that during the process of gameplay – especially in FPS – the gamer is constantly refining his/her skills as s/he is proceeding through a sequence of events, situated within missions containing specific objectives, in order to be able to master the outcome. Further, a typical feature in FPS is that in order to survive you often need to direct all focus onto your movements and to locating – and eliminating – potential enemies before they find you. In this case the ludic experience is of far greater importance than the actual storyline. A nice shot or a particularly efficient massacre is better remembered afterwards than the narrative's 'mission accomplished', and such skillful deeds are also highlighted in films on gamers' personal YouTube channels (and applauded by their viewers) (Kingsepp 2011: 313–14). From a narratological point of view all such achievements contribute to a heroic function, especially as finishing the game means that the player has a) survived, b) exterminated hordes of malevolent enemies and c) accomplished all the tasks set up in the narrative. As a) and b) are prerequisites for c), this indicates that the main focus for the player is on the first two aspects while the overall objectives have a secondary value; they are merely there in order for a) and b) to be meaningful in relation to the narrative frame.

The life-or-death struggle for survival is one of the most prominent grand narratives in Western twentieth-century popular culture. As Gregory Waller writes:

> each new version of the struggle for survival and of the emergence of the fittest is inevitably an exploration and a definition both of struggling and of fitness. Throughout the twentieth century this ongoing exploration has reflected and shaped our understanding of individual heroism and sacrifice and of the ties – beyond family and social roles – that bind one person to another. Stories of survival express and help to create our sense of civilization, and they allow us to witness – with pity, fear, and satisfaction – the process of shedding, stripping away, destroying, or defending civilization.
>
> *(Waller 2010: 355)*

From a narrative point of view, surviving and symbolically saving the world through slaying immense numbers of foes would potentially offer the player a sense of being an important part of a grand epic. However, a memorable gaming experience in FPS is often more about having been really successful in handling the game controller than having experienced some kind of narrative progression. The struggle for survival theme is not, however, the same in a typical RTT/S, as the narrative experience here is about potentially having changed the outcome of historical battles, or even the war. A result of this counterfactual character is that the player is likely to be in much closer contact with the actual historical events, as for a full experience of the game s/he needs to be familiar not only with what really happened, but also how and why it happened. As Atkins recalls, with some unease, from playing *Close Combat II: A Bridge Too Far*, 'in destroying the bridgehead at Arnhem, and stalling the Allied armoured advance well before it reached Nijmegen, I had been responsible, potentially, for altering the course of the war in the West. Bully for me' (Atkins 2003: 1).

A game-fiction, where only the beginning is fixed as a starting point and the rest of the story will evolve during gameplay, implies a conception of time based on algorithms instead of 'mundane' time. When the game is over, the sequence of events experienced by the player during gametime is the game's narrative, which – especially in the case of FPS – is subordinate to the refining of gaming skills. This implies that any notion of simulating an 'authentic experience of the Second World War' is simply impossible, regardless of how much effort has been put into making the weapons and the use of them realistic. We are talking about games, not time-machines. However, this does not disqualify them from being powerful media of cultural memory in relation to the Second World War. What, then, is the specific character of videogames in memory work?

Second World War videogames as virtual sites of memory

The Second World War has for a long time been one of the most popular themes in videogames. A content analysis of military-themed FPS from 1992 to 2010 shows that of the seventy-seven titles in the study 63.6 per cent had the Second World War as their narrative frame (Breuer, Festl and Quandt 2011). I have not found a corresponding study dealing with tactics/strategy games but it is probably not misleading to suggest a similar predominance, especially given the long-established popularity of the Second World War in table-top strategy board games such as *Squad Leader*. As previously discussed, gauging the significance of Second World War videogames as a genre and as a cultural practice of memory involves not just textual analysis but also consideration of players' reception of them. Although the FPS and RTT/S share an overall narrative framework, a focus on military history, a longing for authenticity and a profound interest in weapons, we need to go deeper under this common surface in order to examine how the games communicate, what they say, and to whom.

Second World War games offer representations of the European and other theatres during the war. Although the scenarios are not often characterised by an extraordinary level of detail – except where weaponry is concerned – the games aim to achieve an effect of immersive historicity. While immersion in its general sense is about 'disappearing into' a text, immersive historicity relates to the idea of virtual time-travel (Kingsepp 2006). The aim is to create 'a feeling of fullness, a satiety of experience, which can be taken as reality' (Bolter and Grusin 2002: 53). Wikipedia's description of the multiplayer tactical FPS *Red Orchestra: Ostfront 41–45* is worth quoting from at length for its insights into how cutting-edge FPS strive for realism:

> *Red Orchestra* is notable for its emphasis on realism in comparison to other Second World War-based FPS games. There is no 'crosshair' for a player to aim with in the middle of their screen; instead, the player must either aim down the three-dimensional iron sights, or aim from the hip using the game's free-aim system. The former requires compensating for the breathing of the character and natural sway from holding the gun, while the latter is much quicker but accurate only at very short range. The player must also keep track of their ammo usage mentally unlike many other FPS games, most of

> which use an ammunition counter. Additionally, the player's health status is not represented by 'health points' as many other games use, but by a diagram of the player's body with reddened sections that show where he or she has been wounded; there is no way to recover from wounds, although after a brief period of time, the player will function at 100% again. Receiving wounds will temporarily slow the player down, especially if they receive a wound to the legs or feet; receiving a wound to the hands causes the player to drop their currently held weapon on the ground. Rifles usually kill players in one shot if they connect with the torso or head.[5]

Second World War games come close to actual history in their minute obsession with weaponry and military detail. Names of battles and geographical locations are also important components in anchoring their narrative in historical reality and generating an aura of authenticity. However, for many players this will not be enough to create immersive historicity: achieving the potent experience of time-travel also depends upon one's previous familiarity with mediated Second World War representations. For example, in the creation of 'Nazi-ness' in Nazi headquarters, armament factories and other locations, there is a frequent use of symbols such as the Nazi eagle, swastikas and portraits of Hitler, as well as extensive deployment of *Fraktur* typefaces on signs reading '*Achtung*', '*Gefahr*' and the like; these visual cues are familiar shorthand to many from Second World War fiction films and other popular history forms. The sound of the German language, whether realistic or in its 'film Nazi' version, is also frequently employed in many games, both as an element adding 'Nazi-ness' and as part of the soundscape. On top of this, games can also include obscure details whose meaning is only accessible to different kinds of Second World War 'nerds', something which greatly enhances their appreciation of them (Kingsepp 2006, 2010).

Numerous scholars have noted how games often remediate Second World War films, leading to the conclusion that it is such films rather than the war itself that provide the original for the simulation in Second World War FPS (e.g. Campbell 2008; Kingsepp 2006, 2010; Lukas 2010; Penney 2010; Ramsay 2015; Rejack 2007). This suggests that these games are examples of simulacra and hyperreality in Baudrillard's sense – copies without an identifiable original, where the input of signifiers for the real is so massive that any comparison with 'real reality' is superfluous (Campbell 2008; Kingsepp 2007). The hyperreal quality parallels the claim that not all historical videogames are 'about history'. MacCallum-Stewart and Parsler argue that the core motif of the *CoD* series is instead 'killing things in the fastest and best manner', while the historical context functions 'to offset accusations of violence with the claim that in some part, these events really happened' (MacCallum-Stewart and Parsler 2007: 206). Vorhees cites the games' alignment with US strategic geopolitical interests as an important additional element in their public reception: FPS where American military intervention abroad – whether historical or present-day – is applauded fit 'comfortably within the confines of the discursive formations that give shape to everyday life in America' (Vorhees

2012: 107–8). This fits well with Roland Barthes' concept of myth, connoting a form that underneath its familiar, non-controversial surface is highly ideological. In this sense the main difference between the Second World War in *CoD 1* and the War on Terror in *CoD 4: Modern Warfare* lies merely on the level of signifiers – the weapons, geographical locations and elements identifying the antagonists – while the signified and the codes connecting them to cultural myths remain constant.

For our present purpose, however, it is not really relevant whether the Second World War games are about history or not, as our interest lies in how they function as a practice of remembrance. We have seen that while the historical narrative in RTT/S is open-ended and has the counterfactual as its main rationale for playing the game, the FPS offer a closed, pre-defined narrative which syntagmatically is intimately bound to the different missions that constitute gameplay. What in-game elements are there – besides the stereotypical signs already mentioned – that can function as anchorage between the game-fiction and the real historical events?

Despite all the signifiers of real geographical reality – names of locations and simulations of landscapes, towns and cities familiar from other parts of popular visual culture – historical space in the games has a distinctly hyperreal quality. But does this matter? Second World War games are interactive *tableaux vivants* that can be likened to historical theme parks and historical re-enactments (cf. Lowenthal 2015; Samuel 2012). However, there is – again – a difference between the two game categories: the playful openness to the events in RTT/S encourages reflection, not affirmation or restoration. If they are nostalgic at all, it would be a case of what Svetlana Boym terms reflective nostalgia:

> [T]hese nostalgics discover that the past is not merely that which doesn't exist anymore, but, to quote Henri Bergson, the past 'might act and will act by inserting itself into a present sensation from which it borrows the vitality'. … [T]he past opens up a multitude of potentialities, nonteleological possibilities of historic development.
>
> *(Boym 2001: 50)*

In all games Europe is a place of military invasion and, especially in FPS, other activities directly related to the Second World War such as Nazi secret weapons projects. Marita Sturken's concept 'tourists of history' is very apt in relation to single-player FPS: the action-filled tour through historical game-space is a mediated and re-enacted experience, 'a particular mode through which the American public is encouraged to experience itself as the subject of history … a form of tourism that has as its goal a cathartic "experience" of history' (Sturken 2007: 9). The tourist's detached gaze is that of an innocent outsider, someone who is only visiting and who expects the visit to offer something different from everyday life so that s/he can return back home with new experiences. The innocence of the gamer's visit becomes particularly clear in controversies about videogame violence: it's 'just a game', it's 'not for real'. Moreover, and in any case, the moral imperative is impeccable: protecting what is good against that which is threatening it. This is truly clean war, as all signs of death, suffering and trauma are not even present in many Second World War games, which adds further to their distancing from real reality (Kingsepp 2007; Ramsay 2015). A good gaming experience will produce memories, but can they be regarded as memories of the war? The remembrance aspect implies an experience of mundane time significantly different from gametime.

Historical time in both classes of Second World War games is primarily signified through the use of specific dates in the narrative frame, as shown in the temporal anchoring of both the game as a whole and specific in-game missions in a certain period during the war. Denotative temporal signifiers can also be found in the form of dates in documents giving orders to the player or calendars hanging on walls (Kingsepp 2008 105–110). On a connotative level historical time is also signified by the more or less prominent 'Nazi-ness' of the games, since all things associated with Nazi Germany in the popular imagination are linked to the temporal frame of 1933–45. The presence of the Nazis themselves, of course, further reinforces this association: the appeal of battling these ultimate 'bad guys' is constantly reiterated in my encounters with Second World War gamers and is also apparent in accounts on web forums and in YouTube commentary fields (Kingsepp 2008, 2011). However, the level of visual 'Nazi-ness' varies between games, and while it is high in fantastic FPS such as the *Wolfenstein* games – indicating the importance of Nazi aesthetics in what I have called the Nazi fantastic subgenre – RTT/S and military-themed FPS are in comparison much more restrained. In the latter, the most important temporal signifiers usually build on the authoritative claims from game designers that the different weapons used are realistic and authentic virtual replicas of those actually used in the Second World War. Their function is at once indexical (these are 'real weapons used in the Second World War'), iconic ('these are the exact virtual replicas of them') and, although the number of players who consciously acknowledge this aspect is most probably limited, symbolic ('with these weapons we defeated the Nazis') (Lukas 2010). The thickness of layers of possible readings adds to the games' attractiveness among players.

Sturken's metaphor 'tourists of history' is also useful in considering the generally heavy bias towards a US perspective in FPS games (Breuer, Festl and Quandt 2011). Sturken suggests that the 'mode of the tourist, with its innocent pose and distanced position, evokes the American citizen who participates uncritically in a culture in which notions of good and evil are used to define complex conflicts and tensions' (Sturken 2007: 10). Regardless of the individual player's ethnicity and cultural background, it is the white, male, highly patriotic US American who is being preset as the model character. With this in mind, the analysis of popular history and memory in bestselling FPS as representing and reproducing *US* popular history and memory is certainly accurate. The myth of the Second World War as the 'good war' in which young men from the 'greatest generation' went across the oceans to fight in Europe, North Africa and the Far East, ready to sacrifice their lives for what is Good in the perpetual Manichean battle against Evil, is a characterisation frequently referred to in both scholarly and common discourse on Second World War memory culture (e.g. Allison 2010; Kingsepp 2010; Penney 2010; Ramsay 2015). Its function is to create social bonds and confirm a particular common sense about the historical role of the US in the world. In most of these US-centric games there is no Eastern Front, as there were no Americans there. There is no need to recall the battle for Stalingrad when we have D-Day to ritually celebrate through countless re-enactments in different forms.

Second World War videogames as virtual sites of amnesia

David Lowenthal is not alone in expressing a rather pessimistic view on contemporary Western society's obsession with the past:

> The foreign past gets reduced to exotic sites of tourism or filmic period fantasy .... Legends of origin and endurance, of victory or calamity, project the present back, the past forward. Rather than a foreign country, the past becomes our sanitized own.
>
> *(Lowenthal 2015: 595).*

Such comments certainly apply to many military-themed Second World War FPS where (typically US) cultural myths merge with fantasies of the present, the future and the past. These games are good examples of what Svetlana Boym calls restorative nostalgia, a phenomenon connected to 'antimodern myth-making of history by means of a return to national symbols and myths and, occasionally, through swapping conspiracy theories' (Boym 2001: 41). The belief is that this is not about nostalgia, but rather about the restoration of truth. Both Boym and Sturken describe a conspiratorial worldview in which national/cultural memory reduces the heterogeneity of communicative memory to a fixed, single plot, with clear-cut definitions of us and others, often presented in the form of stereotypes. Sturken likens this to social paranoia, in which conspiracy is seen as the driving force behind historical events: 'In this context, paranoia can be seen as producing a script about the way societies function, a script that understands the world in terms of connectedness and perceives it to be organized beneath the surface' (Sturken 2007: 45).

US-produced, military-themed FPS might be seen to partake of the scripts of social paranoia: certainly, they contribute to the ritual affirmation of the idea that history is a conspiracy and that the US has a divine mission to save the world. But it is also important to consider the exclusions that crafting such a construction entails: what aspects of the wartime past do these games reduce to the subordinate, the silenced, the ignored, the invisible or simply the forgotten?

Two central themes from Second World War history that are practically absent in game contexts are civilians and the Holocaust. The total or effective absence of civilians is striking in the vast majority of FPS games: generally they do not feature at all or are simply very marginal background figures. It is interesting to note that the chief exception here are the fantastic *Wolfenstein* games (and some of its inferior imitators) which do include a number of German civilian characters, such as waitresses and members of a fictive anti-Nazi resistance; moreover, it is not allowed (or possible) to shoot these characters, which demarcates their civilian status. This is in stark contrast to the more 'realistic' games such as *MoH*, where a player is expected to kill everyone who speaks German, regardless of whether they are in uniform or employed in the kitchen. Effacing the combatant/civilian distinction in this way disregards the laws of warfare and also displays a worrying ethnic essentialism: marking out everyone speaking a particular language for death would be intensely problematic in any other context but in many Second World War FPS it is just routine (Kingsepp 2011: 312–13; cf. MacCallum-Stewart and Parsler 2007: 206).

The absence of civilians is one way in which games sanitise the war and its impact, ensuring that important ethically sensitive issues arising from its violence are suppressed; for the same reason other emotionally disturbing elements such as seriously wounded colleagues or their dead bodies seldom feature. This being so, it is scarcely surprising that there is no explicit treatment of, and scarcely even any oblique hints about, the Holocaust in FPS. (Whether representing the Holocaust in such a context would in any event be ethical is a problematic issue left to one side here.) Some RTT/S players do in fact reflect on the absence of the Holocaust in the games, acknowledging this omission as an ethical flaw but also arguing that it renders a true or comprehensive simulation of Second World War military history impossible (Kingsepp 2008). Again, it is only in the fantastic subgenre that the fact of the Nazis being responsible for hideous deeds against human beings is even broached, in the allegoric form of fanatical Nazi scientists trying to create undead supersoldiers. While *Return to Castle Wolfenstein* initially introduced this theme in the shape of cyborg-like monsters, later games mixed it with a creature already established in Nazi exploitation B-movies: the zombie Nazi (Kingsepp 2011: 317–18; Ward 2012). However, it is not probable that players in general make an associative link from zombie Nazis to the Holocaust; somewhat paradoxically, the suppression of the Holocaust may in fact contribute to strengthening the mythical character of the Nazis as embodying absolute evil, but in an unspecified and cosmological way.

Content analysis has found that the protagonists in 82.3 per cent of FPS (not just those based around the Second World War) were US-Americans, with British characters taking second place at 17.2 per cent (Breuer, Festl and Quandt 2011). Due to the majority of games being Second World War-themed, the most common antagonists – at 28.8 per cent – were Germans, followed by Russians – at 15.9 per cent. This is reflected in my own qualitative research in which the basic narratological functions of hero/perpetrator/victim form an important part (Kingsepp 2008). As already mentioned, a major driving force behind today's 'memory boom' is to acknowledge the suffering of victims. Who, then, are the victims in these games, if there are no civilians and no Holocaust? It would be wrong to suggest that zombie Nazis could be in this position; on the contrary, their double character as dehumanised monsters makes their extinction not only ethically desirable but also mandatory in order to save humanity. In fact, as this virtual warfare is in most cases highly sanitised and even the player's own in-game death – if that should happen – is only temporary, it is difficult to find any victims, except for in the RTT/S titles that include aspects of the individual soldier's physical and mental health. These largely echo the common – and evasive – trope from Second World War drama and documentary films in which 'war is hell' mainly for the soldiers involved (Kingsepp 2008).

Player reception deserves a much deeper investigation than it has hitherto received. Although these game-fictions are often simplified and restricted to a number of traditional narratives, this does not imply that players unreflectedly adopt this view on the war. On the contrary, the games can often serve as the beginning of a deeper interest in this part of history (Fisher 2011; Kingsepp 2008). Gamers – along with others interested in the Second World War – compare media texts from different sources with a critical eye, and it is often the most simplified Good vs. Evil narratives, replete with absence or distortion of significant parts of 'real' history, that provoke the reaction to search elsewhere for 'real' facts. In my interviews the majority of FPS players said that they did not consider the games to be about history at all, while RTT/S games were generally appreciated much more highly as ways of dealing with 'real' history (Kingsepp 2008). Moreover, the gamers' national and ethnic backgrounds need to be taken into consideration, as there seems to be significant differences between US and non-US players (Kingsepp 2008; Fisher 2011; Malliet, Thysen and Poels 2011).

Can Second World War game-fictions be regarded as examples of a remembering/forgetting strategy? They certainly imply that the Second World War is important for all to remember, but they don't really explain why, and various different readings are possible. Is it important to remember the war itself, or the fact that American heroes defeated the Nazis? Was the war fought simply because the Nazis were representatives of Evil, and those who are Good and Righteous have an obligation to defend humanity against it? Anyone who claims that single-player FPS such as *MoH* and *CoD* provide history lessons must take into serious consideration the potential for drastic historical over-simplification, and even radical historical revisionism, that lurks within them. From this perspective it can be argued that these games are indeed good examples of this strategy: we are obliged to remember the Second World War through forgetting the real history of it.

It would be possible to argue that the cut scenes in many games – short filmic sequences in between missions or available as bonus material – often contain references to the historical background or even attempt to offer history lessons. However, establishing the actual importance of the cut scenes for players would require in-depth interview research. In my experience, very few Second World War game players bother to pay any attention to the cut scenes, which are felt to interrupt the flow in the gaming experience. Further, the documentary film sequences in the games I have analysed are generally of very poor quality, and an interested player would be more likely to turn to a real documentary film rather than something unsatisfactorily tacked on to an entertaining experience (Kingsepp 2008). If the games are analysed solely as texts, these sequences would seem to be important; but when analysed as game-fictions, and especially combined with a reception analysis, the result is likely to be quite different.

The military-themed games do not only contribute to a sanitised version of the war; by doing so they also performatively acknowledge cultural stereotypes about whose lives are grievable – most obviously those of white, Western (US) male soldiers – and whose are not (see Butler 2009). Equally, if young people with limited knowledge of (or interest in) history play Second World War games and believe the assertions from game producers and reviewers that this is what the war was really like, it is likely to be counterproductive to Western cultural memory's efforts to preserve a special status for the Holocaust. It can be said that the *CoD* series 'positions itself as a memorial, as each historical entry in the franchise is dedicated to the veterans of the Second World War and those who died in combat' (Gish 2010: 176). However, instead of multidirectional memory we get sanitised, non-traumatic mythical memory.

Conclusion

That videogames are in many respects on a par with films and television in their power to mould collective images of the Second World War is clear, especially due to the potential for immersive historicity which makes it possible to speak of virtual time-travel. However, it is important to bear in mind the differences between game types which render them distinct as media of cultural memory. The typical Second World War RTT/S encourages learning about the historical war and reflecting on all its aspects – or at least all those which influence the military outcome. Its memory is potentially of a multidirectional character and although it, too, is influenced by popular Second World War media culture, if there is nostalgia, it would be of the reflective kind. In contrast, the typical Second World War FPS claims to offer authentic experiences of the war, but although the experiences in themselves might feel authentic enough, they are about the Second World War in its mythical, mediated form, the war as simulacrum. Their nostalgic quality is that of restorative nostalgia, familiar from various nationalistic projects in history as well as today. In RTT/S memory work comes closer to living, communicative, even multidirectional memory, while in FPS we encounter the authoritative, fixed narrative of – predominantly US – cultural memory.[6]

The paradox that the Holocaust and civilians as victims are omitted from this narrative is a phenomenon that needs a more thorough examination. Here the hyperreal past is truly 'a foreign country where they do things differently'. This also indicates that although the RTT/S comes closer to the historical war than the FPS, in both cases it is a sanitised version that even surpasses the mythical media version of it: here we have pure war, where the weapons and the use of them for a supposedly higher purpose are all that counts, regardless of context. The strength of myth is that it is taken as something natural, nothing we need to reflect further upon. In Virilio's words, 'People don't recognize the militarized part of their identity, of their consciousness' (Virilio and Lotringer 1997: 26). It has been argued that a strategy of remembering/forgetting is characteristic in the construction of national cultural memory, and many of the games indicate that this is further strengthened by parallel strategies in popular cultural memory. However, these are not unchallenged: Second World War game players are not all distanced tourists in this virtual world. The mythical, unrealistic character of the games can also contribute to critical reflection, knowledge-seeking, dialogue and discussion with others. In that way the games also contribute to the living memory of the war years.

Notes

1 Different sources offer somewhat different figures here, but the general tendency is clear.
2 Unless otherwise stated, all references to *games* will be to digital or videogames using the Second World War as their narrative framework.
3 A summary in English of the main findings is found in Kingsepp 2010.
4 In third person perspective the player is imagined to be right behind the avatar, while the 'god' perspective follows the events from high above.
5 See the Wikipedia entry 'Red Orchestra: Ostfront 41–45' at https://en.wikipedia.org/wiki/Red_Orchestra:_Ostfront_41-45.
6 This conclusion is not shared by all previous writings on the topic; see, for example, Gish 2010.

References

Allison, Tanine. 2010. 'The World War Two Video Game, Adaptation, and Postmodern History'. *Literature/Film Quarterly*, 38, 3: 183–93.

Anderson, Benedict. 2006. *Imagined Communities: Reflections on the Origin and Spread of Nationalism*. Rev. edn. London: Verso.

Assmann, Jan. 2010. 'Communicative and Cultural Memory'. In *A Companion to Cultural Memory Studies*, edited by Astrid Erll and Ansgar Nünning. Berlin: De Gruyter. 109–118.

Atkins, Barry. 2003. *More Than a Game: The Computer Game as Fictional Form*. Manchester: Manchester University Press.

Bolter, Jay and Grusin, Richard. 2002. *Remediation: Understanding New Media*. Cambridge, MA: The MIT Press.

Boym, Svetlana. 2001. *The Future of Nostalgia*. New York, NY: Basic Books.

Breuer, Johannes, Festl, Ruth and Quandt, Thorsten. 2011. 'In the Army Now – Narrative Elements and Realism in Military First-Person Shooters'. *DiGRA 11. Proceedings of the 2011 DiGRA International Conference: Think Design Play*. 1–19. www.digra.org/wp-content/uploads/digital-library/11307.54018.pdf.

Butler, Judith. 2009. *Frames of War – When is Life Grievable?* London: Verso.

Caillois, Roger. 2001 [1958]. *Man, Play and Games*. Translated by Meyer Barash. Urbana, IL: University of Illinois Press.

Campbell, James. 2008. 'Just Less than Total War: Simulating World War II as Ludic Nostalgia'. In *Playing the Past: History and Nostalgia in Video Games*, edited by Zach Whalen and Laurie N. Taylor. Nashville, TN: Vanderbilt University Press. 183–200.

Crogan, Patrick. 2003. 'Gametime: History, Narrative, and Temporality in Combat Flight Simulator 2'. In *The Video Game Theory Reader*, edited by Mark J. P. Woolf and Bernard Perron. London: Routledge. 275–301.

Elliott, Andrew B. R. and Kapell, Matthew Wilhelm. 2013. 'Introduction: To Build a Past That Will "Stand the Test of Time" – Discovering Historical Facts, Assembling Historical Narratives'. In *Playing with the Past: Digital Games and The Simulation of History*, edited by Matthew Wilhelm Kapell and Andrew B. R. Elliott. London: Bloomsbury. 1–29.

Erll, Astrid. 2010. 'Literature, Film, and the Mediality of Cultural Memory'. In *A Companion to Cultural Memory Studies*, edited by Astrid Erll and Ansgar Nünning. Berlin: De Gruyter. 389–98.

Fisher, Stephanie. 2011. 'Playing With World War II: A Small-Scale Study of Learning in Video Games'. *Loading ... The Journal of the Canadian Game Studies Association*, 5, 8: 71–89.

Frasca, Gonzalo. 2003. 'Simulation versus Narrative: Introduction to Ludology'. In *The Video Game Theory Reader*, edited by Mark J. P. Woolf and Bernard Perron. London: Routledge. 221–35.

Gish, Harrison. 2010. 'Playing the Second World War: *Call of Duty* and the Telling of History'. *Eludamos. Journal for Computer Game Culture*, 4, 2: 167–80.

Hirsch, Marianne. 2012. *The Generation of Postmemory: Writing and Visual Culture After the Holocaust*. New York, NY: Columbia University Press.

Kingsepp, Eva. 2006. 'Immersive Historicity in World War II Digital Games'. *Human IT*, 8, 2: 60–89.

Kingsepp, Eva. 2007. 'Fighting Hyperreality with Hyperreality: History and Death in World War II Digital Games'. *Games and Culture*, 2, 4: 366–75.

Kingsepp, Eva. 2008. *Nazityskland i populärkulturen: minne, myt, medier [Nazi Germany in Popular Culture: Memory, Myth, Media]*. Stockholm: Stockholm University.

Kingsepp, Eva. 2010. 'Hitler as our Devil? Nazi Germany in Mainstream Media'. In *Monsters in the Mirror: Representations of Nazism in Post-War Popular Culture*, edited by Sara Buttsworth and Maartje Abbenhuis. Santa Barbara, CA: Praeger. 29–52.

Kingsepp, Eva. 2011. 'Ethics in World War II First Person Shooter Games'. In *Vice City Virtue: Moral Issues in Digital Game Play*, edited by Karolien Poels and Steven Malliet. Leuwen: Acco Academic. 303–23.

Lowenthal, David. 2015. *The Past is a Foreign Country – Revisited*. Cambridge: Cambridge University Press.

Lukas, Scott A. 2010. 'Behind the Barrel: Reading the Video Game Gun'. In *Joystick Soldiers: The Politics of Play in Military Video Games* edited by Nina B. Huntemann and Matthew Thomas Payne. London: Routledge. 75–90.

MacCallum-Stewart, Esther and Parsler, Justin. 2007. 'Controversies: Historicising the Computer Game'. *DiGRA '07. Proceedings of the 2007 DiGRA International Conference: Situated Play*. 203–210. www.digra.org/wp-content/uploads/digital-library/07312.51468.pdf.

Malliet, Steven, Thysen, Tom and Poels, Karolien. 2011. 'Digital Game Rhetoric and Critical Reasoning: The Case of "Grand Theft Auto IV" and "America's Army: Special Forces"'. In *Vice City Virtue: Moral Issues in Digital Game Play*, edited by Karolien Poels and Steven Malliet. Leuwen: Acco Academic. 245–63.

Moscovici, Serge. 2000. 'The Phenomenon of Social Representations'. In *Social Representations: Explorations in Social Psychology*, edited by Gerald Duveen. Cambridge: Polity. 18–77.

Penney, Joel. 2010. '"No Better Way to 'Experience' World War II": Authenticity and Ideology in the *Call of Duty* and *Medal of Honor* Player Communities'. In *Joystick Soldiers: The Politics of Play in Military Video Games* edited by Nina B. Huntemann and Matthew Thomas Payne. London: Routledge. 191–205.

Ramsay, Debra. 2015. 'Brutal Games: *Call of Duty* and the Cultural Narrative of World War II'. *Cinema Journal*, 54, 2: 94–113.

Rejack, Brian. 2007. 'Toward a Virtual Reenactment of History: Video Games and the Recreation of the Past'. *Rethinking History*, 11, 3: 411–25.

Rothberg, Michael. 2009. *Multidirectional Memory: Remembering the Holocaust in the Age of Decolonization*. Stanford, CA: Stanford University Press.

Samuel, Raphael. 2012. *Theatres of Memory: Past and Present in Contemporary Culture*. 2nd edn. London: Verso.

Sturken, Marita. 2007. *Tourists of History: Memory, Kitsch, and Consumerism from Oklahoma City to Ground Zero*. Durham, NC: Duke University Press.

Uricchio, William. 2005. 'Simulation, History, and Computer Games'. In *Handbook of Computer Game Studies*, edited by Joost Raessens and Jeffrey Goldstein. Cambridge, MA: The MIT Press. 327–38.

Virilio, Paul and Lotringer, Sylvère. 1997. *Pure War*. Rev. edn. Translated by Mark Polizotti. New York, NY: Semiotext(e).

Vorhees, Gerald A. 2012. 'Monsters, Nazis, and Tangos: The Normalization of the First-Person Shooter'. In *Guns, Grenades, and Grunts. First-Person Shooter Games*, edited by Gerald A. Vorhees, Joshua Call and Katie Whitlock. London: Continuum. 89–111.

Waller, Gregory A. 2010. *The Living and the Undead: Slaying Vampires, Exterminating Zombies*. Urbana, IL: University of Illinois Press.

Ward, James J. 2012. 'Utterly without Redeeming Social Value? "Nazi Science" Beyond Exploitation Cinema'. In *Nazisploitation! The Nazi Image in Low-Brow Cinema and Culture*, edited by Daniel H. Magilow, Kristin T. Vander Lugt and Elizabeth Bridges. New York, NY: Continuum. 92–112.

Winter, Jay. 2006. *Remembering War: The Great War between Memory and History in the Twentieth Century*. New Haven, CT: Yale University Press.

12

TOUCHING LANDSCAPES? EMBODIED EXPERIENCES OF HOLOCAUST TOURISM AND MEMORY

Tim Cole

In September 2007, Eva Olsson headed back to Europe. Born in Transylvania, Eva and her family were caught up in the mass deportation of Jews living in the expanded borders of wartime Hungary in the spring and summer of 1944. Over sixty years after she had been deported from Satu Mare to Auschwitz, Eva decided to revisit her former hometown and the sites of her and other family members' wartime incarceration. As she prepared for her journey, Eva planned a series of different rituals for each place on her itinerary. In Satu Mare, she wanted to return to 'walk the streets I had known as a child'. At Auschwitz-Birkenau she 'wanted to place a candle on the train tracks inside the camp' in memory of family members killed there. In Buchenwald, where her father had died, she 'wanted to walk on the same ground he last walked on'. In Bergen-Belsen, where she was liberated, Eva hoped 'to pay my respects and say thank you to the soldiers who gave their lives to free us' (Olsson 2008: 3).

As the range of locations and different rituals planned for each suggest, this visit was to be about more than simply sightseeing. It had the kind of purposeful goal of a pilgrimage and also entailed far more senses than sight. Embodied experiences of place were a key concern as Eva planned this trip. In particular, walking assumed a central significance in a number of landscapes as Eva sought a connection with family members who had also walked 'there'. By putting her feet on and into the same streets, tracks and soil that her parents had trod, Eva sought not only to access past place, but also past people. As I explore in this essay, Eva's hopes for embodied connection in and through (re)walking Holocaust landscapes are much more widely shared by a variety of visitors who seek to give what Karen Till calls 'a spatial "fix" to time' by shrinking the distance between past and present through embodied encounter with place (Till 2005: 9).

In the first part of this essay I focus on less familiar Holocaust landscapes than the former camps that Eva visited, beginning with the practices of individuals and groups who have re-walked the road networks where evacuated prisoners were subjected to so-called 'death marches' in the final months of the war. It is not surprising that walking is central to contemporary memory practices in these Holocaust landscapes given that prisoner experiences of these places were as sites passed through on foot rather than lived in. Moreover, the importance of embodied encounter with these places may also be because there is seemingly little to see and so senses other than sight become all the more significant. In the second part of the essay I shift my attention to those sites/sights where there is more to see. While the remaining infrastructure of the former Auschwitz camps is part of the reason why these are sites of mass tourism, it is clear that embodied encounters are significant for a wide variety of visitors who experience Auschwitz in ways beyond the visual. In the final section of the essay I focus on survivors who, like Eva, have decided to revisit the sites of their former incarceration. While there are similarities with the embodied practices of other visitors, the differences raise bigger questions about continuity and change within Holocaust landscapes that have broader implications for the embodied practices of others.

Re-walking the roads

Attempts to connect with an individual's or group's experience in the Holocaust past through re-walking the ground they walked are perhaps most clearly and obviously seen in acts of retracing the evacuation routes that criss-crossed the road networks of Central and Eastern Europe. In the final stages of the war, prisoners were evacuated from camps that lay in the line of the Allied advances into the ever-shrinking Axis zone. The routes of some of these so-called 'death marches' have been re-walked by a handful of survivors accompanied by family members as well as camera crews and directors, as well as by the children of survivors: those dubbed the 'second generation' (Cole 2013b).

In the late spring of 1998 – two years after Daniel Goldhagen's controversial bestseller *Hitler's Willing Executioners* brought the Helmbrechts death march to the attention of an international audience – the Jewish-American photographer Susan Silas retraced the route originally taken by 580 Jewish women from the sub-camp at Helmbrechts to Prachatice in the Czech Republic. The daughter of Hungarian-Jewish survivors, Silas placed her body day after day on the same stretch of road that other Jewish women had over half a century before. Over the course of the twenty-two days that the original march had taken (between 13 April and 4 May), Silas followed the prisoners' route, pausing each night at the spot where the women had stopped fifty-three years earlier. Their being there before her – actually there, on this section of road, on this day fifty-three years before – was of critical importance. While Silas produced a limited edition boxed set of forty-eight prints entitled *Helmbrechts walk, 1998–2003*, she saw the act of re-walking this route as the artwork.[1] As she later explained,

> the art work was my physical presence there – what was important with respect to the marchers and my feelings about them was putting my body in

> that physical space – the images are a tertiary witness to that act. My occupying space and time I wouldn't have occupied had they not been there before me – that was most significant.
>
> *(cited in Kaplan 2008: 115).*

For Dora Apel, it was an attempt at secondary witnessing – a working through of 'relationship to the past by retracing the lives of their parents, grandparents, or unknown ancestors in some way, or even performing the role of Nazi victim' (Apel 2002: 108). A similar retracing of parents' lives can be seen in another artist's project – the following by Lorna Brunstein in her mother Esther's footsteps when she was marched from a labour camp near Hanover to Bergen-Belsen in February 1945. Seventy-one years later to the day, Brunstein retraced these steps, pausing *en route* to gather soil that 'perhaps Esther trod on'.[2]

By re-walking the same route on the same day, both Silas and Brunstein sought the double authenticity that anniversary re-enactment promises. As Brian Conway has written in another context of commemoration of the events of Bloody Sunday in Northern Ireland, 'by ritually re-enacting the original march over the same route at the same time, an attempt is made to obliterate the past-present distinction' (Conway 2007: 106). In the case of re-walking the Bloody Sunday March, the choice of both authentic place – the original route – and authentic time – the anniversary of the original march – is seen to lead to the sweet spot of a telescoping of time in this place of re-marching. These concerns with temporal as well as spatial authenticity appear particularly important in the case of marchers re-walking the less obviously Holocaust sites of the European road network, compared to the more obvious Holocaust sites that an extant camp like Auschwitz presents. It is as if the lack of clear markers of the past – barracks, rails and the ruins of the destroyed crematoria – mean that the reassurance of the temporal proximity of the anniversary is necessary in vindicating a belief that it is possible to connect with past time, past place and past inhabitants.

The significance of a certain authenticity to both timing and route extends – albeit in different ways – to two disparate organisations that position embodied encounters with Holocaust landscapes at the centre of their practices: the March of Life and the March of the Living. The March of Life has focused, like Susan Silas and Lorna Brunstein, on re-walking the road network of Europe which was the site of multiple death marches in the last months of the war. In 2007 the charismatic Christian TOS International Ministries – based in Tübingen and led by Jobst Bittner – undertook their first re-tracing of the route of some of the death marches through Germany. For this initial march, there was an attempt to work – as Silas and Brunstein did – with the anniversary of the original march. Over the course of three days in April, groups walked sections of the route taken by prisoners evacuated in April 1945 from one of the so-called 'Operation Desert' labour camps at Bisingen to Dachau in a 'prayer and memorial march' that was intended to 'leave a mark' on the landscape.[3]

However, there was also another chronology in view, relating less to the anniversary of Holocaust events than to Holocaust memory: the 2007 march ended on the eve of *Yom HaShoah*, the Israeli day of Holocaust remembrance. The following year, in August 2008, this borrowing from Jewish and Israeli chronologies continued, and was further reinforced in the route actually marched. Starting on the eve of *Tish B'Av* – a fast day remembering the destruction of the First and Second Temples – marchers symbolically inscribed a Star of David onto the road network of former East Germany, ending with a service on the Teufelsberg (Devil's Mountain), a man-made hill constructed from the rubble of wartime Berlin. Each day teams walked about seven miles, but rather than tracing specific evacuation routes the focus was on visiting a series of significant sites such as former concentration camps and the villa at Wannsee where plans for the European-wide implementation of the so-called 'final solution of the Jewish question' were discussed in January 1942. The assumption was that former East Germany was 'literally covered' with the routes taken by prisoners being evacuated; therefore 'almost all bigger roads and highways' were 'covered in blood' and were therefore appropriate routes for re-walking.[4]

What both marches in 2007 and 2008 shared were assumptions that the act of re-walking the roads that the death marches had passed along was significant in and of itself. Working with the idea that collective walking through Holocaust landscapes were 'power marches', the organisers saw the possibility of 'reconciliation, forgiveness and restoration' being enacted as individuals walked and prayed together.[5] The need for collective marching was seen to be particularly pressing in the case of the second march centred on former East German territory. Here organisers saw marchers breaking through what they termed 'a double layer of concrete' that 'two dictatorships in a row' had formed through acts of violence and silencing.[6] By mobilising hundreds of pairs of feet on the road network of the former East Germany, March of Life saw the potential to cut through these two layers of concrete and bring about far-reaching transformation.

Although seemingly radically different in origins, the March of the Living shares with the March of Life a sense of the transformative potential of communal marching and the symbolic significance of the Israeli memory calendar. First held in 1988, and an annual event since 1996, the March of the Living brings thousands of Jewish teenagers to Poland on *Yom HaShoah* to march – hand-in-hand and in silence – the three kilometres from the main camp at Auschwitz to the death camp at Birkenau. In part the march attempts to symbolically, if not literally, have Jewish teenagers tread 'in the footsteps of the 6,000,000'.[7] However, as they re-walk this journey to the symbolic centre of the Holocaust – the gas chambers in Birkenau – they are encouraged to re-make this journey and ultimately re-make themselves. As the title of the event – the March of the Living – makes clear, this march is intended not so much to echo and re-enact the death marches, as to re-work them. As teens enrolling on the programme are told,

> As a proud young Marcher, your experience will be in direct contrast to the tragic fate of hundreds of thousands of Jews and others, who were forced by the Nazis to take part in the infamous death Marches, across vast expanses of European terrain, under the harshest of conditions. This time, however, there will be a difference. It will be a March of the Living, with thousands of Jewish youth, like yourself, marching shoulder to shoulder. You will participate in a memorial service at one of the gas chambers/crematoria in Birkenau, which will conclude with the singing of *Hatikvah*, reaffirming *Am Yisrael Chai* – The Jewish People Live.[8]

Singing the Israeli national anthem in the shadows of the gas chamber and marching dressed in the blue and white of Israel and carrying Israeli flags, the Zionist story of rebirth is embodied by these teens who march into this place of destruction and then exit again, ultimately headed for the streets of Jerusalem where they celebrate Israeli Independence Day. (The Poland to Israel itinerary is one repeated by a range of individuals and organisations: see Kugelmass 1993.) For the organisers of the March, the aim is that these embodied encounters with Auschwitz and Jerusalem – as Jewish teens 'walk that walk' – will lead to greater identification both with the victims of the Holocaust and with contemporary Israel.[9]

It is clear from the reflections of former participants approvingly cited in March literature and website resources that experiences of identification with the victims – what Gary Weissman dubs 'fantasies of witnessing'- do take place (Weissman 2004). One marcher explained at length seeing

> the gas chambers, which lay in ruins. The wires that once gave power to these sick buildings stuck out from the ground as if they were tree roots that had been there for hundreds of years. These 'roots' held the secret stories, the wails, and the screams of those six million that perished. They were our history, our roots.
>
> My eyes followed the wires until the end, where my focus blurred until it refocused upon the broken walls around me. There were scratches etched into them. These were the scratches made by those trying desperately to hold on to every last inch of life that they could. These were the scratches of lost hope. As I ran my fingers along the rubble, I felt the cool chill of death pass through my body. I could feel the ridged surface beneath my fingers, each new mark representing a new death. My hand suddenly started to sting, as if the sorrow and pain etched into these imperfections were slicing into my hand and seeping into my heart.[10]

This movement from seeing past place through walking past place to touching past place and so feeling past place and past people is critical to the immersive, embodied and haptic experience of the March of the Living. But these 'fantasies of witnessing' extend beyond the carefully choreographed and highly symbolic rituals of the March of the Living to a broader range of both group and individual visits to the landscapes of the former camps.

Re-walking the camp

In March 2012, I accompanied a group of British teenagers taking part in the 'Lessons from Auschwitz' course organised by the Holocaust Educational Trust (HET) that has a day-long site visit to Auschwitz at its heart.[11] Students make a short visit either to the synagogue or Jewish cemetery in the morning, before touring the museum in the former main camp of Auschwitz and then heading over to the death camp of Auschwitz-Birkenau in the late afternoon and evening. Although our educator briefly drew attention to Holocaust perpetrators when standing by the gallows where the camp commandant Rudolf Höss was executed in Auschwitz in 1947 and to Holocaust collaborators when touching the rail lines under the gateway to Birkenau, the majority of the visit – as for Silas, Brunstein, the March of Life and the March of the Living – seeks to follow in the victims' footsteps. The day itself is structured this way, starting with brief visits to sites of pre-war Jewish life. More significantly, the visit itself is very much framed through the testimony of an Auschwitz survivor who the students listen to in a pre-visit seminar a few days before they go to Auschwitz for themselves. Although the survivor did not physically accompany us to Auschwitz – in the way that survivors play this critical role for March of the Living groups – his words did. As they walked through Birkenau, the students frequently drew on the survivor's story. Walking along the rails towards the former gas chambers, they talked of seeing 'what they' – the survivor's family members *en route* to their deaths – 'saw' and of walking 'the same way' they walked.[12]

The sense of connecting with the victims by inhabiting – albeit for only a few hours – their space reached its apex during the service that marks the end of the day. Gathered around the ruined crematoria, we listened to the words of Sonderkommando member Zalma Gradowski who wrote, 'we will bury our notebooks and diaries deep under the ashes. We have done as much as we could. And you, searching for the truth, you who have lived to see justice and liberty, what will you do?' In the gathering gloom, the effect was very much of hearing one of the victims' voices directly from the past, with our educator reminding us that Gradowski 'is talking to us', since 'we' came 'here to bear witness'.[13] Gradowski's call to action was repeated twelve days later as an 'appropriate send-off' at the end of the post-Auschwitz seminar where students gather to begin thinking about their 'next step projects' to share the 'lessons' they learned at Auschwitz with schoolmates, families and their communities.[14] They do so as individuals who are assumed to have been changed by their encounter with the site: not only are they now 'ambassadors' of Auschwitz, they are also witnesses to what they have seen and heard as they have walked in the victims' footsteps.

By physically taking British students to Auschwitz, the 'Lessons from Auschwitz' programme operates with the assumption, as students were told at the pre-visit seminar, that 'seeing something first hand is different from reading about it in a textbook'.[15] The students themselves talked about their hopes that physically going there would not only help them to grasp the reality of the Holocaust but might also change them, with one hoping to leave Auschwitz a 'better person'.[16] Such thinking pervades the tourist guidebook consensus that Auschwitz is not simply unmissable for anyone visiting Poland, the act of going there in person is potentially transformative. So, Auschwitz is included in the *Rough Guide to Poland*'s '28 things not to miss' alongside a host of other diverse tourist sights. The guidebook's authors argue that it offers 'the profoundest of insights into the nature of human evil': it 'demands to be visited – few who come here will be unchanged by the experience' (Bousfield and Salter 2005: 21). Other guides follow suit, instructing would-be visitors that Auschwitz is 'possibly Poland's most moving sight' (Dydyński 2002: frontispiece), that 'no visitor can leave unmoved' (Omilanowska, Majewski, Czerniewicz-Umer and Townsend 2004: 160), and that, 'if travel elsewhere broadens the mind, struggling around the emotional minefield of Auschwitz must deepen it' (Ward 1988: 50).

Although 'struggling around the emotional minefield of Auschwitz' is clearly imagined as more than simply a visual experience, sites like Auschwitz are presented in part as visual landscapes to be seen and photographed (Cole 2015). As they are guided through the former complex of camps, visitors' initial encounter with Birkenau is from the top of the guard tower where they see (and photograph) the camp stretching into the distance. For the authors of the *Rough Guide*, this initial view of the 'physical scale of the Auschwitz-Birkenau camp is a shock in itself' but a necessary one if visitors are to 'begin to grasp the full enormity of the Nazi death machine' (Salter and McLachlan 1994: 346). That there is so much of the camp left to see is a result of Auschwitz (along with Majdanek) being liberated by the Soviets more or less intact, as well as of the political decision to preserve the physical evidence of its crimes for future generations (Keil 2005). In contrast, the infrastructure in the experimental death camp at Chelmno, and the so-called Operation Reinhard camps of Treblinka, Sobibor and Belzec where Polish Jews were murdered *en masse*, was razed to the ground once the killings were over and the sites planted with trees (Charlesworth 1994). These camps are largely absent from Holocaust tourism. In the case of the *Rough Guide*, they did not feature at all in the first two editions (Salter and McLachlan 1994), and when they did finally appear they did not make it into the region-by-region gazetteer, but were briefly featured in a stand-alone historical box outlining the 'Concentration Camps in Poland' as historical places rather than places to be visited, with the difficulties of reaching these sites made clear (Bousfield and Salter 2005: 418). Auschwitz and Majdanek were recommended not only because their proximity to large cities – Krakow and Lublin – means they are more accessible than the other four, but also because they were more accessible to the tourist imagination given that there are barracks, barbed wire and watch towers, gas chambers and crematoria to see.

The importance of the remaining infrastructure of mass incarceration and killing at these sites means that guidebooks frame Auschwitz and Majdanek as places to see (and believe). At Majdanek, visitors clutching their copy of the *Rough Guide* were instructed to look at the material traces of the camps in order to understand the sheer number of people housed and killed in this place. They were also told to look beyond the boundaries of the camp and note its closeness to Lublin; with a nod to the vexed question of Polish–Jewish relations that ran throughout the guide, the observant visitor would soon realise that 'this was no semi-hidden location that local people could claim or strive to remain in ignorance of …'. However, while visiting the camp was primarily a visual experience, tourists were also encouraged to soak up the atmosphere of the place by 'wandering among the barbed wire and watchtowers' (Salter and McLachlan 1994: 244–5). The language of 'wandering' was repeated when visitors were guided to Auschwitz-Birkenau and instructed to 'wander around the barracks' so that they could 'begin to imagine the absolute terror and degradation of the place' (Salter and McLachlan 1994: 346). In both places a particular kind of walking – slowly and in some ways relatively purposelessly – was seen to offer a way in to the victims' experiences.

The encouragement to use senses other than simply sight was particularly important in places where – like the former death march routes – there was little to see. This was the case at the former camp of Plaszow, close to Krakow, where there were no extant barracks left to 'wander around'. Here, the *Rough Guide* directed visitors to search for the few remaining traces of the camp. Those who 'scramble about in the undergrowth' were promised that they would 'find the remains of the camp gate, blown up by the retreating Nazis in January 1945, and the remains of the quarries dug by camp inmates', and those who made the 'ten-minute walk along paths through the overgrown surroundings' would discover the villa where camp commander Amon Goeth lived. The absence of the infrastructure of the camp was seen to heighten, rather than diminish, the affective experience of this place, with the guidebook authors claiming that 'like all concentration camps the site has an eerie, wilderness atmosphere, all the more so for the lack of buildings'. Moreover, with little to see, the guidebook authors encouraged visitors to literally get down on their hands and knees and 'scratch beneath the surface of the grass-covered mounds', in order to 'find shards of pottery, scraps of metal and cutlery' – tell-tale evidence of its wartime use (Salter and McLachlan 1994: 331). In this place where the architecture of the camp had been razed to the ground, visitors were directed to dig into the soil in order to uncover – and feel – the past (even though this practice surely defied the injunctions now present on local signage to 'respect the grievous history of the site').

Survivors re-walking the camp

The importance of embodied encounter, which characterises everything from artistic practices through organised marches and visits to tourist experiences of contemporary Holocaust landscapes, can also be seen in the return visits of survivors like Eva Olsson to the places of their – and their family members' – incarceration. In part, there are similarities in their practice, particularly in attempts to walk in the footsteps of the victims. However, there are also differences. In particular, it is clear that survivors return to these sites aware that they were places occupied by perpetrators as well as victims. While they do seek to follow in the footsteps of the latter, they perform the absence of the former in striking ways. The absence of the perpetrators in these sites signals the radical changes to these places. While survivors see continuities in Holocaust landscapes, they are also well aware of dramatic changes that mean that these sites are at one and the same time now both the same place and yet also another place altogether.

The importance of continuities can be seen as survivors return to the sites of the former camps in order to walk in the footsteps of the victims not in general but in the familial particular. 'The walk along the track to the memorial was important to me because that's how the victims arrived,' Eva Olsson explained, recalling how: 'when I walked along the track myself, all I could think about … was my family … how they walked' (Olsson 2008: 90). Retelling his return visit to Auschwitz, Andre Mark explained how he 'walked the route where my family walked to their death actually … I walked to the crematoria where I know that's where their life ended.'[17] This desire to retrace the footsteps of family members to the crematoria is one that is widely shared by survivors.[18] Retracing *their* steps and pausing at the gas chambers and crematoria that were never a part of survivors' own personal experience of this camp are important acts of reconnecting with their family's past and, in a sense, with *them*. Eva Olsson left Auschwitz with a sense that 'memories of my mother are stronger now because I had the opportunity to walk around, go into the gas chamber, sit and think, whereas in 1944 it all happened so suddenly' (Olsson 2008: 94–5). As they retell these experiences of visiting Auschwitz, some survivors explain how they saw and felt something and someone here that others cannot see.[19] Returning to the main gateway into Birkenau, Eva explained that she was taken 'right back to that time. I saw a boxcar … my father and brother standing … my mother squatting' (Olsson 2008: 81–3).

As they seek to follow the footsteps of family members killed here, even, in Eva's case, into the gas chamber itself, survivors are conscious that they are going to places for the first time. This sense of seeing something new and entering into places they had never previously been to extends – in this vast complex of camps – far beyond the gas chambers and crematoria. Although Eva had been imprisoned here, she became well aware on her return that 'there was so much more going on at Auschwitz-Birkenau than I had realized when I was there', for then she 'lived in just one barrack, and going to the kitchen to get the soup was as far as I went' (Olsson 2008: 94). But more striking than Eva's sense of being taken by her tour guide to places in the camp that she had never been to before are the deliberate efforts of a number of survivors to either enter places that were out of bounds to prisoners or to inhabit this site in radically different ways. One striking example is the guard tower above the gateway to Auschwitz-Birkenau which was a space that prisoners were never permitted to enter. As they climb the steps and enter this site of surveillance, survivors are not retracing their own or family members' footsteps but are walking in the footsteps of the perpetrators and seeing the camp for the first time through the perpetrators' god-like gaze.

The significance of this, lost on casual tourists who first see Birkenau from this elevated position, is not lost on survivors. Describing the moment when she 'went up' the watchtower in Birkenau, Lilly Ebert recalled that

> it was a funny feeling that you are in this place, you wanted to come and you can go out again and you are in this watchtower where the Germans watched you and we would never have thought of it that we will be in this space, that we can stand in this space.

Looking down from this privileged viewpoint, a number of things struck Lilly. First she was surprised to see that the ground was grey 'not red from blood'. Second, it seemed 'funny to see the place so empty when it was thousands and thousands of people, people couldn't move and now this emptiness' – something also commented on by many others. Third, standing there with her daughter, Lilly

> felt they hadn't succeeded. I am here with my daughter. I am here in your watchtower. I came in for my own will and I will go out from here when I want and with whom I want so you have not succeeded.[20]

Lilly Ebert's sense of the significance of inserting her and her daughter's living bodies into perpetrator space, as and when she wanted, as symbolic of Nazi defeat and Jewish victory is something that carries over into a range of embodied practices adopted by survivors who choose to revisit. Particularly striking in this regard is an interview with Erwin Baum that in the main covered the usual ground of Baum's wartime experiences in Warsaw. However, when describing his return to Poland for the seventy-fifth anniversary celebrations of Janusz Korczak's Jewish orphanage in Warsaw, where he and his brother had lived in the late 1930s, Baum explained how this visit had also offered a chance to return to Auschwitz. As he explained, he and his brother had decided to hire 'a private chauffeur with a car' and go to Auschwitz. Once there, he recalled that, 'I walk in because I want to walk in. And I know on the other side is a guy waiting with a Mercedes for me, and I walk out. I'm liberated.'[21] Whereas his first 'liberation' by American troops who captured the Dachau sub-camp of Allach was experienced passively as a change of management, subjected to the photographing gaze of new owners, his second 'liberation' as he walked out of Auschwitz in 1998 was an active choice. For Baum, the price of a taxi fare – in a prestigious German car no less – from Warsaw to Oświęcim was worth it to show not only that he had made it in this life but also to undertake this symbolic act that lasted only a few minutes of walking in to Auschwitz again with the express purpose of walking out again.

Baum's practice of walking in and walking out again has been adopted by a number of survivors. Michael Zylberberg expressed his long-standing desire: 'before I die to return to those horrible places where I was dragged in as a prisoner.

I wanted to walk in there as a free man and walk out as a free man.' Such was the symbolic importance attached to exiting Auschwitz that Zylberberg had a photograph taken when 'we walked out from Auschwitz ... because this was very important for me'. Showing the photograph to the camera at the end of his Shoah Foundation interview, he explained that: 'the picture shows how I was walking out as a free man of the concentration camp. This was a pilgrimage I always wanted to do and I did it this year.'[22] For Ruth Brand, it was marching 'into the gate' rather than being 'taken as a slave' that was particularly memorable.[23] For David Yeger, the act of walking out of the camp 'got it out of my system. I felt like I'm free.'[24] For Elizabeth Kent it was both entering and exiting Auschwitz of her own volition that was significant, explaining how she

> wanted to walk in there and walk out as a free person. I never was able to do it because everytime I walked in and out there were German soldiers with one and *Arbeit Macht Frei*. I wanted to do it on my own. I wanted to experience that I am free and I am here to tell you about it. And it did happen.[25]

For Nathan Lustman, a sense of freedom came in leaving Auschwitz 'not back through that main gate', but through a section of wire:

> As I walked through I was shuddering like I got a fever ... that had a such a, like a real true freedom walking out of that camp not as a prisoner to Mauthausen but like walking out into true freedom. I really, my whole body was uh, emotional experience walking through those electric charged wires during the war.[26]

The importance of now being able to hold those wires that had once been so murderous was of prime significance to Judith Perlaki who showed a series of post-war photographs at the end of her interview for the Shoah Foundation including one of 'my sister and me holding electric wire – no electricity', taken when they visited the camp in 1991, as Perlaki explained, 'because we wanted to go back as free people'.[27]

For all these survivors, inserting their embodied presence either into new places or familiar places in new ways was to perform a highly significant act of re-making the self. The symbolism of these acts owed much to Auschwitz being on the one hand the very same place and yet on the other hand an entirely different place altogether. The radical changes to this place were clear to someone like Lilly Ebert, who discovered that it was now possible for her to walk up the steps of the guard tower at Birkenau – something she could never have dreamed of doing. But for this act to have symbolic value, it was vital that this was the very same guard tower. In this simultaneously changeless and changing place, Lilly performed acts of liberation and revenge through every step she and her daughter took. The symbolic significance of that mixture of continuity and change comes through in Ann Lenga's reflections on returning to the camp and discovering that

> Auschwitz is the way I left it, the barracks that I was in is still there and I was so victorious of coming in, to be able to say "*Arbeit Macht Frei*, whatever you wanted to do to me you're dead but I'm still a survivor". I can walk the grounds that I was once forbidden and I was very happy to go back there.[28]

As with other survivors, Ann returned to what superficially appeared the same place and yet was also dramatically changed. The perpetrators' absence meant that Ann could trespass into *verboten* space, but in a sense they were still within ghostly earshot and so she directly addressed them. For Ann – and as I suggest she is far from alone among returning survivors – those who they once shared this site with – the perpetrators – are still very much in view and directly addressed, with the fact of return representing an overturning of the previous power relationships within this space.

That sense of different power relationships fundamentally changing the nature of the space, as well as the embodied experience in that place, is something that emerges in Susan Silas' reflections on her own attempts to retrace the route taken by hundreds of Jewish women on the roads that she chose to re-walk. Ultimately she came to realise the impossibility of attaining the experiential authenticity that she sought. It is striking that she chose to title the artwork that she developed *Helmbrechts walk* rather than *Helmbrechts march*. While Erin Hanas sees Silas' renaming as an attempt 'to emphasize the difference between her personal decision to retrace the historic death march and the prisoners' lack of agency', I also read it as a suggestion by Silas of a radically different embodied experience of this landscape (Hanas 2009: 32). Through her act of re-titling Silas explains that while she walked the same roads between Helmbrecht and Prachatice, she was not marched along this route. Walking and marching are, as Tim Ingold points out, very different experiences of place:

> Marching is the form of pedestrian movement that approximates most closely to transport. Unlike the wayfarer whose movement continually responds to an ongoing perceptual monitoring of the country through which he passes, the pedestrian on the march notices nothing. Before his steadfast, unswerving gaze, the country passes unobserved, while his straightened legs and booted feet beat out a purely mechanical oscillation.
>
> *(Ingold 2010: 137)*

Although Silas may have trodden on the same earth, she became well aware that her movement through this landscape as a lone walker rather than part of a mass march meant that it was as if she were in another place altogether; she realised the folly of seeking to touch not only past place but also past people. At the end of her journey, Silas confessed to a 'monumental failure of the imagination' and concluded that she 'didn't find it easier to imagine the plight of these women but harder to imagine' (cited in Kaplan 2008: 115; see also Apel 2002: 149).

Silas' honest reflections are words of caution for those of us who seek to follow in the footsteps of the victims in Holocaust landscapes. She reminds us, as the survivors themselves do, that while these places are superficially the same, they have also fundamentally changed. That landscapes change over time is something of which those who revisit are often all too well aware. For Eva Olsson, the changes to her hometown were so great that she found her visit to Satu Mare a 'devastating' experience. In part, key sites of her childhood memories appeared 'diminished'. While the park was still there, 'the rose arbour where lovers used to sit was gone'. The opera house was still standing but its 'elegance and beauty … was all gone' with the disappearance of the 'velvet drapes' and 'murals'. In the Dacia Hotel 'the lobby wasn't as impressive' as Eva remembered (Olsson 2008: 34–5). But it was not only that places had changed, buildings had also simply disappeared. At the flat where she had lived for most of her childhood, Eva wanted to find the gate to the courtyard as 'a connection with my past', but the apartment building had been torn down and a post office was being built in its place. It was a similar story as Eva sought out the bungalow her family had moved into when she was fourteen. 'Except for the park and the school,' Eva reflected, 'there wasn't one place where I could say, "Yes, I recognize this, I recognize that, that's where I played". All the synagogues my family used to go to are gone' (Olsson 2008: 28–9). The changes to the physical environment were simply too prominent and jarring to allow her to feel the kind of connection with sites/sights of the past that she had sought out through this return visit.

In marked contrast, Eva reflected that she had experienced that kind of connection when she visited her father's hometown of Sighet. Although Eva had wanted, and planned, to go to Sighet – 'the place where her favourite grandfather lived' – as a child, the trip had never happened, and so seventy-three years later she went there for the first time (Olsson 2008: 43). Told by their guide that they 'were walking on streets that my grandfather and father would have walked on many times', Eva 'felt that their spirit was there' (Olsson 2008: 54–5). Unlike her experience of disconnect in the hometown she knew well, Eva felt a connection with past people in a place she had never been to before where visible signs of change were not so pronounced. Sighet was a place where it was much easier for Eva to make a leap of imagination and shrink time in space than it was on the streets of Satu Mare where the signs of discontinuity were jarringly obvious.

Eva's radically different experiences of connection and disconnect in those places she visited for the first time – Sighet and the gas chamber in Auschwitz – and those familiar places like Satu Mare that she returned to are telling. I wonder if many of the contemporary organised and individual practices within Holocaust landscapes that I have explored in this essay 'work' because they are undertaken by organisers and visitors who can (and choose to) make the necessary imaginative leap and see continuities of place more strongly than discontinuities. It is easier for the first time visitor to assume a connection with the past than the returnee who is well aware of how different things are, such that it is almost a different space. In this context, Susan Silas' reflections on her own failure to re-enter the landscape of the death marches are striking for their candid honesty. Most attempts to re-walk the footsteps of the victims are more self-assured about not only the possibility, but also the transformative potential, of such embodied encounters with past time, past place and past people. However, as Silas' reflections suggest, these assumptions of the possibility of short-cutting to direct identification with people in the past through re-entering Holocaust landscapes are at best 'fantasies of witnessing'. Despite all appearances to the contrary, the past remains stubbornly a 'foreign country' (Lowenthal 1985).

Notes

1 To view the images, and for further materials relating to the *Helmbrechts walk 1998–2003* project, see Silas' website at www.helmbrechtswalk.com/.
2 Blog post by Lorna Brunstein at https://forcedwalks.wordpress.com/2016/02/03/belsen-behind-the-barbed-wire/.
3 For details, see the 2007 prayer guide *March of Life* available at http://archiv.marschdeslebens.org/fileadmin/media/MDL/prayerguidemol.pdf. Quotes at pp. 5, 7.
4 For details, see the prayer guide *Marsch des Lebens 2008: Paths of Remembrance along the Tracks of the Death Marches in 1945* available at http://archiv.marschdeslebens.org/fileadmin/media/MDL/doku/media/gebetsleitfaden2008_en.pdf. Quotes at pp. 9, 10, 30.
5 *March of Life*, 29, 7.
6 *Marsch des Lebens*, 11.
7 For details, see the 2016 March of the Living study guide available at https://motl.org/wp-content/uploads/2016/03/MOTL_Study_Guide.pdf. Quote at p. 1.
8 See the leaflet *2017 International March of the Living* available at https://motl.org/wp-content/uploads/2015/06/MOTL-2017-June-28A.pdf. Quote at p. 2.
9 Quote from Malcolm Hoenlein on the March of the Living Canada website at http://marchoftheliving.org/2012/01/30/2012-march-to-reunite-concentration-camp-liberators-and-holocaust-survivors-for-the-first-time/.
10 Speech of Alyse Dan, grandchild of a Holocaust survivor and participant in the 2009 March, on the March of the Living Canada website at http://marchoftheliving.org/speeches/alyse-dan/.
11 I am very grateful to the HET for allowing me to join the 2012 'Lessons from Auschwitz' seminars and visit, and to the educator and students in the group I was part of for giving me permission to quote anonymously from our discussions throughout the course and observe their responses to the site and reflections in pre- and post-visit seminars.
12 Group discussion, HET visit to Auschwitz, 6 March 2012.
13 Closing ceremony, HET visit to Auschwitz, 6 March 2012.
14 HET follow-up seminar, Exeter, 18 March 2012.
15 Introductory talk, HET pre-visit seminar, Exeter, 1 March 2012.
16 Group discussion, HET pre-visit seminar, Exeter, 1 March 2012; Group discussion, HET follow-up seminar, Exeter, 18 March 2012.
17 University of Southern California, Visual History Archive (USC VHA) 7912, interview with Andre Mark. For more on survivor return visits see Cole 2013a.
18 USC VHA 6906, interview with Ruth Mermelstein; USC VHA 38286, interview with Rena Chernoff.
19 USC VHA 2757, interview with Fay Hollander; USC VHA 26356, interview with David Rubin; USC VHA 29370, interview with Sonia Majtlis; USC VHA 44325, interview with Abraham Munk.
20 USC VHA 16120, interview with Lilly Ebert; Cole 2013a.
21 United States Holocaust Memorial Museum Archives RG-50.030*0016, interview with Erwin Baum; USC VHA 8001, interview with Erwin Baum.
22 USC VHA 32519, interview with Michael Zylberberg.

23 USC VHA 36328, interview with Ruth Brand.
24 USC VHA 44062, interview with David Yeger.
25 USC VHA 9161, interview with Elizabeth Kent.
26 USC VHA 1287, interview with Nathan Lustman.
27 USC VHA 11807, interview with Judith Perlaki.
28 USC VHA 29584, interview with Ann Lenga.

References

Apel, Dora. 2002. *Memory Effects: The Holocaust and the Art of Secondary Witnessing*. New Brunswick, NJ: Rutgers University Press.

Bousfield, Jonathan and Salter, Mark. 2005. *The Rough Guide to Poland*. 6th edn. New York, NY: Rough Guides.

Charlesworth, Andrew. 1994. 'Contesting Places of Memory: The Case of Auschwitz'. *Environment and Planning D: Society and Space* 12, 5: 579–93.

Cole, Tim. 2013a. 'Crematoria, Barracks, Gateway: Survivors' Return Visits to the Memory Landscapes of Auschwitz'. *History and Memory*, 25, 2: 102–31.

Cole, Tim. 2013b. 'Holocaust Roadscapes: Retracing the 'Death Marches' in Contemporary Europe'. *Cahiers de geographie du Quebec*, 57, 162: 445–59.

Cole, Tim. 2015. 'Holocaust Tourism: The Strange yet Familiar/the Familiar yet Strange'. In *Revisiting Holocaust Representation in the Post-Witness Era*, edited by Diana Popescu and Tanja Schult. London: Palgrave Macmillan. 93–106.

Conway, Brian. 2007. 'Moving through Time and Space: Performing Bodies in Derry, Northern Ireland'. *Journal of Historical Sociology*, 20, 1/2: 102–25.

Dydyński, Krzysztof. 2002. *Lonely Planet Poland*. 4th edn. Footscray, Victoria: Lonely Planet Publications.

Hanas, Erin. 2009. '"We are all Witnesses": Susan Silas' *Helmbrechts walk*'. *Montage*, 3: 31–41.

Ingold, Tim. 2010. 'Footprints through the Weather-World: Walking, Breathing, Knowing'. *Journal of the Royal Anthropological Institute*, 16, 1: 121–39.

Kaplan, Brett Ashley. 2008. 'Exploring Violence, Amnesia, and the Fascist Forest through Susan Silas and Collier Schorr's Holocaust Art'. *Images*, 2, 1: 110–28.

Keil, Chris. 2005. 'Sightseeing in the Mansions of the Dead'. *Social and Cultural Geography*, 6, 4: 479–94.

Kugelmass, Jack, 1993. 'The Rites of the Tribe: The Meaning of Poland for American Jewish Tourists'. *Yivo Annual*, 21: 395–453.

Lowenthal, David. 1985. *The Past is a Foreign Country*. Cambridge: Cambridge University Press.

Olsson, Eva (with Jacques, Ron). 2008. *Remembering Forever: A Journey of Darkness and Light*. Bracebridge, Ontario: no publisher.

Omilanowska, Malgorzata, Majewski, Jerzy, Czerniewicz-Umer, Teresa and Townsend, Helen. 2004. *Poland: Eyewitness Travel Guides*. 2nd edn. London: Dorling Kindersley.

Salter, Mark and McLachlan, Gordon. 1994. *Poland: The Rough Guide*. 2nd edn. London: Rough Guides.

Till, Karen. 2005. *The New Berlin: Memory, Politics, Place*. Minneapolis, MN: University of Minnesota Press.

Ward, Philip. 1988. *Polish Cities: Travels in Cracow and the South, Gdansk, Malbork, and Warsaw*. Cambridge: Oleander.

Weissman, Gary. 2004. *Fantasies of Witnessing: Postwar Efforts to Experience the Holocaust*. Ithaca, NY: Cornell University Press.

AFTERWORD

Entangled memories of the Second World War

Jie-Hyun Lim

In the midst of the refugee crisis that shook Europe in September 2015, sharp polemics broke out among Polish historians on how to interpret East European apathy, or even antipathy, towards Syrian Islamic refugees. Jan Gross sparked the controversy by claiming that Poland and other East European countries' hostility towards the Islamic refugees was related to a failure to come to terms with their own past, specifically in relation to the Holocaust. Gross argued that greater self-reflexive critical understanding of their own complicity with the Nazis in the murder of Eastern Europe's Jews would have been conducive to a more empathetic attitude toward alien refugees. Having earlier undermined the Polish myth of national innocence in his book *Neighbors* (Gross 2001), Gross now extended his critique of the Polish accomplices in the Holocaust. He even asserted that the Poles murdered more Jews than Germans during the war, which challenged the myth of the unity of the national resistance movement under the German occupation.[1] Leaving aside his somewhat dubious statistics, Gross' main point was that the legacy of the Second World War was casting a long shadow, since East Europeans' failure to grapple with their own complicity in atrocity then was fuelling their contemporary antipathy towards Islamic refugees. Gross' argument was, somewhat paradoxically, echoed in the widespread racist joke in Poland that 'we are ready to accept refugees because we have already got concentration camps' (Abdoulvakhabova *et al.* 2015: 42). The joke alludes to a certain connectivity between anti-Semitism and Islamophobia in Poland.

Polish historians including Aleksander Smolar contested Gross' claims by pointing out that Poland and other East European countries have no colonial past. It was this, they argued, which accounted for any lack of hospitality towards refugees in Poland, because it meant that Poles had had no chance to learn through colonialism how to cohabitate with people of different cultures, religions and race; isolation from the non-communist world in the era of the Cold War had exacerbated the problem.[2] While this argument has a certain superficial plausibility, viewing Polish history through a postcolonial lens casts the issue in a different light. Quite apart from the matter of gentry republican cosmopolitanism in the Polish-Lithuanian Commonwealth, the Second Republic in interwar Poland was a multi-ethnic state, where ethnic Poles formed only about 68.9 per cent of the whole population, with the rest comprising Ukrainians (13.9 per cent), Jews (10 per cent), Belorussians (3.1 per cent), Germans (2.3 per cent) and others. In the words of Janusz Pajewski, the Second Republic of Poland was 'not a nation state but a nationalities state' (Pajewski 1995: 164). Moreover, the government responded to the multicultural demands of various ethnic minorities by setting up the internment camp at Bereza Kartuska in 1934 which was co-organised by Colonel Leon Jarosławski, the head of the Nationalities Section of the Political Department of the Ministry of Internal Affairs. The Second Republic period thus demonstrates that Poles were certainly not unfamiliar with ethnic diversity, and they had encountered it in the course of their own practices of internal colonialism. Thus what has been absent in Poland is not the colonial experience, but critical sensitivity towards that internal colonialism.

By the same token, even in the communist era, hundreds of thousands of Vietnamese people arrived in East Germany, Poland, Czechoslovakia and the Baltic Soviet republics. Many of them worked as guest workers in the 1980s. This testifies to the existence of what has been termed a 'global socialist ecumene' in which transnational flows of ideas, knowledge and cultural artefacts, and the transnational mobility of people, occurred on a quite significant scale. Moreover, this global socialist ecumene did not come to an end even after the collapse of the communist bloc: as 'little Hanoi' in Prague illustrates, a Vietnamese diaspora remains quite visible in today's Eastern Europe. The fact that Poland has accepted 100,000 Chechen refugees or exiles since 1996 shows that it is too simplistic to impute that pervasive Islamophobia is the dominant memory template there. This level of assistance for the Chechen refugees is impressive for a country of Poland's size, even if the humanitarianism was motivated by Russophobia. However, the recent refugee crisis has also seen a dramatic cooling in Polish attitudes towards these Chechen refugees (Abdoulvakhabova *et al.* 2015: 36–9), pointing to an underlying issue. Poland has not been devoid of the experience of living together with people of different cultures, but it does exhibit a deficit of empathetic sensitivity to the 'Other' and respect for heterogeneous cultures, religions and life styles.

These Polish disputes over the refugee question centre on whether anti-Semitic guilt or colonial innocence should be the dominant narrative template underpinning social memory in post-communist Poland. Yet while this often presents as a rivalry, so there are also multiple points of confluence between the Holocaust and colonialism to be found in the East European memory of the Second World War. Michael Rothberg has drawn attention to these confluences through the example of W. E. B. Du Bois' account of his trip to Galicia and Krakow in 1890, written up during the early Cold War (Rothberg 2009: 111–34). Du Bois found his understanding of his own 'race problem' radically revised after encountering 'the Jewish question', an encounter triggered when a Galician cabman in a small town asked him whether he wanted to stop '*unter die Juden*', in a local hotel run by a Jew. In Krakow Du Bois was surprised to find that Polish university teachers and students were hardly aware of the dimensions of the Jewish problem. Finding that antipathy against the Jews over-rode any hostility to himself as a 'Negro', Du Bois discovered that racism is about more than colour prejudice (Du Bois 1996 [1952]: 470). The intersecting histories of Galician Jews and African-Americans in the late nineteenth century, with their common patterns of prejudice, were entangled not so much in the course of history as in the memory of Du Bois.

That sort of confluence of disparate memories embodied by Du Bois is to be found repeatedly in the memoryscape of the Second World War. During his visit to the ruins of the Warsaw ghetto in 1949, Du Bois could hear 'the scream and shots of a race riot in Atlanta and the marching of the Ku Klux Klan'. Du Bois confessed he could get a 'more complete understanding of the Negro problem' through a 'clearer understanding of the Jewish problem in the world' (Du Bois 1996 [1952]: 471). The swift response from African-Americans to the 1948 Genocide Convention is another landmark towards the development of a global critical memory. In a petition delivered to the UN in 1951 entitled 'We Charge Genocide', African-American civil rights activists pinpointed parallels between Nazi perpetrators and perpetrators of racist crimes in the United States and sought global support for an indictment of the United States authorities for genocide against African-Americans. (The petition was not accepted.) Decades later, in November 2014, during the UN Convention against Torture committee review of the United States, a group of eight young activists from Chicago, Illinois, submitted a shadow report using the name 'We Charge Genocide' to address police brutality toward African-Americans.[3]

A further example of mnemonic confluence between the Holocaust and colonialism is the collaboration between Korean American Civic Empowerment and the Kupferberg Holocaust Center of Queensborough Community College, New York. The two jointly organised a meeting of Korean 'comfort women' and Holocaust survivors in the auditorium of Queensborough Community College on 13 December 2011, as the first step in a larger political and educational collaboration. The Holocaust and the 'comfort women' phenomenon intersect mnemonically *a posteriori* in the transnational memory space, though no *de facto* entangled history exists between them. The mnemonic confluence of the Holocaust and 'comfort women', facilitated by the transatlantic and transpacific migration of memory, epitomises the extraterritoriality of the global memory of the Second World War. The performativity of wartime memory is shifting from the national to the transnational, which is exemplified by a monument to Korean 'comfort women' in the Bergen County courthouse in New Jersey. Alongside four other monuments commemorating the victims of African-American slavery, the Holocaust, the Armenian genocide and the Irish potato famine, the memorial stone to Korean 'comfort women', unveiled on 8 March 2013, took its place in the county's 'ring of honor' outside the courthouse as part of a memory island (Lim 2015: 698–9).

About a year after the Queensborough meeting of 'comfort women' and Holocaust survivors, a parallel transnational memory performance took place on 6 December 2012 in Melbourne, Australia. In front of the German consulate, 84-year-old Alf Turner read out an Australian Aborigines' petition protesting against the Nazi's persecution of the Jewish people. Then he handed over the document to the honorary German consul-general as 200 supporters, including Holocaust survivors and members of the Jewish community, watched. The ceremony was actually a re-enactment of one William Cooper's 1938 anti-Nazi protest, made only weeks after *Kristallnacht*. William Cooper, the 77-year-old secretary of the Australian Aboriginal League, an Aboriginal elder of the Yorta Yorta tribe and Alf Turner's grandfather, had led a delegation to deliver a petition condemning the Nazi persecution of the Jews to the German consulate in Melbourne, but the consulate had refused to accept it. Seven decades later, Turner re-presented the petition and completed the mission. (Cooper's show of solidarity with German Jews in 1938 was in stark contrast with the post-war 'White Australia' policy that denied entry visas to Oriental Jews.) Cooper's unique protest against the Nazis has only gained traction in the twenty-first century, reflecting the confluence of postcolonial and Holocaust memory in the global memory space (Lim 2015: 699).

Entangled is the memory, not the history. Memories of unconnected events in the course of the Second World War have met, confronted, cohabitated, reconciled, contested and become entangled in its aftermath. The mnemoscape of the Second World War has changed significantly since the turn of the third millennium, as globalisation – and its surrounding discourses – has impacted on memory. Whereas in the last century memories of the war had been nationalised and territorialised, the current sea change has seen them fragmented and entangled: the global memory space has emerged to challenge the nation state as the legitimate container of collective memories and to rescue the memory of the Second World War from '*la tyrannie du national*'. However, the emergence of global memory space does not simply equate to the de-nationalisation of collective memory. Entangled memories intensify memory contests as well as solidarity among nations, nationalities, ethnicities and races, and in the global memory space they have also been fluctuating between de-territorialisation and re-territorialisation. The global trajectory of war memories is replete with contradictory forces that schizophrenically accelerate both the de-nationalisation and re-nationalisation of memory.

A further significant development in the post-Cold War memory space is the fresh encounter between memories of the Stalinist terror and those of the Holocaust and colonial genocide, creating a triple confluence. The encounter of global memory culture and local sensibilities of the nation and region has become more complicated as the memory avalanche of Stalinist rule in Eastern Europe has reshaped the mnemoscape globally. The collapse of the Cold War system released the oppressed memories of the Stalinist terror and Nazi collaboration in Eastern Europe, which triggered East European versions of the German *Historikerstreit*. The 'fall' also signalled the thaw of frozen memories of colonial atrocities among postcolonial allies of the West as the anti-communist foundations of the alliance between colonisers and colonised crumbled and drained it of meaning. In this triple confluence, war memories became entangled transnationally creating much more than a mere compilation of memories in the global memory space.

The post-Cold War quarrels over history in East Asia and Eastern Europe brought about a seismic change to the global memory space. If the German *Historikerstreit* in the 1980s revolved around the issue of the relativisation of the Holocaust, the post-Cold War equivalents in East Asia and Eastern Europe reproblematised the issue of complicity and collaboration beyond the revelation of colonial atrocities and Stalinist terror. Long suppressed guilt surfaced when the post-communist historians' quarrels signalled a memory shift from accenting victimhood to stressing complicity. This challenged the vision of East Europeans' dual victimisation under Nazism and Stalinism by hinting at their moral sins and political complicity. The process had already begun in 1987 when Jan Błoński published the essay 'The Poor Poles are Looking at the Ghetto' (Błoński 1996). Błoński's seminal essay initiated an argument not about culpability for what Poles had done in the Holocaust, but about their sins of omission. It lifted the Polish discussion on the Holocaust beyond legal positivism to the level of ontological ethics. The debate exposed a deep trauma among those Poles who felt the guilt of being helpless witnesses to the genocide of their Jewish neighbours. By way of remembering sins instead of victimhood, that interpretive move critically unsettled Poles' self-perception as innocent victims.

Błoński's clarion call essay was followed by the publication of Gross' book *Neighbors* in Polish in May 2000, which triggered a veritable Polish *Historikerstreit*. This heated controversy over the Jedwabne massacre brought a genuine moral revolution to post-communist Poland and awakened the sleeping awareness of complicity in the region. But the question of the suppressed guilt that surfaced incubated a conflict between critical and apologetic memory. One could easily detect reluctance among many Poles to admit guilt and complicity. The collective memory culture of apologetic victimhood could not easily accommodate such a drastic metamorphosis from innocent victim to perpetrator of the Jedwabne massacre (or '*Homo Jedvanecus*'). The image of a clean and victimised Poland – of the crucified nation – jarred with acknowledgement of Holocaust guilt (Polonsky and Michlic 2004).

By a similar process, linkages between colonial genocide and the Holocaust have become tangible. A postcolonial critique can link German colonial genocide, the Nazis' Eastern occupation policy and the Holocaust as connected parts of a Euro-colonial and modernising project, even if the relationship is not one of simple linear causation and continuity (Traverso 2003; Moses 2008). As black radical intellectuals have insisted on parallels between Nazi perpetrators and racist perpetrators in the United States, so West European colonialism, fascism and Nazism are seen to have shared many practices, methods and objects. It is intriguing to read István Deák, an eminent American historian of Eastern Europe, suggesting the parallel between Jedwabne and the massacre of innocent African-Americans in Tulsa, Oklahoma at the end of May 1921 (Deák 2004: 422). 'Global memory space', 'cosmopolitan memory culture', 'global collective memory' and 'transnational civic memory' gained a momentum in the mnemonic confluence of postcolonial criticism, post-communist *Historikerstreit* and Holocaust memory.

The global memory space was institutionalised in Stockholm between 27 and 29 January 2000. Twenty-three heads of state, fourteen deputy prime ministers and other representatives from forty-six countries gathered in Stockholm to discuss Holocaust education, remembrance and research. At the end of this history summit meeting, all attendees signed the Stockholm Declaration, which proposed remembrance of the Holocaust as a transnational civic virtue.[4] On 2 August 2000, the German *Bundestag* passed a law to recompense foreign slave workers for their wartime labour. Last but not least, the Women's International War Crimes Tribunal on Japan's Military Sexual Slavery was convened in Tokyo in December 2000. Transnational memory activists agitating on behalf of the former 'comfort women' convicted the dead emperor Hirohito of crimes against humanity. Since 2000, further similar declarations have built up the infrastructure of this global memory space, entrenching multiple confluences: the 2008 Prague Declaration, insisting on the need to remember the crimes of communism, was a direct riposte to its Holocaust-focused predecessor; the Seventy Years' Declaration of January 2012 (the seventieth anniversary of the Wannsee conference) was a return riposte, protesting attempts to posit equivalence between Nazi and Soviet crimes.[5]

The Japanese–Korean agreement for a diplomatic solution of the 'comfort women' issue on 28 December 2015 is suggestive of how the interconnections of the global memory space play out today. Upon the news of the Japanese–Korean agreement, a Bloomberg columnist in the United States wrote that 'our horror about the treatment of the comfort women should steel us to act on behalf of women kidnapped into sexual slavery by Islamic State and Boko Haram'.[6] Just as global sensibilities incited by the sexual violence against women in former Yugoslavia and Rwanda were transposed onto the 'comfort women' in the Women's International War Crimes Tribunal, so global awareness of the suffering of the Korean 'comfort women' raised concerns about the sexual slavery imposed by Islamic State and Boko Haram. And Korean-American memory activists are now actively using the human trafficking issue to raise awareness of the 'comfort women' yet further in the United States. The deployment of cross-referencing memories to vindicate one's own historical authenticity is now a dominant practice in the global memory space.

The Japanese-Korean attempted diplomatic solution to the mnemonic conflict over the 'comfort women' issue also well illustrates how such disputes are intertwined with geopolitics. In East Asia, there has been considerable talk since the turn of the third millennium about the need for a new alliance against China's regional hegemonic ambitions, replacing the former Cold War alliance against the USSR. The waging of the so-called 'Cool War' between China and the United States is seen by many to demand a reformulation of alliance ties between the United States, Japan and South Korea.[7] Yet territorial disputes among China, Japan and Korea, the war of memories over colonial and Second World War-era atrocities and economic rivalry have rendered a putative 'Cool War' alliance problematic. Partnerships and rivalries are in constant flux depending on what is at issue, and American expectations have been particularly confounded by the Sino–Korean alliance against Japan over Second World War memory. The Obama administration's keen concern to encourage – and to exert diplomatic pressure for – Japanese–Korean rapprochement on the 'comfort women' issue must be understood in this context. This is reminiscent of the Cold War logic whereby American Jewry was enjoined to accept rapprochement with West Germany on the grounds that 'Stalin is ready for his "final solution of the Jewish question"' (Novick 2000: 99).

These commonalities aside, there exists a regrettable disparity between European and East Asian memory space: in East Asian memory politics it is difficult to locate any wide-ranging normative quest for transnational civic virtue as exemplified in the Stockholm Declaration. What matters is not whether there is rivalry or a clash of memory, but the nature of the conflict. Divergence, discord, disagreement and tension in the work of remembrance are inevitable, since memory is not homogeneous but heterogeneous. The question is whether the heterogeneity is potentially reconcilable or not. A shared vision of transnational civic virtue in the global memory space would potentially make irreconcilable memory reconcilable. Entangled global memories are open to possibilities of both de-territorialisation and re-territorialisation. Considering the mnemonic confluence of the Holocaust, colonial atrocities and Stalinist terror offers us a topography of the global memory space and guides us as we try to navigate through the complexities of conflicted memories to the destination of cosmopolitan memory.

Notes

1 Bartosz Wieliński, '"Polska nie chce uchodźców, bo nie rozliczyła się ze zbrodni na Żydach". Oburzenie po tekście Grossa', *Wyborcza*, 15 September 2015, http://wyborcza.pl/1,75968,18817369,skandalista-gross.html.
2 Aleksandr Smolar, 'Smolar: Gross szokuje', *Wyborcza*, 16 September 2015, http://wyborcza.pl/1,75968,18824173,smolar-gross-szokuje.html.
3 For further details, see http://wechargegenocide.org/.
4 The text is available on the website of the International Holocaust Remembrance Alliance at www.holocaustremembrance.com/about-us/stockholm-declaration.
5 For the texts see, respectively, www.praguedeclaration.eu/ and www.seventyyearsdeclaration.org/the-declaration/.
6 Noah Feldman, 'Apology Isn't Justice for Korea's "Comfort Women"', *Bloomberg*, 28 December 2015, www.bloombergview.com/articles/2015-12-28/how-korea-s-deal-with-japan-fails-comfort-women-.
7 David Rothkopf, 'The Cool War', *Foreign Policy*, 20 February 2013, http://foreignpolicy.com/2013/02/20/the-cool-war/.

References

Abdoulvakhabova, Malika, Skowron-Nalborczyk, Agata, Strasburger, Stanislaw, Nosowski, Zbigniew and Rymsza, Marek. 2015. 'Dyskusja: czy to nasza sprawa?'. *Więz*, 4, 662: 36–46.

Błoński, Jan. 1996. *Biedny Polacy patrzą na getto*. Kraków: Wydawnictwo Literackie.

Deák, István. 2004. 'Heroes and Victims'. In *The Neighbors Respond: The Controversy over the Jedwabne Massacre in Poland*, edited by Antony Polonsky and Joanna B. Michlic. Princeton, NJ: Princeton University Press. 421–9.

Du Bois, W. E. B. 1996 [1952]. 'The Negro and the Warsaw Ghetto'. In *The Oxford W. E. B. Du Bois Reader*, edited by Eric. J. Sundquist. Oxford: Oxford University Press. 469–73.

Gross, Jan T. 2001. *Neighbors: The Destruction of the Jewish Community in Jedwabne, Poland.* Princeton, NJ: Princeton University Press.

Lim, Jie-Hyun. 2015. 'The Second World War in Global Memory Space'. In *The Cambridge History of the Second World War. Volume III: Total War: Economy, Society and Culture*, edited by Michael Geyer and Adam Tooze. Cambridge: Cambridge University Press. 698–724.

Moses, A. Dirk. ed. 2008. *Empire, Colony, Genocide: Conquest, Occupation, and Subaltern Resistance in World History*. New York, NY: Berghahn.

Novick, Peter. 2000. *The Holocaust in American Life*. Boston, MA: Houghton Mifflin.

Pajewski, Janusz. 1995. *Budowa Drugiej Rzeczypospolitej 1918–26*. Kraków: PAU.

Polonsky, Antony and Michlic, Joanna B. eds. 2004. *The Neighbors Respond: The Controversy over the Jedwabne Massacre in Poland*.Princeton, NJ: Princeton University Press.

Rothberg, Michael. 2009. *Multidirectional Memory: Remembering the Holocaust in the Age of Decolonization*. Stanford, CA: Stanford University Press.

Traverso, Enzo. 2003. *The Origins of Nazi Violence*. Translated by Janet Lloyd. New York, NY: New Press.

INDEX

Note: figures are indicated with an 'f' after the page number